WEST STREET, SHAFTESBURY AVENUE
(Nearest Tube Station: Leicester Square).

Under the management of REANDEAN

THE

REANDEAN
COMPANY

{ST. MART

6ᴰ.

MAJESTY'S
THEATRE

Lessees: Grossmith &
ERS: GEORGE GROSSMITH &

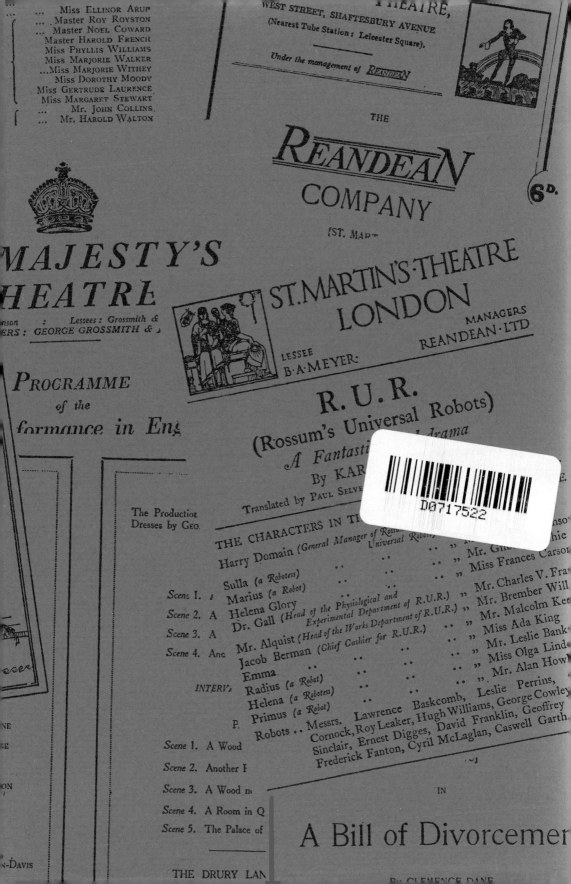

ST. MARTIN'S·THEATRE
LONDON

LESSEE
B·A·MEYER·

MANAGERS
REANDEAN·LTD

PROGRAMME
of the
formance in En

R.U.R.
(Rossum's Universal Robots)
A Fantasti drama

By KAR

Translated by Paul Selve

The Productio
Dresses by Geo.

THE CHARACTERS IN T

Harry Domain (*General Manager of Rossum's Universal Robots*) ... Mr. Gi
Miss Frances Carso

Scene I. Sulla (*a Robotess*) ... Mr. Charles V. Fr
Marius (*a Robot*)
Scene 2. A Helena Glory ... Mr. Brember Will
Dr. Gall (*Head of the Physiological and Experimental Department of R.U.R.*) ... Mr. Malcolm Kee
Scene 3. A Mr. Alquist (*Head of the Works Department of R.U.R.*) ... Miss Ada King
Scene 4. Anc Jacob Berman (*Chief Cashier for R.U.R.*) ... Mr. Leslie Bank
Emma ... Miss Olga Linde
INTERV Radius (*a Robot*) ... Mr. Alan How
Helena (*a Robotess*)
P. Primus (*a Robot*) ... Leslie Perrins,
Robots .. Messrs. Lawrence Baskcomb, George Cowley
Cornock, Roy Leaker, Hugh Williams, Geoffrey
Sinclair, Ernest Digges, David Franklin, Caswell Garth.
Frederick Fanton, Cyril McLaglan,

Scene 1. A Wood
Scene 2. Another F
Scene 3. A Wood n IN
Scene 4. A Room in Q
Scene 5. The Palace of

A Bill of Divorcemen

N-DAVIS

THE DRURY LAN
By CLEMENCE DANE

Seven Ages

The Theatre at War: the official history of ENSA (1956)

Pamphlets

The Theatre in Emergency, I (1939)
The Theatre in Emergency, II (1940)
The Theatre in Reconstruction (1945)

Controller of the Liverpool Repertory Theatre, 1911–13

Basil Dean

SEVEN AGES

An Autobiography 1888–1927

HUTCHINSON OF LONDON

HUTCHINSON & CO (*Publishers*) LTD
178–202 Great Portland Street, London W1

London Melbourne Sydney
Auckland Johannesburg Cape Town
and agencies throughout the world

First published 1970

*This book has been set in Garamond type, printed in Great Britain
on antique wove paper by Anchor Press, and
bound by Wm. Brendon, both of Tiptree, Essex*

ISBN 0 09 104240 2

to
three
women

Acknowledgements

I am greatly indebted to Raymond Mander and Joe Mitchenson
for supplementing my pictorial records with selections from
their famous Theatre Collection.
A copyright letter from Bernard Shaw is published by permission
of the Society of Authors on behalf of the Shaw Estate.
Extracts from letters from John Galsworthy and Arnold Bennett
appear by permission of the respective literary executors.
I desire to acknowledge the debt I owe to my family and the many
friends and acquaintances whose information and encouragement
have helped me to write this book. Above all, I owe much to
my secretary, Miss Berta Nicoll, whose patient research and
unflagging interest have been an invaluable contribution to
the work.

Contents

Illustrations

This is the story of my life and of my career in the theatre: of the many rich experiences and sharp disappointments that I have sustained during the course of it and the rare personalities I have encountered. I shall seek to tell the truth and nothing but the truth, yet not the whole truth for that is impossible. There are secret places in a man's heart that he had best keep to himself. Furthermore, truth must always be a relative term in autobiography since one cannot recapture with accuracy the mental approach and hard enthusiasm of one's youth, nor the confidence and energy of the middle years. I suppose the ideal method would be to write a volume in retrospect every ten years or so, but that supposes a degree of public interest and a supply of book-print pleasing to fancy but not in accordance with fact.

One
Childhood

Once upon a time I was the little boy with the apple on his head in the William Tell story. It was a play in our garden and my elder brother was William. Fortunately for me, my brother's marksmanship was inaccurate. The arrow ploughed a furrow just under my right eye to the alarm and distress of my mother. My own alarm was naturally greater. Family legend recounts a still earlier appearance, this time as a Christmas pudding, my brother having stuck sultanas over my eyes and mouth and in my nose and ears as I lay in my cot. Naturally I cannot be expected to recall such an undignified performance. All my early attempts at impersonation had disastrous endings. Upon another occasion I went to a children's Christmas ball in the local town hall, attired as a Chinese mandarin, complete with a scalp wig and long pigtail attached. The ball was an important annual event,so much so that my father used to engage a friendly barber to come and make us all up. (This was my introduction to the smell of grease-paint, which I thought delicious, especially the cocoa butter.) Alas! No one had realised what a gross temptation a bobbing pigtail would be to all the other little boys, especially when viewed from behind. My wig ended up as a football during the first 'Highland Schottische'. I was 'dissolved' in tears, and so was the grease-paint. I decided never to be a Chinaman again. The said event took place some six or seven years after I was born at Croydon, in the year 1888, to be exact, in a little Regency cottage called Holly Lodge, one of several built originally to house coachmen and gardeners on the North Park estate, whose green fields still bounded Croydon to the north. It must have been an extensive property, for it was guarded by five sets of lodge gates. To us children it was a vast territory which we were permitted to explore only at haymaking time. The elderly lady who lived alone in the large Georgian mansion at the centre of the property, like a spider surrounded by her web of parklands, market gardens and cottages, was seldom to be seen. When she died the estate was broken up and our cottage went with it. So we moved to a larger house on another part of the estate. The only features of Holly Lodge that I remember were its deep porch with pointed lead roof and latticed sides smothered in climbing roses and the narrow path that led up to it through the long front garden.

Croydon in the nineties was still a pleasant market town, although the fate of North Park was soon to be repeated on all its boundaries as the southward London sprawl continued. In our nursery there used to hang a charming little oil sketch showing the sign of the Greyhound Inn suspended across the top of the narrow High Street. This marked the first ten-mile stage of the old London to Brighton coach road. By the time I was old enough to observe such matters the old sign was still there but at the side of the road. Thursday was market day, when sheep and cattle were driven through the streets to market. Old trees lingered in the side roads, and at the northern end of the town rows of great elms separated the dwindling farms and market gardens from the London road. There were big granite horse-troughs at the top of High Street and in the North End outside Sainsbury's where the suburban reputation of the famous provision firm was first laid. On hot summer days I loved to watch the big draught horses sucking up the clear water with gurgling enjoyment until I was dragged away by tiresome grown-ups.

There were chunky little horse-trams which ran on iron rails laid among cobblestones down the centre of the street, over which the horses slithered and splashed in wet weather. There were passing places at intervals. Sometimes two trams found themselves on the same track, and there would be loud argument between the drivers before one of them was forced to retreat. Either side of the cobble-stones the badly made road was thick with mud in winter. The western end of the tram-track was not far from our house. I used to gape at the pair of horses being led round by their driver amid the stream of traffic while trying to make up my mind whether to visit Sisley's the sweetshop at one corner or the corn-chandler's at the other. Sisley's was immensely popular with the children of every class because the sweets were nearly all home-made. Some of them you could see actually being made in the rear of the shop. There was one delicious sweet known as coconut toffee, which was sold in enormous quantities to voracious schoolboys at four ounces for one penny. At the corn-chandler's we used to buy monkey-nuts and sweet dried beans which we called locusts.

Gradually, as the town grew and farms and market gardens and parklands disappeared from all its boundaries, the tram-tracks were extended to all points of the compass. Wooden blocks began to replace the cobblestones and mud; yet not entirely, for the horse-droppings made the wood blocks slippery in wet weather. The next step in the town's progress to suburban prominence was taken when the horse-trams disappeared altogether and overhead electric wires supplied the traction to a tramway system that extended far beyond the original confines of the borough.

There were several railway stations: West Croydon, which stood well back from the road with gardens and trees in front of it, and under the trees usually three or four carriages waiting for hire. We used this station for local journeys to London and to outlying villages such as Sutton and Epsom beyond. East Croydon was a much more adventurous place, for that station carried us much further afield, to places like Brighton and Worthing and Eastbourne, while South Croydon was one station nearer to those magical places. These stations were served mainly by the London, Brighton and South Coast Railway. Even in those days boys loved to collect the names of its spanking bright yellow engines, and the sheds where they were housed. Central Station was the original terminus, running deep below ground into the heart of the town. It was a mysterious place to me, since no trains ever ran from it. One half of its site had already been used for the fine new town hall opened in 1896, which I thought was the grandest building I had ever seen. Locally, it was regarded as a piece of gross municipal extravagance; the other half of the site consisted of sidings, shrouded in trees, and gravel pits still being worked. Today the Ashcroft Theatre and Fairfield Halls have completed the take-over.

2

My father came of yeoman stock. Most of his forbears were farmers and country people generally. When the industrial revolution threatened to rob them of the good life in British agriculture they began to drift into the towns or joined the stream of early settlers to Australia. One branch took root in Tasmania. His mother's family, Haslock by name, had been settled for many generations in the Stansted district of Essex. His father was a tall, stately old man with an aura of gentle loneliness about him, as though he still mourned the loss of his wife, Philadelphia. Nevertheless, she had borne him twelve children, only three of whom survived, my father and his two sisters, all persons of independent character. My younger Aunt Nellie might easily have been the model for Shaw's *Major Barbara*. She became a prominent Salvationist and quite late in life married Dunbar Smith, the architect who built the first Westminster Theatre. From this side of my family I inherited a love of independence and a fundamental sympathy, too, with the worker's point of view, whether of hand or head.

On the maternal side I am of mixed ancestry, French and Dutch as well as English. The families concerned lived in Kent. The English strain was provided by one of the established county families, but there was nothing about them of particular interest to this story. The Dutch family was originally called Van Duynk (I am not sure of the correct spelling) which was later anglicised into Dunk. They must have arrived in this country at a very early date, for the legend is that one of them was a civic dignitary during the reign of Queen Anne. They were hop-factors with important interests in London and Kent.

The French strain comes from a Huguenot family named de Winton, who left France in an open boat at the time of the massacre of St. Bartholomew, landing at Dover in the dead of night with nothing but the family jewellery to sustain them against an uncertain future. So the legend runs. They remained in Kent. Early in the nineteenth century they were settled at Nettlestead Court in the village of Wateringbury, still bearing the arms of the de Winton family, although the French prefix of rank had long since been dropped. When my grandfather married the hop-factor's daughter—she was beautiful—he did so in the teeth of his family's opposition. In due time the young couple were established in a place of their own, a lovely Georgian house called Congelow, in the nearby village of Yalding, where my mother, eldest of six healthy children, was born in the year 1853. Grandfather Winton lived in the style befitting a country gentleman of the period, leaving the tilling of his farmlands to his bailiff, enjoying shooting parties with his friends, riding to hounds on his strawberry mare most days of the week in the hunting season. (My mother had difficulty in convincing me of the truth of that part of the story, for I could not believe in the existence of an animal of such a colour.) His bride had little time to share in his activities, for she had her six children in quick succession, the youngest being still an infant when my grandfather caught cold whilst out hunting, or so it was put about, and in six months was dead— of a galloping consumption, according to the medical description of the time. In a burst of confidence one day my mother told me what actually occurred. He had become involved in a romantic scrape, had been set upon by an outraged rival in a country lane one wintry afternoon returning from the hunt, dragged from his mare, assaulted and left by the roadside. It was the shock to his nervous system as much as the chill which caused his death whilst still in his early thirties. . . . The diverse elements in my heredity, Puritan on the one hand and a more Catholic view of life on the other, proved difficult to reconcile when I grew up.

Grandfather Winton's death changed the family prospects. With great courage my grandmother turned her back upon her country life and removed to a large house on the outskirts of Croydon, just then emerging from its chrysalis state as a small market town, thereafter to devote herself to the upbringing of her children. Unfortunately, she had not allowed for the unorthodox business methods of her uncle, the family trustee, known to us as 'wicked Great-Uncle Henry'. Eventually it was discovered that he had misappropriated some £80,000 of the hop-factor's trust funds. It says much for the integrity of my Dutch forbears that when this was found out a family conference was held to decide what action should be taken. In due course Great-Uncle Henry went to gaol.

Mrs Winton was forced to abandon some at least of her social ambitions; she removed herself and her family to the opposite end of the town. No sooner had she settled in her new home on the edge of North Park, where no jerry-builder had yet set his feet, than her eldest daughter met and fell in love with the young man next door, my father. This seemed to the unfortunate widow to be yet another family disaster. The young man was in trade— 'something in the City'—and not at all suitable. What was to be done? The exasperated lady quite lost her head, held impassioned interviews with the young man's father and, despite his good-humoured advice, forbade the young man the house and promptly cut off her daughter's dress allowance. She forgot the heritage of

B

constancy she had passed on to her daughter. A battle of wills ensued. The two houses were divided by high walls with the park-land beyond. There were secret meetings over the wall at night: Juliet's balcony scene without the balcony. My father had no need for anxiety over my mother's resolution. She always had enough courage and initiative to sustain the two of them. Rather than sub-mit to the parental will, she departed for Eastbourne, there to become an instructress in art and music at an exclusive seminary for young ladies, a post for which she was singularly ill-equipped. Her health gave way under the severe rationing system imposed in that high-class establishment, 'Dothegirls' Hall. She was forced to return home, where she lay supine from spinal weakness for many months. Finally, the physicians took a hand in warning my grand-mother of the probable outcome of this Victorian variation upon the Romeo and Juliet theme. Whereupon with grim reluctance the old lady allowed her daughter to know her own mind. It was one thing to relent and quite another to forgive and understand; this she never did. However, the lovers were happily married at the Croydon Parish Church on January the 16th, 1882, and, in spite of all their ups and downs and material disappointments, remained so until the end of their days more than fifty years later.

3

The marriage began blissfully enough. My father installed his bride in a comfortable house with a large garden in Selhurst, at that time a quiet sub-rural area not yet swallowed up in the South London sprawl, nowadays a dreary suburb. Thence at week-ends he delighted in driving my mother about the vestigial countryside in his smart gig: Victorian equivalent of the modern 'mini' car. Being essentially simple-minded, it was not surprising that he early met with disaster in his business affairs. One evening shortly after the arrival of their first child, my elder brother, my father returned home with the news that the partner in his growing business—he was a cigarette manufacturer amongst other things, and is so named on my birth certificate—had absconded with a large part of the firm's funds. The shock of this betrayal might have killed him but for my mother's sensible handling of the situation. She told me once with some pride how she had won praise from the family doctor for packing him off to bed, where he slept for twenty-four hours on end, my mother's love and courage taking the place of modern sedation.

His firm was forced into liquidation. Long years afterwards I discovered by accident that he had spent the next ten years of his life quietly paying each of the firm's creditors in full. And he did so without complaint of any sort because that was how he saw his duty. The justice of the matter may be questioned in view of his growing responsibilities, for he left the burden of poverty to be borne mainly by his young wife, and presented his children with vistas of opportunity denied to them. As they grew up they wondered at his lack of success and resented their mother's incessant struggle with the problem of ways and means. Yet he remained silent and sought no praise for what he was doing. Most families have their skeletons, but not all of them are hidden in cupboards. Ours was a skeleton that rattled its bones throughout my school years.

My father was not a clever man. His mental processes were directed along singularly narrow lines. As a member of the Church of England, he placed his own exact interpretation upon its teachings and accepted its dogma without question. I do not think he ever bothered to read a religious book except the Bible. He was content to abide by the rules. If he had been directly challenged as a fundamentalist he probably would have evaded the issue: 'Ours not to reason why' should be the guiding principle for everybody.

For many years he conducted the Mission of the Good Shepherd in the worst quarter of the town where there was much drinking and violence. He was so well known and respected that even the bawling women's voices were hushed as he went by. That tiny mission hall is a vivid memory: its rows of reversible school desks—the place was a school for slum children on week-days—the raised platform at the far end on which stood the altar, always beautifully decorated with flowers, and a sizable organ, only partly concealed by a curtain which billowed violently under the vigorous arm thrusts of the boy pumping air into the machine. I recall, too, the penetrating smell of horse manure that on hot summer evenings floated in through the range of wide-open windows down one side of the hall from the livery stables next door, where rows of tired bus horses stood under house arrest for twenty-four hours.

My father loved the everyday life and gossip of the Church and was never so happy as when he could invite some clergyman or other to Sunday lunch or supper after evensong; and the higher the rank of the guest, the better he seemed to be pleased. I believe we once achieved a bishop, and the rural dean was a frequent visitor. Without question my father lived a life of practical Christianity, as he saw it. He was a happy man and died widely respected.

4

The quality that I remember best about my mother was her unquenchable spirit. Her husband's failure so early in their married life had been a blow to her pride. Nevertheless, she devoted herself unremittingly to the physical care of her home and family. At the same time spiritually, but not in any religious sense, she bore her husband aloft and prevented the household from sinking beneath the weight of his solemnity. The combination of energy in practical matters with a vigorous imagination would have made her a successful man of affairs. For example, when her share of the depleted family trust came her way, I well recall her announcement that as flying was obviously going to be the great development of the future, she proposed to invest some of the money in an aviation company that had just put out its first prospectus. By way of contrast, my father's reaction to the exploit of M. Blériot in flying the Channel had been to remark sourly that 'if we had been intended to fly, God would have provided us with wings'. I half expected my mother to burst out laughing, but she remained silent. I already suspected her of a degree of agnosticism after overhearing her quick rejoinder to my aunt's sly reference to my father's excessive piety: 'All that praying wears out his trousers.' A friend who knew her intimately once described her to me as 'Elizabethan', which I felt was an apt description.

I especially remember her playing and singing on the nursery piano on Sunday evenings, the only day in the week when she allowed herself such indulgence, except, of course, at parties. She had a warm soprano voice, well trained and full of tune, and sang to her own accompaniment the old ballads such as Haydn's eighteenth-century setting of 'My Mother Bids me Bind my Hair', 'Robin Adair', 'On the Banks of Allan Water' and 'Cherry Ripe'. There was one ballad which began 'I stood on the bridge at midnight, the clocks were striking the hour'; it was too sentimental even for our generation and caused such hilarity that my mother gave up singing it. There were gayer songs, too, such as 'Linger Longer Loo', which Yvette Guilbert brought to this country, and the popular tunes of Leslie Stuart. Sometimes she would sing hymns. My favourite was 'Abide with Me', which she sang with such pathos that I was for ever pestering her to repeat it, and she would teasingly ask me why. My reply that she made it sound better than in church pleased her. The hymn-singing was also an effective excuse for staying up late.

At times physical weakness overcame her, then her spirits seemed to flag under the weight of routine anxieties. She would remind us of all that we owed to her. I wished she would not, but then I was too young to appreciate her need of an understanding deeper than husbandly consideration. From the first there was close affinity between us, more so than with the rest of her children, so that she would often talk to me of her family and her early life, adding always her views as to the position in the world which she expected her children to occupy, especially myself. Thus, by letting me see quite clearly which of her children she hoped would justify her life of self-effacement, she stoked the fire of my ambition so efficiently that I became obsessed with the length of the journey I had to make and the shortness of the time in which to accomplish it. There was another direction in which I learned the lesson of her life, and all too well. The early and persistent anxiety about money gradually bred in her a neurosis that I inherited along with the rest of her message. I was not conscious of it at the time, but it was to affect adversely some of my decisions later on.

Only thrice in my life had I seen her in tears: once when she came into the nursery one morning early, weeping softly for the loss of her baby son. I had not seen a grown-up person crying before, and it shocked me. The second occasion was when I left home for good, and finally towards the end of her life. She was sitting upright in her high-backed armchair, struggling for breath. I sat beside her, silent, while the unspoken question trembled between us: was she really going to die? Then as she gazed fondly at me her eyes slowly filled with tears. Above all there remains for me a vision of courage of that steadfast feminine quality that claims instant respect wherever a man may meet it, a courage that never once gave way to the day of her death in 1937 at the age of eighty-four.

5

There must be some connection between records of idleness in childhood and exceptional activity afterwards that run through the stories of those who have achieved success. And I think it lies in just that squirrel-storage of early impressions obtained by dawdling, which is a natural process and stands the child in good stead later on. Yet it can so easily be nagged out of existence. In my time anxious mothers and fretful nursemaids were forever chivvying their charges down the long avenue of unfolding childhood to the gates of the schoolhouse. Anyway, as a child I loved to dawdle, especially on foggy autumn afternoons under the orange green of the gas lamps. Thus I began unconsciously to develop the habit of seeing persons and events as pictures in the mind. I can recall the places and groupings of individuals in occurrences long past, see the colours and hear the voices, although many names are now forgotten. The facility persisted so that my first impressions of an author's script came to me in picture form, and were seldom altered by subsequent study.

My earliest pictures are of every sort: my grandmother's house and garden; the Victorian drawing-room with its water-colours, little gilt-legged tables and china figurines in glass-fronted cabinets and the scent of pot-pourri; the shining mahogany and silver in the dining-room; the hall lavatory behind a blue glass door, with its too commodious pan, flushed by means of a heavy pull-up handle, and decorated with a blue willow pattern of a Chinese peasant in a funny hat, crossing a bamboo bridge; was he on his way to do what I was doing? I wondered. When the time came to disperse the old lady's treasures there was a family tiff because an aunt had foolishly destroyed the family tree that used to hang in the same downstairs lavatory, suitably placed, no doubt, for adult reflection upon the mutability of human affairs.

The garden was full of the scent of moss roses, dark-eyed scabious, the bluest of blue cornflowers, night stocks, mignonette and all manner of sweet-smelling things: above all, the delicious fragrance of musk, a plant long since lost to our gardens. Over all there lingers the aura of a white-haired old lady, dressed in mauve or grey silk brocade, with a white lace cap on her head, seated behind a silver tea-service: a picture that fades to the sound of solemn whispering at the time of her death.

The life of the street provided endless fascination. There was the muffin-man, striding along the pavement on Sunday afternoons in the misty half-light of winter, ringing his little bell, and balancing something like a butler's tray on his head. Beneath a green baize cover (to keep in the warmth) and a white muslin cloth lay the delicious muffins and crumpets. I can see myself staring longingly out at the gathering darkness, listening for the approaching bell. Often the lamplighter would appear about the same time, lighting up each lamp in turn by means of a taper at the end of a long pole. He was always in a hurry to beat the darkness, and was later supplied with a bicycle. That must have been the origin of the Victorian exhortation to errand boys to 'run like a lamplighter'. The crossing sweeper at the end of our road had a wooden leg and a medal hanging from his shabby coat. He swept his crossing especially clean at Christmas time, with little whorls of mud for decoration, because that meant sixpence instead of the usual penny. One character that I remember well was an Italian ice-cream vendor named Filippo Capecci, who had marked out the district where we lived as his special territory. On hot summer days we regarded his gaily-painted handcart, with its big zinc container slung between its wheels like a miniature milk float, with longing eyes. But his cry, 'Hokey, pokey, penny a lump!' went unheeded, for we were warned never to go near or to buy his ices: 'he was Italian and therefore what he sold was certain to be unclean.' Butcher boys in their blue aprons whistled and sang as they bore on their shoulders big joints of meat on long wooden trays for delivery at the tradesmen's entrances. Looking back it seems to me that all these familiar figures and the bus-drivers, tram-drivers, railway porters and chimney sweeps were cheery, laughing people. Perhaps they reserved their dark looks for the grown-ups.

I remember the day when I sat perched on my father's shoulder watching the old Queen drive up Constitution Hill during her Diamond Jubilee, tiny reflections of the June sunshine rippling like liquid jewels from the jiggling swords and lances of the Indian princes riding behind as escort.

I remember watching the returning crowds on Derby Day, from the top of a high garden wall: four-in-hands, drays, waggonettes, dogcarts, victorias, landaus, vehicles of every sort for high and low, not excluding the costermongers in pearls and feathers urging their donkeys to keep pace: a continuing stream that passed on through the hours of fading daylight. The din was prodigious, with the hoarse cries of ragged children rising above the noise of the traffic as they dodged in and out, barefoot, shouting: 'Throw out yer mouldy coppers. Throw out yer mouldy coppers!'

In the average Victorian nursery little attention was paid to matters of diet. Food was often badly cooked, but the children were forced to eat it whether they liked it or not. There seemed to be an open conspiracy to force as much sloppy vegetable and still more abominable tapioca pudding down our throats as possible. Consequently, we gourmandised the more attractive and less digestible foods, which in my case led inexorably to a monthly round of bilious attacks, accompanied by nightmares when I would imagine myself growing progressively bigger and bigger amidst a swirling cloud of sheets and blankets. When I woke up screaming, my mother would be peering anxiously at me, holding a lighted candle in her hand, with my father in the background. 'He's been over-eating again,' my father would say, but I preferred my mother's comment that I was highly strung.

However, most of the memories of my childhood are as gay and brightly coloured as the figures in the toy theatre handed down to me from my grandfather. This was a complete model of a nineteenth-century theatre, with sliding grooves for the scenery, trap-doors, a roller curtain, fire-pans for burning red, blue and green fire in the wings. There was always difficulty over the blue fire because the little Victorian toyshop round the corner so rarely had it in stock. A row of practical footlights, fed from a trough of colza oil, completed the equipment. The stuffy, sweet smell of that oil lingers in memory as it did in the nursery atmosphere. A large repertoire of plays had been accumulated, many of them dating from the early years of the century when both the drawing and colouring of the scenes and figures were so beautifully done that today they are highly prized by collectors. Some of the figures were drawn as portraits of famous players of the period. One particularly ravishing creature that I loved was Morgiana in *The Forty Thieves*; she had tiny lustres sewn on to her various costumes and head-dresses. On that model stage I presented everything, from nautical drama with sinking pirate ships and cutters of the Royal Navy to the rescue, manned by sailors in hard hats and stiff pigtails (*Red Rover*), or a fast-moving panorama of the road to York, contrived by winding a painted back-cloth behind a galloping highwayman on a black horse (*Dick Turpin*), to an elaborate transformation scene at the end of a legend (*The Maid and the Magpie*). I contrived extra lighting effects by the use of candles in the wings. There was also a bull's-eye lantern with coloured glasses for limelight. Performances had to be given in the dark, so nursery routine was disorganised, particularly when the 'gala' performances took place. These were achieved by the simple process of throwing several plays together, books, scenes and characters, in one glorious hotchpotch. The gala performance might go on all day long, with results utterly incomprehensible, but this did not seem to trouble my small sister, faithful audience of one of all my play-making. She was content to peer for hours through that little cardboard proscenium. Her small eager face with its ringletted curls lighted by the flickering candles would have made a worthwhile subject for an artist. Yet woe betide her if she tried to interrupt the performance! And woe betide anyone who opened the door suddenly and destroyed my lighting effects! There would be tantrums for the rest of the day. . . .

I like to think that I absorbed some of the essential mystery that is Theatre in the long hours I spent playing in that way. And what enchanted hours they were!

6

Within its Victorian limitations our family life was a full and happy one. Parties were encouraged at all times. There was one that I never forgot. It was given by my mother's closest friend, who lived in a big Victorian house with a large family and a still larger garden. There were many parties there, both summer and winter, but I did not enjoy them very much. There was such an air of restraint swaddling her kindness—the good lady was sternly religious—and this restraint was reflected in the deportment of the nannies, those mirrors of Victorian respectability. On this occasion, a hot summer's day, one of the little boys, either a guest or one of the family, had been teasing me all the afternoon, mocking my inability to do things as well as he did. During the sumptuous tea, laid out on the lawn, he began to boast of all the characters he was going to be after tea; he would be Robin Hood, Lord Nelson, and I can't recall who else. Suddenly I lost my temper and shouted back: 'And I'm going to be G-G-God Almighty.' There was a horrified silence. The nannies duly reported the matter to Mrs. Wilkinson. I was hurriedly removed from contact with the other children, and on the following Sunday I was sent three times to church.

Both my parents loved gardens and flowers. We never knew what it was to be without a large garden to play in. Gardeners appeared at infrequent intervals, but for the most part my father did all but the heavy work. My mother's special joy was her rock garden. She once offered me sixpence if I would weed it for her. Returning from paying a call she found three of my small friends hard at work upon the appointed task with myself seated upon the topmost crag directing operations. Apparently I had told them they would get a most scrumptious tea in return for their efforts. I was, of course, to pocket the sixpence.

I made my first appearance in public at the ripe age of eight during one of the winter entertainments—penny readings they were called then—which my father organised for his mission. Dressed in a blue jersey and shorts, I recited a poem called 'The Enchanted Shirt' which was so vociferously applauded that I was forced to give an encore. Seizing the *Standard Reciter* from which I had taken my recitation, I hastily turned over the pages and started to read David Copperfield's encounter with the waiter. The spectacle of myself, very round and plump, with the heavy volume propped against my waist-belt, hugely delighted the rough audience. All went well until I reached the word 'akimbo', which I thought was a misprint. My mother from one side of the stage and my father from the other whispered energetically, but in my fright the two versions sounded quite different. Then the audience began to titter. However, I struggled to the end and left the stage amid thunderous applause but scared in my secret self at such a narrow escape from failure.

I never forgot the thrill of my first sight of the sea, that mysterious blue void at the end of a long narrow street in Brighton. I felt I was walking to the edge of the world. A later visit to Eastbourne introduced me to the delights of sea-bathing, as then understood. I shared a horrible contraption known as a bathing machine with my father. We climbed into the vehicle above the level of the tide, and, as we undressed, an aged horse towed us joltingly into the waves. My father's stern admonition not to be a cry-baby but to hang on to the rope and jump in, keeping clear of the wheels or I might bruise myself, frightened me extremely. As I surveyed the grey waters swirling round the machine, made still more uninviting by the floating horse-droppings, and watched the fat ladies bobbing up and down, the wind ballooning the voluminous wrappings of their modesty, I decided that either I must learn to swim properly or not at all.

The visit to my first pantomime holds an enchanted memory of a grand mechanical shipwreck. This took place in semi-darkness—'so that the audience won't see how it is done,' whispered my mother. When the lights came up again Crusoe had been washed ashore. He (she, really) lay fast asleep at the foot of a front-cloth depicting golden sands and palm trees. 'He' was spotlessly attired from head to foot in white, complete with feather parasol and the coolie hat from Indo-China, that apparently the part demands. I thought it the most beautiful picture I had ever seen. When my mother asked if I was enjoying myself, my eyes filled with tears and I could not say a word, so she just squeezed my hand. The stage of a theatre is a mysterious place, full of shadows and secrets of long ago. The spirit of make-believe that informs its proceedings can only make its presence felt in an atmosphere of faith and love.

7

Our parents never discussed religion in our presence. Faith was taken for granted, as we listened to the merits and demerits of the local incumbents, referred to impersonally by the consecrated names of their churches: St. Matthew's was too low and SS. Michael and All Angels somewhat on the high side. Non-conformists were looked at askance as being of a slightly inferior order of faith. As for the Catholics they were beyond the pale. When someone reported that So-and-so had 'gone over to Rome' an expression of doom spread over my father's face, and the conversation became hushed in the face of spiritual emergency. To exemplify and, as it were, reinforce the religious teaching we were assumed to have imbibed, certain moral precepts were handed down to us, chief of which was that punishment would overtake every sinner sooner or later. The public house, descendant of the gin palace of Dickens' day, was the ruin of the working class. (For some unexplained reason the country inn was more respectable.) An alternative fate awaited life's failures: the prison or the workhouse.

The Church of SS. Michael and All Angels was our usual place of worship. This example of late Victorian architecture, only half completed when we attended there, has been much admired by

John Betjeman. Across the road was the newly built Pembroke Hall where, later, I was to make various youthful appearances as an amateur actor and which, fifty years on, was to emerge from suburban obscurity to become London's first professional Theatre-in-the-Round. To the right of that again was the family home of the Watneys, the brewing family, at whose head was old Mr. Watney, a pillar of the new church and one of its churchwardens.

We were taken to church twice each Sunday, in the morning and in the evening, and no excuses were valid, except illness definitely ascertained, so that gradually I grew to hate the approach of that day with its irksome routine. My mother drew the line at afternoon Sunday School, although I suspect her objection was based on the fact that this was usually attended by the 'lower orders', to whom my father felt we should set an example. Instead, therefore, we had to memorise and recite the Collect for the day. Immediately after lunch we departed to our bedrooms, there to accomplish the memorising process. Then one by one we would lean over the banisters and call out 'ready' in shrill tones. I can still see myself, standing nervously before my father, hands behind my back, repeating words which had little meaning because my mental energies were divided between anxiety not to make a mistake and anticipation of freedom to play with my toy theatre. There was one particularly long Collect which I hated, but oh! the glee with which I observed the approach of the shortest one of all for one of the many 'Sundays after Trinity'.

Quite early in my nursery days the thought of Hell Fire began to worry me. I pictured a vast bonfire of red and orange flame into which naughty little boys were flung headlong. I wondered, too, how God found room upstairs for the immortal souls He was continually creating, and how terribly overcrowded Heaven would become if the Day of Judgment were too long delayed. I was too young to distinguish between dogma and truth, or to understand how faith can transcend logic, although even in my earliest years I could feel the fascination of ritual well performed.

One day—I must have been about ten years old—something clicked in my mind and I knew without fear of contradiction that the Angels of Heaven were mere abstractions, and that the fires of Hell had been extinguished for ever. Later on I discovered, like everyone else, that there are terrestrial hells which one can make for oneself. My mind was now free to work things out without that paralysing fear. This I proceeded to do secretly and, in my own way, even while enjoying the ritual of the church. I spent hours with my immature speculations whilst others were living in a simple communion of hearts with the Ideal or singing dull hymns out of tune. Eventually, the routine of family prayers on Sunday evenings, recited in unison and led by my father in his best clerical manner, filled me with such shyness that to this day the recollection causes me acute embarrassment. Little did my father know of the turbulence in my heart as I knelt beside him. It would have grieved him greatly to see a member of his growing family so obviously falling from Grace.

Two
School

My schooling began in the usual manner at dame school, conducted
by two maiden ladies in a large Victorian mansion situated a few
doors away from my grandmother's house. I can remember nothing
of my time there, except my first interview, standing in the middle of
what seemed a vast drawing-room, being fussed over by the principals while tears kept coming into my eyes because I was unable to
scratch the chilblains on my toes, encased in a new pair of black
boots. I mastered the three R's without much difficulty, but my
mother surveyed a larger field for my education. Her own impulse
towards self-expression had been submerged in a sea of day-to-day
anxieties and, since she had failed to arouse any interest in cultural
matters in her older children, she now turned her attention to me.
Since I was forever chanting snatches of popular songs picked up
from the barrel-organs and hurdy-gurdies to my younger sister—and
she mocking me for my mistakes:

> 'Jack's the boy for work,
> Jack's the boy for play,
> (And) Jack's the boy when girls are sad,
> To kiss the (smack) tears away.'

> 'O, Tommy (Tommy) Atkins,
> You're a good and hearty man,
> (You're a good'un, heart and hand)
> You're a credit to your country
> And to all your native land,'

my mother concluded that I must have some music in me, but, since inability to sing in tune was an obvious deterrent, singing was abandoned in favour of the pianoforte. Various unprepossessing females were hired to give me lessons, but I hated their weekly visits and the demands for daily practice. There was one creature, bearing the magical initials L.R.A.M. after her name, whom my mother was confident would overcome my reluctance. I resented her bad breath and pink nose as much as her fussy demands upon my attention by the use of a ruler over my chilblained fingers. So I early developed a technique for terminating the proceedings by mistaking her shins for the pedals.

Another horror was a children's art class that claimed to give special attention to free-hand drawing. These lessons, too, were abandoned in despair. The only painting at which I ever achieved any success was that of my own face, for which purpose by a process of exchange and barter I acquired some grease-paint and a brochure entitled *The Art of Make-up* which laid down confident rules for all types of disguise, as for instance: 'For sailors and all ruddy characters use No. 4 grease-paint', and again: 'The Chinese are invariably yellow and should be made up accordingly.'

Even a sense of rhythm was apparently denied to me, for my progress at the dancing classes conducted by Miss Hancorne James, on behalf of Mrs. Wordsworth, fashionable instructress of the day, was virtually nil. Once in each term the formidable principal came down from London to view progress, dressed in black velvet and carrying a long silver-mounted cane. She invariably singled me out for special attention, tapping my clumsy feet with the cane while the titters of the other children trickled like cold water down the back of my Little Lord Fauntleroy suit of black velvet. After much trial and mostly in error, I managed to circumnavigate the hall in the polka or the barn dance but never in the valse. . . . In the end my mother gave up wasting money on the attempt to arouse my interest in artistic matters or to inculcate the social graces in me.

Next, a leap forward to my time at a preparatory school, run by a certain Mr. Hawes, a pleasant, bustling Irishman, not at all averse to the use of the cane. The only other master of whom I have any recollection was a wild young man from Trinity College, Dublin, who refereed our football and taught us history with his tongue in his cheek, as much as to say: 'Well, you can believe it or not, but at least you will pay attention.' During the Second World War I met him again as a distinguished Harley Street specialist, employed on government service, which was an astonishing translation until he explained that he had taught us so as to earn enough money to continue his medical studies. It never occurs to children that those who teach them have lives and ambitions quite separate from their own.

By this time I was a pudgy round-faced little boy, hating all organised games, except football, much addicted to dreaming, and often teased for 'burying my nose' in books. Instinctively I sought out the most dramatic and exciting stories, preferring the Brothers Grimm to Hans Andersen, and rejecting the *Boy's Own Paper*, full of useful 'do-it-yourself' information, in favour of its rival, *Chums*, with its bloodthirsty stories and violent illustrations. There was the usual procession of children's classics such as *Swiss Family Robinson*, *Peter Penniless* and the stories of R. M. Ballantyne, superseded in turn by the historical romances of G. A. Henty. Despite their titles cunningly devised to attract boys (*With Clive in India, The Tiger of Mysore*, etc.) I found out after a little while that they were all written to a formula, and suddenly they weren't interesting any longer. However, I duly arrived at Dickens and Thackeray, and did not entirely avoid Scott. Then upon a memorable wet afternoon I encountered Mr. Sherlock Holmes beneath the light blue cover of the *Strand Magazine*, with its hansom cab bowling down Fleet Street and the shouting newsboy holding up the contents sheet. The atmosphere of suspense created by that first story was so strong that I lay awake all night, shivering in contemplation of the deadly dangers lurking behind the wardrobe. When my mother found out about it I was forbidden to read any more Sherlock Holmes, but this was too much. I retired to the most unlikely and therefore safest place. Seated on the throne, I read the latest issue. Sometimes I was too frightened to come out afterwards, so that my mother thought I had been taken ill 'in there'. Ultimately, the ban was withdrawn provided I learnt my Sunday Collect first.

In one direction my father was singularly enlightened, for he encouraged us to go to the theatre whenever funds would allow. He made no objection when my brother took me to the old Theatre Royal, known locally as 'The Blood Tub'. It was at the bottom of Crown Hill, the roughest quarter of Croydon. We used to push our way along the crowded street, with gas-lit stalls lining the kerb on either side, listen to the hoarse cries of the stallholders mingling with the arguments of the customers in one prolonged shout of salesmanship, and arrive eventually at the pit door of the theatre. Such Hogarthian surroundings were a fitting introduction to the lurid melodrama within: *The Silver King, Soldiers of the Queen, The Lights of London*, Grace Warner in *Sappho* and Sam Livesey in *The Village Blacksmith*. When the doors were opened we would go tumbling and jostling our way down the narrow stone staircase to reach the front row of the pit by hurdling the intervening benches. The place had a strangely evocative smell, compounded of leaky gas jets, scene painter's size, grease-paint and powder, beer and tobacco; it lingers in my nostrils still. Soon we would hear the cheerful cries of boys with baskets selling 'O'nges! Choclit! O'nges! Choclit! Programme!' The audience liked their situations strong and full-flavoured, blood and plenty of it. They were rowdy, generous in applause, ready to take sides with the heroine at any time, expressing joy at 'Villainy unmasked, Virtue rewarded' by thumping on the floor with their heavy boots. This was the bear-pit public whose ancestors Shakespeare knew. In spite of the contrived situations in the plays the theatre was loved; it was a place of assembly for shared enjoyment irrespective of what took place on the stage.

2

I was still at prep school when the second Boer War broke out, its opening stages marked by the usual British characteristics of lack of preparation, blind confidence and early disaster. We schoolboys shared in the excitement of the time as we watched the procession of C.I.V.* marching down the Strand in new khaki uniforms and slouched hats on their way to victory. We chanted the chorus of Rudyard Kipling's *The Absent-Minded Beggar* and collected effigies of our favourite generals, printed on little ivorine buttons with the Union Jack in the background. They were supplied with safety-pins so that you could, if you wished, wear your heart upon your sleeve, so to speak. We ran an 'Exchange and Mart' system for the discarding of duplicates and the acquisition of rarities. The names come back to me: Wauchope, Gateacre, Kelly-Kenny, Sir George White (locked up in Ladysmith), Buller, Methuen, French and Baden-Powell: all but the latter cheating us of our hopes of victory. My brother was at home recovering from measles when it was announced that Roberts and Kitchener (military idols of the nation) were being

* City of London Imperial Volunteers.

C

sent out. I found him sitting up in bed, excitedly waving the newspaper. 'It won't be long now,' he said. On the night that Mafeking was relieved hysteria took over, and a new word was added to the language. I remember my shocked parents telling us how they had seen quite respectable people piling furniture on the street bonfires.

I had my first brush with popular science when the sixth form at my prep school was given a practical demonstration of the latest wonder, the phonograph. The lecturer arrived with a clumsy apparatus consisting mainly of a large brass cylinder made to revolve beneath a fixed microphone with a little tin mouthpiece attached. When tubes coated with silver foil were slipped over the cylinder and certain adjustments made it was possible to hear our own voices reproduced in faint, tinny accents. Some years later my father acquired an expensive gramophone in discharge of a bad debt. It was equipped with a huge aluminium speaker and a collection of discs, including the earliest recordings made by Melba and Caruso. There were also a number of orchestral pieces, one of which so caught my fancy that I played it over and over again until my younger sister was moved to protest. The piece was 'Gymnopedie' by Erik Satie. In later years I often regretted the lost opportunity of acquiring a basic knowledge of the theory and practice of music, due to a teacher's lack of understanding and my own laziness.

3

One glorious May morning I found myself among a group of rather forlorn little boys standing under the giant elms that lined the playing fields at Whitgift, watching the older boys laughing and greeting each other on the first day of the new term. Overhead the rooks wheeled and dipped and cawed; everything expressing the joy of spring. For a few vivid moments I was lost in a sense of abstract beauty, until summoned by a junior master to join the file of boys in the cloisters on their way in to Big School for prayers. In recollection I regard this as my first aesthetic experience, which is perhaps why it remains so clearly etched in my memory.

The Whitgift Foundation, created by the Archbishop of that name in the reign of Queen Elizabeth, consisted at that time of the Grammar School, which occupied a large area in the very centre of the town, an Elizabethan 'hospital for aged pensioners' perched on top of Crown Hill, its beautiful quadrangle of flint and brick already under fire as a tiresome obstruction on the town's main traffic route, but sufficiently regarded to arouse local citizens to successful defence against successive agitations for its removal; and Middle School, housed in the roughest quarter of the town. With schoolboy snobbery we regarded Middle School as a much lower form of educational life than our own. Its fees were lower, too. The two schools kept rigidly to themselves, except occasionally when resentment surged up Crown Hill. Then street fighting would break out, much to the annoyance of parents and masters. All aspects of the Whitgift Foundation were a source of pride to the townspeople of that time, and the stream of boys bearing the Archbishop's mitre on their caps was a familiar afternoon sight in the High Street.

When I joined the school its outlook upon education was conventional and class-conscious without the saving grace of a great institution like Eton whose scholars face the world with an ease of manner that stays with them for life. It combined a thorough grounding in elementary classics and English literature with the achievement of a respectable games standard in competition with public schools of similar size. Some of the masters were long past the age of retirement and scholarship was at a low ebb. Consequently the school governors had recently decided upon a shake-up and announced the appointment of a new headmaster. It was for that reason that my entry into the school had been delayed beyond the normal age. So I found myself in Form IV A, presided over by a master called Dodd, who possessed a stentorian voice and marshalled our attention rather like recruits on the barrack square. Facts imparted by his method were never forgotten.

The new head, S. O. Andrew, was destined to leave an indelible mark upon the place and to raise its status among junior public schools. His opening address in Big School had a tremendous impact. His downright attack upon the general slackness of the place, including such matters as the appearance of schoolboy graffiti on some of the urinals—a word I had never heard before— delivered in rasping North Country accents, took us all by surprise. At first we thought him a bounder to mention such things, but he speedily shook us out of that. A posse of new masters appeared with him, who promptly set about modernising the place, dividing Upper School into classical and science sides, and encouraging interhouse rivalry of every sort.

Whitgift's reputation for games, especially cricket, was higher than its achievements in scholarship. This may have been due to the fact that the sons of the Reverend Crawford, an early master, had been educated there. My brother used to show me score-cards with a monotonous list of centuries scored by them against important public schools. I am no student of *Wisden*, but I believe that both V. F. S. and Jack Crawford subsequently played for Surrey. But our reputation in the national game must have begun still earlier, for I have a distinct recollection of seeing Dr. W. G. Grace with his great beard emerging from the pavilion to bat on Big Field when I was taken there as a tiny boy by my father, for many years the senior Old Whitgiftian living. In this matter of cricket I was no conformist, for I detested the game. My hatred of it arose from the simple fact that owing to poor eyesight I could never see the ball until either it hit me in the stomach or broke my fingernails when I tried to catch it. When I was very small my brother used to bowl 'yorkers' at me because he said I was a little 'funk', which was true. One of these gave me a black eye which lasted for weeks, and converted my nervousness at cricket into a minor complex.

Football was a different matter. I enjoyed rugger because then I did have a chance of seeing the ball occasionally. I played for my house and soon reached the School Second XV, playing beside Arthur Tedder* who was my junior by about a year. I remember him as a boy of great charm with a good-humoured smile and an imperturbable manner. Another of my contemporaries bearing a name familiar to the general public was Dudley Bowater of the famous paper-making family. His claim to distinction lay not so much on the football field as in his immaculate clothes. They were made in Savile Row surely, and the envy of us all!

The School Cadet Corps, later renamed the O.T.C., wore uniforms of dark green, pork-pie hats with chin-straps, bandoliers and cartouche cases of black patent leather and black leggings laced up with string. We were armed with carbines dating from the Crimean War. Drill was elementary, mainly conducted by a retired sergeant-major on behalf of the arts master who was nominally in charge. Whenever the latter was on parade the sergeant-major put up a tremendous show of discipline to which we valiantly responded. Off parade he was friendly and relaxed, full of tall stories of the North West Frontier.

* The future Marshal of the Royal Air Force, Lord Tedder.

I remain grateful to the O.T.C. in one respect, for it was during firing practice on the morris tube range that my disability was at last discovered. During the shoot-off to select our team to compete for the Ashburton Shield at Bisley, which the school had won once— and still looked up to as a great achievement—I began by scoring several bulls, but when the cards were sent up for inspection lo! I had been peppering the target of the boy firing next to me. My target was unscathed, which drew a torrent of heavy sarcasm from the sergeant-major.

4

Now I come to a turning-point in my story, not apparent at the time but clear enough in retrospect. A sharp attack of rheumatic fever kept me from school for the whole of one term. I returned to find several changes in the teaching staff. Senior classes in English literature and history were now being taken by a new man, Norman Frazer, a brilliant teacher, who opened the minds of his pupils to these subjects in a manner quite different from the teaching methods then current.

Frazer was a man of average height with iron-grey hair and a small reddish beard. He had a brusque sarcastic manner and a waspish tongue at the first sign of insubordination. Above all, his manner of teaching was dynamic. Once your attention was engaged he never let go. For instance, he might be dealing with some dull portion of overfamiliar Plantagenet history. Suddenly, the historical dummies come alive, jump as it were from behind the arras, character illuminated and motives explained. It was like that throughout the term as he took us rapidly through Green's *Short History* in what he called a preliminary canter. By the end I believe the whole class understood the significance of the major events of our history. It was the same with literature. For example, as with most boys of my day, my mind was slammed tight against Shakespeare because of the detestable exercise then prevalent in English schools of making us analyse and parse extracts from the plays, a process rather like dissecting a corpse and then expecting it to spring to life again. Frazer led me along the path to understanding and then enjoyment with a firm hand. I date the beginning of my intellectual progress from his time.

There was one other boy in the English VIth whom Frazer influenced in a similar way. His name was Robert Keable. Son of a Nonconformist minister, tallish, red-haired and quick-tempered, he was already giving signs of the temperament that was to lead him away from the beaten track of his contemporaries. We had been friends since preparatory schooldays, and now ran neck and neck in the race for Frazer's encouragement. Sometimes Frazer would invite us to read our essays aloud, and sometimes he would quote from them himself. Keable and I used to go round to his rooms for tea and talks, seeking information about books, firing questions to test his opinions on this and that, and then comparing notes as we walked home together. It was hero-worship in an advanced form.

5

The time had now come for me to think about a career. Dazzled by the romantic notions which Frazer's dynamism had aroused, I saw myself in some important post influencing history in the making, without any clear idea what that might be. I began to look forward as eagerly to Oxford as Bob Keable did to Cambridge, and to work with an energy that astonished Frazer. He lent me books, made the necessary enquiries as to university scholarships, and backed up the headmaster's assurance of my future success. My mother began an anxious search for influential friends or relations who might help things along, but my father kept noticeably silent. I concluded that he wasn't really interested in what might happen to me, or else that he was haunted by the spectre of his bankruptcy. When the blow fell which ruined my hopes of a scholastic career, I was quite unprepared. My father told me he could not afford to keep me at the university for the necessary three years, notwithstanding any scholarships that I might win. In those days these were fewer and the doors of opportunity for members of impoverished middle-class families much harder to push open. As my elder brother had not been to a university and was now carving out a successful commercial career for himself in the City my father saw no reason why I should receive different treatment. I was bitterly resentful. It never occurred to me that he doubted my ability on current showing to win a place in the difficult Civil Service examinations.

We had now removed to Sanderstead, a few miles from Croydon. At that time it was a small village at the beginning of the Surrey Downs, with some cottages and a nice old church on the top of the hill and at its foot one or two new houses surrounded by acres of undulating cornfields and coppices of beechwood. We occupied one of these new houses with a large garden, part of it left uncultivated as woodland, where my father could indulge his passion for gardening. The whole district is now a dormitory suburb, but when I knew it one still walked through the waving corn to the railway station.

Next door to us there lived Howard Page, a young businessman with his very attractive wife and twin sons. Over the fence, the heads of the two households exchanged plants and bulbs and confidences as to the future careers of their progeny. Page had another hobby besides gardening, a passion for motor-cycling, then in its infancy. He had acquired a second-hand 4 h.p. Triumph, a machine of an early type in which the mixture of petrol and air was controlled by hand. For some reason or other Page never mastered the trick of this. He would drag the back wheel of the cycle on to its stand and sit in the saddle pedalling like mad, at the same time fiddling with the carburetter in an effort to coax an explosion out of the mixture. There would be a succession of long and short coughs like the Morse code, followed by hiccoughs and sighs as the engine lost compression, and then a long pause before another attempt. Alternatively, parts of the machine would be strewn in a widening circle about his lawn whilst he cheerfully disembowelled various parts of the engine. Occasionally, there would be a desperate sortie out into the road, followed by a crestfallen return. I was never able to laugh very much at Harry Tate's motoring sketch after that. I had seen a much funnier performance.

Our neighbour was the junior partner in a small but influential firm that conducted mysterious operations in the Money Market. This seemed to my father an intriguing possibility for his younger son, especially as it had to do with a commodity that had eluded him throughout his life. Gradually, from the various hints that were dropped, I learned the fate that was being prepared for me, but I was determined to avoid being swallowed up in the maw of City life.

The opening of new chemistry and physics laboratories at the school suggested a convenient escape route. I suddenly announced that I wanted to become an analytical chemist, and went to Mr. Frazer one day and told him, without giving the situation away—

I had enough family pride for that—I wanted to transfer to the newly formed Science VIth. He thought I had taken leave of my senses, and tried to dissuade me. My father, sensing the depth of my disappointment over the university, allowed me to stay on at school for an extra term or two to give my desperate experiment a chance. Joining me in the class were three senior boys, all of whom I assume achieved distinction in their chosen fields. For me it was just a leap from one illusion to another. I was searching, searching without really knowing what I was looking for. However, I trusted to my ability to remember what I did not understand. The truth is I was still in a romantic turmoil about my career and now saw myself making wonderful discoveries that would benefit both mankind and my own pocket. How this was to be achieved by uncovering glass jars filled with sulphuretted hydrogen during lectures, or squirting distilled water over the laboratory assistant, did not occur to me. All adolescents dislike being cross-questioned, and in my state of mind my father's well-meaning enquiries as to my progress in science made matters worse. The whole business was foolish to a degree and could have had but one end. Once my parents realised I was wasting my time I was told I must leave school at the end of the term and start life in the City, whether I liked it or not.

In spite of all the upset I finally left school in an unexpected blaze of glory after playing the leading part of Dick Bultitude in Anstey's play *Vice Versa*, the play chosen that Christmas for our annual performance in aid of the school charities. Playing opposite me in the girl's part was Arthur Tedder, who also played my better half on the school football field, where we danced attendance on the rugger scrum. My acting was accounted a great success, even the unapproachable Head, Dr. Andrew, pausing in the cloisters the following morning to congratulate me and to wish me well in my career. At that time I had no thought of going on the stage and did not take the Head's good wishes in that sense. So I left school without any sense of direction and with my ambition smothered in a cloud of resentment.

Three
Crossing the bridge

For the first month or two after I joined the hurrying crowd of
bowler hats on their daily journey across dirty old London Bridge I
felt completely at a loss. There were few women to be seen in the
City then. Those that had business there used the horse-buses,
leaving businessmen and their clerks to their brief exercise. On
November days everybody walked through the yellow-green murk.
On wet days if one ventured too near the kerb one could be liberally
splashed with the London compost, part liquified horse-manure,
part ordinary mud.

The familiar image of Howard Page, red in the face and sweating,
pedalling away like mad on his jacked-up motor-cycle, was now
transformed into an elegant figure in silk hat, short black coat and
shepherd's plaid trousers, rushing in and out of the office in pursuit
of fractional percentages on fairy-tale sums of money. The senior
partner, Mr. Granville, was an awesome person who seldom spoke
to the clerks, leaving all matters of office routine to Page, while
he gave his attention to maintaining personal relations with the
merchant bankers and heads of discount houses who were his clients.
His shambling walk and a mode of dress, untidy within conventional limits, suggested a professor engaged in remote areas of
research rather than the solid prosperity of the Money Market.
When the shooting season began he was often absent from the office
for days at a time, returning when sport had been good with presents
of partridge and pheasant for our chief clerk. Coste was a perky, neat
little Cockney, who had begun his life with the firm as the office
boy, was now the mainstay of the place and destined to achieve

eventually a partnership. He showed me much kindness and covered up my worst errors of omission. I wondered about the clerks who were senior to me; their prospects seemed dim. But those were the days of colonial expansion when thousands of young men, lacking privilege at home, found fortune if not fame in our burgeoning dominions.

The office, with its shabby mahogany and horse-hair furniture, blazing coal fires and grimy light reflectors attached to the outside of the windows to catch the stray beams of light that found their way into the tiny courtyard, was like a scene out of Dickens. Smells everywhere: first thing in the morning of brown Windsor soap after the Mrs. Mopps had done their worst, and laden dustbins lining the passages and interior courtyards; at lunch-time of sizzling chops and steaks from the nearby chop-houses; all day long a pervasive smell of soot. The street scene reminded me of the cover of the *Strand Magazine*: hansom cabs, newsboys carrying bundles of papers under their arms, contents bills held in front of them like aprons, shouting the latest editions as they dodged in and out amongst the gaily-coloured horse-buses—royal blue for Waterloo, red to Hammersmith and a white one to Putney; street scavengers (so they were called for all their blue overalls and slouch hats) with brush and pan pouncing upon the horse-droppings, sometimes awaiting the event right under the animal's feet; cheesemongers, bun and coffee shops, wine shops: finally the surge home across London Bridge. Everywhere the feel of prosperity, good humour, hearty eating, hearty living. Indeed, the whole of my brief incursion into City life takes on a warm glow as I think of it, although it was drab enough at the time.

The conferences that went on in the partner's room—although the business was a prosperous one the premises consisted of only two rooms—remained as mysterious to me as did the more obvious routine of the firm's operations. Apparently speed in conveying messages, cheques and securities to the various offices in the Money Market was essential. The clerk told to collect the news of the Bank Rate every Thursday was expected to rush at high speed from Threadneedle Street through the alleys behind Cornhill to the office in Gracechurch Street where the partners waited impatiently. Personally, I never felt any inclination to hurry as I could not persuade myself to any interest in the merry-go-round and frequently got into hot water in consequence. On days when the rate was changed, provided the change was in the firm's favour, the atmosphere in the office became hilarious, like an old fashioned billiard-room in a country hotel on market day, full of smoke, bustle and rough fun that sometimes ended in an actual scrimmage on the floor in which the younger partners joined. On specified days in the week the partners would take their lunch in the inner room. Then waiters from one of the many chop-houses in the area—the Bell Tavern, Simpson's in Cornhill, Birch's, Crosby Hall, and the George and Vulture near Lombard Street, and several more—would call round for orders and later bring in battered old tin trays laden with succulent chops, or steaks, fried potatoes and pewter tankards of beer. Upon one occasion the waiter failed to turn up and I was told to go and fetch the meal. As my own lunch usually consisted of coffee and sandwiches at a little bun shop round the corner, I felt a twitching of the stomach as I bore the rich-smelling food into the office. It was an exceptionally busy day, and the partners hurried out to interview the discount houses, leaving half-eaten meals on their plates. When Howard Page returned he jokingly offered me the coagulated remains of the chump chop he had left to keep warm by the office fire. I can remember the hot flush on my face as the other clerks roared with laughter at the joke. This humiliated me more than having to carry the trays. At that moment I felt no gratitude at all to Page for what my father called 'giving me a start in life'.

A few days later I was told to take a cheque for one million pounds to a certain bank. The cashier grinned at me and said: 'Aren't you thrilled to be carrying all that money about, my boy?' 'No,' I snapped back, and walked out, thinking, 'I shall never be any good at this job. I have always hated arithmetic. I must get out.'

At home I now became resentful and secretive, thinking of ways of escape to the golden lands of opportunity; anywhere away from the rut of City life, perhaps to join my brother in India or a cousin in Canada where the Government offer of 160 free acres sounded like easy riches. There had recently come to live near us Joseph Flint, a bluff Yorkshireman who had been retired from his post as district manager of the old Niger Company. Disappointed of the larger responsibilities he had hoped for when the territory came under the Colonial Office—the award of the C.M.G. was no compensation—Flint sought consolation in London club life. Out of regard for my mother, whom he greatly admired, he took me under his wing, trotting me round the West End, introducing me as his nephew at the Oriental Club then in Hanover Square. His fascinating stories of early days on the Niger River, of journeys up-country in native canoes to open new trading stations, of the language of the drums, of the constant battle against malaria, fought in those days with whisky and quinine, of cannibalism, and dangerous barter with native chiefs; in short, all the mysterious atmosphere that still shrouded 'darkest Africa' in Edwardian times set me off again. But while 'Uncle Joe' sympathised with my refusal to accept my present fate, he was scornful when I suggested that I, too, might seek a fortune in Africa. Thus, to all my romantic enquiries I received firm and commonsense replies.

2

During the winter months I became more and more involved with amateur dramatic clubs, appearing as a 'guest player' with one or two of them and later reviving an organisation that had originally been founded in 1880 with the high-sounding title of the Charity Aid Entertainment Society. We were an enthusiastic band who pledged ourselves to give performances in aid of any charity whose application for help had been accepted by the committee. A small percentage of the 'gate', plus acting subscriptions, sufficed for the expenses. In the two brief seasons of its revival the little society gave performances in various suburbs and for many causes. Also, I took up fencing, not as a deliberate training for the stage, but because I imagined in a vague sort of way that all successful actors were expert swordsmen. A lengthy series of private lessons with the sergeant-major of the school O.T.C. made serious inroads into my meagre salary, but at least made me proficient in the use of foils.

In the summer I went every night after the office was closed to the West End to join the gallery queues waiting to see the current plays, then catching the last train home and walking from the station through the fields, not at all admiring the natural scene but concentrating upon the stage scene I had just left, and vaguely formulating a criticism of each play, which later I set down in writing. I regret I have not these criticisms now. They would have supplied useful information about the plays and actors I saw at that time. In the short space of a few weeks I must have been in every gallery in London.

I was now in the second year of my existence among those

kindly City people, yet I remained as ignorant of the principles that governed their business as on the first day I walked through the swingdoor of the outer office. Subconsciously, I suppose, my mind was preoccupied with thinking about the possibilities of a stage career, but I had not the faintest idea how to set about it.

3

The summit of my playgoing was reached on a night in June, 1906, when my brother and I sat on camp stools under the great colonnade of the Theatre Royal, Drury Lane, waiting to go into the Ellen Terry Jubilee Matinée on the following afternoon. It must have been one of the earliest instances of an all-night theatre queue. My brother and I were determined to get good seats in the pit (at ten shillings each). We arrived at nine o'clock in the evening, to find some thirty or forty people there before us. By midnight news of the queue had drawn the town. The street leading to the stage-door was crowded with playgoers returning home, including the *haut monde* from the Grand Opera Season, with market idlers and people of every sort, all come to gape and see the fun. Many of the great ones of the stage, who were to do honour to Ellen Terry on the morrow, joined the throng until the canvas was as crowded and varied as Frith's 'Derby Day'. Hawkers sold us oranges and sweets and fetched mugs of hot coffee, while the hansom cabbies drove up and down, cracking their whips and throwing chaff at the crowd like confetti. The word went round that Ellen herself had arrived to see the queue. Little gusts of cheers blew up and down the waiting line as she drove jingling past. Gradually, the sight-seers drifted away, leaving us to the longest time of waiting. Soon the first of the great lumbering market carts began to arrive, adding a general confusion of horse to humanity. As the dawn stretched above the roof-tops the summer air blew clammy breaths of spring cabbage and fresh turned earth up and down the street. The market stalls were made ready for the new day.

We stormed into the pit about noon, only to find it had been reduced to half its size to make room for additional stalls. Many of those who had waited confidently all night found themselves jammed tightly into standing rows at the back. Late-comers were sent away in hundreds. There were angry shouts and cries against the management. Some of the rougher elements began to break up the seating. My brother and I had secured places in the centre of the second row, but we were not sure that we were going to be allowed to stay there. Appeals from the attendants and assistant managers were drowned in the hubbub.

Eventually, Arthur Collins had to be sent for. He came stalking down the centre aisle in the stalls in top-hat and frock-coat, waving his arms and appealing for quiet. When the din subsided, he pointed out that the pit had been reduced in size ('No pit left, guv'nor!') in order to make as much money as possible for 'our beloved Ellen'. ('Hear, hear! Boo! Quite right! Boo! Bet she knows nothing about it. Three cheers for our Ellen!') Eventually order was restored. Collins went back to his lunch at the Savoy and we settled down to a further two hours' wait.

Only a few memories of that tribute to the greatest female personality on the English stage since Mrs. Siddons remain in my mind. The rest is a jumble of scenery, cheers and waving programmes. Clearest recollection of all is of Ellen making her entrance as Beatrice in a scene from *Much Ado About Nothing*—Beerbohm Tree was the Benedick—and of how the other actors stood stockstill, watching the great actress receive her welcome. Many of them must have been in tears, as were the audience, standing on their seats and in the aisles, waving top-hats, programmes, bouquets, anything that was to hand. A little while later the welcome broke out again, as she spoke the lines so associated with her that they had become as it were her signature tune:

> '. . . but then there was a star danced,
> and under that was I born.'

Later there was Charles Wyndham in the drinking scene from *The School for Scandal*—I think George Alexander was the 'Careless'— with Ben Davies singing 'Here's to the maiden of bashful fifteen', and Edward Terry as Moses. Wyndham's style and charm compensated for the fact that he was much too old for the part. Then came Coquelin aîné and Coquelin fils, acting a duologue from Molière in front of a flapping front-cloth, both attired in frock-coats and looking like two black crows in argument, one short and fat and the other tall and thin. The French dialogue received flattering laughter from the stalls and cheerfully uncomprehending titters from the pit. Towards six o'clock came the final tribute when Ellen Terry stood in the middle of the stage embowered with flowers and surrounded by what seemed to be the entire theatrical profession. The cheering and the speeches went on and on. For my part I sat and stared at a stately woman dressed all in black, standing motionless amongst the brilliant crowd on the stage. It was Eleonora Duse. Unlike Sarah Bernhardt, no question of rival importance or dignity had troubled her; she had made a special journey from Italy to be present.

4

Subconsciously, my mind was now made up. In consequence, my work at the office began to improve, so much so that one day Page invited me into the inner sanctum where he and his partners were enjoying their after-lunch cigars. He made me a pleasant little speech; out of the high regard he had for my mother and the fact that I was doing so much better in the office, the firm had decided to double my salary from forty to eighty pounds per annum. He hoped this would encourage me to continue with my present energy, and that I would enjoy being with them for a long time, and so on and so forth. I thanked him and left the room. Over my office tea I decided I could not delay any longer. Plans had to be made. The unexpected kindness of the partners had cleared the air. As I had no intention of remaining with the firm it was not right to mislead them by taking the extra money and saying nothing. Besides, I should need much more money! Dreaming of a world made up of loving kindness, I decided to appeal to these two prosperous gentlemen to help me to become an actor!

The next day I waited until after they had finished their lunch, and then went in and told my story. I had decided to go on the stage, but I could not do so until I had saved a little more money, and would they please make it at least a hundred pounds per annum. I can still see the partners spluttering over their coffee at my impudence. 'What! What! What!' said one. 'Most certainly not,' said the other.

As I ignominiously left the room I realised I had burnt my boats. The news would travel quickly across the garden fence to my father. I borrowed some money from the chief clerk and hurried to a shop in St. Martin's Lane where I had espied an elaborate make-up box in the window. I bought the box, filled it with a large assortment of grease-paints of every colour and hue, returned home and announced my decision to go on the stage. I make no apology for myself for this rather childish approach to my ambition. If I did not know anyone connected with the theatre, at least I could buy myself some grease-paints!

The practical problem of how to make contact with a world so remote still had to be solved. Three Whitgiftians had achieved prominence on the London stage, Leon Quartermaine, his brother Charles, and, more recently, Harcourt Williams, who was only a year or so senior to my brother, so I worried him into seeing me, which he did one Sunday afternoon. My first task was to convince him that I was in earnest, but all I could get in reply was that if he heard of anything suitable he would let me know, a phrase that was to become all too familiar to me. Two theatrical papers, *The Stage* and *The Era*, carried columns of advertisements each week, announcing vacancies in provincial companies, and an even larger number from actors offering their services. They were couched in a language all their own, doubtless designed to assist the conduct of business but very confusing to a beginner. I pestered Harcourt Williams week after week for advice as to which of them to answer. His replies were always salutary, warning me against advertisements written from obscure addresses containing promises that suitable applicants would be given full instruction in the art of acting on payment of a premium. The majority of the profession still held the view that acting could not be taught; it was an Eleusinian Mystery whose neophytes were expected to learn its secrets at the expense of the public.

The last time I went to see Harcourt Williams he mentioned casually that Benson's leading man, Cyril Keightley, was about to form a company of his own to tour in Old English comedies; he would have many Old Bensonians with him. Why not write to him? He would write, too. This seemed like the break-through. After an agonising wait Keightley replied to my letter, pointing out that he did not pay salaries to amateurs, at the same time inviting me to call at his house in Kensington during my lunch break to read a small part in a new play to be included in the repertoire. He sat there with a cheerful grin while I stumbled through a few sentences. Indeed, he seemed to regard the whole matter as a huge joke, possibly because of my complete disregard for the facts of the situation. However, at the end of the reading he handed me my first theatrical contract, under which I undertook to give eight performances per week for the sum of one guinea. I also bound myself to obey a variety of rules and regulations. For instance, if I should ever be more than ten minutes late for rehearsal I was liable to be fined two-and-six. I almost ran back to the City, handed in my resignation to the partners and proudly informed the outer office that I was about to become a professional actor, that in fact I had already signed my first contract! . . . Thus it was that I found my way to the career that must have been at the back of my mind all the time.

5

The excitement of going on the stage carried me successfully through occasional moods of anxiety at the thought of leaving home, especially when my mother, to whom I was devoted in a hard, ambitious sort of way, came to see me off at the local station. There had always been a secret understanding between us that one day I would break away. Now the time had come. Yet shyness put a barrier between us and prevented me from putting my thoughts into words, while she stood on the platform with tears in her eyes, waving me goodbye and holding my dog, who was whining and struggling to join me in the carriage.

Cyril Keightley was an Australian of great charm and easy manners. His company was composed of Old Bensonians and members of the equally well-known Compton Comedy Company, which had recently been disbanded. They all appeared to be on excellent terms with one another, full of little jokes, and exchanging useful information about good theatrical addresses to be found on the tour. The Bensonians with their traditional outlook of good fellowship suffered my presence as the youngest member of the company with easy tolerance, and the Compton ladies gave me fleeting smiles of encouragement. As I stepped on to the stage of the Opera House, Cheltenham, on September 3rd, 1906, in an extremely silly costume drama entitled *Miles Carew, Highwayman*, I had no reason to fear that my honeymoon with the theatre would prove disappointing.

Initial anxieties about finding lodgings and maintaining myself on a weekly salary of one guinea without drawing upon my slender reserves were removed when Henry Crocker, our stage manager,

D

invited me to share rooms with him and his assistant. Crocker, who had been Edward Compton's stage manager and was married to one of his daughters, knew well how to avoid the worst discomforts of touring. Some of these were unexpected. Brought up in the strict Victorian tradition in which women were still supposed to be without natural functions, at all events as far as their behaviour in public was concerned, I found it embarrassing to be told to wait my turn as I made my way to the outside lavatory past the landlady's daughters in the crowded kitchen.

In addition to their tradition of cricket and football as a means of healthy exercise for actors the Bensonians brought with them a love of practical jokes which added to the genial atmosphere. Inevitably, I suppose, I was made the victim of one of them. It occurred just before our first Saturday matinée. Anxious to learn all I could I had offered my services as an additional stage manager, and this was to be my first spell of duty in the prompt corner. In those days the theatre curtain was usually made of canvas, upon which the local scenic artist had indulged his taste for fantasy, such as scantily draped ladies in pseudo-Grecian costume and hair-do's, posing amidst the broken columns of ruined temples. This display of scenic art, known to all stage managers as the act drop, was controlled from the prompt corner by a tinkling little bell or a buzzer. On this Saturday afternoon the overture had begun, and Henry Crocker was standing beside me in the prompt corner, dressed for his part in the play. Suddenly he turned to me: 'Have you got the key of the act drop ready?' 'No,' I said blankly. 'Good God, the flyman must have it,' said Crocker, 'run and get it quickly.'

I rushed up several flights of stone steps and eventually reached what I was told was the fly floor where a shirt-sleeved functionary regarded me sourly. 'Where's the key?' I asked breathlessly. 'What key?' 'The key of the act drop, of course.' He must have been in the game, the rascal, for he just turned his back, and said Mr. Keightley had it.

Back I tore down the steps to No. 1 dressing-room, which the actor-manager was just leaving to make his first entrance. 'What's the matter?' he said, as I rushed towards him. When I told him, he laughed, and brushed past me on to the stage, leaving Mr. Crocker to ring up the curtain and me to recover my wits as best I could.

I was determined that nothing like that should happen to me again. So I set out to learn all about the technical workings of a stage, pestering the master carpenters of the various theatres we visited for explanations as to why they did certain things in certain ways. Property masters were another useful source of information with their innumerable stories of resource in moments of crisis; so, too, were their property rooms, choked to the ceiling with all manner of gleanings: dilapidated bits of furniture of every conceivable period, old pantomime masks, bric-à-brac old and new, all testifying to the proud claim of every property master to be the most skilled scrounger and borrower in the town. Much of the stuff did not appear to have been turned over for years; it would have been a rich harvest for any acquisitive antique dealer. My curiosity vastly amused Baliol Holloway, an actor of charm, fine presence and great possibility, to whom ultimate fulfilment was to be denied because of the nineteenth-century style of acting in which he had been reared and which he was never able entirely to shake off.

6

The romantic haze through which I was viewing everything coloured my first impressions, but I soon tired of the interminable stage gossip, although it was often funny and sometimes malicious. I began to wonder whether I could ever really belong to a world bounded solely by the footlights and the dressing-room. There was one member of the company who stood apart from the others. This was Iden Payne, whose help and encouragement were to influence my career so profoundly. With his long fair hair, fresh complexion and pince-nez glasses, he looked more like a medical student than an actor. In the intervals of rehearsal and in the dressing-room he seemed always to be reading. When he did join in the conversation his light clear voice enunciated ideas completely at odds with the commonplace talk of the others, who listened in silence and with raised eyebrows. I was fascinated. We began to talk, or rather he talked and I listened, while he set about converting me from my middle-class acceptance of the social order to a more critical outlook. I began to realise I had been living within a kind of mental closed circuit ever since my mood of sulky rebellion at home. He spoke about William Morris and the beginnings of Socialism. Thoreau's *Walden* was the first book he lent me, then Walt Whitman's *Leaves of Grass*. Soon he had me reading Blatchford's *Britain for the British*, Prince Kropotkin's *Field, Factory and Workshop*,

and Samuel Butler's *Erehwon*. He introduced me to Ibsen, the early
Shaw, H. G. Wells, and a world of free-thinking literature previously
unknown to me. I was eager to absorb all the new ideas, not always,
I fear, with a complete understanding of their implications. We
argued endlessly, setting the world to rights both politically and
economically at least once a week.

Next I was persuaded into vegetarianism. Like my mentor, I
began to live on fresh fruit and vegetables, wholemeal bread and
various kinds of butter made from nuts. I was introduced to vegetarian steaks, though why they were so named was puzzling. I
was shown physical exercises designed to control breathing and to
improve enunciation. All this was an expression of Payne's belief in
a disciplined life for the actor. Although our association at that time
lasted only for a few months it occurred precisely at the right
juncture for me. I was resuming my education after a brief flirtation
with 'the City'. Looking back, I must acknowledge what a good
and sensitive tutor Payne was. His work in founding Miss Horniman's company in Manchester and his ultimate career in America
exemplified this.

7

Long before the end of the tour I began to worry about my next
engagement. An early visit to Blackmore's Theatrical Agency in
London, the only one of any note at that time, was a miserable
experience. The clerk who sat in the outer office had earned himself
a scabrous reputation for curt dismissal of unwanted applicants.
'Nothing today, thank you,' he would mutter without even looking
up at the leading lady with faded make-up, nervously waving an
appointment card. The crowded outer room and the array of eager
faces looking up expectantly whenever the inner door opened and
a manager emerged to dart across the room into the street, to avoid
the appealing glances of the unemployed standing about in groups,
was a picture I have never forgotten. My brief interview with the
dreaded Mr. Blackmore, a dark and dapper little man with cruel
eyes, was short and dismissive. I vowed I would never go to see
him again.

Thanks to a generously worded letter from Cyril Keightley I
found myself journeying to Bury St. Edmunds on the night of

December 30th, 1906, to join a new company formed by Florence Glossop-Harris, daughter of the famous Sir Augustus Harris of Drury Lane, at the instigation of her recently acquired husband, Frank Cellier. The repertoire had been chosen with both eyes upon the parts in which the leading lady most fancied herself, such as Juliet, Beatrice and Viola from the Shakespearean canon; in romantic drama a new translation of *La Dame aux Camélias*, and a dramatic version of *Carmen*.

Florence Glossop-Harris was an indifferent actress, and certainly no Carmen! She had assembled a company of similar indifferent quality. Most of the women were younger than herself, but they were kindly and hard-working, dispensing an aura of faded optimism that invoked sympathy but failed to conceal a lack of talent. The men spent their odd moments during rehearsals gossiping in the nearest pub, whence they could be sent for by the stage manager. Apart from Frank Cellier, who became a very good actor indeed, there was obviously no future in store for any of them.

The complete repertoire was presented or, more accurately, thrown upon the stage during the first six weeks of the tour. Yet I can remember little of it, neither the performances nor how the engagement ended, whether by my own choice, or by notice given. The only memory that persists is of myself humping a heavy gladstone bag through the deserted streets of Bury St. Edmunds where we were due to open the tour on the following day with a matinée of *Carmen*. (The lovely Theatre Royal is today happily rescued from its prolonged degradation as a beer warehouse.) The city was under deep snow and strangely quiet until a church clock struck ten. It was New Year's Eve. I had been given two addresses of lodgings. At the first I was refused. I stood outside in the snow with my bag on the pavement, feeling like one of the orphans of the storm. But at the second address, a cottage in a side-street, the woman was friendly and soon made me feel at home in her sitting-room. I looked forward hopefully to my second engagement, for which the salary had been increased to twenty-five shillings per week.

8

Next I joined Ian Maclaren's Shakespeare Company at a salary of thirty shillings a week. I was going up in the world. Maclaren was a competent work-horse of an actor, devoid of subtlety, with a good voice and a certain straightforward charm. He travelled with a buxom wife, even more simple minded than her spouse, who played all Shakespeare's heroines with buoyant inadequacy. Occasionally their children appeared, travelling with them through the holiday time and later packed off whence they had come to resume their schooling. The company included one experienced actor, recruited from melodrama, who shared the manager's acting burdens playing Iago to his Othello, for instance, also two or three elderly 'Shakespeareans', acting in the style of the previous century, and a bunch of eager youngsters like myself, openly competing for the parts left over. My chief rival in this regard was George Relph. At our first encounter we fell to arguing the respective merits of Rosencrantz and Guildenstern, generally referred to as Salmon and Gluckstein. We left our bone of contention on the mat when we found ourselves promoted to Laertes and Horatio respectively.

Maclaren made no attempt to produce any of the plays; he was intellectually incapable of doing so. We had to learn in the rough and tumble of experience. Often there were acrimonious disputes in the dressing-room on matters of technique. Upon one occasion I received practical instruction in the importance of conviction in acting. We were playing *Hamlet*, and an argument arose because the previous night the leading lady had tangled up her words and said something rather silly, and the audience had laughed. Listening to the discussion was our oldest actor; he once had played Hamlet, was now playing the King, and would doubtless finish up as the Second Gravedigger. 'You can say anything, my boy,' he interrupted me, 'provided you say it with proper conviction. Now I'll bet you a pint of beer that I will say something quite absurd in the next act, and no one will laugh.'

Rashly, I took the bet. Nothing happened until just before the duel between Hamlet and Laertes, when the King concludes his instructions to the duellists with the words: 'And you, the others, bear a wary eye.' Fixing me with a glassy stare—I was playing Horatio—the old actor said: 'And you, the others, wear a beery eye.' This was received in stony silence by the audience. When I returned to the dressing-room our King was waiting for me. All he said was: 'Laddie, my pint.'

In the matter of voice production we had the example of the older actors constantly before us. Nearly all of them possessed fine, resonant voices, a physical attribute that had nothing to do with the intelligence or otherwise of their performances. Cynics have declared that those rich fruity voices were the result of the quantities of stout that were consumed. Certainly those actors drank the stuff in enormous quantities. But, in fact, it was the habit of speaking with the vocal chords fully relaxed and the words formed well forward in the mouth, plus the continual practice of full-blooded speech that gave the voices their range and variety. I was early warned of the dangers of exactly the reverse process, of tightening the vocal chords, which old troupers called 'speaking on the rough', and soon acquired the ability to make heavy demands upon the voice without fatigue.

Our stage manager was a humorous, hard-working Cockney in a perpetual state of uxorious quarrel with his wife, a plain, cheerful woman who supervised the wardrobe and made occasional appearances in the court scenes, as a 'waiting gentlewoman', gallantly holding a property lyre upside down. For spear-carriers and the like we relied upon local talent, summoned to attend at the stage-door at 9 a.m. each Monday morning. It was part of the stage manager's duty to put them through their paces, and sometimes I would help him, while he made unflattering comments under his breath. 'Gawd! Falstaff's ragged bloody army again' was usually his opening remark.

The company travelled with a minimum of scenery, mostly shabby pieces required for particular plays. Otherwise we relied mainly upon the stock scenery still to be found even in quite minor theatres, a carry-over from the days when provincial entertainment was largely autonomous, when the success of the local Theatre Royal, especially at pantomime time, was the status symbol of each community. Our wardrobe was limited and the effort to share what was available equally among the company often led to surprising incongruities, resembling not so much an accurate representation of an historical period as a parade of fashion. I remember a heated argument with George Relph as to who was to wear the only suit of chain-mail the company possessed. Finally, honours were divided, George wearing the suit for Laertes and I for Cassio, compensating for my lack of girth by a complicated system of bootlaces arranged so as to make active movement and a quick discard equally possible. This was 'Shakespeare on a shoestring'.

9

That we were able to please at all was due to our uncritical audiences, but whenever we appeared before a more sophisticated public, as in the university towns, the financial results were disastrous. This was a serious matter, for Maclaren had no reserves. We were in a constant state of anxiety lest he should be unable to pay salaries when Friday night came round. When business was poor this was the sole topic in the dressing-rooms. Often we would peer through a tiny peephole in the centre of the curtain and count the house during the overture. To find the salaries for his company was only one of Maclaren's anxieties. Would his share of the takings provide enough cash to take him and his company on to the next date, or would he have to leave his scenery behind as security for money borrowed from the local manager? Whenever there was the prospect of a week 'out', because no booking had been secured, Maclaren could be seen surreptitiously scanning the columns of *The Stage* for advertisements of vacant dates. Upon one occasion there was less than a week between us and unemployment.

Maclaren's efforts in difficult times to avoid meeting his weekly obligations to his company were varied and ingenious. Sometimes they included his total disappearance from view. Towards the end of my stay with the company we played for three nights at Oxford. It was out of term, and business had been bad. Maclaren paid no salaries on the Friday night. I was desperate, as I'd only a few shillings left. I got up very early on the Saturday morning and waylaid him just as he was leaving his lodgings. He was startled out of his wits by the sudden apparition of one of his actors at that early hour. So when I insisted upon my salary, otherwise I could not pay my landlady, he produced two gold pieces from his pocket, a pound and a ten shillings, dropped them reluctantly into the palm of my hand, and hurried away without saying a word. I felt ashamed of my truculence, but the cheerful clink of the coins had made it worth while.

10

Life on tour was not exactly the romantic struggle I had imagined; away from the theatre it appeared sordid and uninspiring. I was left with a lasting impression of tedious railway journeys and uncomfortable lodgings. Few of the cross-country trains had corridors. Occasionally a lavatory was discovered attached to a single compartment; this was allotted to the women; the men had their own way of dealing with the calls of nature. Late journeys were completed in semi-darkness which the gas jets, encased in glass bowls in the roof, seemed only to accentuate; sometimes the gas escaped; often there was no gas at all. The railway companies did their best to provide heating by means of small metal canisters of hot water, guaranteed to cause chilblains rather than to provide warmth. Dining-cars were non-existent, but luncheon-baskets, made of brown wicker with the name of the railway and the station of issue stamped on a zinc plate on the lid, were available for those who could afford them. The women usually provided themselves with sandwiches, relying upon the men to rush out at the first important junction (usually Crewe, the universal rendezvous for actors travelling on Sunday) to buy them cups of tea or coffee. The men stood each other pints of beer in the suddenly crowded refreshment rooms, and shouted exuberant greetings to their acquaintances in other companies, often followed by devastating criticisms as they made their way back to the train.

There was virtually no opportunity for sustained reading. The women gossiped, while flicking over the pages of the latest novel, or drawing attention to some item of theatre news in the Sunday papers. The men played cards, spreading a blanket or overcoat between them over their knees to form a table. I resented the ceaseless chatter but I was too young and inexperienced to realise that behind the gaiety and the smutty humour there was courage, as well as anxiety as to an uncertain future, when savings would have to be spent in advertising one's lack of employment disguised beneath the euphemism of 'resting'.

It is not to be wondered at that after such tedious journeys, often made more so by being shunted into and out of sidings to await connections, the provincial actor's first thought was of his lodgings, especially if the train were late and the hot meal, ordered in advance, likely to be spoiled. Hence the importance attached to good addresses in the towns he visited. Those where he was assured of a comfortable bed, reasonably good cooking, and, above all, a cheerful welcome from his landlady, were jealously guarded secrets. To forestall another member of the company in securing such a lodging was a more likely cause of friction than rivalry in the theatre.

Our advance man was a tough character, who spent the greater part of his time distributing display bills among the public houses, fish and chip shops, etc., in exchange for complimentary seats for the opening night. Sometimes he would paste the bills up himself. But he was always waiting on the platform at our journey's end, ready to report on the box-office prospects for the coming week, and with a list of addresses for those who had not booked their rooms in advance. One disastrous experience taught me that a drink with this character in his favourite pub under a pretence of good fellowship was something not to be omitted. It came about in this way. We arrived late one night at Maesteg, a small mining community in South Wales, where we were to play for three nights. The advance man, waiting on the platform as usual, warned us that lodgings were not easy to come by. I had foolishly kept aloof from his convivialities hitherto, so I came last on his list. With a flicker of hesitation which I remembered afterwards he gave me the address of a villa with the attractive name of 'Starlight Glen', and told me to try my luck.

The landlady, a soft-spoken Welshwoman, seemed decent enough. When she showed me to the bedroom with a large illuminated text over the head of the bed: 'God is love', I thought I was in luck, but there was little love in that stormy villa. Returning from the theatre late the same evening—we'd arrived in the morning—I went straight up to bed, tired out. I turned down the quilt. I was appalled at the amount of insect life embedded in the blanket; they were like currants in a cake. I retreated to an armchair and to my overcoat. Discomfort reached its peak on the Saturday night when a drunken brawl between husband and wife broke furiously over the little house like a thunderstorm, threatening to jerk 'God is love' clean away from the wall!

The following morning we set out on another protracted journey which involved a long wait at a railway junction. It was bleak March weather, snow and sleet in plenty. As I stood shivering on the platform, feeling and looking acutely miserable, our oldest actor came towards me and tried to cheer me up. He was wearing a frock-coat, grey flannel trousers, canvas shoes, and a bowler hat; he had a spare pair of boots wrapped up in a copy of *The Stage* under his arm. His manner was unmistakable evidence of his former eminence as a tragedian, although he was now only the rather corpulent second comedian of our company. His chaps were blue with cold, but his deep resonant voice was full of confidence as he boomed at me: 'Cheer up, laddie; The acting profession is the finest profession to that of a gentleman that I know.' And he meant it.

Most of the older actors seemed happy enough to remain in the provincial rut, never raising their eyes beyond the immediate bounds of anxiety lest pantomime time should throw them out of work. True, some of them would be playing demon king, but then there was usually only one demon in each Christmas tale. This was not my idea at all. I was determined to get out as quickly as possible. As a first step I made several attempts to join Benson's company. Although the zenith of his influence had passed, his company was still a magnet to draw ambitious actors out of the crowd. I made my final attempt while we were playing in Harrogate. Benson was at Leeds, so I wrote to him for an appointment. He replied that he would see me during the Thursday matinée. I carefully prepared a scene from *As You Like It*, and duly repaired to Leeds where, to my horror, I discovered that Benson himself was playing Orlando that afternoon. I had nothing else ready, and so when Benson saw me in his dressing-room after the matinée I proceeded to give him my version of how the part should be played—with disastrous results to myself!

II

During my first year on the stage I became involved in an agitation to revitalise the Actors' Association, to persuade it to abandon its attitude of gentility and to adopt the principles of trades unionism in the struggle to improve the actor's lot. One of the main planks in our platform was the demand for a minimum wage of two pounds per week. I wrote long letters to *The Stage* every week in support of the campaign. As the agitation developed I found myself drawn into heated controversy with Dr. Distin Maddick, an eccentric and wealthy gentleman who had built the Scala on the site of the old

Prince of Wales' Theatre, just off Tottenham Court Road. The correspondence became so heated that I wrote to Bernard Shaw for advice. He sent me a draft answer, together with the wise advice, written in pencil on a torn-out page of an exercise book; 'Don't fight D. M. on the points on which he is thoroughly right— stick to his errors, G. B. S.' I still possess that document.

Broadly speaking, there was little time for anything but acting, and in that matter I grew more and more impatient of my lack of progress. I became over-earnest, indulging my old habit of day-dreaming. The brief encounter with Iden Payne had encouraged me to question prevailing views. Yet it was foolish to try to stand apart from the others; it could only lead to misunderstanding and spite. So I did my best to conform—as who would not, to escape un-popularity?—and at the same time despised my subservience to an outlook upon life with which I disagreed. Looking back, it is easy to see how much of the fun of that life I missed.

I began to take long walks, not always in the beautiful country-side, sometimes among the slag-heaps and smoke of industrial areas to indulge in dreaming and introspection. There was one special day that stands out in memory. We had left the mining towns of South Wales, and arrived three days before Easter at Leamington Spa where we were to open on Easter Monday. I decided to make a pilgrimage to Stratford-on-Avon on Good Friday. It was warm and sunny, one of those rare spring days in England that no other country can match. Relaxing after the walk from Leamington, with no food to speak of—I was still determinedly vegetarian— I sat down by the river's edge in a field just short of the town. In the distance I could see the top of the tower of what I took to be the Memorial Theatre. The sun was hot, larks were singing in the sky, the river was full and ruffling in the breeze, and all round there was spring growth. I had been reading Thomas Hardy and thought of his 'dreaming spires'. I fell into a mood of intense long-ing. Worthwhile achievement seemed such a very long way away: Would I ever act in Shakespeare's birthplace? Later, I walked to the theatre and stood and gazed, much as I had done as a schoolboy at the magical names posted up outside Drury Lane Theatre at pantomime time. There was no certainty in my mind as I trudged back to my cheerful lodging in Leamington, reaching there in the last of the spring daylight.

Four
Manchester

I

Soon after I joined Maclaren I heard from Iden Payne, telling me that a certain Miss Horniman, a name I scarcely knew, had appointed him to manage the Abbey Theatre in Dublin for the Irish Players. Payne never spoke much about his experiences there, but his gentle rationality must soon have clashed with the Catholic genius of the players. A month or two later he wrote again telling me that Miss Horniman had withdrawn her support of the Abbey Theatre and appointed him to form a company of English players to be based on Manchester, where she could express her reforming zeal for the theatre free of the bothersome Irish. The letter ended with an offer to join the new company at a salary of thirty-five shillings per week. So I was still going up in the world! For the second and, as it proved, the last time, Iden Payne was to set my feet on the right road and thus to influence my career.

Manchester at the beginning of the century was a city of thrusting prosperity, the result of a union of Lancashire shrewdness with the meticulous efficiency of a considerable German community, engaged mainly in the textile and chemical trades. Through fog and rain, the confident citizens strode about their affairs, asserting in speech and manner their conviction that what Manchester thinks today, London will think tomorrow, while heavy horse-drawn drays, laden with great bales of cotton, rumbled ceaselessly over the cobbled streets.

The city also had a vicarious reputation for musical appreciation, due to its enthusiastic support of the Hallé Orchestra mainly by its German residents. Typical of their confident taste at the time was the reply of the great Richter when asked why he never played any French music: 'There is no French music.'

By 1907 the Midland Hotel had become the social centre of this commercial metropolis. Here class distinctions, not of birth but of money, were judiciously maintained by the prices charged in different parts of the hotel for identical services. The Octagon Court was at the centre of this centre, so to speak. Here to the discreet sounds of a palm court orchestra the mill-owners' wives met for tea and gossip, or waited, dressed to the highest provincial standards, for their husbands to take them to theatre or social occasion; here younger members of the same families met their fiancées and discussed wedding plans. In the Winter Garden, built at a significantly lower level, life was noisier and cheaper. There boys met girls, not always of the same class, and cheerful talk with friendly waiters was an accepted practice. A well-patronised German bar at one side of the hotel served businessmen in a hurry with excellent lager beer, both 'helles' and 'dunkles' and with schinkenbrot.

Among the other facilities the hotel offered was a spacious banqueting hall for formal celebrations of progress in business and trade, with or without benefit of women, and, most surprising of all, a theatre. Although little more than a stage set at one end of a great oblong ballroom, with rows of boxes down the sides, and hence quite unsuitable for use as an intimate theatre, this had nevertheless proved a useful Christmas-time home for Pélissier's Follies. It was now about to accommodate a theatrical enterprise of a very different sort, for a letter had recently appeared in the Manchester press announcing Miss Horniman's intention to found a repertory company in the city under the management of Iden Payne. Pending the acquisition of a theatre of its own her company was to give preliminary performances in the Midland Hotel Theatre. The *Manchester Guardian* gave solid encouragement to the plan, while the other papers uttered faint chirrups of praise for the unknown lady's boldness, while the arrival of a heterogeneous group of quite unknown players was regarded with scepticism by a public already well supplied with theatrical entertainment from London.

The company was made up largely of idealists, anxious to reform the art of acting and, incidentally, the world at the same time, but who did not possess the abilities to achieve a fraction of such aims. I was the junior member of the troupe, allowed to play waiters and servants, and only then when the supply of other actors to take such parts gave out; but I was kept busy enough as the assistant stage manager. The opening play was *David Ballard*, written by Charles McEvoy, the first of a new generation of writers for the English Theatre with whom I was to be closely associated in the future.

Charles, brother of Ambrose McEvoy, the painter, was an extraordinary character, in physical appearance more of a caricature than a normal person. His long, twisted face, with bulbous eyes and tiny chin beard, was like a note of interrogation. Possessed of a ferocious Cockney accent and a great sense of humour, he lived in a caravan and boasted his knowledge and love of the nomadic life. His appearance at rehearsal in corduroys complete with moleskin waistcoat and a red handkerchief tied round his neck was decidedly *outré* in those days but would pass unnoticed in a modern 'trendy' crowd. There was a restaurant scene in the second act, so I was early initiated into the mystery of substitute meals on the stage, deceptive in appearance, unpalatable, but otherwise harmless. At least once a week during that first season there would be full dress occasions in the banqueting hall, from which succulent smells would be wafted round the stage just before the curtain went up. This I found trying, for I was living on a Spartan diet and feeling hungry most of the time. Theatrical lodgings were mostly concentrated in a group of streets towards the end of Oxford Road, the best known of which was Ackers Street, where several of us lodged. I was at Number 32, provided with what was called a combined room, i.e. sitting-room and bedroom in one. It was quite a long walk back from the theatre, and even late at night every other shop along Oxford Road seemed to be selling tripe and onions, or frying fish. The smells were discouraging to an appetite disciplined by the strict vegetarianism to which I still clung.

The Horniman players were so unlike their usual lodgers that the landladies of Ackers Street began to spread rumours: we were very peculiar people indeed, 'atheists and I don't know what else, living on nuts and things'. It was even rumoured that we indulged in what was then called 'free love', whereas in point of fact we were just a group of rather highbrow over-earnest young actors and actresses, living on humble salaries and with our noses just slightly tilted upwards since we were, after all, somewhat different from the ordinary run of touring actor, or at least we thought we were. It was due to the persistence of these old wives' tales quite as much as to the left-wing tendencies of our authors that we lived in a state of *apartheid* for the first year, more so even than the actors who came up from London to play in Shakespeare and pantomime at Christmas.

Our first audiences were so thin that I feared I should be soon out of a job; but Miss Horniman seemed quite unperturbed, sitting up in one of the side boxes at every performance and staring at the rows of empty seats with a grim smile. There was always present a sprinkling of extreme opinion in politics, art, letters, what you will; but the few members of the general public who strayed into the performances usually left in disgust after the first act. They had no idea what it was all about. At the end of the season we went to Preston for a week, where the audiences were even more dumbfounded; then we returned to Manchester for an odd week or so before finally being turned out to make way once more for Pelissier's Follies. By this time I had no immediate anxiety because Miss Horniman had already announced the purchase of the Gaiety Theatre, and her intention to remodel it and set about the achievement of her aims in the ensuing autumn.

2

At the end of that first season we went on tour, visiting towns somewhat off the usual track of touring companies where theatres were prepared to risk a three-day flirtation with the new drama; Greenock and Bury in Lancashire were two of them. Like most young actors of the time I detested the menial implication of being made an assistant stage manager. That girls could do the job as well, if not better, had not yet occurred to anyone. I resented, too the fact that my reputation for reliability was keeping better parts at arm's length. Our stage manager was experienced but forgetful, and sly. His favourite trick at rehearsal, when Payne's angry shouts from the dress circle called him to answer for some omission or other, was to poke his head round the prompt corner, and after making sure I was out of earshot, reply: 'I'm afraid I left that to Mr. Dean.' (In those days everyone was either Mr. or Miss in the theatre; only gradually did Christian names come into general use.) Throughout this period the company was being steadily enlarged and strengthened. I watched the process with mixed feelings, wondering how much the new talents would retard my own progress. But obscurity came to a sudden end for me when Miss Horniman invited William Poel to make a special production of *Measure for Measure* for Easter.

Poel had founded the Elizabethan Stage Society in 1881 for the express purpose of restoring the plays to their original shape and performing them in the manner that Shakespeare knew. His simplified settings restored flexibility and speed to the performances—some scene changes were indicated only by the drawing of a curtain—and this enabled the plays to be played in full. Hitherto, the demands for ever more elaborate scenery had forced the actor-managers to reduce the number of scenes and alter their running-order to give time for the stage-hands to push the increasingly solid constructions about the stage. With the cuts restored, Shakespeare's technique, which had been made to seem tortuous and clumsy, now appeared in all its suppleness and variety. The swift, almost continuous performances, to which we are now accustomed, owe their origin to Poel's pioneer work.

Poel also wrought great improvement in the standards of verse-speaking, which were then at a low ebb. He selected his cast entirely from the point of view of the suitability of their voices, taking each actor in turn and showing him how to maintain speed and rhythm without loss of meaning. He would recite the speeches line by line, picking out one or perhaps two words in each line for dominant emphasis, and exaggerating the stresses for purposes of example. Only when he felt that each actor fully comprehended his system would he allow the company to rehearse together.

The younger members of the Horniman Company laughed much at this strange elderly gentleman, with his flowing hair and long ascetic face. In his Inverness cape, with black hat and black woollen gloves, he looked more like a professor at a theological seminary than a man of the theatre. We neither realised nor cared that his methods had begun to revolutionise the art of Shakespearean presentation. As for the older actors, they were vitriolic in their anger at being treated like schoolboys. This was not production as they understood it; it was tutoring. There were loud dressing-room protests, and noisy caricatures of the rehearsals by the comedians. Lewis Casson, who had joined the company in January, had his own fine competence in verse-speaking; he refused to accept the eccentricities and lost the chance of playing the Duke. Clarence Derwent, another senior member of the company, also walked out.

Poel liked my voice, and so I was cast for the part of Claudio. I was given strenuous daily instruction during the week we were playing in Dublin. I can see Poel now in his hotel sitting-room, holding the book in his left hand and tapping out the stresses on

E

his knee with the long fingers of his right hand, while W. B. Yeats, his beautiful sensitive face and flapping hair the complete make-up of the poet, and J. M. Synge, red-faced and bucolic, sat on chairs at the other side of the room, waiting for the lesson to be over to take Poel out to lunch, an invitation which he appeared to have forgotten, because closing the book, he embarked upon a long discussion with Yeats about how Shakespeare should be spoken, while Synge sat silent and thoughtful.

This was my first big chance. I thought my whole career depended upon the verdict, but the result, it seems, was equivocal, for my little pocket diary contains the laconic entry for April 11, 1908: '2 p.m. The eventful day! 11 p.m. only moderate success!' *The Manchester Courier* said my elocution was 'the best of the night', but C. E. Montague in the *Manchester Guardian* accused me of shouting. But after all, I thought, it was something to be mentioned by that great critic, his columns of fine prose seldom including the names of the actors whose work should have been their inspiration.

In Easter week we gave several performances at the Memorial Theatre, Stratford-on-Avon. The appearance of Manchester 'provincials' at the annual Shakespeare season was perhaps more of a shock to the haughty Bensonians than the unexpected quality of our performances. . . . Time is the drag upon ambition's heels. The months spent in touring had seemed endless, yet it was less than a year since I lay in the meadow by the Avon, wondering whether I should ever act in the Memorial Theatre.

3

The company soon acquired many of the characteristics of a permanent ensemble, although one or two of the older men seemed to have little understanding or belief in Miss Horniman's aims, and openly sneered at the political message which they suspected each new play to contain. To avoid argument I pretended to agree with them, a piece of duplicity of which I was secretly ashamed. Lewis Casson, older than most of the company, thirteen years in my case, set us all a good example with a sense of mission that extended beyond the theatre to the world in general. He kept aloof at first, but after a month or so I found out that he, too, read the *Clarion* newspaper, and supported its editor's vigorous campaign on behalf of the underprivileged. The paper represented that side of the early Socialist movement that was inspired by William Morris, Robert Owen, and others, the side that admired H. G. Wells—his writings were the popular science fiction of our day—and held Bernard Shaw in awe. Yet it was failing to carry the trade unions with it. Its youthful supporters were called Clarionettes. Blatchford opened the primary school doors to art, literature and 'the open road', all the joys, in fact, of which he claimed the working class had been deprived by the industrial revolution.

Each year a cycling 'meet' was held over the Easter holidays in some pleasant locality, when troops of young men and women bicycled in from all parts of the country to greet Clarionettes from other towns, to enjoy music, to sing uplifting songs, and to listen to speeches from Blatchford, H. M. Hyndman and other leaders. Fraternity was the password; Norfolk jackets and red ties for the boys, tweed skirts, white blouses and more red ties for the girls, were signals for recognition. My innate radicalism responded eagerly to the ideals and the enthusiasm, but less intelligently perhaps than Casson's more sedate approval.

During the run of *Measure for Measure* he and I hurried over to Shrewsbury, where that year's 'meet' was being held, to appear in the opening Good Friday concert. We gave the tent scene from *Julius Caesar*, standing on the bare stage, in Norfolk jackets, of course. Lewis was Cassius and I was Brutus, but I was hopelessly outclassed by Lewis's fine voice and rapid delivery of the lines. He kept muttering under his breath while I was speaking: 'Faster, faster.' As the hall rang with shouts of 'More! More!' I felt Cassius had won the argument in spite of Shakespeare.

Less than a month after our descent upon Shrewsbury—Campbell-Bannerman having died in Downing Street and Winston Churchill been defeated in Manchester by Joynson-Hicks in the ensuing election—Casson and I went to a big Sunday rally in the Free Trade Hall to hear R. B. Cunninghame-Graham, H. M. Hyndman (in his customary frock-coat), Robert Blatchford and a freebooting rabble-rouser named Victor Grayson, who shot like a comet past the extreme left of the political spectrum. My subsequent meeting with Blatchford was a disappointment; his writings had not prepared me for encounter with such a dull personality.

Sybil Thorndike did not join us until July, on the West Pier, Brighton. (We were touring until the Gaiety Theatre should be ready for us.) Sybil brought to the company her own special quality of enthusiasm and a personality better suited to the serenity of the cathedral close than to the stridency of Grand Guignol or the thunder of Greek tragedy. Her Candida was the finest I ever saw. We spent a joyful fortnight, swimming off the pier every morning and scandalising holiday audiences with Shaw's *Widowers' Houses* at night. Sybil joined our swimming party with glee; but neither we nor the lonely stunt man who dived off the pier-head on a bicycle twice daily was the centre of attraction for the onlookers; that was Marie Lloyd, plopping intrepidly into the deep sea in a billowing costume to a chorus of laughter and chaff from her music-hall companions.

A senior member of the company who quickly established himself as its most gifted actor was Charles Bibby, an old Bensonian whose brilliant career was cut short by his death in the First World War. Among later additions to the company were two unusual characters, both, I should judge, outside the main stream of the professional theatre. Henry Austin was a mysterious creature with a charming personality and no knowledge whatever of the technique of acting. I judged that some financial disaster lay concealed behind that smiling weatherbeaten face, adorned with a rimless monocle, for he played all his parts in the same suit of clothes—and got away with it! Miss Darragh was another mystery. She joined us in the spring of 1908. A highly intelligent and educated woman, she was known always in conversation and programme announcements simply as Miss Darragh. A good figure, *bien corsetée* in the Edwardian style, was set off by a head of hair dressed in the same style. Her acting was reminiscent of Marie Tempest, yet had about it always a suggestion of the amateur. Rumour had it that she had once been the wife of an Indian civil servant and had surrendered to the temptation surrounding amateur theatricals in Simla. Like Henry Austin, she lived apart from the rest of the company. Unlike him she was not the subject of secret amusement, but of genuine respect. She was destined to alter the course of my career in a few years' time.

Some of Payne's early acquaintances came to augment the company, including Ian Maclaren who showed no embarrassment at meeting me, so lately a junior member of his troupe, but then I was no longer one of his actor-creditors. Esmé Percy appeared in our first Christmas production, *The Knight of the Burning Pestle* by Beaumont and Fletcher. His engagement caused surprise and not a little curiosity among the company because of his sensational success at His Majesty's Theatre in London, and because of some startling stories about his flamboyant behaviour. How could this exotic flower hope to flourish in Miss Horniman's prim herbaceous border?

Percy gave an immediate answer to that question when he arrived in Manchester at the end of a long journey from Venice. Rooms had been booked for him in Didsbury, a suburb of the city. When he awoke next morning he observed first one hearse and then another going past the window; he had been lodged opposite the local cemetery. His protests drew a blithe response from his landlady: 'Well, we all have to go that way sooner or later, don't we?' But Percy was unprepared for his own early departure, and told Miss Horniman he couldn't possibly stay in such a dreadful place. 'Why, I've just come from Venice!' 'We have canals here, too, you know,' replied Miss Horniman, quite unmoved. His appearance as Ralph on the first night, mounted on a fat, white pony, waving a wooden sword and shouting, was a sensational success with the audience, but not with me, because the wretched animal treated me to an odoriferous shower before Ralph had time to utter a word: a case of first night nerves!

Percy had been educated partly in Brussels. Subsequently, he studied for a short while with Sarah Bernhardt in Paris, a fact of which he was very proud. He spoke fluent French. His gay precocity must have cheered her ageing heart; the cordial message endorsed upon her photograph, which he took everywhere with him, certainly suggested so. He was devoted to his mother, a pretty, charming Frenchwoman who lived outside marriage with a well-known Society moneylender. Percy's frequent reference to the devotion of his parents to each other in the face of all worldly obstacles reminded me somehow or other of La Dame aux Camélias. Perhaps Percy's Gallic temperament embroidered the story a little, for in spite of all pretence I think he felt his illegitimacy keenly. In the course of time he became more or less integrated with the rest of us, although I always felt that his flamboyance and orotund manner of speech remained out of scale with the realistic acting that Payne favoured. Off the stage, his gay Latinity was always in laughable contrast with the assemblage of rather drab personalities that Payne had collected to further Miss Horniman's mission of reform. For my part, I thought him a charming, mischievous and highly talented personality, and I was grateful for what I learned in his company.

On my twenty-first birthday I invited Percy to have supper with me at the Midland Hotel after the show. He asked me why I was so glum and depressed. I could not give him the reason. Among the letters I had received that morning was one from my mother, so full of piety and homely precept that I felt embarrassed not to be able to respond in similar terms.

4

I was now living in Chorlton-cum-Hardy, a suburb still in course of development. The view from my bedroom window was of cornfields, sodden and flattened by a singularly wet August. Twelve months of Ackers Street, with its rows of soot-blackened houses, spotlessly hearthstoned thresholds, and noisy squabbles in the backyard had been more than enough. Two spinsters, the Misses Roberts, former housekeepers to a wealthy bachelor in Carlisle, were now fussing over me. They were also keeping the old gentle-man's memory bright and shining in the lovely mahogany furniture he had bequeathed to them.

By this time I had begun to carve out my own style of playing light comedy parts which was bringing me some popularity. I began to receive letters and requests for photographs, and soon discovered behind the highbrow talk of my stage-door acquaintances warmth and romance in plenty. Fortunately, the magic of the theatre was strong in me, and I was determined not to allow myself to become involved. Somehow or other I managed to keep out of serious sexual mischief. I fell in love with an adorable little dancer, very young and gentle, with soft brown eyes and voice to match. She came to Manchester with a troupe of young ladies of the ut-most gentility, giving Elizabethan songs and dances. Although I never voiced my feelings I knew they were reciprocated. It was an idyll of youth and inexperience that lasted for a year and more, but the frequent interruptions of her professional engagements, in-cluding one with Professor Reinhardt in Berlin, finally brought it to an end. Yet, wherever she may be, I know that its memory has stayed with her as it has with me.

5

After my success in *Measure for Measure* my acting began to improve although I was always conscious of the fact that the more romantic or emotional I felt, the less convincing I became. It was a different matter in the field of light comedy where I eventually established myself as our leading player. The break-through came when I was given the part of Jack Barthwick in *The Silver Box*, John Galsworthy's first play, about to receive its first provincial production. During early rehearsals I fumbled in my efforts to find the right approach to the character, but when Galsworthy arrived he took me on one side and whispered the opening lines of my part so revealingly that I had no further trouble.

My part of Jack Barthwick made a great hit with undergraduate audiences everywhere, especially in Oxford, where my appearance at a college party would be greeted with shouts of 'Crackers, please, Dad', in imitation of the way I spoke those lines. During one of our early visits I had noted how the young bloods were abandoning boots in favour of shoes for general wear. (This was the origin of the trade description, 'Oxford shoe'.) Upon a subsequent occasion I noted with pride that a haberdasher's window in the High displayed 'Jack Barthwick' socks. That was because I had seized upon this trend and was now appearing in a suit specially designed for me by a fashionable West End tailor, with trousers of a length to give every opportunity for ankle display! Even in the staider atmosphere of Edinburgh my young reprobate made similar appeal. One student, member of a famous Scottish family, presented me with a lovely little silver box which I treasured for nearly fifty years. It was stolen eventually by a burglar, thus repeating in real life the main incident in the Galsworthy play.

It was in *The Silver Box* that Ada King laid the foundations of an international reputation as a character actress, especially in downtrodden parts. Her performance as Mrs. Jones, the charwoman, was acclaimed everywhere. In private life she seemed to revel in misery, which could be irritating, but when salted with her own brand of bitter humour was condoned as eccentricity. Throughout her years with the Horniman Company she lived with Spartan economy in single rooms, her one indulgence being the purchase every Saturday of a flagon of Australian Burgundy with which to solace her lonely week-ends. I greatly enjoyed playing the Rev. Lexy Mill to her Prossie in *Candida*, with Sybil to beam at us from the fireplace. But woe betide me if I should attempt any liberties with my part that might interfere with the applause on her exit in the last act. After her death I was deeply moved to find she had left me the little black cat which she always kept by her dressing-room mirror, and over which we used to wish ourselves luck on first nights all those years ago.

6

After two years in Manchester, we made a rather diffident first appearance in London, arriving at the little Coronet Theatre in Notting Hill Gate in June, 1909. We were an immediate success. The season, originally planned for two weeks, had to be extended by a further week. The critics were ecstatic over Mona Limerick, Payne's wife, a young woman of striking beauty and personality about whom Max Beerbohm was constrained to write a special article in the *Saturday Review*. 'I've known of no other actress who would tear a passion to tatters quite as she did'. Every muscle in her body quivered with emotion as she rasped out her words with tightened vocal chords. Shaw admired her performance in *Widowers' Houses* greatly, demonstrating the influence of Barry Sullivan on his taste in such matters, as his unflagging support of Esmé Percy's bravura performances in his plays was to do later. But we in the company noted with dismay the damage Mona was doing to her voice by not producing it properly, and the failure of her husband to discipline her at rehearsals. The promise of a great tragic actress was never fulfilled. She lived in seclusion for many years, and died quite recently.

The quality of the ensemble was specially noted by E. A. Baughan, dramatic critic of the *Daily News*:

'I was astonished by the ease and naturalness of their acting. Each member of the company was playing his or her part entirely from the point of view of the character and its place in the scheme of the drama. . . .'

William Archer, doyen of the dramatic critics of that time, whose humourless translations of Ibsen had held back the great Norwegian's arrival on the English stage for a decade, wrote:

'I wish to express my deliberate opinion that this Manchester movement is the most important fact in our theatrical history since the opening of the Vedrenne-Barker campaign at the Court Theatre.'

The reaction of the critics confirmed us all in our estimation of ourselves as in a class apart from ordinary companies, which is only another way of saying that a corporate consciousness had been developed. But as individuals we were soon disillusioned. A year or so later when on the introduction of Galsworthy I sought a London engagement with the Frohman Repertory Season at the Duke of York's Theatre, Dion Boucicault made it plain that we might pass muster when acting together as a company, but as individuals we were things of nought.

7

Throughout my time in Manchester I was obsessed with the need to complete my education—a foolish thought, come to think of it, since one's education is never completed. I read everything I could lay my hands on: scientific and medical books, history, poetry, the important novels I had missed or been too lazy to finish; but I confess George Meredith's *Diana of the Crossways* defeated me. I bought the *English Review*, so full of good things during the first years of its existence, and read the *New Age*, edited by a remarkable character named A. R. Orage. I also noted the dramatic criticisms of one Jacob Tonson, who later turned out to be Arnold Bennett. I ranged as far as German philosophy, reading Kant, Schelling, Schopenhauer and, finally, to top up the feast of reason, Nietzsche's *Also Sprach Zarathustra*, all of course in English translation. What benefit I derived from such un-guided voracity is obscure; it may have helped me to think for myself, but not much else beside. Percy was fascinated by these efforts at self-education, so unlike his own indolent cleverness. My excursions into German philosophy especially amused him. One day he produced a copy of Krafft-Ebbing's *Psychopathia Sexualis* which he said he had just read, not, I suspected, with intellectual interest, but because the examples of sexual perversion given in the book tickled his sense of humour.

Life was opening out for me in other ways, too. My head had always been full of romantic notions, ever since those early literary flourishes which Norman Frazer had read out in Sixth Form, a recollection that still makes me shiver. My feeling for English coun-try life and character had been fostered by the discovery of Thomas

Hardy while I was still at school. I became an addict, reading the Wessex novels over and over again, and buying copies of defunct magazines containing some of Hardy's early stories. I even went as far as Max Gate in Dorset on my bicycle to gape and worship at that rather disappointing shrine. Passing by the great houses en route, I loved to people them with families of my own making, to imagine the love passages, ecstasies and disappointments of men and women long gone to dust. Soon I was seeing not 'sermons in stones' but drama everywhere.

8

Still in thrall to Thomas Hardy's Wessex, I spent several vacations in Seatown, a fishing hamlet near Chideock in Dorset, which at that time consisted of a few thatched cottages nestling in a fold of the downs, and a lovely Regency villa at the head of the valley, summer home of Ada Reeve, the musical comedy star, whom I occasionally espied from afar, sunning on the verandah in white muslin with parasol to match. I stayed in the cottage of the leading fisherman, a man called Young. It was a rough life and I loved it. I had already acquired a copy of William Barnes' *Poems of Rural Life in the Dorset Dialect*, and used to recite successfully many of those gentle Arcadian verses to my northern friends. Now I set out to master the current dialect which I found to be full of archaic turns of speech, very little changed from those in the Wessex novels; for example, 'thee' and 'thy' were still in common use. Some of the fishermen's speech was so thick with intonation that it was difficult to follow all that was said. But I found I had a quick ear for phonetics and, very soon, Higgins-like, I was filling my notebook with useful information.

The following is part of an account of the village scene that I wrote at the time and sent to Galsworthy for his criticism and comment:

'. . . There was great excitement when the mackerel shoals came in, usually in June and September. Then fishermen from neighbouring villages would come over to help man their neighbours' boats. A look-out would be posted on Golden Cap, a cliff on one side of the village, high above the little inn of tarred weatherboard, which I was assured used to be a smugglers' resort. When the "skools" were "in", the look-out gave a peculiar cry which the fishermen recognised at once, running down by the little stream that meandered past their cottages to bury itself beneath the shingle, and clambering into two heavy seine boats which they rowed with great speed to meet in a semi-circle, one man standing in the stern of each boat shooting the nets. One end of each seine was left ashore, and when the boats had completed the semi-circle the nets were hauled from either end. This was when the shoals were big. At other times one seine boat only would be used. If the draught was a heavy one there would be much excitement, and the fishermen's wives would come running down to help haul in and fill deep wicker baskets with the silver fish, which would later be taken to the fish-market at Bridport by carrier. Sometimes the fish buyers, having heard that the mackerel were "in", would be waiting on shore and strike their bargains there and then.

I was not strong enough to man the heavy oars of the seine boats, but at other times I would go out with George Young and his two partners, lobster-potting and blinning. Upon one occasion because of the tides we set out at four o'clock in the morning; it was very rough, and I was feeling pretty sick, especially when invited to share the crew's breakfast, consisting of cider, rough enough to take the roof off one's mouth, and blue Dorset cheese, a meal which left me soon afterwards.

When we got back about mid-day, a glorious day of blue sky and hot sun, and not a sound but the noise of the gulls and clacketty-clack of the reaping machines, George Young's wife sat me down to a special meal of mackerel, stuffed with gooseberries and breadcrumbs fried with thyme, while George produced out of a secret cupboard some special cider which he said was ten years old. (All the fishermen at that time made cider from their own apples.) It had the generous quality of port wine. I drank about half a pint of it, and in a short while was staggering across the road, offering to help the men and women gathering the harvest. When I woke under a haystack it must have been about eight o'clock in the evening; stars were beginning to appear in a cloudless sky. My escapade was the joke of the village for the rest of my stay.'

9

Inevitably, my first attempt at playwriting was set in the West Country. Typing it out on an old-fashioned Blick typewriter, letter by letter, I had no clear plan for its destiny. However, had not Miss Horniman loudly proclaimed her intention to encourage new English dramatists 'to write better than the Irish'? Indeed, we seldom saw her in the daytime without a bundle of scripts clutched defiantly under her arm as public proof of constancy, as she boarded her daily bus to the Manchester suburb where she lived in modest theatrical lodgings. So there was no harm in my trying. I sent the play to Miss Horniman.

During rehearsal a few days later I noticed her standing at the side of the stage beaming at me. My heart gave a thump. Could this really be—I had scarcely time to say good morning before she burst out:

'I feel very proud! I've just been turned out of the Octagon Court.'

'What on earth for?' I asked.

'Smoking in public,' she said proudly, waving a Turkish cigarette in its long holder in the air. She must have seen that I looked disappointed. So she added quite casually:

'Oh, by the way, I like your little play.'

'Do you really?' I said excitedly.

'H'm, h'm.' She nodded, and walked away.

When Iden Payne accepted the play he told me I must produce it myself because it was written in dialect. This was a daunting prospect for a junior member of the company. We were to rehearse at Carlisle during the company's visit prior to the opening of the reconstructed Gaiety. Lewis Casson was cast for the young lover and Sybil Thorndike for the girl, and there were two older characters. I have a clear memory of the wide peaceful streets of the city before industrialisation sullied its aspect, and of the bright rain-washed atmosphere as I set out for the first rehearsal on that August morning with my heart thumping like a rickety gas engine. I arrived at the theatre to find the actors having a brisk argument among themselves in a corner. But when Sybil saw me she immediately turned to the others with that all-embracing gesture of hers, and said: 'Now come along, don't be silly. Let's all help the young man to have a success.'

My play was called *Marriages are Made in Heaven*; it brought Lewis and Sybil acting together for the first time, gave me my first chance as a producer and my first thrill at hearing words I had written spoken by other actors, and raised the curtain for the first time in the rebuilt Manchester Gaiety; also, it received a surprisingly good notice from James Agate in the *Manchester Guardian*, the first that I received from that distinguished critic. Thus a premier occasion upon several counts!

The little play was well liked everywhere and remained in the Horniman repertory for several years. I wrote another West Country curtain-raiser, equally successful, called *Mother To Be*, a title that was a tactless anticipation of events for its two leading players, Charles Bibby and Hilda Bruce-Potter, who had just become engaged. On the first night I was called twice before the curtain. In her letter of congratulation Miss Horniman wrote:

> 'I hope that next time you won't look so anxious when you are called so heartily as you were the other evening. You have done better already than some who have made big names—so please go ahead bravely.'

This was no compensation for having my first full-length play rejected at the same time.

My next short play gave Percy an opportunity to act the lover in a drawing-room, which he mistook for a china shop. Another was extremely grim, too grim in fact for Miss Horniman. I sent it to the Stage Society, the only experimental theatre at that time. The opinions of its reading committee were mixed. Professor Gilbert Murray, Dr. Wheeler and some other member were enthusiastically for it. But Bernard Shaw said it was 'just dirt and drunkenness'. The time for the drama of the kitchen sink was not yet. Another one-act play was lost by Iden Payne. When I told him I had no copy he mildly suggested I should write it again. This I had not the heart to do.

During our fourth season—there were two seasons in each calendar year—Galsworthy's *Strife* was produced. From then on his plays occupied an increasingly important position in the company's repertoire. I always looked forward to his appearance at rehearsals. His air of critical detachment and his upright athletic figure, clad always in well-cut tweeds, seemed to reflect the characteristics of his plays, as we afterwards came to know them: liberal in their criticism of the social order, conservative of all that was best in the life of the English countryside. I longed to talk to him about my own efforts as a playwright, and wondered whether I dare ask him to come out to Chorlton after rehearsal to listen to one of them. After all, he had been pleased with my Jack Barthwick, and my rooms were quite comfortable. Eventually I made my request, very nervously, because I had no idea what thoughts were hidden behind that quizzical eye-glass. But J.G. met me half-way and agreed to come. Thereafter, during his visits to Manchester I would march him dauntlessly to the Central Station after rehearsal for a journey of some fifteen minutes or so to Chorlton, and thence by a brisk short walk to my lodging. A hasty cup of tea, with cakes especially baked for the occasion by Miss Roberts, and then we would sit down to discuss whatever piece of writing I was engaged upon.

After one of these visits he took away with him my first completed three-act play. A week or so later he sent it back from his home in Devon with much of the dialogue rewritten in pencil in his own clear handwriting. I boggled at the alterations, and proceeded to rub out most of them, which strikes me now as a singular piece of foolishness. Recently, reading again Mottram's *Life and Letters*, I realised that Galsworthy's first reaction to the criticism of his friends had also been resistance, but he had the sense to weigh their suggestions and eventually to profit by their advice, whereas I stolidly rejected his.

10

For some time there had existed a caucus of young businessmen who used to meet informally in the lunch hour in one of the domino-infested cafés off Market Street, there to argue contumaciously about matters of public interest. The group regarded themselves as part of the northern intelligentsia who had pioneered reform in the past, and would do so again. No one was well off, except in the matter of high spirits and a zest for the bones of contention. After the Gaiety opened the group turned the searchlight of its criticism on to us. As membership increased a room was reserved for regular lunch-time meetings at the Swan Inn, next door to the theatre and opposite the Theatre Royal. Thereafter, the group nicknamed themselves the Swan Club. There were no rules, no subscriptions and no credentials beyond an ability to speak one's mind and to be ready for instant contradiction; it was a catalyst of lively intelligence playing upon a variety of interests. I was the only actor to be invited to join, but as we had only half an hour's break at lunch-time, I could not sit through all the meetings; those I did attend left a lively memory.

Some of the 'Swans', tired of criticising, began to try their hands at writing plays themselves. Two went on to achieve national success, Stanley Houghton and Harold Brighouse; others wrote plays specifically for the Gaiety. Houghton won his success sooner than Brighouse. There was as much fuss over the arrival of *Hindle Wakes* in London as there has been over John Osborne's *Look Back in Anger*. It was part of the intellectual snobbery of the club to profess contempt for commercial success. Houghton, a gentle, kindly creature, smiled away chaff that contained more than a tinge of envy. His character was not strong enough to withstand such overwhelming success. His health broke down and he died without further achievement. Brighouse on the other hand has attained a permanent niche in the gallery of English dramatists by the inclusion of *Hobson's Choice* in the repertoire of the National Theatre.

II

They were halcyon days at the Gaiety, with famous authors descending upon us from time to time, columns of well-written criticism (of the plays, rarely the players) in the *Manchester Guardian*, and a growing nucleus of support, most of which sat in the upper circle or thronged the sixpenny gallery. Our audiences included students of every shade of opinion, intellectuals from the University, vegetarians, nature lovers, week-end hikers in the Derbyshire hills, and general marchers in the advance guard of public opinion. But in spite of all enthusiasm, critical and otherwise, our private lives were curiously circumscribed. We had no contact at all with the daily round of the city. The legend of extremism set buzzing during that first season in the Midland Hotel persisted, so that we were ignored by the wealthy members of the community; not that this caused any concern: we were too busy. Our contacts remained with those who sat in the loftier seats in the theatre.

The routine of work was exacting: we rehearsed from 10.30 to 4 p.m. with only half an hour's interval for lunch, then a scamper through the rain to tram or train to one's lodgings, then back through the rain once more for the evening performance. Miss Horniman did what she could to make things easier for her company. It was she who insisted that there should be a break in the middle of the morning for coffee, which she sent in at her own expense from the Midland Hotel. Thus, the established routine of the mid-morning coffee-break during rehearsals owes its origin to Miss Horniman. Another example of her concern comes to mind: *An Enemy of the People* contains a dinner scene in the second act. For the sake of realism, actual food was proposed. The business manager wanted to deduct the cost of the meal from our salaries. Esmé Percy took the matter to Miss Horniman, who calmly replied that no such thing would happen. Thereafter, we ate a hearty meal of hot roast beef with trimmings at every performance, and enjoyed ourselves so much that we forgot our cues, and the prompter gave up in despair.

Her benign influence is best illustrated by the good feeling that existed among us. I can recall no quarrels or jealousies of any consequence. This unanimity of purpose, which critics noted at the time, enormously increased the company's impact. Possibly it was because of Miss Horniman's utterly selfless motives that the influence of her company extended far beyond the scope and duration of its work.

Miss Horniman's public attitudes undoubtedly betrayed her masculine trend. This may explain in part the affinity she felt for sensitive minds like W. B. Yeats, and the strong regard, not to say affection, she had for Iden Payne. In the light of modern psychology her later disagreements with Lewis Casson, a more definite and masculine character, become understandable. When her enterprise was about to be closed down because of the First World War, and she was asked if she intended to be present at the final performance, she wrote its epitaph in words of superb courage: 'Of course I shall be there. Every corpse must attend its own funeral.' A mordant remark matching Sheridan's at the burning of Drury Lane Theatre.

12

By the summer of 1910 the Horniman Company had reached the zenith of its achievement, never to be overpassed. The credit for

Above   My parents
Below left   My first audience
Below right   I acquire a bicycle

Miss Horniman and some
of her authors

Above right   John Galsworthy
Below left   Charles McEvoy
Below right   John Masefield

The first Horniman Company included Miss Darragh, Ada King, Hilda
Bruce-Potter, B. Iden Payne (the director), Charles Bibby, Lewis Casson,
and myself

this belonged to Iden Payne. I do not recall that he bothered us very much over technique, but he had a flair for letting people have their heads and yet, somehow, guiding them into a kind of emotional unity that was a complete expression of the play's purpose. The ensemble effects thus produced revolutionised the style of acting that had existed hitherto. Those of us who survive regard our time at the Gaiety with special warmth, for it was the only theatre in the land where the art of the ensemble was deliberately cultivated.

For my part I felt I was riding high on a full tide of achievement when everything about my parts seemed to click into place in my mind: the voice I should use, how I should dress and walk, my relations with the other characters and, above all, an inner understanding of how my man lived and had his being. I felt I was on my way to a true understanding of the actor's art, although it might be years before I could acquire complete mastery.

We concluded the season with a successful visit to Cambridge, followed by a positively triumphant fortnight at Oxford. During my first year of touring I had made no attempt to get into touch with my school contemporaries at either university because, frankly, I was ashamed of being in such poor companies. In any case our visits were made mostly out of term, which was just as well. Now, all was changed. School friends were seeking me out and inducting me into various undergraduate circles. It is commonly said that early friendships are the most lasting. This was certainly so in my case. At Cambridge I met again Arthur Tedder, later to become Deputy Supreme Commander to General Eisenhower, in which position he was to lend powerful support to my plans for entertaining our troops during the Second World War. Robert Keable was there, too, in an emotional mood of preparation for the Church, which he entered in due course. But the urge to write, strongly felt in his schooldays, gradually overcame his sense of dedication. He left the Church to become a popular novelist. One of his books, *Simon Called Peter*, became a best seller; it was thought to be very daring in its day. Later he went to live in the South Seas with an Australian wife. I met him once or twice on his return to England after the First World War, when he tried to persuade me to join his *dolce vita*. The last news I had of him was from Alec Waugh at a luncheon club in New York, who told me that he was living in common-law marriage with a Tahitian of good family. But the life of pleasure was too much for him. He died young. Keable's personal problem was the age-old conflict between sex and religion—in his case

F

fought out upon unconventional lines. I also met Clive Carey and Robert Crichton who helped me to appreciate the importance of music and rhythm in the theatre. At Oxford I made many new friends apart from those I had known at school including Desmond Young who crowned an adventurous career by being captured by Field Marshal Rommel and then writing a best-selling biography of him. One invitation, to breakfast I think it was, came from an undergraduate at Oriel and led to the most enduring friendship of my life. Roger Ould was reading law and using his spare time to acquire a half-blue for boxing. A cherubic countenance that would wrinkle up with zestful enthusiasm at the slightest provocation seemed to deny his pugilism. Neither of us had any sense of destiny at this chance meeting.

By this time the undergraduate audiences were greeting me with a round of applause on my first entrance in *The Silver Box*: exhilarating but dangerous, because personal receptions were frowned upon by the management. From the warmth of my welcome I began to think there was no need to bother about my future with the company. It would be merely a question of what salary I was to receive. However, I thought I had better find out, so towards the end of the week I marched confidently up to Iden Payne, standing in the lobby of the New Theatre, to put my question. When he told me I would not be re-engaged for the autumn I was flabbergasted. Why? I asked. Well, I had been long enough with the company; I had learned all I could learn with them. I should try my luck elsewhere. It was no compensation to be told I might make a curtain speech of farewell on the last night.

Payne's action was incomprehensible to me. Perhaps he thought there was some risk of my acquiring star rating, which might upset the balance of the ensemble. Whatever the reason for it, the sudden blow effectively restored my sense of proportion. More than that, it revived all my uncertainties about the future. Perhaps I was not going to be a success after all?

Five
Liverpool

Suddenly cut off from what had promised to be a career of mounting achievement I felt lost. All the familiar surroundings of home appeared to have shrunk in size, which I suppose is a common enough experience. It was unlikely I should succeed in placing any of my plays for a long time to come, so work had to be found somehow. I went to as many West End theatres as I could afford, watching the performances, and haunting the stage-doors, hoping to find a niche of employment that would help me to climb. My money was disappearing so fast that I began to worry. Fortunately, I found a little bistro run by a jolly Frenchman just behind the Palace Theatre, rough but clean, bare boards, unstarched linen tablecloths—where one could get a three-course lunch; soup, meat or fish, cheese and a bottle of vin (*très*) ordinaire for one-and-six. Eventually I decided to swallow my pride and go once more to the hated Blackmore Agency. The waiting-room was full of the unsuccessful. When my name was called gossip ceased, and envious stares followed me into Mr. Blackmore's sanctum. To my astonishment I was told that Mr. Hall Caine wanted to see me that afternoon at his flat in Whitehall Court. That interview had an air of fantasy about it. First, a parlour-maid took my card, then a male secretary ('gold-stick-in-waiting') asked my name, and, finally, after a decorous interval during which the deep silence that pervaded the flat made me feel nervous, I was ushered into the presence. Hall Caine dressed all in black was seated in a high-backed chair that looked as if it had been rescued from the property room of the Lyceum Theatre. He had white hair, a small pointed beard and Machiavellian eyebrows; and certainly looked the part of the arch-poseur of literary Godfearing, which in fact he was. He described in solemn whispers the small part of a priest that he invited me to play in his latest melodrama: also, would I care to understudy his son, Derwent, in the leading part? The salary was to be eight pounds a week, exactly double my recent salary with the Horniman Company. When he learned I had some pretensions to authorship he declared with an air of high generosity that he would welcome any suggestions I might make to improve the scene I was to be in. I fell into the trap, and went home to re-write most of the fustian rubbish it contained. But at the first rehearsal I received a curt reminder that as an author of twenty-five years' experience, he thought he knew best. The play opened at the Shakespeare Theatre in Liverpool. I was sacked at the end of the first week for not speaking the author's lines. Keeping this humiliation to myself, I continued the search for opportunity on the West End stage, but it seemed impossible for a provincial actor to cross the road to the economic safety that lay beyond the stage-door of a London theatre; the traffic signals were all against him.

Some hazy ideas of mine about an Art Theatre for London were welcomed with enthusiasm by J. T. Grein, dramatic critic of the *Sunday Times*, and with caution by William Archer. Hamilton Fyfe, then writing for the *Daily Mail*, invited me to Sunday lunch at his country cottage near Brooklands to discuss the plan. Our talk was interrupted by the arrival of Hawker, a young airman very much in the news at that time. The new excitement of flying blew all thoughts of the theatre out of the window. After lunch we went to Brooklands, where Hawker offered to take me for what he called 'a flip' round the aerodrome in his machine. Still hugging thoughts of my Art Theatre project, I refused, and thus missed the opportunity of a flight with one of the pioneers of flying.

Countering my moods of frustration, Galsworthy wrote me wise, restraining letters when I thought of abandoning the stage and going abroad. Even Joseph Flint, that tough old adventurer, was against that idea. Then one day I received a telegram from Miss Darragh. There was a chance of 'doing repertory' in Liverpool. 'Please come at once.' Just that and no more. It seemed a wild gamble. I should have to borrow the money for my train fare, and for my stay in the city. I had an intuition that this might be a turning point, yet I hesitated to take the risk. I decided to toss for it. My future was to depend upon the toss of a coin; or was it? I spun the coin and lost the call. Muttering 'threes' to myself, I spun the coin again, then again and again. Each time I lost. Finally, exasperated by this Delphic failure, I packed my bag, borrowed some money from my mother and caught the next train.

2

Miss Darragh met me at the station. With her was Charles Kenyon, a wealthy young mill-owner, who was also an amateur actor of some repute, with the ambition to turn professional. The strangest concatenation of circumstances had brought us together. For some time past ardent Liverpool playgoers had been journeying regularly to Manchester to see the plays at the Gaiety, returning home by the last train, full of enthusiasm for the good things they had seen enacted there. Recently they had begun to agitate for a similar enterprise in their own city. Letters had appeared in the Press, and a playgoers' society been formed. Soon professors from the University, led by Charles Reilly, the energetic principal of the recently founded and already famous Liverpool School of Architecture, had joined in the agitation. Next, town and gown were tacitly joined when Professor Reilly became Chairman of the Playgoers' Society. Then Alfred Wareing made an offer to bring his Glasgow Repertory Company to Liverpool for a six weeks' experimental season. This was eagerly accepted, and a guarantee fund against loss was raised by prominent people in the city. The plan came unstuck when Wareing, already beset by financial difficulties in Scotland, fell ill and cancelled his offer. In Manchester meanwhile, Kenyon, a close friend of Miss Darragh, had been offering to finance her plans to leave the Gaiety and form her own company. She had often hinted to me that this was something in which I might have a share. Now a friendly telegram from Wareing, announcing his withdrawal, had brought her hot-foot to Liverpool, myself following in response to her summons. And that is how the three of us came together to plan our 'experimental season' for Liverpool.

It was apparent from the start that Kenyon was infatuated with Miss Darragh. Indeed, he made no secret of it, constantly reminding me that, although he expected good parts for himself in the plays, her personal success was his main interest in the scheme, and I must never forget it. But I had my own views about that. I always knew when he had been pressing his suit, for his eyes would suddenly fill with tears of frustration, even while we were discussing business details. It was most embarrassing. I always suspected that Miss Darragh held the poor man aloof, not as a matter of cool calculation, but because she was not free to do otherwise. There was always an aura of Anglo-Indian entanglement about her. But I had to tread warily round a personal situation that might have wrecked our plans.

Our chances of success seemed flimsy indeed. We knew no one in the city. All we had to go on was the suggestion contained in the Wareing telegram that we should get into touch with Professor Reilly. But we did not know the Professor's address and had to look it up in the telephone book. While Miss Darragh went off to interview him, I was told to see the editor of the *Liverpool Daily Post*. At the newspaper office I met Alan Jeans, son of Alexander, the managing editor of the paper. Alan passed me on to his younger brother, Ronald, then working in a stockbroker's office, who proved to be the vital link in a chain of interest stretching from the enthusiastic Playgoers' Society and the lively professors at the University right up to the editorial chair of the newspaper, where Sir Edward Russell, veteran journalist and admirer of Henry Irving, still nominally presided. With his approval, egged on by Ronald Jeans, the *Liverpool Daily Post* went all out to publicise and support our plan, pointing out that upon the success of the promised Six Weeks' Experimental Season depended the prospect of a permanent repertory theatre for the city. The rival newspapers soon joined in; even the *Manchester Guardian*, not to be outdone, gave us a qualified blessing. Impressed by the newspaper backing, no less than by Kenyon's offer of five hundred pounds working capital, the original guarantors agreed to transfer their support to our enterprise. As soon as these money matters were settled I went off to London in search of plays and players.

The London theatre scene was an intimidating prospect to an unknown provincial actor in search of managerial status. I felt a distinct fluttering at the pit of my stomach as the train drew into Euston. Plays must be the first consideration, so I appealed for help to John Galsworthy, who responded warmly. He agreed to let us open with *Strife* (after first taking the precaution of writing to Manchester to ask whether I was capable of the responsibility). Next he secured us the practical support of J. M. Barrie and John Masefield, from whom I obtained *The Twelve Pound Look* and *Nan* respectively. My talks with leading critics during the previous autumn now bore fruit; J. T. Grein gave the plan an enthusiastic welcome in the *Sunday Times*, E. F. Spence wrote a column in the *Westminster Gazette*, and William Archer publicly acknowledged its significance by coming to Liverpool for the opening night. Actors, always with a nose for good opportunity, were naturally influenced by this grand show of approval. I had no difficulty in recruiting the company. The leading man was C. M. Hallard, a West End actor of established reputation and strong mannerisms, who endured my tentative suggestions at rehearsal with impatient politeness. Meanwhile in Manchester Miss Horniman, her crusading spirit aroused, had persuaded some of those she was pleased to call her Manchester authors to give us plays, including Allan Monkhouse and Harold Brighouse. She loaned the scenery for all but one of the productions, and released some actors to complete the casts, including Whitford Kane to play Roberts in *Strife*.

Rehearsals took place in a small room at the top of the shabby old Kelly's Theatre, in Paradise Street, re-named after himself by W. W. Kelly, the redoubtable Irishman who had toured W. G. Wills' melodrama *A Royal Divorce* (with his wife, Edith Cole, in the leading part) for so long that some of its lines had become bywords with the audience, especially 'Not tonight, Josephine'. Work was constantly interrupted by meetings, conferences and interviews as I struggled for a measure of authority over a company of actors brought together for the first time, some of them very senior indeed. Fortunately, Galsworthy, visiting us in the final stages, approved of what had been done. I have no recollection at all of the quality of the performances. Today I find myself reading those unfailingly laudatory notices with a high degree of scepticism.

The audience on the opening night, February 20th, 1911, represented all aspects of life in the city: the Lord Mayor and his lady, of course, mayors and aldermen of neighbouring towns and boroughs, two visiting judges of the High Court, and, on the social side, representatives of the great shipping families still reigning in the city. Some came partly out of curiosity or in response to editorial indoctrination, and some partly to justify the publication of their names in the list of guarantors. Professors of the University, led by Charles Reilly, sat side by side with leading dramatic critics from London and the North. In one box sat the fifth Lord Derby, that magnum-sized personality whose word was second law throughout Lancashire, and, opposite him, Miss Horniman, in her finest brocade and wearing her breastplate of opals, came to watch the inauguration of her first self-governing colony.

The printed list at the University Club supper which followed was headed by Granville Barker, who was to propose 'The Repertory Theatre', but he failed to appear. His attendance at the same club the previous year to speak on the same subject had been a failure, largely because with commendable honesty he had pointed out that the theatre would probably lose money each week, whereupon his wealthy listeners had decided to think again before loosening one end of their purse-strings. Fortunately, on this occasion there were plenty of enthusiastic speech-makers to cover the embarrassment caused by his absence. Galsworthy repeated the plea he had made at the end of the performance for 'the establishment of a permanent repertory theatre in the city to encourage the strong, true and vital in art'. Miss Horniman repeated her parrot-cry for a 'civilised' theatre, and Lord Derby, obviously out of his depth, warmed all hearts with bonhomie.

Following that opening night, our tale of unbroken success is briefly told. All concerned seemed to be borne aloft upon one great surge of enthusiasm. Crowded audiences were the order at each performance, including the two weeks of *Strife*, this despite the protest of a prominent V.I.P. at being invited to such 'a damned Socialist play'. Paradise Street had never before welcomed such a stream of distinguished visitors. Even hard-headed businessmen began to wonder whether, after all, there might not be some promise for the future in all the enthusiasm. The season closed to deafening applause with another distinguished author, John Masefield this time, to give the final nod of metropolitan approval. The ovation given to the players as they assembled on the stage exceeded that of the opening night. I was called, and was able to announce the decision to establish a permanent repertory theatre in Liverpool. (Vociferous cheers.) Professor Reilly was then introduced as the chairman of the proposed company. (More cheers.) The actors were then joined by all the stage staff (I had insisted upon this), Auld Lang Syne was sung, and everyone trooped out of the theatre, convinced that all that remained was to raise some money and build the theatre as quickly as possible, certainly in time for the autumn!

Financially, our success was greater far than anything we had hoped for. Neither the Liverpool guarantee fund, nor Kenyon's money had been called upon. In fact, Kenyon made some eight hundred pounds profit, one-half of which he gave to Miss Darragh, £100 to myself—the first cheque I ever received for such an amount —and distributed the remainder among the members of the company. 'Yes, the experimental season had been a huge success,' everyone declared. 'No doubt the new theatre will be, too.'

3

Liverpool at the turn of the century was a city of noticeable contrasts, in attitudes quite as much as in physical aspects. Civic pride expressed itself in founding art galleries, libraries and a new university, to say nothing of planning a great cathedral, even while it neglected such domestic issues as slum clearance. At the apex, as it were, of the city's prosperity, there was the rebuilt Adelphi Hotel, its modern wonders, especially the plumbing, proudly displayed to troupes of admiring visitors by young Arthur Towle, about to inherit his father's reputation for railway hotel management. Past that hotel clanging tramcars hurtled themselves over the stone setts on their way down to the comparative peace of the riverside, where swishing little ferries, crowded with commuters, churned their way past great liners anchored in the river. Even the weather was vagarious and uncertain; rain clouds racing from the sou'west alternated with days of sea mist and fog, when screaming gulls and hooting sirens punctuated the silence.

The great shipping families were still the hierarchy of the city's commercial life, its leaders, too, in the social round. As Ramsay Muir, one of the University's professors actively interesting himself in the repertory theatre, and eventually to become one of its directors, wrote later: 'In the early years of this century there was a real vitality, a fizz and a go, in Liverpool.' It was with the same high confidence, helped no doubt by the astonishing success of our experimental season, that the fund-raising campaign began. It was led by that notable 'fizzer', Professor Reilly, without whose ebullient enthusiasm and persistent refusal to look economic facts in the face the scheme might never have got off the ground. For weeks after the experimental season closed Liverpool seemed to eat, drink and breathe nothing but repertory. The only discordant note amongst an otherwise unanimous press was sounded by a small satirical magazine, called *The Liverpool Porcupine*, which justified its name by publishing prickly little paragraphs, referring contemptuously to 'the over-enthusiastic repertorists'. There were lectures, newspaper articles and what used to be called 'bun-fights' (taking the place of the modern cocktail party), at which opinions and promises of financial support were eagerly canvassed, the first to be disregarded if they were unfavourable, and the second pursued relentlessly to the moment of signature on the cheque. The wives and daughters of future directors were prominent at these gatherings, revelling in the latest topic of conversation; it was a case of 'repertory, repertory, all the way'.

Miss Darragh was well to the fore on all social occasions, fashionably dressed in the Edwardian style which suited her, and wearing the smart hats of the period with a panache that was not lost upon the provincial ladies. Kenyon rarely appeared, which left her free to exercise her fascinations elsewhere, notably with Professor Reilly in an Elinor Glyn-like interview in her private sitting-room at the Adelphi Hotel. The lady had a cold, explained the porter. But this did nothing to advance her claim to head the new enterprise. Just the reverse, for hostesses resented this dangerous intrusion into the domestic entourage, and set about adjusting their husbands' ideas accordingly, arguing, sensibly enough, that this was a movement best managed by a young man rather than by a middle-aged actress of undoubted charm. I was asked point-blank whether I was prepared to run the theatre without Miss Darragh, otherwise the promoters must look elsewhere. I could see no viability in the Darragh-Kenyon axis, nothing but enormous difficulties when it came to choosing and casting the plays. So, after a stormy interview with Kenyon, I agreed. Pangs of conscience still assail me as I write this, for I was never able to repay the debt I owed to Miss Darragh.

Amid all the junketings our prospective directors never lost sight of the objective, which was to have a repertory theatre of some sort by the autumn. But it was soon obvious that a new building was out of the question; it would cost too much and take too long. Mr. Kelly, snuffing the air of opulence surrounding the guarantors, offered to sell the lease of either of his two theatres, the Shakespeare or Kelly's, neither of which was doing well at the time. The committee did not fancy Kelly's: they said the seats were uncomfortable, but they asked me to look over the Shakespeare. Fortunately, Kelly opened his mouth too wide, and so the trap of overhousing our enterprise was avoided. There were days when it seemed as though the opportunity of a lifetime would slip from me. Eventually, the Star Theatre in Williamson Square, once an old-time music-hall, complete with chairman and waiters, and now a home for melodrama, came on offer. It was owned by one Harris Fineberg, who had sold the property once before, and then taken it back at a knock-down price when the enterprise failed. Perhaps he thought he could repeat the process. While negotiations were going on I spent many dreary hours in the theatre bar, half-drugged by the fumes of the beer cellar behind me, listening to Fineberg's tall stories about himself, and trying to persuade him to lower his terms. My naïve enthusiasm must have had a contrary effect. The purchase price was finally agreed at £28,000, of which £20,000 was to be left on mortgage. An option was obtained and the deposit paid. I was to have my opportunity after all.

The architect chosen to plan the reconstruction was Professor Stanley Adshead, first Professor of Town Planning at the University, and a brilliant architect in his own right. A large friendly man with a sense of humour, he proved an excellent foil to the excitable Charles Reilly, whose frequent attempts at interference he did not hesitate to slap down with firm good humour. When I told the committee the stage was too small for repertory purposes, they approached the City Council, secured the closure of a passage at the rear of the building and bought property beyond it for dressing-rooms. Nevertheless, in the prevailing climate of ignorance there was likely to be a tussle to prevent too much money being spent on the auditorium to the exclusion of stage requirements. By a happy chance, sound technical knowledge and a ready sympathy with my ideas were at my elbow.

4

My meeting with George Harris occurred during the experimental season—a chance encounter that in retrospect seems to have been preordained, a part of personal destiny. The garden scenery for the second act of *The Cassilis Engagement* by St. John Hankin had been loaned to us by Miss Horniman, but when we set it up for the dress rehearsal it proved to be barely presentable, and there were no flower-beds. Whoever heard of an English garden without flower-beds! I rang up Robinson, a well-known property-maker in Liverpool, whose premises were appropriately named 'The Ark', to supply the deficiency. Shortly afterwards, a friendly, quiet young man with a sardonic smile and a heavy birthmark which had the appearance of a permanent black eye, a defect about which I was to discover he was extremely sensitive, walked on to the stage. This was George Harris. He watched me trying to arrange the flower-beds he had brought with him. Then, as my language became unprintable, he added his own salty comments. Soon we began chatting, mocking the silly scenic conventions of the day: the ridiculous foliage borders looking like 'washing on the line', and the flapping landscapes at the back. Should there not be more light and air on the stage? Agreed. So we tore down the backcloths and threw away the borders, mentally speaking, of course. And why did scenery always look so flat and dull under the electric light? New painting techniques must be thought out, said George. I cannot remember how that dress rehearsal was ever begun or ended. All I care to remember is that for the rest of the season, and for weeks afterwards, we theorised and argued together and worked out plans for the new playhouse. The more we talked the more I realised how fortunate I was in having made Harris's acquaintance. I determined to wean him from his bread and butter employment at 'The Ark', and to attach his star to mine; whether ascending or descending, time alone would show.

George was so wrapped up in the theatre that if I had been told he was born in the manager's office it would have caused no surprise. In fact, that was not far from the truth. When quite a tiny child he was dressed up and carried on to the stage of the newly built Shakespeare Theatre by his father, who was manager there. At the age of thirteen he was attending art classes and at fifteen apprenticed to a well-known local scene-painter. At the same time he became a student at the Liverpool University School of Architecture and Applied Arts, where he soon became the star pupil at Augustus John's weekly life-classes. An artist-craftsman of the highest quality, he was to become my closest friend and collaborator in the years ahead.

5

While I was in London in January engaging the company I had seen
Max Reinhardt's production of *Sumurŭn*. This production in which
colour, light and movement were combined to such brilliant effect
followed closely upon the enormous upsurge of interest in stage décor
that had been aroused in Western Europe by the designs of Bakst,
Benois and others. I was immensely impressed and as I could do
little good waiting about in Liverpool while the fund-raising campaign got under way, I decided to go to Germany to seek out
the great man himself. So, with what was left of the £100 Kenyon
had given me out of his profits, I set off, leaving George Harris to
keep his eye on Adshead. Fortunately, this worked very well.
George's sardonic wit appealed as much to Adshead as did his
evident technical mastery.

Reinhardt was about to present his production of *Oedipus Rex*
at the Circus Schumann in Frankfurt. I made my way there, arriving
in time for the first performance. The Circus held nearly five thousand
people and was crammed to the doors. I was completely carried
away by the emotional impact of that stupendous production as I
listened to the powerful German voices and watched the vast arena
filling with the well-drilled crowd chanting 'Oedipus! Oedipus!'
under the coloured searchlights. This was an arena performance at
full stretch. Thus modern experiments in this type of staging
were ante-dated some fifty years by Max Reinhardt.

After the performance I sat in the garden of the Grand Hotel,
Frankfurter Hof, amid a flurry of white-aproned waiters carrying
huge beer mugs, the air filled with the scent of lime trees and cigar
smoke. (All countries have their characteristic scents, perhaps
noticeable only by foreign visitors.) Reinhardt must have been
amused by the spectacle of an impecunious young Englishman
trying to follow the desultory remarks of Felix Hollaender, von
Hofmannsthal and others seated at the little iron tables. He gave me
his autograph on a hotel postcard (which I still possess) and invited
me to follow him to the Deutsches Theater in Berlin. There I was
permitted to watch him rehearsing a revival of *Sumurŭn* with the
lovely Leopoldine Konstantin as Die Tanzerin and Camilla Eiben-
schütz as Sumurŭn. Then I went next door to the Kammerspiele to
see a moving performance of Wedekind's *Frühlings Erwachen*. I

was allowed to wander round both theatres, noting the technical equipment, especially the use of a plaster dome in place of the usual painted back-cloths. Illuminated from one central point at a considerable distance away, this produced effects of space and light quite unlike anything to be seen at home at that time. I decided to introduce some of these technical advances on to our stage.

My elementary knowledge of the language and my ignorance of the social customs of the Germans gave me an awkward moment after one of Reinhardt's first nights. He invited me to join him and some of his associates at supper at the Café Horcher, the most expensive restaurant in Berlin. Max sat at the head of a long table, surrounded by a goodly company of famous players: Else Heims, to whom he was still married, Moissi, Bassermann, Gertrud Eysold, Paul Wegener, Max Pallenberg: I was flattered to be in such wonderful company. The meal was excellent, and so was the 'Rhenish', but I was horrified when I saw waiters going to each member of the party in turn with a little piece of paper on a plate. Apparently this was the normal German custom on such occasions; each guest pays his own bill. Good heavens! Have I enough money for my share? The thought sent shivers down my back, and still does. Hurriedly, I fingered the notes and coins in my pocket, as I listened to my neighbour's small talk with a vacant stare induced by mental arithmetic. I had just enough. But I had to walk back to my hotel, use the last of my traveller's cheques to pay the bill, and catch an early train, arriving in England starving but enthusiastic. It was fortunate I had taken a return ticket.

6

Back in Liverpool I found Reilly and Adshead locked in bitter argument over estimates that were far in excess of what had been anticipated. Reilly, waving his silver cigarette case, a favourite gesture when excited, was especially insistent upon the conversion of the old beer cellar into a foyer where people could circulate and discuss the play in the interval. He found an unexpected advocate in myself, for I had been greatly impressed by the *lange pause* of the German theatres, when seemingly the whole audience rose from their seats and hurried to the buffets to swallow ham sandwiches and drink lager beer, and to stroll up and down creaking corridors, discussing the play. There is no doubt Reilly was in advance of his time over the foyer, but he gave me no return support over my lighting plans, referring contemptuously to them as 'this lighting nonsense'. However, he became acquiescent when they eventually proved their value at the box office.

The begging campaign had been going all too slowly while I was away. I began to wonder whether the great opportunity would slip from me. But Reilly with great courage insisted upon the issue of a prospectus, naming ten leading citizens of Liverpool, each of them prominent in his own sphere, as the first Board of Directors. (Two more names were added after publication.) The prospectus was heralded with trumpet blasts of newspaper publicity, summoning the good citizens of Liverpool for their souls' sake to follow the example of these ten good men and true and take up as many one pound shares as possible. The impetus lasted only a few days, then the size and rate of subscription began to dwindle again. It was clear that a host of small subscribers, however valuable they might be in sustaining the theatre in its nursling days, could not provide all the initial capital needed. A determined assault upon the business world was decided upon, led as before by the undaunted Reilly.

He told me to write to the first Lord Leverhulme, then Sir William Lever, inviting him to become a shareholder, but when I showed him the reply, an abrupt refusal, Reilly said he could not possibly take No for an answer. So upon a chilly Saturday afternoon we journeyed out to Thornton Hough, Reilly confidently anticipating a promise of £5,000. Sir William was well used to Reilly's tactics by now, having previously succumbed with many benefactions to the new University, including the purchase of the lovely Bluecoat Buildings to house the School of Architecture. Reilly did most of the talking, while Sir William just stood in front of the huge coal fire, staring me out of countenance with his large blue eyes. Presently tea was brought in by butler and parlourmaid in the stately manner of the time: silver tea-pot and spirit kettle upon a large silver tray, silver tea-caddy, silver dish for scones, and silver tea-knives, all set gleaming in front of Lady Lever, who had been quietly knitting. After she had made the tea, there came the homely summons: 'Now, William, come and 'ave the tea before it spoils.' Eventually, with much reluctance, Sir William promised to subscribe for five hundred one-pound shares. 'Disappointing,' said Reilly briskly as we left the house, 'but it might have been worse.'

I spent hours tapping out letters to authors on an aged typewriter lent me by a supporter, telling them of our forthcoming happy event and asking at least for their moral support if their plays were not available. Bernard Shaw warned me not to ask authors for money, and Galsworthy excused himself by explaining that he had recently 'outrun the constable'. I still have the encouraging letter which W. S. Gilbert wrote me. It must have been one of the last from his pen, for two days later he died in his own lake at Grims Dyke swimming to the aid of Winifred Emery's niece. I also typed soothing letters to impatient actors, anxious to know if their autumn engagements were assured. Professor Reilly assumed that his duties as chairman included close supervision of every letter I wrote, so it was not long before I and my borrowed typewriter and my packets of stationery were removed to a studio in the School of Architecture, where I met the present Lord Holford, then a student working to win the Prix de Rome.

One of the earliest supporters of the experimental season had been Alec Rea, a junior partner in the prosperous family business of R. & J. H. Rea, coal-factors. Originally converted to interest in the repertory movement by Ronald Jeans during their daily journeys across the river to their respective offices, and encouraged by his vivacious young American wife, Marguerite, Rea now became deeply involved. He used to invite me to meet him at the Exchange Club where his business friends ate hasty lunches while listening with amused expressions on their faces to my fairy tales of how much a repertory theatre would add to the amenities of their city. Then they would hurry off to more important matters, forgetting our conversation almost before they had left the building.

In the few days that remained before the subscription lists closed, John Shute, another businessman active in the theatre's cause, harried the members of the Liverpool Cotton Exchange, where he was a leading and popular figure, to 'pay up and lose their money like gentlemen', while other campaigners grabbed cheques from reluctant hands and hurried with them to the bank. In a last rallying call for victory Sir Edward Russell was induced to write yet another signed article for the *Daily Post*. Only in the nick of time, as it were, was sufficient money raised—£13,000 out of the £23,000 asked for in the prospectus—to justify the directors in proceeding to allotment. The campaign had lasted less than a month. No other city in the country would have done better at that time.

Top
Left Rev 'Lexy' Mill: *Candida*

Right Jack Barthwick: *The Silver Box*

Centre
Left Jasper: *The Knight of the Burning Pestle*

Right Claudio: *Measure for Measure*

Below
Left Paris: *Romeo and Juliet*

Right Walter King, gamekeeper: *When the Devil was Ill*

Parts I played with the Horniman Company 1907–10

Above First performance in Liverpool of Galsworthy's *Strife*. The six weeks' experimental season at Kelly's Theatre led to the founding of the Repertory Theatre

Below Dress rehearsal of *You Never Can Tell*. The Repertory Company included Ronald Squire, J. H. Roberts, Estelle Winwood and Dorothy Massingham: I stand aside, waiting to give notes after the photograph is taken

7

When summer came I jumped at the chance of escape from the chairman's exacting company by accepting an invitation to stay with Harry Lowerison, one of the small band of idealists gathered round Robert Blatchford. He was running a co-educational school at Heacham on the Norfolk coast. Professor Reilly demurred, saying he had invited Granville Barker to come and address the directors on how to run the theatre, and as he had not yet fixed the date I should wait. After my long experience in Manchester I felt I was better qualified to run a provincial repertory theatre than Barker, so I said nothing, waited a few days, and then, as no word came, caught the train. Soon I was busy helping the boys and girls of Ruskin School to prepare an open-air performance of a *Midsummer Night's Dream*. It was great fun rehearsing such intelligent youngsters, destined, some of them, to play their parts on the political stage of the country. But a peremptory summons to return to Liverpool to receive Granville Barker soon reminded me of my own political situation. I felt the time had come to assert myself, else my work for the theatre would lack all independent judgment. So I stayed away. When I returned to Liverpool the air was frosty with Reilly's disapproval. Although I did not realise it at the time my unwise gesture of defiance was to set the pattern of our future relations.

Part of that wonderful summer I spent with a group of friends from Birkenhead at Abersoch in North Wales, swimming, fishing, and sometimes sailing to Bardsey or the more distant Puffin Island, usually storm-bound but that summer squatting peacefully day after day on seas so calm that the cries of the sea-birds quite drowned the gurgle of the water in and out among the rocks. At sunset we walked on the Welsh hills under the brightening stars, reading Keats and Shelley. Some of the odes of William Watson were good for shouting over the cliff-tops. One member of the party, charming and witty, often looked quizzically at me, wondering how much of this was simply histrionics and how much inspired by personal feelings for her daughter. I was not prepared to enlighten her, and she was wise enough not to ask, content merely to encourage us all to enjoy idyllic moments that might never return. That was also her wise advice when I had news that bricks from our theatre site had been

G

used as ammunition by the rioting unemployed. 'What if the rioters have stolen your bricks? You can't prevent them now,' she said. 'Stay where you are.' I returned eventually to find that the opening of the theatre, planned for October, would now have to be postponed by one month.

8

At last all was ready, constructional difficulties overcome and the inevitable last-minute delays sufficiently estimated to enable us to fix the opening date. I gave this out, together with the programme for the first half of the season at the October session of the Liverpool Playgoers' Society, an extremely active body of enthusiasts, with Professor Reilly at its head and Oscar Waddington, a young chemist's assistant as its secretary. The Liverpool press gave the announcement a warm welcome, except the Liverpool *Porcupine*, which acted up to its title by publishing a column of sarcasm at my expense that brought angry letters from its readers. Two formal openings were decided upon. The first, to take place on November 11th (1911) would be mainly for our shareholders—there were now 1200 of them—who would be given priority at the box-office; the second, on Monday, 13th, would be a civic function, presided over by the Lord Mayor. Liverpool society turned out in force on the Saturday night, drawn partly by curiosity to see how its money had been spent, and partly by the unerring instinct of the smart set ever to be in the right place at the right time. Here was a gathering not to be missed, regardless of what took place on the stage. Certainly, the spectacle which awaited them was pleasant enough. The discreet colours of the auditorium (ivory, cerise and gold), the huge banks of flowers massed at vantage points (a gift from a wealthy patron), and, above all, the latest fashions of the women, well set off by the white ties and tails of the men; all was fully commented upon in the social columns. The story in the *Liverpool Courier* read like a description of an eighteenth-century rout:

'Society, wearing its prettiest frocks, occupied boxes and stalls and circles. Muspratts, Forwoods, Holts, Batesons, Willinks were there. The two boxes were occupied—on the one side by Rathbones and on the other by Bowrings. Professors and doctors, student folk and businessmen, journalists and authors, and men of law were gathered together to speed the new house of drama. Professor Reilly was the hero of the evening.'

A souvenir programme was designed by a member of the School of Architecture, in which the hopes and aims of the management were tersely stated! 'The immediate success of this venture will be the individual responsibility of every member of the audience. Dividends will be limited to six per cent.' Suggestions and complaints were to be addressed to me personally. All this raised more quills on the Liverpool *Porcupine*.

The performance began with the National Anthem. (In my time the Anthem was played only at the opening of a new theatre, or when royalty was present, thus creating a sense of occasion in the audience and quite a degree of excitement amongst the players.) Our patriotic duty done, the red and gold tableau curtains parted to disclose Aida Jenoure, a senior member of the new company, attired as 'The Tragic Muse, after Joshua Reynolds', but looking more like a nineteenth-century Britannia slightly gone at the knees, to recite verses especially written for the occasion by John Masefield. The play was *The Admirable Crichton*, by J. M. Barrie, given in the scenery of the original London production, which took our inexperienced stage-hands so long to arrange, that I had to go in front of the curtain and apologise for the length of the stage waits. This taught me my first lesson in management. In future we must make simple productions of our own rather than hire elaborate scenery from London and, in addition, have to pay for its repair. However, the long waits were no disaster on this occasion since they gave the rank and fashion time to troop into the new foyer to gossip and to admire their surroundings. The quality of the performance received little attention.

Liverpool seemed to give up the entire week-end to contemplation of its latest civic achievement. Throughout Sunday the theatre was thronged with visitors. Parties were led by Professor Reilly into the new foyer, where they collided with similar parties in charge of Professor Adshead, whose ample gestures brushed aside the flatteries showered upon him above the clatter of tea-cups. At Monday's performance all was repeated as before, the social atmosphere increased rather than diminished by the presence of Lord Derby, the city aldermen, the mayors of neighbouring boroughs, and much minor bumbledom, all in full regalia. The banks of flowers were still there, and so, too, was the enthusiasm of the audience.

No sooner had I seen the last of our distinguished guests on their
way to the celebration supper in the banqueting hall of the Adelphi
Hotel than I heard the sound of a fire-engine approaching the rear of
the theatre. I turned back to find the auditorium full of smoke and
firemen trailing hoses over our new stalls carpet. A fool had tossed
a lighted cigarette into a rubbish-filled wastepaper basket in the
manager's office. It took several gallons of water to extinguish the
blaze. When I reached the hotel the company was already seated
(two hundred and fifteen persons, all of high or middle, none of
low, degree). After a hurried word of explanation to the chairman
who promptly persuaded the editors present to keep the news out
of their papers, I took my place, acutely aware of my sooty shirt
front and unable to remember more than a phrase or two of my
carefully prepared reply to Lord Derby's toast to the new enterprise,
coupled with my name.

Miss Horniman, seated on my right, glanced at my frightened
face as I rose to speak. 'Cheer up,' she whispered. 'This is only the
beginning.' How right she was!

9

After such a successful night one might suppose that the future
would be all sweetness and light. This was not the case. Financially
speaking, the infant's arrival had been so premature that its survival
was a continuing source of anxiety. It began its existence with
literally no working capital at all. All the money that remained
after Fineberg had been satisfied was swallowed up in the work of
reconstructing the theatre, so we were dependent upon what came
in each week at the box-office which, despite the high percentage of
attendances to begin with, was insufficient. The takings had to be
helped out by additional bank guarantees, provided by the wealthier
directors.

The saying that money is the root of all evil was reversed in our
case, for it was the lack of it which led to battles royal among the
directors. Every Thursday they assembled in the front office, fresh
from dealing with their own affairs, and eager to give the theatre
the benefit of their special expertise. Attendances were regular and
enthusiastic. But conflicts of opinion soon caused schism in the
board-room. On the left were those who supported the chairman's

Who is Basil? What is Dean?
  That all the world applauds him.
He but ventures on the scene
  And Liverpool rewards him
With a post that's no wise mean,
With a post that's no wise mean.

                    etc., etc.

Voice permitting and the Shades of
Shakespeare and Schubert propitiated,
this song may be warbled to the air of
Who is Silvia.

*The 'Repertory' Dean. An early
caricature by George Harris*

desire for experiment—but without expense! To the right were those
who agreed to any production likely to improve the bank balance,
regardless of its ultimate effects on the theatre's reputation. The
small group who understood my desire to steer a middle course were
the 'crossbenchers' of the assembly. There were three of them:
Ronald Jeans, who cared so deeply that he would turn deathly
pale and inarticulate whenever a policy he believed in was under
fire, Sewell Bacon, proprietor of the leading fashion store, from
whom I cadged a set of velvet draperies, thirty feet high, for our
productions of poetic drama, and Alec Rea, my staunchest ally.
My lifelong friendship with Alec was forged during those early
battles.

At first the directors did not select the plays: they merely vetoed
them. There were often pitched battles before final decisions were
reached. Suggestions put forward at the chairman's behest were
usually thought to be too advanced by the business members of the
board. Commercial plays to redress an adverse verdict at the box-
office were torn quietly apart by the University members. The
astonishing amount of tension and excitement which the meetings
aroused was doubtless good for the theatre; it certainly was for me.
In the years to come I was to be grateful for the vigorous grooming

in responsibility that I received. After a while, the chairman feeling his feet, began more to control than to guide the arguments. When results were good at the box-office he would forget the anxieties of the previous meeting and chide me for not being more venturesome. The trouble was that Reilly was fundamentally a teacher, a professor. Artists were a breed he did not understand, neither how they thought and worked nor how to handle them. At the risk of contradicting myself, I must add however that he did act as a sort of gadfly, injecting the antidote of intelligent criticism into the complacent tea-cup-and-saucer atmosphere which invaded the theatre whenever business was good.

10

In spite of financial stringencies we had no reason to be ashamed of our programme for the first season. We gave plays by Sheridan (*The Critic* was our first Christmas production, in which I played Mr. Puff), by Galsworthy, who was represented by *Justice*, in which Irene Rooke and Milton Rosmer repeated the performances they had given in the Horniman production, and by Ibsen, *Pillars of Society*, in which we obtained such startling effects with our plaster background during the big storm at sea, which we had taken care to make visible through huge windows at the back, that everybody in Liverpool wanted to see it. We did tremendous business for a fortnight. Even *Porcupine*, which had declared that 'Ibsen in Liverpool was tantamount to box-office death', admitted that this was the first commercial success ever achieved by Ibsen in Liverpool. There were comedies by Bernard Shaw, Harold Brighouse and St. John Hankin, also by Haddon Chambers and other dramatists not bred in the repertory stable. We also produced new plays by Charles McEvoy and Allan Monkhouse.

The social atmosphere created by the opening festivities lingered about the theatre throughout the season. When well-known authors came to the first nights of their plays the occupants of the stalls usually wore full evening dress, the men in white tie and tails, the ladies *en grande tenue*. At the first performance of *The Honeymoon*, with Arnold Bennett present in a white lace shirt-front appropriate to the occasion, an electric cable fused outside the stage-door most inconveniently during the climax of the last act, tossing great paving-stones into the air and filling the stage with smoke. Hearing the swish of skirts and the banging of tip-up seats, I went on to the stage to stop the rush for the exit doors and found myself caricatured by Ronald Jeans in the *Daily Post* next morning as the saviour of a theatre panic! After first nights there would be animated discussions at supper parties in the University Club, where the left-wingers congregated, or in the private rooms of the Idle Hour Club, hired by the Dozen Club, a coterie of crossbenchers who were my personal supporters. Right-wingers usually went straight home.

The sense of occasion was undoubtedly fostered by Reilly's foyer. At first slightly embarrassed audiences had to be encouraged to leave their seats by switching on blue signal lights at either side of the proscenium, but, eventually, the audience grew accustomed to a social habit that has contributed much to the long-term success of the theatre. For many years the interval gatherings in the Playhouse foyer were to remain unique in the provinces. Here Maud Carpenter, who began as an assistant box-office clerk and part-time secretary to myself, was enabled to exercise her special talent for making everyone feel at home, and so to become the best front-of-house manager in the country. Amid all the cross-currents of opinion there set in motion, it was just as well that her basic ignorance of drama proved a useful safeguard against any tendency to meddle with the work of the producer.

II

Our first company was full of lively talent, too lively at times. Ronald Squire, Estelle Winwood, Dion Titheradge, J. H. Roberts, and many others come to mind, all of them young, keen and destined for success. Among the students Miles Malleson spent his first year on the stage with us, and soon gave evidence of a rare talent for eccentric comedy. The work was grindingly hard, and gave virtually no opportunity for social relaxation of any kind. Small wonder that the company became decidedly obstreperous towards the end of the season, some of them only too ready to pounce upon my hesitations, and mischievously to exploit my inexperience. But by this time I had learned two lessons; firstly, to discipline myself before I could expect discipline from others, and, secondly, to drive my team with a loose rein, since nearly all of them were senior to me either in age or experience, or both. And I took secret pleasure in the thought that I had been able to offer engagements to several players who had been friendly and encouraging to me in my touring days.

There are always bright spirits in a theatrical company, ready to be the ringleaders in any mischief that is going. Ronnie Squire was one of them. His sharp sense of humour brightened many a long hour at rehearsal. Upon one occasion I engaged an extremely beautiful but rather sexy young woman to play opposite him. During rehearsals it became obvious that Ronnie was much attracted to our new leading lady. After a triumphal final performance on the Saturday night Ronnie took her off to Chester for the weekend.

On the following Monday I went on to the stage to begin rehearsals of the next play, and heard Ronnie describing the experience to a cluster of young men. 'She was absolutely marvellous,' he enthused. 'Too much for me, really.' His eyes twinkled with merriment. 'Too much?' queried someone. 'Why, yes,' said Ronnie, 'we'd had a wonderful night. I was absolutely exhausted. Then she woke me up early in the morning and wanted some more.' 'What did you do?' someone asked. 'Oh, I simply said, "What! On Sunday morning? Don't be disgusting!"'

In my own case there was little opportunity for social relaxation of any kind, as each successive task overtook its predecessor. The nervous strain was due as much to my struggles in the boardroom as to the unceasing work of rehearsals. At every meeting I had to furnish estimates of production and running costs for the next play, figures on which I was always closely cross-examined. It is extremely difficult to estimate the costs of stage production closely; there are too many imponderables. The knife-edge accuracy demanded by the chairman was well-nigh impossible. Eventually, I was reduced to such a state of nerves that rehearsals on Thursday mornings became an agonising distraction. As the hour of the board meeting approached I became more and more nervous and less and less attentive to the actors. Yet this was the most important day of the week preceding a dress rehearsal on the Friday. On the rare occasions when there were no estimates to present I felt like a schoolboy with an unexpected half-holiday, and thoroughly enjoyed the rehearsals.

The routine of casting, rehearsing, arguing costs and waiting on box-office results was seldom interrupted by events beyond the stage-door. However, one such occasion was the sinking of the *Titanic*. Liverpool was aghast at one of the great sea tragedies of modern times. Confidence was further shaken when it became known that the conduct of the head of one of their great shipping lines was being called into question. Upon a day when the scandal-mongering was at it height I was lunching with Alec Rea at the Exchange Club. We met Bruce Ismay in the cloakroom, and were shocked by the utter misery on his face as he nodded to the embarrassed greetings of fellow-members. A matinée for the Lord Mayor's Disaster Fund was given at our theatre by all the companies then appearing in the city. It began with the *Tannhäuser* overture, performed by the combined orchestras of all the theatres under the baton of Eugene Goossens, then a junior conductor travelling with the Carl Rosa Opera Company. This was the first of our many meetings in professional co-operation and private friendship.

As the season drew towards its close I seemed to be heading for a breakdown. My friends the Reas were seriously concerned. Marguerite Rea was one of those rare women to whom illness is a challenge that must be met immediately. I was taken to their home on Windermere, where relief from the alien atmosphere of theatrical lodgings plus the gallons of hot milk that she bade me swallow brought sleep to my jangled nerves. Matters were not made any easier by the increasing tendency of certain directors to go behind my back to the actors to grumble at my shortcomings and to discuss plans for putting matters right. (In his autobiography published many years later Reilly admitted that perhaps this was a mistake!) An incident during the dress rehearsal of *You Never Can Tell* well illustrates the state of affairs. Arthur Chesney, brother of Edmund Gwenn, and a better actor, but lacking Gwenn's application, was playing the waiter. I was giving out some notes from the front of the stalls. When I spoke to Chesney, he looked down at me with a cheeky grin and said, 'Come up here if you want to talk to me, young man.' Ronnie Squire, who was playing Valentine, had a shocking memory which he tried to conceal by the wildest improvisations. Whenever I protested he merely chuckled and said something that made us all laugh. I still have a cartoon of him standing behind a sofa, being prompted from both sides of the stage at once with the words, 'My God!', to which he replies, 'What did you say?' His performance remained an elusive paraphrase of what Shaw had written, and got me into serious trouble with the author.

You Never Can Tell was followed by a special week of *Captain Brassbound's Conversion*, permission for which Shaw had given to Charles Charrington, an amateur actor long past his prime, in order that his wife, Janet Achurch, might play Lady Cicely. G.B.S. had once declared that she was the greatest tragic actress of the age. Why she should want to play Lady Cicely I could not imagine, unless to show that a tragedy queen could also play comedy. In any case, she was not long past the zenith of her powers. Charrington refused all help over the production, and went his own way. The result was a shambles. I saw only the dress rehearsal. The next morning I went abroad to seek fresh inspiration in Germany, taking George Harris with me. Before leaving I arranged an exchange visit with Miss Horniman: our composite company to go to Manchester to play the two Shaw plays. Unfortunately, the author, visiting Manchester for some Fabian lectures during that week, popped into the Gaiety to watch his Janet struggling with Lady Cicely, and—worse still!—on the following night to watch Ronald Squire perform his antics of memory as Valentine. Shaw was horrified and threw the entire blame on me. Months later when I wrote to him for permission to produce *Arms and the Man* during our second season. I received a letter which I have always kept as a useful corn-plaster to soften the hard edge of my conceit:

'Dear Basil Dean,
    You really mustn't ask me to allow you to murder *Arms and the Man*. The truth of the matter is, you have no producer. If you do the production yourself, believe me when I assure you that you are the most infamous producer as yet born on this planet. The performance of *You Never Can Tell* at Manchester made me swear that I would never let another play of mine come within ten miles of the Liverpool Repertory Theatre. There were all the materials for an excellent performance, and it was the worst on record. *Brassbound* I say nothing about: you must know that it was utterly disgraceful, and that it would have been an open calamity if Miss Achurch had not pulled it through.
    I daresay you don't believe me; but when you have had twenty years' experience you will know better. Anyhow I not only refuse *Arms and the Man* most vehemently, but solemnly forbid you ever again to produce a play of mine on any terms or under any circumstances whatever.

It is no use your arguing about it, as I leave the country to-morrow and shall not be back until the middle of September.

Yours faithfully,

G. BERNARD SHAW'

12

While the modest beginnings of my reputation as a producer were being shattered by the goings-on in Manchester, George and I were having an exhilarating time in Berlin. Reinhardt was amused that his English disciple had turned up again with enthusiasm unabated, introduced George to his designer, Ernst Stern, while Ordynski, the theatre's *dramaturg*, arranged visits for us to other famous theatres, where we saw interesting productions of Ibsen, Hauptmann and the usual German classics. In Munich my contact with the director of the Kunstler Theater was to bear fruit later on. Next, to the Burg Theater in Vienna where the productions were overwhelmed by an excess of hydraulic machinery. Here George and I parted company, he to return to misty Liverpool and I to the pursuit of romance under the dazzling blue sky of Italy.

The little town of Riva at the end of Lake Garda was full of strutting Austrian soldiers confronting Italian bersaglieri on the opposite shore. The officers wore a third epaulette, on the backside, the only officer corps in Europe to do so. Scandalous tongues declared the privilege was granted them for their talent in running away. In fact, it was to gratify their ageing emperor's passion for gold lace. As a peaceful citizen of the greatest empire in the world, accustomed to travel in Europe without obligation of passport I thought the military display faintly ridiculous, failing to understand its portent. The beautiful surroundings, almost empty of tourists since it was between seasons, seemed just the place for a siege of hearts. But keys to guarded fortresses are not readily surrendered! I had to learn patience. The family moved on, I with them, first to Fasano on the Italian side of the Lake and thence to Baveno on Lake Maggiore. There I raised the siege, and hurried home to face Professor Reilly and reality.

13

I had now made up my mind to follow a different policy from that of the Horniman Company, whose plays had acquired the somewhat pejorative title of 'the Manchester Drama'. I wanted to bring more light and colour into the theatre. I was bored with drabness. But I needed to tread warily because of the ambivalence of the chairman's attitude. Support would probably be forthcoming for new writing, especially in poetic drama, but not for new ways of presenting it. My overworked state at the end of the first season had given him a reasonable excuse for clipping my wings. While I was away a second producer had been chosen from among the company, Lawrence Hanray, a misanthropic but capable actor with a talent for writing light music. (In a letter to me, reporting later events, George Harris wrote: 'Hanray should be given wings and called a grouse.') Also, Lascelles Abercrombie, the poet, had been appointed as play-reader at the munificent salary of a guinea a week. He was to report on all plays. This was no good augury for future peace, but George and I kept our counsel. I strengthened the company on the female side, adding Eileen Thorndike (who might well have rivalled the achievements of her sister, Sybil, had she lived), Dorothy Massingham and Maire O'Neill to the team, while George went on painting realistic scenery in the little paint-room behind the dressing-rooms.

The season opened with *The Importance of Being Earnest*. Then Lilian Braithwaite and C. Aubrey Smith came up to try out a new play which they were to do later in London. This, my first encounter with London stars, was intimidating. They seemed to live in a rarefied atmosphere of their own, scarcely bothering to notice the rest of us poor mortals.

My first real opportunity to 'have a go' came through a casual talk with Barry Jackson. During the previous Holy Week he and John Drinkwater had brought to us the Pilgrim Players, an amateur group from Birmingham. One day Barry showed me some children's sketches which the group had performed the previous Christmas under the general title of *Fifinella*. They were full of charming ideas: just the things for us next Christmas, I thought. I suggested we should collaborate in developing the sketches into a full-length play. I had noted Barry's comparative indifference to the financially disastrous results of his group's summer visit, and knowing full well

that our directors would not find the money for the sort of production I had in mind, I further proposed that Barry should finance
the production. He was delighted at the thought of having his ideas
presented on the professional stage. So we spent two or three weeks
in summer lodgings at Aberystwyth, which he had taken for his
mother, to whom he was devoted. On fine days we sat on the pebbly
beach, sunning ourselves after a chilly bathe, and on wet days on
either side of an enormous aspidistra in the bow window of the
'first-floor front', arguing suggestions and discussing new lyrics.

During the autumn the pressure of work was not made any lighter
by the crazy state of the theatre's finances. My private life was in
turmoil, too, where I apparently had made no progress. On sleepless
nights my thoughts were in two places at once: the working half
of me obsessed with the rising temperature of the theatre's politics,
and the other half wondering which of my rivals was making the
most progress across the river. The silly night thoughts ran on:
how many dances had she gone to this week? And then the switch
back again: what should I have said or not said at this afternoon's
board meeting? Eventually, the conflict of anxieties overbore me.
Once again my friends, backed up by Barry Jackson, stepped in
and insisted either that I should take a sea voyage or give up the
idea of producing *Fifinella* at Christmas. Barry, usually a self-
sufficient person who kept his ideas and his money to himself,
most generously offered to help me with the fare. On a foggy day
in November I stood at the rail of *S.S. Alcantara*, about to begin
her maiden voyage to South America, while Barry and his great
friend, Scott Sunderland (part of our bargain was that Scott should
join the *Fifinella* cast), waved me goodbye from the jetty. We called
at Estoril, Vigo Bay, and Corunna. I left the ship at Lisbon to
return by homeward steamer, refreshed and eager to begin my
Christmas task.

There was much to be done. First of all, the music: I invited
Norman Hayes, composer of Judge Parry's *Katawampus*, to do this
for me. The results were tuneful but commonplace, a mistake that
was to prevent *Fifinella* from becoming the perennial success it deserved. Among the lively pack of stage children provided by Italia
Conti was one, Gertrude Lawrence, a rather plain child with pigtails, who seemed to feel the thrill even more than the rest of us,
jumping in and out of stage traps intended not for her but for the
Demon King—a fanciful version of the conventional character,
played by Baliol Holloway in his best Shakespearean manner.

George Harris seized his chance with both hands. The main scene, described on the programme as The Top of the Hill We All Know Well, with a twisted oak tree at its summit silhouetted against a full moon pendant in a vivid blue sky, was a sensation. Nothing like it had been seen before in Liverpool. In the branches of the tree sat The Owl with blinking yellow-green eyes, a part played and sung by Eric Blore, subsequently to become a star in the long line of English butlers to emerge in Hollywood films. Robert Crichton, who had abandoned his Cambridge studies to follow his passion for the Russian ballet by becoming a professional dancer, danced The East Wind admirably. The Man in the Moon, played by Clive Carey, flew out of the moon just as the children expected, to sing in an enchanting tenor voice:

'The Man in the Moon from his globe of light
Sees many queer things as he rides through the night
A world of joy, a world of pain,
Laughter and tears, love in the lane.'

The success which the production achieved is a matter of local theatre history.

14

Our Christmas success raised morale all round. Everyone looked forward to the spring season with confidence. The chairman supported my plan to stage D'Annunzio's *Francesca da Rimini*, provided I could get Mrs. Patrick Campbell to appear in the name part. I asked Esmé Percy who knew her well, to suggest it. In reply Percy said Mrs. Pat was flattered to be asked but unfortunately she was at present in a nursing home. He added an amusing description of the first night of *Der Rosenkavalier* at Covent Garden, a notable musical event in the Edwardian era:

'The *most* perfect musical thrill I have had since I first heard *Tristan*. Covent Garden was packed: a deposed king, many deposed courtesans, and two classes of "Society", those who borrow at 60 per cent and those who lend at 60 per cent. . . .'

I then put forward another idea that I had cherished for some time, Hauptmann's dream play *Hannele*.* This, too, was welcomed, but when the time came to approve the estimated cost there was sharp argument in the board-room. The discussion took on a faintly religious tinge. Robert Hield, editor of the *Liverpool Courier* and an ardent Catholic, strongly urged the production. His advocacy was unexpectedly backed up by 'Jack' Shute, another Catholic, formerly one of my sharpest critics, now on my side in this matter. Reilly had no religious compulsions; he disliked the proposition because of the expense, but he could not very well oppose the vice-chairman to whom the theatre already owed so much.

We worked out a number of new ideas for the production, some of them I must admit distinctly 'Reinhardtian'. For instance, I made the figure of Death, shrouded in black gauze, stalk down the middle of the stalls and on to the stage to solemn music (composed by Arnold Clibborn, a Liverpool organist) played by an augmented orchestra. This created quite a hullabaloo among elderly ladies at matinées. There were other effects, great and small, such as draped scenes of great height and ghostly lighting designed to enhance the appearance of the child Hannele as she lay in her crystal coffin. The rehearsals were protracted and eventful, to say the least. For Maire O'Neill's entrance as the Angel of Mercy heavenly music was provided, but when the cue came she was nowhere to be seen. The orchestra broke off raggedly, leaving the trombone to sound a final note of sombre comment. The company waited expectantly, while I sent various members of the staff to search for her. When she appeared twenty minutes later, she forestalled my angry protests by hurling her long flaxen wig in my face, shouting: 'How the hell d'you expect me to play an Angel of Mercy in that?' I learned afterwards that, tired of waiting, she had sneaked away to dine at the Adelphi Hotel with her fiancé, G. H. Mair, then a dramatic critic on the *Manchester Guardian*, and a personal friend of mine since my Jack Barthwick days, but not upon this occasion!

It was in this production that Gertrude Lawrence and Noël Coward first acted together, appearing as members of the Angelic Chorus in the dream sequences, although from their subsequent careers it does not seem that either of them was markedly influenced by the experience. Gertie was just over fourteen: 'Old enough for

*Years later I heard that *Hannele* had been one of Stanislavsky's greatest successes in Moscow—in 1896, some years before the Moscow Art Theatre was founded. Had I known this at the time it might have lessened the chairman's opposition.

licence,' as she pertly remarked to her new playmate. She suffered her first professional heartbreak when she discovered that her surname had been spelled with a 'u' instead of a 'w' in the programme. Noël was a pimply, knobbly-kneed youngster with an assured manner.

The chorus, four girls and four boys, also included Harold French and Roy Royston, the latter a cheeky little urchin whose remark to Baliol Holloway arriving late for rehearsal one day—he was playing the Deity in Hannele's dream—'Hurry up, Jesus, you're late,' earned him the sharpest of reprimands from me. George Harris dressed the children in little Greek kirtles, with silver leaves in their hair and long palm-leaf fans in their hands. During Hannele's dream the Angels were ranged in a single line across the front of the stage, waving their fans slowly to and fro as they sang, 'Sleep, baby sleep, the hills are white with sheep.' All went well at the final dress rehearsal until suddenly Italia Conti's shrill voice was heard above the orchestra: 'Noël! Noël! What on earth are you doing?' He was waving his fan violently above his head instead of rhythmically like the others. I stopped the orchestra for the second time that evening. In the sudden silence Noël stepped forward and in a piping voice said: 'Please, Miss Conti, may I leave the room?'

15

Hannele is full of German sentimentality that today would be dismissed as old-fashioned nursery stuff. But apparently I managed to impart a degree of religious fervour into the production for it was regarded in Liverpool as a personal triumph. My supporters felt justified of their faith in me. Soon I found myself cocooned in their friendship. These were the days of motoring clubs. Towards winter's end ladies and gentlemen, swathed in coats, mufflers and caps (heavy veils for the women), began to emerge on Sundays to test the capacities of their cars, especially the hill-climbing, often risking their necks on roads cambered for horse traffic. Lunch would be taken at one or other of the well-known hotels famous for their superior English cooking. Over coffee, the club members would sit round, gossiping, while chauffeurs in knee-breeches and polished black leggings, some with cockades in their caps, relics of the coachman's day, gathered in knots at the door, arguing the merits of their respective chargers: De Dion Bouton versus Panhard Levasseur, or possibly Wolseley, and so on. Sometimes the returning cars would chase each other like homing pigeons. In the dry spring weather the hedgerows were soon white with dust.

I was frequently asked to join these family trips to the beauty spots of North Wales. I would sit in the back of the car, swathed in rugs, drinking in the rushing mountain air like wine. As the pendulum swung away from theatre worries, my mind was filled with romantic notions that took no account of compatability, but by the time the car began its homeward run along the straight road from Chester to Birkenhead I was usually half asleep, waking only to hear the chauffeur shout excitedly that we were doing fifty!

On a particular Sunday evening in late spring, I sat with my girl friend in front of the fire in the music-room of her parents' home, no! not the log fire of romance, but an enclosed anthracite stove roaring behind its mica window-panes, drinking in her praise for my *Hannele*. A lump rose in my throat as I fumbled to reply. There was a long, long silence. And then suddenly the barriers were down. Simply, quite simply, I heard words spoken that I had longed to hear. The next moment a chill feeling struck me—a sense of the responsibility. It was only momentary. We agreed to keep our promises secret for the time being. As we entered the dining-room to join the Sunday supper party I remember my future father-in-law staring suspiciously at our flushed faces, following this with a rather helpless glance at his wife who was smiling more brightly than was her habit. These are the moments when women acquire superior vitality while men look on, embarrassed by yet another hapless surrender.

16

I had achieved two productions that were long remembered in the city. But the chairman thought I had outwitted him over *Hannele*, which was true enough. He also bitterly resented my failure to secure Stanley Houghton's *Hindle Wakes* for the theatre. He thought it an error of judgment on my part, and said so in his autobiography. This was not the case. Stanley, a close friend of Manchester days, sent me the play before anyone else. I regarded it as his major achievement, and said so. But we had no actors capable of presenting

H

his closely observed Lancashire characters, whereas Miss Horniman's Company was notably suited to do so, as their subsequent production of the play abundantly proved. I knew it was only a question of time before the axe would fall. One Thursday afternoon after a long and solemn meeting, from which I was excluded, the board gave me notice to quit at the end of the season.

Lascelles Abercrombie, with whom I had reached a close affinity after the production of his play, *The Adder* (a conjunction of minds not anticipated by the chairman) wrote caustically of my dismissal:

'. . . I am profoundly grieved that all our schemes for Liverpool must come to nothing. For I suppose that's what will happen with you gone. But of course the theatre had an absurd constitution from the start and was given over to the Devil before it began. I am sorry you cannot regenerate it, but you know what Schiller says about stupidity? . . . ? (What did Schiller say?)'

The Liverpool Playhouse, so re-named after I left, is now the oldest repertory theatre in the country. The fact that it was the first to be publicly owned and controlled by a board of directors has been the source both of its strength and of its weakness. Only when there has been complete *rapport* between the chairman and the producer (now called the artistic director) has the record been one of lasting success. At other times there has been too much boardroom and not enough green-room in the theatre's record.

Now I was once again being sent back to square one: a most unwelcome journey! My future prospects looked decidedly grim, and were not made any brighter by the presents of silver cigar and cigarette boxes which I received from the directors and the actors. I was virtually unknown in London, and the position I had occupied would make it difficult to take up acting again. Moreover, there was my private situation to be considered: Should I not release my fiancée from her promise? I stayed with the Alec Reas for a week or two to recover my breath and to make up my mind what to do. On the very day that I decided to leave, sensing that I had outstayed my welcome, there came a letter from Sir Herbert Tree's general manager, offering me an engagement on the staff of His Majesty's Theatre. I sat staring at the letter while Alec read his morning newspaper propped up on a little silver easel, and as he rose to leave I told him the news. 'When will you go?' he asked abruptly. (I was right: I had stayed long enough.) 'Today,' I replied.

Six

'My beautiful theatre'

The West End stage seemed an intimidating prospect, in spite of
the offer of a year's engagement from Sir Herbert Tree. In the days
of actor-manager supremacy His Majesty's Theatre was looked
upon as the Royal Academy of the British stage, a regard earned
by its prolonged record of lavish production. It was in accord with
the dignity of its proceedings that a uniformed lift attendant conveyed me aloft, past several dressing-room and office floors to the
private sanctum in the dome of the theatre for my interview
with 'the Chief'. The first thing I noticed about the great man were
his large blue eyes which regarded me whimsically while Henry
Dana, the general manager of the theatre, began to shoot questions
at me. One poser was, had I ever produced Shakespeare? 'No, I
had not.' More and more questions followed in rapid succession.
Evidently, this dried-up little man with the air of a senior civil
servant, regarded the proposed entry of an unknown provincial
into this holy of theatrical holies as just another of his chief's
whimsical touches.

Meanwhile Tree sat doodling on the back of an envelope. Presently, he broke into the conversation with a disconcerting conundrum:
'When is a repertory theatre not a repertory theatre!' Before I had
time to reply, he answered his own question: 'When it's a success, of
course.' Then with a chuckle at his own wit he hurriedly made for
the lift, obviously regarding my engagement as a matter of minor
importance. My little castle of opportunity began quickly to tumble.
. . . Yet I must have made some impression because the Chief
was reported as saying to Dana subsequently: 'That young man will

get on, by hook or by crook. I hope it'll be hook, but I expect it'll be crook.'

On my first day at the theatre Tree had taken me to lunch at his house in All Soul's Place to meet Lady Tree and her three daughters, Viola, Iris and Felicity. I must have made a poor impression; I was tongue-tied most of the time. Viola said I owed my engagement to her—she had seen my production of *A Florentine Tragedy* in Liverpool—and explained with a disarming vagueness that closely resembled her father's, 'Daddy is out of touch with new things in the theatre. You must give him new ideas and all that.' Tree had gurgled with amusement, while Lady Tree and his other daughters stared at his latest acquisition with an air of considerable doubt.

My appointment was as assistant producer; at least it was so stated on the programme, but I soon learned that the rest of the staff regarded my presence much as Dana had done when engaging me. When I joined rehearsals were already in progress for *Joseph and His Brethren*, the Bible story, written in terms of dramatic spe-tacle by Louis Napoleon Parker, a skilful play carpenter, better known to the general public as the organiser of a rash of historical pageants that had recently erupted in various parts of the country. Parker was deaf and carried a little black box which he planted on the prompt table in front of him. He also possessed an ear trumpet for casual use, fastened to the handle of his walking-stick. The con-traptions limited communication. Rehearsals seemed to be conducted in a very haphazard manner. Parker was obviously experienced in the marshalling of crowds and the ordering of scenes, so Tree let him have his own way, only reserving to himself and his leading lady the right to do as they pleased. Any tentative suggestions I made about the acting were either disregarded because Parker failed to hear them or were brushed aside with courteous warnings by the stage management: 'Better keep your ideas to yourself; the Chief knows best.' The thought was devastating. Later, I found out that Tree rarely allowed his staff to say much at rehearsals. Even when doing so, he usually rejected their suggestions, later re-gurgitating them, much embroidered by his own fertile imagination. Tree accepted, in fact basked in, the admiration of his staff, at the same time making his way through the maze of their conflicting in-terests and keeping all frustrations under control with a ceaseless stream of witticisms.

There were days when rehearsals became social occasions, when Lady Tree and one or more of her daughters, accompanied perhaps by 'the Manners girls', as they were familiarly known in the theatre, might be seen *and* heard, voicing loud comments from the stalls. Sometimes the beautiful Duchess of Rutland on her way to a luncheon engagement would join her daughters. Lady Tree was gifted with a sharp tongue and an even sharper wit which did not add to the harmony of the proceedings. When Tree, conscious of his society onlookers, began to embellish his part with fanciful ideas, she would call out with a devastating air of innocence: 'Herbert, what are you doing that for?' There would be a gentle ripple of laughter from the onlookers, and tears of vexation would come into Tree's eyes.

As *Joseph and his Brethren* lumbered slowly into production, I was bewildered by the orderly procession of experts: stage-managers, carpenters, electricians, costumiers and wardrobe staff criss-crossing each other on their interrelated duties, all with a quiet assurance born of the knowledge that they were working for the most important theatrical personage in London. On the first night the back of the stage resembled a nomadic encampment as strings of camels, donkeys and goats were marshalled for this triumph of stage realism!

2

On the technical side, not a whisper of new ideas had been allowed past the stage-door so far. Conventional scenery was still being provided by Joseph Harker, whose technique was in the direct line of descent from the great scene painters of the nineteenth century: Telbin, Clarkson Stanfield and the rest. Borders were still hanging across the stage in ridiculous profusion, and the only evidence that this was the stage of London's premier theatre lay in the proliferation of arc lamps, used to supplement the rows of batten lights. There were more of them than I had ever seen in use before. Since each lamp or, at most, each pair of lamps required a man to 'feed' it during performance, the cost must have been considerable even for those days. When I talked to the staff about the possibility of bringing more life and colour to the scene by the use of modern equipment it was plain that they resented my interference in such matters.

Before I left Liverpool Barry Jackson had confided to me that he intended to build his own theatre in Birmingham and offered me a generous fee to act as technical director in charge of stage construction. I gave his architect, S. N. Cooke, an introduction to the

director of the Kunstler Theater in Munich, and it was upon that
theatre's plan and the general information acquired during his visit
to Germany that Cooke designed the Birmingham Repertory
Theatre. I protested to Jackson that the site he had acquired was
too small and would handicap his enterprise without reducing its
running costs—a mistake that civic theatre enthusiasts still make,
to their lasting regret when their enterprises begin to succeed—and
that I disliked the steep, single-tier auditorium that had been planned
in consequence. This would create difficulties of projection for the
actor. For the stage I borrowed some of the new ideas that I had
seen in Germany, including a plaster dome and the Fortuny lighting
system.* After my modest steps towards scenic reform in Liverpool
and Birmingham, I rashly assumed there would be opportunities for
further development with Tree. But in persuading Cooke to design
a cyclorama for His Majesty's on the lines of the one just completed
at Birmingham, I overstepped the mark. Neither Tree nor any of
his henchmen were interested in the technical developments that
were taking place on the Continent. So it was embarrassing to have
to return Cooke's claim for fees and expenses.

3

My frustrations were confined strictly to what went on inside the
theatre. Outside, the prospect was widening in various directions.
I was now sharing a flat in a down-at-heels terrace house in South-
wick Street, Hyde Park, with Robert Crichton. (His real name was
Maltby. He was the son of an archdeacon living in Nottingham-
shire.) Our brief acquaintance at Cambridge had developed into mutual regard when he came up to Liverpool to dance in *Fifinella* for
me. Our landlord was a Rachmanite individual, who gave us some
awkward moments whenever we were late with the rent, which was
all too frequent. Bobby was completely given over to his ambition
to join the Russian ballet, spending all his working hours in dance
training and the balance of his slender allowance from his father on

* Fortuny was an Italian electrical engineer who had brought out a system
of cyclorama lighting which consisted in the main of rows of automatic arcs,
the light being projected through various coloured silks travelling on rollers
controlled by tracker wires. The effects obtained by these means were exceptionally soft and beautiful.

admissions to the Covent Garden Gallery. I became his convert
and joined him there whenever I could. The gallery patrons regarded
themselves as the most representative audience of the London
season. There we all were, packed like ecstatic sardines—if you will
pardon the description—artists, music-lovers, balletomanes, call us
what you will, except 'fans'—we were too sophisticated for that,
sharing the same aesthetic excitements, such visions of movement
and colour as were never before known. Everyone seemed to know
everyone else. In the intervals greetings rang out from one side
of the gallery to the other and echoed down the passages where
students discussed the latest gymnastics, their feet tapping with
joy.

I have the programmes of some of those early visits. Nijinsky,
Bolm, Karsavina, Federova, Fokine, Cecchetti, with Pierre Monteux
conducting: the names fall off the tongue like recollected items of a
delicious feast. What visions of grace and beauty they conjure up!
It is impossible ever to forget Nijinsky's leap through the window
in *Le Spectre de la Rose*, or that bounce on the head during his
death-throes as a slave in *Scheherazade*! How on earth did he do it?
Sometimes, after the ballet we sat among the red plush, the mirrors
and cast-iron Victoriana of the old Café Royal, listening to the
rattle of dominoes and the occasional roar of Augustus John,
arguing with one of his entourage, a rival painter perhaps, or more
often a lady friend.

Another pathway was opened up for me by 'Eddie' Marsh, a
remarkable civil servant, so ardently alive to new artistic impulses
that he spent his entire life, and most of his substance, on their
encouragement. His tufted eyebrows, squeaky voice, monocle and
irrepressible enthusiasm lurked behind all Winston Churchill's
official occasions at that time and at week-ends enlivened the country
houses of his intelligent and sophisticated friends. His compulsive
friendships with the young artists and poets of the new Georgian age
have earned him an assured place in our social history. I met him
first when the Horniman Company came to London. He had been
to see *The Silver Box* and wrote to me afterwards to say how much
he had admired my 'Jack Barthwick'. Now that I had come to
London he invited me to go to first nights with him—Granville
Barker's production of *A Midsummer Night's Dream* at the Savoy
Theatre was one occasion—encouraging me to throw off my pro-
vincialism and to meet others of the new generation who, like
myself, were fighting for recognition. How well I remember those

rooms in Raymond Buildings, Gray's Inn, the walls so crowded with examples of the new spirit in painting that his latest acquisitions were hung on the doors. Here I listened goggle-eyed to the talk of the Georgian poets, renewed acquaintance with Lascelles Abercrombie and met Wilfred Wilson Gibson and Gordon Bottomley, one of whose blank verse dramas I was to produce later on. Here I met Ivor Novello, then in the extreme youth of his promise. Soon I was round at Harold Monro's Poetry Bookshop in Gray's Inn Road, buying *New Numbers* and *The Blue Review*. Once I lunched in the flat above with Katherine Mansfield, whose quiet talk and resigned air suggested a character out of Chekhov, and Middleton Murry, whose domination of his partner made me feel uncomfortable.

I can recall few experiences outside this 'brave new world' that I had set out to explore, although the memory of a certain naval engagement can still raise a tremor. At a party somewhere I met the gunnery officer in H.M.S. *Implacable*, an old pre-Dreadnought battleship, then lying at Sheerness, and he had invited me to spend the week-end on board. There I was introduced to the captain who in turn introduced me to the potency of 'black velvet', served in tankards before lunch! So fortified, and in response to a ward-room challenge, I essayed to climb the foretop, a lofty look-out reached by a narrow and vertical iron ladder. This I achieved unaided, but I had to be helped down after a hasty look at the tiny speck of deck beneath me. I landed safely with shaking knees and greasy clothes, still dizzy with fresh air and champagne, to the delight of the assembled ward-room.

Not all my evenings were free for private delight. Occasionally when the mood took him, Tree would insist upon my accompanying him to the Garrick Club after the evening performance. I might be dog-tired and anxious to go to bed, but it was useless to protest, for a major planet in the theatrical firmament naturally expects to be accompanied by satellites. In the coffee-room we would sit at the centre table, running almost the length of the room, very imposing with its white damask cloth, great silver loving-cups and gleaming candelabra. While Tree ate his supper of raw Westphalian ham and marmalade, I sat half asleep listening to the gossip of Pinero, Squire Bancroft, John Hare and other knights of Thespis. Meanwhile Dunn, the dignified wine waiter—an ex-naval man and conscientious in-fighter amongst the members' left-overs in the club buttery—his breast emblazoned with the silver chain of his office, padded round the table discreetly filling glasses. Discussion and argument would go on until long past midnight, when the eminences would slip away one by one, the tinkling bells of hansom cabs and the clip-clopping of horses over the wooden paving in the otherwise silent street signalling their departure.

Colouring my thoughts about the future was the romance of my engagement, still kept secret from a formidable father-in-law until a moment judged to be propitious. My fiancée came often to London with her mother to talk excitedly over our future plans. Home-making was something neither of us knew anything about, but a smiling, sympathetic mother-in-law-to-be was at hand to smoothe all doubts and difficulties. Florence Van Gruisen, sister of Rufus Isaacs, possessed in special degree a genius for living. Intelligent, witty, gay, with a keen appreciation of the latest trends in painting music and the arts generally—herself an amateur painter of talent—she seemed to be meeting life at all points of the compass, save perhaps from one direction only. Sheltered always from material care, she saw no reason why her daughter's life should not be similarly ordered. Consequently, she made no attempt to prepare her for the social changes that were already making their appearance. Her blind spot was to involve me in difficulties later on, but at that time I was happily basking in her affectionate encouragement. Summoned by my future father-in-law to his suite at the Savoy Hotel on his return from a business trip abroad, I expected a stormy interview. Instead I was met with a handshake and a friendly chuckle. Apparently our situation had been known to him months before. Only one awkward question was there to answer: 'Are you prepared to support a wife on a salary of £500 a year?' My confident affirmative made a good impression, but solved no problems.

4

Tree's next production was a piece of confectionery called *The Darling of the Gods*, manufactured by David Belasco in America. I was determined not to endure the agonies of frustration for a second time, so after the first day or two I quietly abandoned my silent stance behind the prompt table and went in search of a better way of justifying my salary. I retired to a little office on the fourth floor to eat into the pile of plays that had accumulated since

the departure of its former incumbent, Frederick Whelen.* Soon
Viola came in search of me, only to stare reproachfully when she
saw me reading plays instead of providing the modern influence
downstairs that she had hoped for.

Play-reading was frustrating, too, because it was only with the
greatest difficulty that Tree could be persuaded to so much as glance
at a new play. He preferred to have it read to him, usually by the
author, in the presence of members of his staff. Even the plays
commissioned from Comyns Carr and Louis Parker had to be read
aloud, however much they may have been discussed beforehand,
because this 'bespoke' playwriting called for several 'fittings' before
the Chief was satisfied with his part. Reading took place in the
dome, which on closer acquaintance I discovered was fitted out as
the Chief's private headquarters. The main room was furnished
in the style of a medieval banqueting hall, with long refectory table
and oaken benches, the walls panelled with scenes from Tree's
production of *Macbeth*, painted by Charles Buchel, which I always
thought conveyed a bodeful message. Here Tree would lay his
'Banquo's ghost' of finance by giving supper to financiers and other
important persons, also to distinguished foreign artists visiting
London. Beyond the double-doors of the banqueting 'chamber'
was the Chief's inner sanctum, where he had his imposing desk,
well-furnished bookshelves and an open fireplace, complete with
log fire.

I was present at a typical session when E. Temple Thurston,
popular novelist of the day, was invited to read his play to us.
It was a depressing affair because not only was the play wordy and
dull, read with precise emphasis by an author manifesting his
nervousness by drinking tumblers of cold water at the end of each
scene, but also because everyone present knew before the reading
began that the play would not be produced by us. (In fact, our
next production had already been decided upon.) With all the appearances of rapt attention Tree spent his time making funny
drawings on the backs of envelopes and flinging them across the
table to those nearest him, or scribbling business queries to his chain-
smoking manager.

However, play-reading did bring me into touch with many of the
younger people who were influencing the literature of the time,

* There is a curious mistake in Hesketh Pearson's book on Beerbohm Tree.
He refers to Frederick Whelen being on the staff of the theatre when *Pygmalion*
was produced. This is incorrect. Whelen had left and I had taken his place.

among whom were Jack Squire and Edward Shanks. I had bought their *English Review* from the first number, and had first read Joseph Conrad in its pages. I was in correspondence with D. H. Lawrence about one of his plays; I signed a contract with Michael Lykiardo-pulos, Secretary to the Moscow Art Theatre, to adapt a popular Polish play of the time entitled *Eros and Psyche* by Julius Julafsky. Then one morning in the autumn of 1913 the greatest prize of all came my way. The bulky package had all the appearance of being just one more of those voluminous outpourings that it was part of my lot to read. With it there was a hastily scribbled note from Viola saying: 'Please give this wonderful play special attention; we wanted Daddy to read it but he says it's too long.' The play was *Hassan* by James Elroy Flecker, one of the group of Georgian poets gathering under the urbane encouragement of Eddie Marsh. Viola and her husband, Alan Parsons, a brilliant young man who forsook the Civil Service for journalism, had joined his circle, and it was Eddie Marsh who had brought the play to their notice.

For weeks I could not persuade Tree to read *Hassan*. Finally, he did read it, grumbling at its length. In the end he told me that the part would not suit him. The matter must not be allowed to rest there. Even in its existing form the play was clearly one of major importance. I offered to give Flecker what help I could in reducing the manuscript to manageable proportions and in steering the play through to subsequent production. By this time he had been compelled to abandon his consular post at Damascus and to retire to Davos to wrestle with what was to prove his fatal illness. My offer was made to him through Eddie Marsh, who had already given the poet much wise advice in the early stages of the writing. Flecker first agreed and then refused my proposal: a change of mind due rather pathetically to a momentary improvement in his illness which made him think he could carry out the work himself. Finally, he gave way to Eddie's pleading and accepted. I began my modest undertaking knowing nothing of the desperate efforts the poet was making to hold on to life until he should see his master-piece fulfilled before an audience. It was the knowledge that his time was short that made Flecker begin the work of revision without waiting for my technical recommendations. So the work proceeded on two fronts as it were. Our revisions crossed each other in the post.

5

There were other 'odd jobs' that the Chief, rather slyly I always thought, expected me to do, apart from reading plays, such as drafting his speeches and being on call to receive V.I.P.s in the ante-room to his dressing-room at the end of performances. Even this menial task had its minor compensations. I remember gaping at Gladys Cooper whilst she was being interviewed for a part in *The Darling of the Gods,* and thinking her the most beautiful creature I had ever seen. On matinée days Claude Beerbohm would climb up to me and ask whether there was any chance of seeing the Chief at the next interval. Claude, jauntily dressed always and sporting a gold-mounted malacca cane, would leave his interviews with the Chief sometimes with a grin of satisfaction on his face, at other times with a sullen look of disappointment, but Tree always had an air of embarrassment when I went in to see him afterwards.

The company always knew when a formal luncheon was in the day's programme. On such occasions the Chief would appear at rehearsals in a frock-coat and silk hat. In his pocket might be a crumpled copy of the speech I had drafted, which he would fish out from time to time, alter and scribble over with a pencil borrowed from the stage-manager, while the rest of the cast stood respectfully by, waiting for the great man to resume rehearsal. As the lunch hour approached, a look of abstraction would gather in his large blue eyes. Then when he caught sight of Trebell, his faithful valet, lurking by the prompt table, he would suddenly snatch his hat with a muttered, 'Sorry, I must go', hurry through the swing doors and into a waiting cab, leaving the cast all standing.

At Christmas the Chief gave me leave of absence to go to Manchester to reproduce *Fifinella* at the Gaiety Theatre. Barry Jackson was by this time absorbed in plans and expenditure for his Birmingham Theatre and was unwilling to finance the revival. However, Algernon Greig, a young enthusiast who had joined the Liverpool Company straight from the O.U.D.S. in the spring, seemed anxious to sow some managerial wild-oats, so Barry made the scenery and dresses available to him on easy terms. We had a strong cast and business was good, but not quite so good as at Liverpool. Nevertheless, I began to dream of a West End production the following Christmas, and of ways of achieving this. With typical whimsicality

Tree had once boasted to me that he was the only manager who possessed the distinction of having refused both *Peter Pan* and *The Blue Bird*. But Graham Robertson's *Pinkie and the Fairies* had been a matinée success at His Majesty's a few years previously, so why not try him with *Fifinella*? With this in mind I resolved to persuade the Chief to go up to Manchester to see a matinée performance. The plan was supported by Stanley Bell, the stage director, who was secretly amused by my effrontery. To everyone's surprise the Chief agreed to go. It seems scarcely credible as I recall it, but he caught the breakfast train to Manchester Central where he was welcomed by the station-master in frock-coat and silk hat, and conducted by me to the Lord Mayor's Parlour for a civic luncheon arranged in his honour. He made an amusing speech, and then hurried to the Gaiety Theatre for the matinée at two o'clock. The visit had been well publicised, and the theatre was packed. The childish side of his nature was delighted with all the fuss, so much so that I had to prise him out of his seat before the short third act was over to ensure that he caught the four o'clock express out of Central Station, where the door of his reserved compartment was once more ceremoniously held open for him by the station-master, still in his silk hat. From St. Pancras he was driven to the theatre in a special cab, making up as he went along. Throughout that astonishing day Tree's blue eyes never ceased to twinkle with amusement. Perhaps he was tickled by this early confirmation of the prophecy he had made to Henry Dana after my interview: it was certainly a case of 'by hook or by crook'.

Back in London (January, 1914) I received an urgent letter from Granville Barker, then in the middle of a programme of repertory at the Savoy Theatre. The actor who had been playing Jack Barthwick was ill with jaundice: would I take up my old part for a few performances? Tree consented, and so I found myself once more playing the irresponsible Jack. This was a relief from current frustration even though I appeared to be progressing backwards.

6

One day in the spring of 1914 Viola brought into my office an advance copy of Bernard Shaw's latest play, *Pygmalion*. Although it had been written with Mrs. Patrick Campbell in mind—indeed, she already regarded it as 'her' play—Viola wanted my help to persuade her father to take the play and act Higgins. So far he had shied away from the idea, possibly because he was afraid Shaw might criticise him as harshly as he had criticised Henry Irving. (In the event Shaw treated him as a big baby and laughed at his eccentricities.) After a show of reluctance Tree agreed to discuss the matter with Shaw over the telephone. I was deputed to make the call. It was just after a matinée of *The Darling of the Gods*. The Chief was taking his make-up off when I went to tell him that Shaw was on the line in the ante-room. He looked up with a frightened face, like a child scared out of its wits. It might be a ticklish business to persuade Shaw to accept him as Professor Higgins. However, he picked up the telephone and after some badinage they proceeded to business. 'Oh, no, no, no, Tree,' I overheard Shaw say. 'Yer much too old. Wouldn't hear of it!' However, eventually, everything was settled, as Shaw doubtless intended all along that it should be. Thus it was that Bernard Shaw, the most distinguished left-wing dramatist of the day, entered the most right-wing theatrical establishment in London.

What followed was fascinating to watch, so I resumed my daily stance behind the prompt table. Here were three strong personalities manœuvring for position all the time: Tree to see that his interests as a star at the head of his own theatre were properly conserved; Mrs. Campbell to see that she got the best out of her opportunities as Eliza Doolittle, and Shaw to see that his play was faithfully presented.

From what transpired at rehearsals Shaw did not appear to be greatly concerned with the aesthetics of production, such as scenery, dresses, lighting effects and so forth; the intellectual side was his abiding interest. He used to say: 'I like my lines spouted; like Shakespeare.' (The actor he had idolised in his youth was Barry Sullivan, he of the 'silver voice'.) This did not mean that he wanted the actors to behave in an extravagant manner. He simply wanted his lines well heard. One might say briefly that Shaw produced from mind and ear; the mind to secure understanding and the ear for the music of the splendid English he wrote. It is also worth noting that his study of phonetics did not range far. He showed little interest in any of the dialects beyond the Home Counties, such as Lancashire, Yorkshire or the West Country. Characters such as Lickcheese in *Widower's Houses*, Doolittle in *Pygmalion* and Burgess in *Candida* are written in the idiom of London's streets during his time. However, this restricted interest, understandable perhaps in an Anglo-Irishman, was used entirely for comic purposes.

All went well for the first fortnight or so. The actors read their parts in leisurely fashion, but Shaw was plainly baffled by the theatre's rambling method of putting a play on the stage instead of with the precise ideas that he had acquired from his close association with Granville Barker. Nevertheless, he appeared to enjoy the frequent passages-at-arms between Tree and Mrs. Campbell; but he would always intervene whenever the situation threatened to get out of hand, as for instance, when either of them wanted to alter lines or threatened the introduction of an outrageous piece of business. Then a battle royal would ensue, while company and staff waited in the ringside seats for a decision.

Upon one occasion when Mrs. Campbell objected to Tree's interpolating business which was not in the script—he was always one for doing that sort of thing, partly to disconcert his partner, and partly because he could not repress his love of mischief—she suddenly, without any warning, picked up one of Higgins's slippers, and threw it right in Tree's face; it drew blood, and his watery blue eyes became more watery than usual. She was momentarily shocked and began to apologise. 'That's perfectly all right,' said Tree. 'It's very good business. We'll keep it in!' I was never allowed to take part in the arguments, save when Tree, wanting support, would fling an arm round my shoulders and forcibly propel me into the conversation. I was too frightened to bandy words with the great G.B.S. But upon one occasion, when Tree turned to me, Shaw exclaimed: 'What's he got to do with it?' Said Tree: 'He's my assistant producer.' 'Well, he's not going to produce my play,' said Shaw.

One day there came a major crisis. One of the routine duties which I shared with the stage director was to ring up the dome and tell the Chief when all the cast were assembled and everything ready for rehearsal. On this particular morning I had to tell him:

'Chief, I'm sorry, but Mrs. Campbell isn't coming today.'

'What's that? What's that?' muttered Tree, sleepily. 'What d'you say?'

'Mrs. Campbell has gone away to marry George Cornwallis West.'

'Oh, my God!' exclaimed Tree.

I can see her now on the day of her return, standing erect and formidable in front of the inner swing doors of the stage entrance, dressed Edwardian style in sable toque and tippet, adorned with a large bunch of Parma violets, and carrying a little dog. I ran to the house telephone:

'Chief, she's back!'

'Good! I'm coming down,' said Tree. A few moments later he emerged from the lift, his large blue eyes blazing. He stared at 'Mrs. Pat', momentarily nonplussed by her monumental calm. 'So, you're back then,' he said lamely. 'Yes,' she replied without a moment's hesitation. 'George is a golden man. Now let's rehearse.' That was the only apology she made.

The rehearsals lasted nine weeks in all. How much of the delay was due to Mrs. Pat's absence, how much to Tree's leisurely methods and how much to the interminable arguments between the three protagonists in the struggle for production must remain a matter of imprecise calculation. Towards the end tempers were becoming frayed; Tree's little jokes were growing stale and Mrs. Campbell's tantrums a decided bore, while Shaw's irrepressible energy was getting on the nerves of both stars. It was his habit to stride across St. James's Park and enter the theatre by the Charles Street stage-door, full of health and vigour. On a particular morning both Mrs. Campbell and Tree were waiting for him. Both had 'a morning after the night before' look about them. Shaw came briskly on to the stage in his Norfolk jacket and Inverness cape, carrying the large loose-leaved notebook in which he wrote rehearsal notes in his immaculate handwriting.

'Good morning, good morning,' he said.

'Good morning, Bernard,' said Mrs. Campbell, looking balefully at him. She always called him Bernard at rehearsal, reserving the nickname 'Joey' for less public occasions. 'What do you want to do today?'

'I think,' he said, 'we'll take your love scene in the last act, and I'll go to the back of the pit and I won't interrupt ye at all, and then I'll come down and tell you both how bad ye are, ha, ha!'

The joke was not appreciated. However, Shaw retired to the back of the pit, while Mrs. Campbell and Tree struggled valiantly through the love scene, both much too plump for their parts. At the end of the scene, Mrs. Campbell put her hand under her chin to shield her eyes from the glare of the footlights—we always rehearsed with the footlights on because Tree said a dark, empty theatre was full of ghosts—and called out:

'Are you there, Bernard?'

'I'm here,' he said, and came down the centre of the stalls.

'Is that any better?' Mrs. Campbell asked.

'It's terrible. It isn't a bit like it. I don't want your flamboyant personality. I want an ordinary London flower-girl in love. That's the part I've written and that's the part I want.'

'Love!' exclaimed Mrs. Campbell indignantly, 'what do you know about love? One of these days you'll eat a beefsteak and then God help all the women!'

The first dress rehearsal began with a mishap. Stanley Bell had devised a rain curtain. He had won his argument against my suggestion that the downpour could be just as effectively presented by the use of light and sound effects as by the use of real water. He was supported by the author who was all for water and plenty of splash! Unfortunately, the rain curtain refused to work until a technician took a wrench and gave the stop-cock a mighty twist, when it spurted in all directions, drenching Tree, to his intense annoyance and the vast amusement of both Mrs. Campbell and Shaw. Tree sulked for the rest of the rehearsal.

On the first night everybody was on tiptoe with expectation. Would Mrs. Campbell really say 'bloody' on the stage? Rumours of a public protest at the threatened depravity had been circulating. When the moment came I was standing in the prompt corner with Stanley Bell. We heard a sharp intake of breath, and then a vast sigh of relief. The trumpets of Shaw had at last breached the walls of the Lord Chamberlain's Jericho.

7

We were married, Esther Van Gruisen and I, on April 30th, 1914. For months beforehand we had been living in a dream world. How else could I, with my thermometer of financial stability registering zero, have contemplated success with someone so young and attractive and so completely fenced off from the hard business of career-making? How else could she have dared the exchange of family affection and middle-class comfort for my dedicated life in the theatre? Ours was no flare-up of sexual attraction; it was a slow growth of intellectual sympathy that gradually acquired the glow of romance as the months went by, a glow that warped judgment and set aside the ordinary business of life. Neither of us had faced up to what we expected of the other. Yet we both longed

I

passionately for a unity of thought and feeling without knowing how to achieve it. World events and our own circumstances were eventually to place it beyond our reaching.

Any doubts that remained before we thrust our hands into the lucky-dip on that sunny last day of April were washed away in champagne, the exuberant good wishes of my theatre friends, and more restrained greetings from her relations, obviously deploring a *mésalliance*. I remember how dark and overcast the sky became during the customary speeches in the open marquee on the lawn behind the house, but clearest recollection of all was of my mother waiting among the sea of upturned faces at the foot of the stairs for our departure; it stands out in memory like a blown-up item in a press photograph. As she flung her arms round me and whispered something I did not hear, I can recall the pang of remorse I felt for the years of my seeming indifference. A few minutes later we were driven away to Chester by the family chauffeur to catch the mail train to London, and thence to Italy.

My brother had gone ahead with the luggage. This he had placed carefully in an otherwise empty luggage-van, but on arrival at Euston one of the new suitcases had disappeared. I spent most of the evening on the telephone, trying to find Bobbie Crichton. Eventually, about midnight, Bobbie returned to his flat, and agreed to present himself at the Grosvenor Hotel at eight in the morning to receive money and a list of articles for purchase, including a new suitcase. Booked to leave Victoria by the Continental Express at ten o'clock, we waited anxiously at the barrier for his return with the necessary articles. He came running towards us just as the first whistle blew. Our honeymoon was saved—by a suitcase and a sponge bag! The honeymoon is by popular conspiracy declared to be the happiest time of one's life. It rarely turns out so. Problems of adjustment that soon begin to make their appearance are apt to dispel the romance of travel in another's company. Yet I would not say that our first weeks in each other's company were any less successful than those of thousands of others.

Arriving at Fasano, on Lake Garda, the second of my mishaps reared its expensive head. In lifting a heavy iron table on the balcony outside our room I allowed the unexpectedly loose marble top to slip through my fingers. It crashed in several pieces on the stone floor. Almost before I had ceased to contemplate the disaster an infuriated manager appeared from seeming nowhere and assailed me with a volley of German-Italian and a bill for several hundred lire.

The scene was worthy of operetta in the best Italian style. In Verona a gala performance of *Romeo and Juliet* in the open-air theatre was ruined for me by mosquitoes, reminding me, not for the first or last time, of the special predilection of that abominable insect for my person. In Venice we aroused the wrath of a fat German woman whom I had espied in a corner of our hotel-restaurant on the morning of our arrival, consuming vast quantities of cold sausage of various hues. Her bedroom was divided from ours by a paper-thin partition. Our happy laughter, following upon champagne and a moonlit gondola ride, drove her to furious tapping on the wall and shouts of '*Ich will schlafen*', which in turn drove us into more laughter. The indignant phrase became the signal for hilarity between us for the rest of our honeymoon. Incidents such as these—there were many more—served only to punctuate our happy discovery of each other. Deeper issues lay beneath the surface. We left them there.

In the course of correspondence with Flecker earlier in the year, we had both become anxious for personal contact, he in order to speed up the work and I to meet a poet whose work I deeply admired. So when I wrote that I was shortly getting married and might be going to the Italian lakes for the honeymoon, he at once replied that he and his wife would be staying at Locarno in the same month, and would wait for us there. But when we arrived they had already left, leaving behind a message that with the advance of spring the climate had become too warm and relaxing, so they had been forced to return to Davos. Flecker's letter ended with a pathetic appeal to join them at Davos. I felt this to be impossible under the circumstances. Evading my wife's inquiries as to my sudden preoccupation, I secretly wrote my refusal. Although I had no doubt at all of my wife's response this was a decision no bride should be asked to share. Had I recognised the moment as my only opportunity of seeing Flecker alive I might have acted differently, and not have been left with such a lasting regret.

8

We were back in London before May was out, in time for the production of *The Love Cheats*, my first three-act play which Miss Horniman had refused in Manchester but which, after I had carried out some re-writing on the advice of John Galsworthy, was now to be produced at the Coronet Theatre in Notting Hill Gate on Monday, June 1st. This was the last week of the current Horniman season, which in turn was to be the last of a noteworthy series. The notices for my play were moderately good, but I had realised by this time that it was too derivative, too much influenced by infatuation for Thomas Hardy.

The London season was especially glamorous that year. At least it seemed so, viewed through our romantic eyes; or, perhaps this is only a trick of memory distorted by the overwhelming events that followed. The newly-painted mansions in the London squares with awnings of gaily-striped canvas appearing in front of each great house in turn to shelter the arrival and departure of guests fulfilling the Season's programme of balls, dinner dances and receptions; window-boxes everywhere gay with flowers: all this was the apotheosis of wealth and splendour at the heart of the British Empire. Of course, we were only on the fringe of these high social events, but at least we could enjoy our evenings in the gallery at Drury Lane, where the Russian Ballet was again keeping the town in a whirl of excitement.

The influence of the Ballet spread rapidly to the interior decorators. The most influential disciple was Paul Poiret of Paris, whose decorative schemes included carpets, furnishing fabrics and light fittings specially manufactured in France at high cost. He was the leader of a minor revolution in taste that was eventually to remove much of the Edwardian clutter from our middle-class homes. Poiret's London agent was Marcel Boulestin, who combined this activity with running his Restaurant Français, a popular meeting place for the younger artistic set, where the *spécialité de la maison* was Omelette Boulestin. Excited by the new trend, I suggested that our flat should be decorated in Poiret style, a suggestion that was accepted without demur by my wife's relations who were going to bear the cost. Boulestin secured the most wonderful patterns from Paris, from which we chose the most expensive; he also undertook to supervise the work in our absence.

All was ready and waiting when we returned from Italy. The dining-room had black walls and a black ceiling, glass pendant fittings in bright orange, and Sheraton chairs, upholstered in a sort of trousering of black, grey and orange, a design that was Poiret's special pride. The sitting-room was decorated in pale blue, and the curtains had a lovely design of pink flowers printed on linen. The result was the envy of our friends and a source of amusement to

our elders. Among the guests at our flat-warming were Eddie
Marsh, Bobby Crichton, Geoffrey Toye, later to become Sir Thomas
Beecham's deputy at Covent Garden, and his pretty wife, Doris
Lytton, Viola and Alan Parsons, and George Harris. Unfortunately
the party was something of a disaster. Neither my wife nor
I knew anything about the domestic facts of life; our ignorance of
such matters as catering was profound. However, we bought a
dozen or so bottles of white wine (cocktails were almost unknown),
and on the morning of the party I set out for Appendrodt's, a
German delicatessen in Piccadilly Circus, to purchase one leber-
wurst, a sausage for which the shop was famous. Our guests made
the usual noises in praise of the décor, and seemed to enjoy our
hospitality, but we were nonplussed by the subsequent silence.
Eventually, I wormed the truth out of Eddie Marsh: 'My dear, it
was that liver sausage! We were terribly ill afterwards, all of us.'

In the face of added responsibility I began to worry about the
future. Since Tree was unlikely to take up his option upon my further services, where was my next engagement to come from?
Future prospects hung like a huge question mark in the air. I had
not forgotten my early dream of founding an art theatre for London. An amused but imperturbable listener to my ideas was 'Joe'
Langton, senior partner in a famous firm of solicitors, and Tree's
legal adviser. He agreed to make enquiries as to the availability of
a certain theatre that I thought suitable. This was something of a
confidence trick on my part, pure fantasy if you prefer, since I had
no financial prospects whatever. I can only assume that Joe thought
my wife's influential relations were behind us, which was not the
case.

On June 6th Eddie gave a party at Raymond Buildings for Rupert
Brooke soon after his return from the South Seas. The rooms were
crowded with artists and musicians eager to welcome home the
young poet, and full of talk about their own plans. It was a gathering-
together of wondrous promise, Eddie Marsh's pledge of their
future achievements. No fault of his that world events were to
prevent its fulfilment. I remember that party particularly well,
because of an exciting talk with Brooke about my most pressing castle
in the air, an art theatre for London, in which the new poetry would
be given its head. Avoiding the crowded rooms, we went out on to
the landing and sat on the stone steps discussing possibilities and
talking in excited, staccato tones, as is the way at young parties. I
extracted his promise to write a poetic drama for the new theatre.

9

Towards the end of July we joined friends and relations in a family holiday at Lulworth Cove, where there was quite a gathering of English families on holiday. The weather was perfect. We swam and danced; we played cricket and rounders, and chased each other over the downs in childish games with a kind of feckless excitement. Maybe we stopped occasionally to stare at the gathering war-clouds but we certainly did not comprehend their dark significance. That was the business of professionals. But over the first August week-end the mood changed. Fun and games disappeared overnight, and newspapers were filled with the news of general mobilisation and other items in the international drama.

Twice a day we left the Cove and marched up the downs to where an old coastguard was manning a look-out. His post was equipped with an ancient telephone for communication with the coastguard station along the coast. Judging by the protracted winding of the handle necessary to elicit any response, it was already giving signs of that special neurosis that was to attack all wartime telephones. We pestered the old salt with questions whenever we caught him scanning the horizon through a large telescope on a stand, expecting German torpedo boats to emerge from every distant smoke flurry. His replies were vague and suspenseful: 'British tramp, out of Newcastle most likely.' Then another squint through his glass: 'That one's French, bound for Southampton', etc., etc. We hung on his words, especially after an unduly prolonged stare through the telescope. Of course he was without any accurate information, but he must have enjoyed a sense of importance.

Two or three days after the declaration of war, on the Wednesday I think it was, one of our party, just finished with Rugby and due to go to university in the autumn, came down to breakfast with the decision to enlist. The suddenness of his announcement silenced us all for a moment. Then his parents, alternating between shock and bewilderment, tried various arguments to dissuade him, but no! he must go immediately. Listening to the hectic arguments made me realise in a dim sort of way that this was going to be a different kind of war from those we had read about in the history books. This was to be a war in which everyone must play a part. To most of the young men of my generation it came as a shock that we would shortly be expected to go out and shoot people.

Returning to London I found that *Pygmalion* had come to an end. *Drake*, a patriotic spectacle by Louis N. Parker, was about to take its place. Rehearsals had already begun, but I had no part in them because this was a revival. The play's requirements were already well known to the permanent staff. This was to be followed by a dramatised version of *David Copperfield*, by Louis Parker, in which Tree gave superb character studies of both Dan'l Peggotty and Mr. Micawber. The author had everything worked out down to the smallest technical detail. I was left with nothing to do.

An appeal had been made for special constables to patrol power stations, railway junctions, etc., and so I joined the queue at Covent Garden, waiting to be sworn in. What was to be the effect of our presence at these nerve centres was not made clear to us. Were visitations to be expected from German spies armed with bombs? Armed with a police whistle and a truncheon, I was told to keep an eye on a pumping station just off Oxford Street, sharing with our stage director the duty of relieving at certain hours of the day a poor little wisp of a man, whose sole greeting each time I went to relieve him was to point to his flies, thickly coated with crystals, and mutter: 'Diabetes,' and then shuffle away.

After a week or two of this duty I began to fidget. So many of the young artists I had known or admired had gone: Rupert Brooke, Harold Chapin, Dennis Browne, and oh, many many more. Even Bobbie Crichton was talking of abandoning his flat and the barre. I grew increasingly restless and unable to sleep. One particularly hot night in August I turned round in bed to find my wife awake, too. 'I think I shall go,' I said. After a long silence she said quite simply: 'I knew that's what you were thinking. I shan't stop you.'

I was given a territorial commission in the Cheshire Regiment and posted to the battalion in which my brother-in-law was already serving. He must have greatly exaggerated the military knowledge I had acquired in my school O.T.C. to have obtained such a quick response to his recommendation, or maybe the authorities were willing to take on anybody at that time? Anyway, before the month of September was gone, I obtained a well-cut uniform from my 'Jack Barthwick' tailor in the West End, purchased an infantry sword with a beautifully damascened blade and a .450 revolver, both second-hand, and paraded, thus fully equipped, in the prompt corner of His Majesty's Theatre, waiting to say goodbye to the

Chief at the end of the last act of *Drake*, the first member of his staff to appear before him thus attired. I had been taken aback by the readiness with which he had agreed to release me from the remaining weeks of my contract. Now we were both relieved that an engagement so mutually unsatisfactory had come to an end.

The next day, saying more goodbyes, I ran into Joe Langton, who was plainly astonished at my transformation. 'I've been looking for you', he said, slowly adjusting his eye-glass and drawing from his breast-pocket a long envelope. 'Here's a draft lease of the Savoy Theatre. Rental for the first seven years fifty pounds a week.' I was so full of my new career that I scarcely took in what he was saying, although I did remember to thank him for his trouble. The disappointment I would normally have felt was drowned in a wave of patriotic enthusiasm. Within a matter of days my wife and I closed our flat and went north to stay with her parents.

10

Shortly after my arrival at the depôt the colonel announced in the mess that all newly commissioned officers would attend a lecture on army discipline from Regimental Sergeant-Major Whiteley, a hard-drinking, hard-swearing professional type that I thought had disappeared from the British Army after Waterloo. He had been called up from reserve to assist in whipping the new battalion into shape. Whiteley was in constant pain from a spinal wound received in one of our colonial wars, possibly fighting against the Boers, and this put a sharp edge to his wicked humour. He also suffered from a perpetual sniff which he used as a form of emphasis. He began his lecture—speaking the title in two syllables, thus, Diss-(sniff)-cipplin, with a straightforward account of this military attribute as understood by the professional army. 'Tell you what it is, gentlemen, Diss-(sniff)-cipplin is the (sniff) backbone of the British H'armee. Now my company officer when I was serving in India, *coo*, he was a soldier; he knew about Diss-(sniff)-cipplin; expected you to go into action just like you was on parade.' He proceeded to what he obviously considered to be the definitive illustration of his point: 'You see, gentlemen, it's like this: My company orficer (sniff) if he was to say to me, Sar'nt Whiteley, I want Jesus Christ 'ere in twenty minutes, dead or alive, 'Ee'd be there, gentlemen. 'Ee'd be there! Now that's what I calls Diss-cipplin.' The colonel disapproved of 'barrack-room ballads' for young officers—many of us were straight from public school. R.S.M. Whiteley gave no more lectures.

When the summer was nearly over we were moved out of the depot and put under canvas 'somewhere' in North Wales. With the coming of the autumn rains the trenches which we dug round each tent were soon filled with up to three feet of water. We began a long acquaintance with duckboards! Finally, shortly before Christmas, conditions under canvas became impossible. We were moved into billets at Aberystwyth. There we began to develop company rivalry, not only in field exercises, but in recreation, such as football teams and so forth: part of the process of welding our band of raw recruits into the semblance of a fighting unit.

My 'B' Company rapidly forged ahead in smartness of turn-out. We also earned top marks from the colonel for a series of weekly concerts, given in a local café. These were dutifully attended by the colonel and his senior major, an immensely stout person, whose efforts to mount a restive horse by the aid of a kitchen-chair were a severe strain upon battalion discipline, especially since included in our ranks were several natural 'comics' from Merseyside. The following autumn we were sent to Park Hall, Oswestry, one of the vast hutted camps then being built all over Britain. With the waywardness that sometimes afflicts public departments the huts were built in the summer and the roads in the winter. In consequence, the macadam sank into the earth as fast as it was laid down.

11

As more and more of my friends were swallowed up in the mud of Flanders or shot to pieces at Gallipoli, prolonged silence acting as the tell-tale, my former life receded into the background. Late in December, 1914, I received a letter from Eddie Marsh: Viola was enquiring about *Hassan* on behalf of Matheson Lang who might find the money to produce it. What were my plans? I was not going to let go of my prize. I replied to the effect that it would be most unwise to produce the play in wartime, and that I intended to produce it immediately the war was over. In fact, in response to a despairing postcard from Flecker, written at the end of November,

I had risked the wartime post and sent out to Davos my final suggestions. But the poet died in January, 1915, with his revision of the last act unfinished.* A year or so later Henry Dana wrote from His Majesty's Theatre, enquiring the whereabouts of the manuscript of a play (he had forgotten its name) by 'a man called Flecker'. I heard indirectly that the enquiry was on behalf of Oscar Asche. It gave me exquisite pleasure to inform Dana that the future of *Hassan* was settled. These were only two of the many hostages I gave to Fortune over *Hassan* during the next few years without in the least knowing how I was going to redeem them.

My eldest son was born early in 1916 and in the summer my wife and child moved out to lodgings in a small Welsh village called Pant, where I visited them as often as I could, driving a recently acquired Triumph motor-cycle at such desperate speed out of camp that my company sergeant-major gave me a private talking-to for risking my neck unnecessarily.

I continued to hear occasionally from Bobbie Crichton. He was the last of my associates to disappear into the void; he was killed on the Western Front in 1916 while serving with the Rifle Brigade. News of his death made me realise that my own journey into the unknown might be short, too. So it might have been but for my involvement with troop entertainment. In deference to the wishes of my commanding officer I began to give regular shows in the canteens of our division. Conditions were primitive, the main concern of the private contractors who ran them being to sell their beer. But the new citizen army demanded amenities other than the gallons of beer supplied to thirsty professional soldiers. Entertainment was one of them. I devised a scheme whereby each battalion of the two divisions in our camp should contribute towards the cost of building and running a full-scale garrison theatre on professional lines. Eventually complaints about the canteens and the excessive profits the contractors were making became so widespread that the Government was forced into action. It was decided that in future canteens would be run by a central authority with power to fix prices and allocate profits in the interests of the troops. Thus was formed the Army Canteen Committee, later to become the N.A.C.B.† and, finally, the present-day NAAFI.‡ How my modest scheme was swept into the net, myself with it, and how it grew

* His last letters to me are reproduced in the acting edition of *Hassan*.
† Navy and Army Canteen Board.
‡ Navy, Army and Air Force Institutes.

into a world-wide organisation that was to make a substantial contribution to national morale in the Second World War has been described in detail elsewhere.

12

After a brief spell at West Command Headquarters in Chester, I and my scheme were moved to London and embodied in the new canteen organisation. Thus, it was that in 1917 my wife and I found ourselves back in the flat in St. John's Wood with a son. We counted ourselves fortunate to regain our first home while the war was still raging.

Having escaped the Flanders trenches by a hair's breadth, as it were, I gave myself up completely to what I regarded as my war mission. . . . This sounds trite; it is none the less true. I became a dedicated person, with little thought for private relationships. I was often away visiting camps up and down the country, leaving my wife to grapple with unaccustomed domestic problems. Returning home late at night, exhausted and usually silent, I had no companionship to give her. In the autumn George Harris came down from Liverpool to join the branch, where he designed stages, scenery, costumes, programme covers and posters with a furious speed and a technical facility that I have only once seen equalled, and that was by Rex Whistler: savage cartoons too, that were a bitter comment on the futility of war. He came to live with us temporarily, which did not make things easier for my wife. Eventually, tiring of the difficulties, she began to spend an increasing amount of time with her parents, now living in the Surrey countryside. It seemed reasonable enough at first, but after a while it became increasingly difficult to suppress feelings of irritation, even anger, at her absence.

In the face of the dreadful casualty lists which were plunging our elders into the deepest anxieties, we of the younger generation sought relief wherever we could find it; not so much in drink as in dancing and sex. This was the beginning of the dancing craze that swept the country, and was to last well into the twenties. George and I began to visit Rector's, an underground night-club in Tottenham Court Road, as well as the socially superior Murray's. Rector's was a sleazy sort of place. The subdued lights, the dance rhythm spun out not with the loud insistent beat that is the modern fashion in such places, but softly and seductively from bands at either end of the black polished floor, the illuminated blocks of ice with electric fans blowing coolness into the stale-scented air, the frank sex of the girls and the hard appraising looks of young officers in uniform (others braving the provost marshal were in dinner-jackets) all contributed to an exhilarating wickedness. This was the Garden of Eden, and here was the forbidden fruit. So it was with us, as with thousands of other young marriages, that wartime conditions were straining our relations, a fact that neither of us appreciated at the time.

Seven
ReandeaN

I

As the end of the war drew near everybody began looking to the
future: the troops to the day of demobilisation: civilians to recovering their peace-time jobs or finding something better. Already at the branch our more important volunteers were drifting
away to look after their own concerns. It was time I began to look
after mine. Then one day, out of the blue, Fortune touched me on the
shoulder. I had been lunching with Alec Rea, wartime chairman of
the Liverpool Playhouse. As we stood on the pavement outside
the Hyde Park Grill Room—my headquarters were just opposite
in Knightsbridge—he asked me what I proposed to do after I was
demobilised. I said I had not yet decided, adding rather deceitfully
that there was plenty of time: I would not be demobilised until
the following year. Then quite simply, without any fuss, he said
that if the idea was of any interest to me he was willing to provide
the capital for a new theatrical company, adding the gentle rider
that he had always liked my work. I was struck dumb. 'Think it
over and let me know,' said Alec, his eyes twinkling. The next
minute he was disappearing towards Piccadilly in a battered wartime taxi, leaving me on the pavement, stunned by this thumping
piece of good fortune. Had I dreamed for a hundred years I could
not have imagined an opportunity more suited to my circumstances.

Of course, I accepted, and at once began looking round the staff
of the Entertainment Branch for future associates. The first person
I thought of was George Harris. He responded enthusiastically. I
needed a business manager whom I could trust. My choice fell
upon E. P. Clift, who was doing an excellent job as manager of the

latest garrison theatre at Catterick Camp. He jumped at the chance, and thereafter wove himself in and out of my story with persistent self-interest, as will be seen. Meanwhile, Alec busied himself with the legal formalities of registering our company, to which he gave the anagrammatical name of ReandeaN, always printed with capital letters at either end. People scoffed at first to see this name at the head of our playbills, accompanied by our signet, a silhouette of Histrion bowing behind a row of footlights, designed by George Harris, which he irreverently nicknamed Basil Hamlet. Eventually the public came to accept it as the hallmark of an efficient presentation.

I had no set ideas as to how to begin operations, nor how to formulate a policy. I just felt an urge to replace the ramshackle productions of the wartime theatre by the standards of acting and homogeneity of production in which I had been trained. This could only be achieved by having a semi-permanent company. Such a company would be like a football team; the longer they worked together the more likelihood there was of scoring goals. The analogy was never far from my mind, and I was to tell the actors so later on. But to reassert lost standards was not enough. I wanted to revive the sense of dedication possessed by the now vanished actor-managers. Pride in their theatres had been their sustaining virtue, often superior to the merit of the plays they produced. So my plan went far beyond the encouragement of a team spirit. It called for unity of style and purpose, expressed by actors, musicians, artists and technicians, all equally concerned with bringing an author's work to life upon the stage. Only by establishing a 'joint and several' will to succeed would it be possible to combat the malaise that had overtaken the theatre during the war. Inspiring the new company with these ideals would not be easy. Actors trooping back from the battlefields and munition factories were discomfited, more anxious about future employment than present perfection.

2

The search for plays and players, and for a theatre to put them in, had to be pursued simultaneously, if we were not to be brushed aside in the post-war scramble. First the plays: new dramatists not having appeared on the scene, I turned to those I had known before the war. I had lost touch with John Galsworthy. The author who came next to mind was Arnold Bennett, whose early plays I had produced at the Liverpool Playhouse. He made an appointment to see me in his private sitting-room at the Royal Thames Yacht Club in Piccadilly on a cold afternoon in December, 1918. He looked a picture of misery, seated huddled up in a wicker armchair in front of an inadequate fire, wearing carpet slippers. Every now and then he would shovel coke from an old Victorian scuttle in an endeavour to coax more warmth into that unfriendly room.

When I asked him to write a play for us he suggested a play he had written about Don Juan. Alec thought it too expensive for our first essay. I approached J. B. Pinker, Bennett's agent, but he said it would be at least a year before Bennett could deliver a commissioned play. I was growing alarmed. It was now March, 1919, nearly six months since Alec Rea's generous offer; virtually no progress had been made in the search for those three keys to fortune: the plays, the players, and a theatre. In a fit of desperation I acquired two light comedies, but no sooner had I announced their purchase than Bennett wrote to say he could let us have a play based on his novel *Sacred and Profane Love*. He had another offer for the play, but was willing to let me read it. This type of salesmanship was to be expected of authors' agents, but not from Arnold Bennett. However, we bought *Sacred and Profane Love*, and decided to make it our first London production.

Next, as to the company: Bennett's play called for star performers in the leading parts, but the ensemble I had in mind would have to be built up slowly by a process of careful selection from among actors I already knew and admired. That is why the names of many of those I had worked with in Liverpool and Manchester appeared in our first cast lists: they formed the nucleus of the permanent ReandeaN Company.

We needed a home of our own before we could establish ourselves within the close circle of West End managers. This proved the hardest task of all. The war had destroyed the actor-manager system and thrown up in its place a rash of speculation. Gambling in theatre rents became the sport of woollen merchants from Bradford, tycoons from the steel-making belt or not too straightforward Jewish speculators. One tycoon, although he did not deserve such a grandiloquent title, was Edward Laurillard, an intelligent, uneducated man who acquired a theatre-owning empire known as Grossmith & Laurillard. Later, when speculation died down, his empire crumbled, and he died in comparative poverty, sponging on his friends. We suffered a brisk education in the economic facts of theatre life as practised by theatre proprietors. Another ringleader in the game was the late A. E. Abrahams, a bill-posting tycoon who might be described as speculator-extraordinary in theatre leases at that time. During the war he had acquired a number of them which he sublet to other speculators. These gentlemen, having no intention of committing the folly of producing plays themselves, passed the obligation on to others. Short-term rentals became exorbitant. It looked as if we might have to give up the idea of a permanent home, and content ourselves with a temporary resting place.

While the search for a theatre was going on I obtained leave—I was still in uniform—to pay a hurried visit to Berlin to renew my contacts with the German theatre. Although the war had been over for six months or more, travel was still subject to long delays. The journey took me over twenty hours. I stayed at the Hotel Adlon, already on the way to recovering its peacetime magnificence. There I found Esmé Percy, wearing his kilt as an officer of the Highland Light Infantry with a somewhat Latin air. He was a member of a mysterious British Mission charged with the duty of securing the personal safety of certain members of the Kaiser's family. This information he conveyed to me by a series of winks and hints.

The German theatre was suffering from post-war chaos even greater than our own, and Reinhardt was away in Vienna. On the last day of my visit I was walking down the Unter den Linden when I met an acquaintance, Captain Codrington, son of Major-General Codrington, Commanding London District. He was returning from Constantinople and asked me when I was going home.

'Tomorrow,' I said. 'Beastly journey! They empty you out at the Dutch frontier in the middle of the night.'

'Oh!' he said, 'you don't want to do that. I'm flying home. Why not come too?'

My heart sank.

Above   The Skin Game. The Hornblower 'outsiders', Edmund Gwenn, Mary Clare and Malcolm Keen, confront the privileged Hillcrists (Helen Haye, Athole Stewart, Meggie Albanesi)

Centre left   The Blue Lagoon. Under full sail for Australia. Paddy (Edward Rigby) plays to the children while their guardian (Hesketh Pearson) talks to the captain.

Right   Fire at sea

Below   Faith Celli and Harold French discover sex in front of the Great Stone Man

The first two ReandeaN successes: *The Skin Game* and *The Blue Lagoon*

Au théâtre St. Martin
salut amical de la
part du théâtre Artistique
de Moscou et de la part
de C Stanislavsky
1926 – 20 – II Moscou

Above left   Constantin Stanislavsky
Above right   Professor Max Reinhardt (Deutsches theater, Berlin)
Centre   A. Lunacharski (Minister of Education, U.S.S.R., 1926)
Below, from left to right
James Elroy Flecker
William Archer
Anton Chekhov (the dramatist's nephew) as Hamlet

Pictures on my office wall

'Come along,' he said, 'and we'll book seats.'

We went to the booking office of Daimler Airways which had just opened a service with single-engined monoplanes. To my great relief we were told that all the seats were booked. I think the planes only carried four or five passengers anyway.

'Never mind,' said Codrington cheerily, 'we'll come back after lunch. There are sure to be cancellations.'

Unwillingly, I went back with him after lunch to find that all bookings had been cancelled because the weather had worsened. At 9 a.m. the next morning I was standing in the entrance hall of the hotel, waiting for the bus to take us to Templehof, and watching the rain come pelting down. Then I noticed a small man, with a patch over one eye, also watching and waiting. He was wearing a raincoat and carrying a little attaché case.

'Are you flying, too?' I asked.

'Don't be a bloody fool,' whispered Codrington, 'that's the pilot!'

'Good God!' I exclaimed. 'Only one eye?' This was the famous Captain Hinchcliffe who lost his life in 1928 flying the Atlantic with Elsie Mackay.

My recollections of the journey home remain vivid. Ten minutes after take-off we got into difficulty over one of the Prussian pine forests; we went round and round in circles and I began to feel unsafe, although I had been strapped into a wicker chair with a deep seat.

'Anything wrong?' I shouted.

'Air pocket,' replied Hinchcliffe.

When the aircraft began to bank in readiness to come down at Hamburg—my first experience of that manœuvre—I felt as though I and my stomach were about to part company. As we left the aircraft and hurried across the grass through the rain to a Nissen hut which did duty for the office, Hinchcliffe asked me what squadron I belonged to. When I told him the truth he exclaimed: 'Good heavens! Is this your first time up? Come and have a brandy.'

Later we came down at Bremen and Amsterdam, finally arriving at Croydon Airport at 7.30 in the evening, having left Berlin at about 9.30 a.m. I felt very shaky but secretly relieved as we left Croydon Airport.

On my return there was still no news of a theatre and Alec Rea was impatient to make a start. Then one day Viola Tree told me she was planning to spend her share of her father's estate in re-establishing the traditions of His Majesty's Theatre at the Aldwych, which, after rough experiences as a Y.M.C.A. Centre during the war, was

K

now being patched up. Mr. Abrahams, owner of the head lease, sitting back as usual, had sublet the theatre to Mr. Cochran. The latter, happy to add a little speculation to his expert showmanship, was willing to sublet the theatre to Miss Tree, but she was obviously out of her managerial depth, so when she told me that Gerald du Maurier had invited her to act with him I persuaded her to let me open the Aldwych with our Bennett play, while she sent off to act at Wyndham's.

Meanwhile, Alec arranged for us to pay a three weeks' visit to the Liverpool Playhouse, playing one of our light comedies for the first fortnight to give time for the final rehearsals of *Sacred and Profane Love*, to be given in the third week.

3

Brought up in the traditions of the Horniman Company, where respect for authorship was paramount, I was nevertheless unprepared for the flood of letters and telegrams that poured in from Bennett, dealing with every aspect of the production. For leading lady he preferred Sybil Thorndike to Madge Titheradge, and would have nothing to do with Iris Hoey, who eventually played the part quite admirably. He wanted Esmé Percy for the virtuoso because he could play the piano. He would only accept Franklin Dyall as a substitute provided I engaged a young pianist from Paris to play the piano off-stage. Since the virtuoso suffered from drug addiction I was instructed to read Crothers' *Morphinism*, especially the passages he had marked. George Harris was closely instructed upon details of design, e.g. 'the prevailing colours of Victorian rooms were green, magenta (a rich crimson) and blue; the total width of each pair of double-doors would be about four feet six inches to five feet, etc.' George was highly amused at this airing of the technical knowledge which Bennett had picked up down Hammersmith way.

Bennett was easy to deal with at the Liverpool rehearsals, although he never ceased to remind me how fortunate we were to have secured such a brilliant play for our first programme. But at the final dress rehearsals in London calm deserted him. While the scenery was being set for the second act, a sitting-room in a Paris hotel, he wandered on to the stage, where he started an argument with Harris about the finger-plates on the doors; they ought to be bronze.

George lost his temper, so Arnold returned to the auditorium via the pass-door. He marched down the centre aisle of the stalls to where I was sitting, his thumbs in the armholes of his waistcoat, a favourite gesture, his cockatoo-like coif more than usually erect.

'What's the matter?' I asked.

'W-w-w-well,' spluttered Arnold, 'your M-M-Mr. Harris has just told me to get off the bloody stage, a-a—and he's quite right!'

During the scene between the virtuoso and his mistress which followed, Arnold, seated immediately in front of me, became even more fidgety. After a while he beckoned me forward with his finger. 'I d-d-don't l-l-like her,' he stuttered, pointing at the actress. 'She's too hard!'

The scene went on a little longer and again he beckoned me forward, pointing his finger again at the actress: 'Is th- h-that girl a v-v-virgin?' he asked, 'I really don't know,' I said. 'I suppose so.' A slight pause. Then Arnold: 'Oh, c-c-can't th-th-that be altered?'

The fashionable first-night audience assembling in the foyer of the Aldwych Theatre observed a large reproduction of Titian's masterpiece thoughtfully borrowed by Viola Tree, although she had neither read nor seen our play. This misled to anticipation of a more colourful atmosphere than Arnold's prosaic piece could provide. The Lord Chamberlain's representative on the other hand was much relieved to observe that our title was symbolical. The reception was vociferous. There were loud and insistent calls for 'author'. Bennett, having somewhat disingenuously declared that nothing would induce him to take a call, I, being inexperienced in these matters, thought I should step forward and explain that the author was not in the house. Whereupon Bennett suddenly poked his head through the double doors at the back, swathed in a large opera cloak. He was greeted with a roar of laughter and promptly disappeared.

Despite the author's confident prognostications and the columns of criticism that appeared about the play, the results at the box-office were equivocal. Commercial success being our immediate target, this first shot was a near miss!

4

Before the box-office results of the Bennett play declared themselves we announced a Christmas production of *Fifinella* at the Scala

Theatre. We hoped to repeat the success which this unpretentious piece had won in the North of England before the war. But the atmosphere of Imperial Rome in the too-magnificent auditorium seemed to overawe the children and to chill their enjoyment; or, possibly, it was that the heating plant was not functioning properly.

There was a distinguished first-night audience, one daily paper reporting that: 'Mr. and Mrs. Asquith had a large party with them in a box, including Master Anthony, who looks quite grown up, except for his boyish hair.' Attendances were good over the immediate holiday period, but they fell away in January. Our hopes of establishing *Fifinella* in the short list of children's annual favourites were disappointed. So there it was, another near miss!

Undaunted by my lack of success, Alec Rea continued his search for a permanent home. His eye lighted upon the St. Martin's, London's newest theatre, built immediately before the war by B. A. Meyer for Lord Willoughby de Broke, and opened in 1916 by C. B. Cochran, whose attempt to introduce an all-stalls floor, price one guinea, had failed. The public regarded this as outrageous, seeing that hitherto the highest price, apart from opera, had been twelve-and-six. The theatre had managed to achieve one rather oblique success, an English translation of Brieux's *Damaged Goods*, dealing with the subject of venereal disease. This was heavily patronised by Australian troops on leave, come to stare glumly at their own possible fate. Cochran was quite willing to sell us his lease, which had nineteen-and-a-half years to run, but he wanted £20,000 for it. Alec thought this an extortionate demand. However, enthusiasm overcame his business caution.

Our long association with the theatre began on February 11th, 1920, with the production of one of the light comedies that I had purchased, which ran for two weeks only and was succeeded by another, *Over Sunday*, first produced in Liverpool. The leading man was Clive Brook, who came straight from France to give a polished comedy performance. Unfortunately, that play also ran for two weeks only. Clive, having acquired a wife from among our 'undergraduates', left us to seek his El Dorado in Hollywood. We were now in serious case. Not only had we acquired a reputation for short runs, but we had managed to confirm the St. Martin's record in that respect, which was worse. Actors were openly saying: 'Oh nothing will ever go in that place.' The popular press took to commiserating with the actors for having to work for such an unfortunate management. I suppose I deserved it. After all, four failures—

two near misses, and two completely off target—was pretty poor shooting.

Alec came into the office every morning, looking increasingly scared as he contemplated the speed with which our funds were melting away. Yet he refused to give in, and remained valiant in support for which I always remained grateful. But I could not expect him to continue to finance my blunders indefinitely. I spent sleepless nights cursing my folly in not adhering to my original intention to produce only plays of artistic integrity. To adhere to that policy was the obvious course, but it called for moral courage because our funds were nearly exhausted, and yet another failure would almost certainly put an end to ReandeaN for good.

5

Once again Fortune brushed me lightly on the cheek. While we were preparing Bennett's play I received the following note from John Galsworthy, with whom I had lost touch during the war:

> Aug 8 1919
> Grove Lodge,
> Hampstead, N.W.

My dear Dean,
    Where are you? And are you nearer starting a theatre yet? Let me hear your news.

> Best wishes,
> Yours sincerely,
> JOHN GALSWORTHY.

I did not appreciate the significance of his enquiry until some weeks later when he rang up to ask if I would care to read his new play. This was *The Skin Game*, the contract for which was signed on December 10th, 1919. That we did not make this play our opening production at the St. Martin's was further proof of the extent to which my judgment had strayed. However, hesitations were out from now on. *The Skin Game* was produced on April 21st, 1920, nine days before the contract was due to lapse.

Biographers have suggested that Galsworthy both cast and produced his own plays. This was not so. Naturally, in view of my previous association with him, first as actor, then as producer, I always respected his views. Beginning with *The Skin Game*, a kind of routine of preparation was established, with full discussion of the principal characters and of the actors suggested to play them. There was never any serious difference of opinion between us.

Three established West End artists were included in the cast, Athole Stewart and Helen Haye for Mr. and Mrs. Hillcrist, representing the landed gentry, and Edmund Gwenn, to play Hornblower, heading the family of outsiders. Hornblower's daughter-in-law, Chloe, was played by Mary Clare. Her warm Irish temperament and delightful sense of humour were to make valuable contributions to many future ReandeaN productions. She was one of a number of young players that I grappled to us to form our semi-permanent company. There were others, too, who began their successful careers with me at this time. I think especially of J. H. Roberts, whose gentle retiring personality kept him from ultimate stardom, but who was to contribute many superb character studies, and of Malcolm Keen, whose fine voice and presence had made the success of several N.A.C.B. companies during the war. He brought strength and vitality to our ensemble. Later, some members of the original Horniman Company joined us; their names will appear in due course.

Foremost among our younger recruits was Meggie Albanesi, a young actress, barely twenty when I first met her, who was destined to influence my own career as well as the development of the ReandeaN Company. Here it is necessary to digress somewhat to provide the background to events that were to justify that statement. . . . Meggie was the daughter of Carlo Albanesi, Italian by birth and English by adoption, who taught the violin at the Royal Academy of Music, and of his wife, Maria, a novelist of modest talent. After the usual fumblings during which she studied both violin and piano, Meggie scored her initial success by winning the Bancroft Gold Medal at R.A.D.A. She was seventeen, the same age as Lady Teazle, the part which won her the medal. She began her professional career by playing a tiny part in a revival of *A Pair of Spectacles*, at Wyndham's Theatre, the run being cut short by air raids during the war. I asked her to come and see me during her engagement as understudy to Faith Celli in *Dear Brutus* at Wyndham's.

Our first meeting was not a success. She was listless and full of complaint against Gerald du Maurier for not giving her a chance to act. I remember wondering what it was about her that had made so many people urge me to send for her. She was not beautiful, appealingly young, yes, but not beautiful: a small dark head set firmly upon a short rather dumpy body, hands broad and strong like a man's, a voice inclined to hoarseness. What was it then? Her eyes? Yes, that was it! The most expressive eyes I had seen in any actress.

When I sent for her a second time, having the ingenue part of Jill Hillcrist in *The Skin Game* in mind, she had just made a sensational success in a special performance of *The Rising Sun*, an English adaptation of the Dutch play by Heijermans. She had been presented to Ellen Terry at the end of the performance, and been warmly praised by the critics the following morning. She was rather offhand when I invited her to join our company. It seemed as though our acquaintance were going to develop into open hostility. I thought her conceited and said so. She thought me too managerial. I suppose I was. It was all very foolish. The second interview terminated even more abruptly than the first. We often laughed together over it afterwards. Fortunately, I persisted, and eventually convinced her that in our ensemble she really would have the opportunities she so ardently desired. It did not take long to realise what a prize the theatre had secured, although none of us foresaw that this young actress was destined to streak comet-like across the theatre sky; nor were we sensible of the dangers that lay in the private path of one who was essentially a giver. In her performance as Jill there was an extraordinary quality of stillness, which had the effect of concentrating attention upon her whenever the drama seemed to demand it, although Desmond MacCarthy criticised her for being too stiff. 'She should allow herself more movement', he wrote. This advice, thrown off in the course of writing his review, was an illustration of something I was to notice frequently during the course of my career, namely, the inability of some critics, foremost in their appreciation of the literary qualities of a play, to note where writing ceases and the techniques of acting and production take over.

The presence of authors at rehearsal never bothered me, accustomed as I had been to seeing them about the theatre in the heyday of the Horniman Company. In fact, I encouraged them to come to the ReandeaN rehearsals and to talk over their parts with the actors. At times their advice bordered upon fantasy, as, for example, when Galsworthy went up to Mary Clare after her emotional exit in the second act of *The Skin Game*, and whispered in her ear: 'Miss Clare, I would like you to make your exit from that scene rather like a duck crossing the road after a thunderstorm.' At the end of the rehearsal

Mary was still to be heard muttering Irish obscenities in a dark corner of the stage.

The first-night reception was tumultuous: no other description fits. While the critics hurried off to Fleet Street, the author, following the custom of the day, had to make a brief speech of thanks before the audience could be constrained to disperse, only to re-group themselves excitedly on the narrow pavement outside. The reviews were mixed. The popular press hailed the play as an exciting melo-drama, while some of the more serious papers were shocked that Galsworthy should have dared to write such an evident commercial success! The play became the hit of the season.

6

The St. Martin's was ideal for the production of realistic plays. But the theatre was too small, both auditorium and stage, for the other ideas that I had cherished ever since my first talks with Max Reinhardt in Germany. Productions calling for an imaginative use of light and colour would require a larger theatre and a more commodious stage.

Before *The Skin Game* was produced I had been shown a rough dramatisation of H. de Vere Stacpoole's best-seller, *The Blue Lagoon*, prepared by Charlton Mann, business manager of the Adelphi Theatre. He had managed to retain most of the charm of this boy-and girl idyll on a South Sea island. Realising its possibilities in spectacular staging, I decided to produce the play at the old Prince of Wales' Theatre.

Stacpoole, a kindly Anglo-Irishman with a genial sense of humour, had been living on the financial surface of his *Blue Lagoon* for years, and made no bones about it. The fact that someone was prepared to risk putting the story on the stage he regarded as huge fun. The scenario—it was really more like a film script than a play—contained a number of short spectacular scenes; these had to be linked together with music, for which I turned to Clive Carey, busily training opera students at the Royal College. He composed some charming atmo-spheric links for me, which were played by an indifferent orchestra.

Casting the play was not as difficult as I had anticipated. Dick and Emmeline, as children, were played by two adorable pupils of the Italia Conti School; as adolescents we had Harold French, now grown into a handsome youth since his appearance in company with Noël Coward and Gertrude Lawrence as the Angelic Chorus in my Liverpool production of *Hannele*, and Faith Celli, still basking in the praise she received for her lovely performance as the Dream Child in *Dear Brutus*. Since that time she had become sexually self-conscious, and this made things difficult when it came to costuming her for the part. Emmeline was supposed to have grown up on this tropic island in a state of nature. George Harris, with this in mind, had designed a dress of imitation plantain leaves, strung together with necklaces of seashells. Before the first dress rehearsal Miss Celli protested at the inadequacy of the dress, rolling it up in her hand like a dishcloth, and declaring that the audience would be able to see the shape of her breasts. I told her not to be prudish but to go away and put the dress on at once, adding as a parting shot that they were quite nice breasts! She eventually reappeared in a bead frock which she had somehow contrived for herself. She looked like a cabaret girl dressed for a speciality dance. George was furious, the actress tearful but undaunted. Between them they performed a sort of strip-tease in the wings, while the rest of the cast which included Roy Byford and Allan Jeayes, waited for the outcome. The part of the father, a key rôle, was played by Hesketh Pearson. His Boswellian talents were not yet apparent, neither were his abilities as an actor, but I was bound to agree with him that his part in *The Blue Lagoon* was a dull one.

Harris's scenery was simple, but highly coloured. There was a lagoon of royal blue, a coral reef with a green-blue open sea beyond; a mound and a few palm trees for the island. The stone idol, essential to the story, was twenty-feet in height, a cross between Easter Island and Jacob Epstein—a magnificent example of the property maker's craft. To complete the picture of wide skies and bright sunlight we had an enormous cyclorama, to light which I used automatic arcs placed in semi-circular housings with grooved fronts to take colours.* When the typhoon struck the island the palm trees were lashed to fury (by fixing them to eccentric rockers underneath the stage), and the sea surged over the coral reef in billows of green silk, sewn into long airtight bags, inflated by a pulsating blower, with green lamps inside to give luminosity. There were scenes on the deck of the ship, on the open sea with the ship ablaze (eventually to sink below the horizon), and a long-boat with

* This equipment was later developed and put on the market by a well-known German firm of lighting engineers.

the two children in it, being rowed away by an old sailor (Edward Rigby). For this most successful piece of stage realism we devised a machine to toss the yards of painted canvas up and down (taking the place of the boys who used to perform this service for *Robinson Crusoe* in the Victorian pantomimes). Everybody wanted to know how we achieved such marvellous effects on such a comparatively small stage. In fact, all that Harris had done was to adapt the well-thought-out technical tricks of the theatres of long ago.

The play was produced on the 27th August, 1920, and was an enormous success both with the Press and the public. There were ecstatic descriptions of the production. 'Quite unlike anything we have had in the London theatres before', wrote *The Times*, which sounds rather childish today, but it has to be remembered that films were young in fact and still juvenile in outlook, and there was no colour.

7

During the next year or two there was a sickening alternation between success and failure. Fortunately, the former outweighed the latter to a considerable extent. All the same, I was secretly rather proud of our distinguished failures. The first of them followed hard upon *The Skin Game*. This was *The Wonderful Visit*—a dramatisation by St. John Ervine of a novel written by H. G. Wells in 1895. H. G. did not put in an appearance at the rehearsals but St. John Ervine sat with me throughout, obviously enjoying the proceedings but saying little. His only grievance was that I never allowed him enough time to eat his lunch. Casting entirely within the ensemble was not possible, so I strengthened the list by engaging for a key part Miss Compton, aunt of Fay, and wife of R. C. Carton, a successful Edwardian dramatist. An actress accomplished in the best traditions of the Compton family, she was now at the end of her career and alas! suffering from failing memory, a disability that I brushed aside because of her unique personality. On the first night, when three parts of the way through the key scene in the second act, she doubled back to the beginning and started all over again. The play never regained its equilibrium after such a toppling of the audience's attention.

Still walking the tight-rope between success and failure I decided that my only course was to go forward boldly. That way there was less risk of another tumble. So I chose *A Bill of Divorcement*, a first play by Clemence Dane, a young writer who had already attracted the attention of the literary critics with two early novels. This moving play would have stood no chance of acceptance by a commercial management because the subject of madness was taboo on the London stage.

Rehearsals went well. By now the company were tackling each new production with increasing confidence, and our two guest players, Lilian Braithwaite and C. Aubrey Smith, forbearing to shine as individuals, gave themselves up to the family atmosphere of the play without reserve. There is a feeling of special certainty about the preparation of a play destined for success; it persists in spite of one's pretence at ignoring it. The converse is also true, when nothing seems to feel right, and the manager or producer vainly strives to forget his forebodings. Time and time again such premonitions have been confirmed. The actors, too, often get the message, however surprised they may be when the public endorses it. They were more than surprised on this particular first night: they were overwhelmed. The principal recipients of the frantic applause were the author and Meggie Albanesi in the part of Sydney Fairfield, the only instance within my memory of a young actress achieving an international reputation by virtue of her performance in a single play. Never can I forget the utterly poignant scene in the last act when, having sent her lover out of her life for the sake of her crazed father, Sydney turns in bitter anguish and cries out: 'Oh, Mummy, I'm not hard. I'm not hard!' Nor can I forget the reception which followed at the play's end, the audience shouting 'Meggie, we want Meggie' after the fashion of modern teenagers, and the critics standing in their places waving their programmes. The actress stepped forward again and again, limp with fright and nervous exhaustion. I was the first to greet her in her dressing-room, just as I had been the last to leave it before the play began. She flung her arms round me and burst into tears. Neither of us spoke. It was then that I began to realise how much gentleness and self-doubt and yet steely determination to give and give of her best lay concealed behind that abrupt manner.

The author too, was called on to the stage. She began with the usual cliché, 'I can't make speeches,' a remark immediately interrupted by a joyous shout from the upper circle, 'But you *can* write a play, Miss Dane.' The notices were exuberant, although A. B.

Walkley in *The Times* wrote a column of gentle mockery of Miss Dane's 'argument', doubting whether the daughter's sacrifice of 'happiness' in order to look after her father would have worked out in real life, but even that highly sophisticated critic could not refrain from ending his notice with paeans of praise for Meggie. A. P. Herbert headed his notice in the *Westminster Gazette* with simple finality: 'A great play.' Amid such excitement I naturally thought we were at the zenith of achievement. However, there was still better to come, but not immediately.

8

This success made me more than ever determined to cling on to *Hassan*. So soon as ReandeaN was formed I had written to the poet's widow in Paris telling her the good news and suggesting she might like to come to London some time to discuss the production. She had arrived in June, expecting a production that autumn. Thereafter, every new ReandeaN production was followed by an urgent enquiry from Paris for news of *Hassan*. To avoid these importunities Mr. A. P. Watt, the agent, was asked to draw up an agreement that would secure to us the dramatic rights for twelve months in exchange for an advance royalty payment to Mme Flecker. It was a desperate gamble on my part, for I had not the faintest notion where to look for the large sum of money that I realised would be required. From now on, to add to my embarrassment, whenever ReandeaN had a success, there was Mme Flecker waiting on the doorstep!

Apart from the question of finance I began to worry about the actual production. The poet had always wanted music. I felt that only a composer of the first rank could do justice to the work. This involved me in animated discussion in musical circles, where I was at a disadvantage, having no knowledge of music, only a great love of it. Nevertheless, from the outset I had my own ideas as to the appropriate type of music, and where it should occur. While various English composers were being considered Mme Flecker wrote from Paris proposing Maurice Ravel. Her argument that 'a composer with a name like his will look well on the programme, whether his music be suitable or not, which very few people can tell' did not impress me. I agreed to her suggestion with some reluc-

tance, because Ravel knew no English, and this might make collaboration difficult. But the composer shilly-shallied too much; he was
busy writing an opera; he had other compositions in mind; how much
music was required? Finally, might he read the play in French?

While we were waiting for a decision Harris and I began study
sessions on scenery and costumes. Talks were held in the evenings
when interruptions were fewer. Upon one occasion, leaving the
office rather late, as we passed by Covent Garden my eye caught
sight of a poster announcing the performance that night of *A
Village Romeo and Juliet* by Frederick Delius. I had recently read a
notice of this little-known opera and, on a sudden impulse, persuaded
George to come in and listen to it. We crept into the back of a box
and soon found ourselves immersed in the glorious music of 'The
Walk to the Paradise Garden'. Never had I heard such a fountain of
sound. I was enthralled. I turned to George and said: 'This is the
man I want for *Hassan*.' I wrote off the next day to Mme Flecker
and told her that I was not going to wait any longer for Ravel's
decision. I had made up my mind. I wanted Frederick Delius.
I asked her to find out whether he would be interested. She
replied that he was interested, adding: 'judging from his appearance
—a bundle of quivering and spasmodic nerves—he is possibly a
very good musician'.

I decided to go to France to see the composer and to take Harris
with me. From Paris we set out for Grez-sur-Loing. It was a sunny
day in July, a day of pictures in the memory: the village street
quiet in the summer's heat, then the clanging bell while we waited
at the door of the villa; in the cool interior Mme Delius, a tall,
gracious hostess, waiting to give us luncheon and, after coffee in
the lovely walled garden, to show us her pictures. Above all, there
remains the vivid impression of the maestro himself. Delius was
unlike the popular idea of a composer. His thin, ascetic face and
precise diction suggested a professor, perhaps of philosophy,
rather than a musician, while his faint North Country accent and
brisk manner hinted at business training. We went through the play
together, Delius agreeing without demur to the amount of music I
required and the places where it should occur. The composer proved
to be extremely businesslike in negotiation, totally rejecting the
first draft agreement and making so many alterations in the final
one sent to him that Clift was constrained to remark that this was
'the most difficult gentleman I've ever had to deal with'. Before the
agreement was signed there was last-minute correspondence over

the size of the orchestra. I had suggested twenty-one players, the composer demanded many more. Eventually we finished up with thirty-four.

The press announcement which followed the signing drew a letter of strong protest from John Galsworthy, who was travelling abroad with Ada, suffering one of her recurrent periods of malaise. I should have consulted him before I made the decision, he wrote. It was a disastrous mistake, etc. etc. The letter aroused the strangest emotion in me. Although I could advance no argument in support of what I had done, yet I felt that J.G. had made a fool of himself, so I tore up the letter, not wanting anybody to know. I wish I had kept it. . . . The greater part of the music was delivered with what I regarded as unwelcome speed, since I was still without concrete plans for the production. The additional interludes that I had to extract from a loudly protesting composer are among the most enchanting items in a score that did more to bring Delius to the notice of his countrymen than all his previous work.

9

When I first came to London I had all the provincial player's awe of his lofty cousin, the West End actor. Ridiculous, really, in modern eyes, but there! He had reached Mecca while we were still struggling along the dusty road outside. It was with this attitude of mind that I used to encounter Owen Nares seated on top of a bus in the Finchley Road en route for the West End. The sole protection against the weather was a little tarpaulin apron which one put across one's knees when it rained. Owen usually sat right in front above the driver, where he could study his part without fear of interruption. I was much too shy then to make myself known to this handsome matinée idol, but now I found myself offering him an engagement to play the lead in a light comedy by Gertrude Jennings, which I had decided to produce at the Aldwych Theatre, where Viola Tree was facing serious difficulties with her rental overlord, C. B. Cochran. This was what in modern business jargon might be described as 'a holding operation'. My long-term intention was, of course, to produce *Hassan* there. The comedy foreshadowed the arrival of the famous Aldwych farces a year or two later, but, alas! it did not anticipate their success, even though two stalwarts of that later company, Mary Brough and Sydney Fairbrother, were both in the cast. We produced the play on a Saturday night, which was foolish because in those days gallery audiences were an exuberant lot. Early in the proceedings one of the first-nighters developed a loud sneeze, which was followed by whispers of 'Shut up!' The affliction, recurring at intervals, led to a susurration of giggles from all parts of the gallery. The hysteria reached such a pitch that at the end of the performance the applause of the reserved seats was drowned by loud and persisting booing from the gallery. This roused Lady Tree to remark with her usual acid wit: 'We used to say the success of a new play was on the knees of the gods, but now it depends on their sneeze.'

In the afternoons we gave a series of matinées of *The New Morality*, a brilliant light comedy by Harold Chapin, preceded by a grim piece by John Galsworthy called *The First and the Last*. I chose it to give Meggie the opportunity of playing Wanda, a Polish waif. She gave a devastating performance, partnered by Owen Nares. I hold the little play especially in memory because it was during those few matinées that the affair, if one may use a tarnished word to describe the pathetic idyll, between Meggie and Owen began. Later, Owen went away on tour. Meggie sent him a letter in which she poured out her feelings with all the abandon of her passionate nature. Owen's wife, the actress Marie Polini, coming early to the theatre where they were playing, took the letter from the rack and read it. Sharp in defence of her own, she made Owen, always weak in her hands, return the letter and tell Meggie that he would 'never again' see her alone, and she must not write to him. The brutality of this turning-off broke Meggie's heart. It is necessary to bring this story to light, for it explains, some would say justifies, much of what followed. . . . Our attempt to step into Viola Tree's financial shoes was a failure; they were too big for us.

10

My next and more distinguished failure was Clemence Dane's *Will Shakespeare*, staged at the now destroyed Shaftesbury Theatre. This play, written in the white heat of her initial success as a dramatist, contains some of Clemence Dane's most passionate writing for the theatre, the blank verse spoken by Queen Elizabeth in the final

Early woodcut by George Harris for the limited edition

scene being especially notable. The play gave George and I an opportunity to develop still further our ideas for new staging. The old Shaftesbury Theatre had a very high roof, so we planned the whole production inside draperies fifty feet high. They were made of hessian, dyed a deep purple and stencilled in black and dull gold, with Tudor crowns and roses. For the last act in the Palace of Westminster there was nothing on the stage but a throne chair on a dais within an alcove of curtains looped high, and a small writing table and stool. At the back a flagstaff on the balcony flew Queen Elizabeth's personal standard. Below was a vista of old London. The diminutive shaking figure of Haidée Wright, seated on her throne, speaking the Queen's grandiloquent lines with demonic energy, had a thrilling effect, and nightly stirred the audience to interruptive applause. The décor was probably the best of Harris's early achievements.

We had a fine cast including two notable 'Shakespeareans', Arthur Whitby and Claude Rains, who were ably backed up by members of our permanent company,* especially Mary Clare as Mary Fitton.

At the final dress rehearsal, Philip Merivale, who was playing Shakespeare, was so dull and depressing in the first act that Clemence Dane went round to De Hems' oyster bar and bought quantities of oysters, champagne, and stout for a supper party in the dressing-rooms. While George and I struggled with technicalities, the exhausted actors feasted. The result was that Merivale played the remaining acts magnificently and bamboozled us all into thinking we had a success. This was the reverse of the old theatrical saying that a bad dress-rehearsal means a good first night. In the event Merivale played Shakespeare as a man who had given up life's struggle before ever he left Stratford.

* It was under my management that (Dame) Flora Robson made her first appearance on the London stage as one of the visions in Act One.

Above With the author at rehearsal: Malcolm Keen, Lilian Braithwaite, Meggie Albanesi, C. Aubrey Smith

Below Meggie overhears her mother's rejection of her lover

A Bill of Divorcement, Clemence Dane's first and most successful play

Above left   Will Shakespeare with Mary Fitton at the virginal: Philip Merivale and Mary Clare

Above right   Henslowe presents a petition from the players to Queen Elizabeth: Haidée Wright, Arthur Whitby

Below   The Audience Chamber at Whitehall

Will Shakespeare: Clemence Dane's 'Invention'. It offended the popular conception of Shakespeare

The basic weakness of the play was that Shakespeare was presented in un-heroic guise, a weakling dominated by women; first by Anne Hathaway, next by Mary Fitton, finally by Queen Elizabeth herself, who in the last scene was made to goad him into writing *Twelfth Night*. The British public would not accept this view of our national poet, and the play failed. Most of the literary critics condemned the play because the 'invention' was not near enough to the known facts of Shakespeare's life. Many well-known literary figures of the day joined in the castigation of poor Clemence Dane: Edward Shanks in *The Outlook*, William Poel, of course, and even Owen Seaman in *Punch*. St. John Ervine, in the *Observer*, began his two-column criticism with a pun: 'Miss Dane's Defence' (reminiscent, of course, of the Henry Arthur Jones play) and proceeded to a long and savage attack, so much so that on the following Sunday John Galsworthy wrote a long letter in the author's defence. This led to such a spate of words that the editor was forced to close the correspondence two weeks later with a final three-column answer from St. John Ervine.

Among those who spoke up for the play were Hugh Walpole, Gordon Selfridge, Mrs. Patrick Campbell, and even dear Ellen Terry, who described it as 'a great play, greatly acted'. Feelings run high when so much that has been put into a production is dismissed in a few sentences. I made the youthful manager's mistake of attacking the critics for their lack of understanding, a self-indulgence to which actors, producers and managers are all prone from time to time. The outcry stirred the ordinary public in support. Business improved over the Christmas holidays, but not enough to pay expenses. It was a flash in the pan. We made preparations to withdraw the production, which roused Clemence Dane to offer us £2,000 of her own money to keep the play going. This news found its way into the papers. 'Cheers' and 'Bravos' greeted her appearance at both matinée and evening performances at the end of the week. We thought we had won through, but there was only sixty-two pounds in the house on the following Monday. The play had to close. . . .

As a creative artist in sculpture and painting, as well as in the theatre, Clemence Dane's work was always nobly proportioned, even though it fell short occasionally of the complete success that was her aim. . . . In later years her writing seemed oftentimes out of scale with its subject-matter. I think she was happiest living on the high veldt of her imagination.

L

11

Time now to recall more of my private story. This I do with the utmost reluctance, for the mists of failure dimmed the bright colours in which it began. In retrospect, too, the inevitability of it all saddens me.

After the Armistice my father-in-law had bought for us the lease of a house in St. John's Wood, which Ernest Joseph, chief architect to the Canteen Board, offered to re-furbish. We accepted his ideas, contaminated though they appeared to be by prolonged contact with the requirements of the N.A.A.F.I. institutes. I can remember little of his alterations, except two new doors of polished mahogany plywood, unpanelled, very incongruous among the mouldings and cornices of a house built under Regency influence early in Victoria's reign. Another recollection is of an elaborate bath which the outgoing tenant had left behind. It had a glass-encased shower at one end, with a multiplicity of taps designed to squirt water in every direction, which it succeeded in doing, sometimes with unexpected results. There was a little study below stairs where I worked out new productions on the model stage which my mother had treasured since nursery days. The most satisfactory feature was the well-proportioned drawing-room, which had two pairs of French windows in the wall facing south. This gave the room a spacious look. We had virtually no furniture for it, save a baby-grand piano, given to my wife as a wedding present. Neither of us could play the instrument, but in those days it was considered uncivilised to be without a piano in the home. We did manage a hair carpet, and I obtained a lovely crystal chandelier from the theatre by paying the balance of the hire-purchase money at the end of the run of one of the plays.

A friend from the garrison theatre time was Harold Samuel, a virtuoso noted for his playing of Bach. He came regularly to dine with us, and after dinner would sit down and give a Bach recital on our baby-grand. It must have amused him to see us seated side by side on an old packing-case covered with an Indian shawl at one end of the room, while at the other end he played on and on, privately enjoying his mastery of the music. The lack of furniture increased the resonance of the room. We might have been seated in the front row of a concert hall.

In that house we began our home-making, all else having been only wartime lodgments. Here my wife set herself to repair the hair-line cracks that had begun to appear in our hitherto close relationship. Our marriage, begun in a mood of idyllic happiness, was based upon romantic notions that had little relation to the practical problems with which we were now faced. After years of dreaming and hoping for opportunity the fever of dedication that possessed me froze the personal side of my life into a state of inertia. There were days when I felt as though I should burst with frustrated ambition. I wanted my wife to come into the market-place to join the battle. It was impossible she should do so. I was foolish to expect it.

In social attitudes we were prisoners of our generation, subject to its inhibitions and taboos. Frank discussion beforehand of such matters as family planning would have been considered indelicate. I was unprepared for the challenge of divided interest with which parental responsibilities confronted me. Now, two generations later, I find myself applauding the frankness of young people in discussing sexual matters, although it does not seem that in the world of the theatre at any rate this has led to more successful solutions of marital problems than was the case with our inhibited approach.

12

While I was worrying over the failure of *Will Shakespeare* I received an unexpected call from Galsworthy. He had looked in to tell me he had written two new plays; one of them, called *Windows*, he brought with him. 'What good fortune,' I thought: But after I had read it—well, I was still worrying! Might I read the other play? I asked diffidently. J.G. said he had half-promised it to Leon M. Lion. But there is no harm in my reading it, surely? The play was *Loyalties*. After I had read it I lay awake at night, thinking I must have that play! I pleaded so hard with Galsworthy, reminding him that ReandeaN had brought him his first commercial success, that eventually he agreed to make the change.

Loyalties was somewhat under length, so I obtained permission to play J. M. Barrie's *Shall We Join the Ladies?* with it. This brilliant spoof had been performed only once before, at a benefit performance at the Academy of Dramatic Art in Gower Street—not yet in receipt of the royal prefix. Which of the two plays should come first in the programme? Here was a delicate question of precedence. Barrie and Galsworthy were good friends: neither wished to be regarded as the rival of the other. A certain amount of manœuvring for position followed. I wanted *Shall We Join the Ladies?* to come last. This would enable me to borrow Leslie Faber, Gladys Cooper's leading man at the Playhouse, to play Mr. Smith—the part created at the Academy matinée by Dion Boucicault. J.G. objected to the arrangement, so Barrie wrote to him: Does it strike you that a three-act play which, on the surface, is all the time giving its audience the problem, who committed the theft, should not be preceded by a one-act play whose problem is, who committed the murder?'

The issue was finally settled with honours even: Barrie's play should come last for a few weeks only, when Faber would speed from one theatre to the other, like the music-hall stars used to do. When Gladys Cooper changed her programme at the Playhouse, this playing order would no longer be possible, so Gilbert Ritchie, a member of our permanent company, took Faber's place, and the Barrie play was then put first.

Both plays had lengthy male casts; also there were eight women in the Barrie play but only three in *Loyalties*. This meant that our permanent company would have to be much enlarged. Even so, some of the players would have to play more than one part, a process called 'doubling', much frowned upon in the West End, where it was regarded as a cheap device of the provincial theatre. Among those specially engaged for *Loyalties* were Ernest Milton, giving the finest performance of his long and distinguished career as De Levis, Eric Maturin, acting the desperate gallantry of Captain Dansey, D.S.O., both on and off the stage; and Dawson Milward who made General Canynge a commanding figure, while Lady Tree resumed the part in the Barrie play that she had created at the special performance.

Following precedent, both authors attended rehearsals of their plays. Barrie listened shyly behind the scenery, but whenever I turned to him for advice he was usually to be seen disappearing through the stalls exit. Some of the girls teasingly asked him who had done the murder and when he was going to write the remaining acts. He became evasive, although he did allow me to describe it on the programme as 'The first act of a new play in three acts'. The fact is he had written the playlet as a party joke, a huge question mark, without any intention of supplying an answer.

Galsworthy was by now a familiar figure in our theatre. He knew most of the company personally, and thoroughly enjoyed himself in the beneficent atmosphere of collaboration. One might almost say that he was our paterfamilias, expressing interest not only in the progress of individual members of the company but in the future prospects and education of my own growing family. Indeed, we had become so 'Galsworthian' that we gave our youngest son the name of Jolyon, after the character in *The Forsyte Saga*. My wife told him about this during the final dress rehearsal of *Loyalties*. His terse reply was: 'Ah, yes? But it's not Jŏlyon, it's Jōlyon,' to which Max Beerbohm commented, 'Since your son is the only living Jolyon you have every right to pronounce his name how you like.'

During the preparation of the play I had to watch out for J.G.'s known weakness for understatement. This predilection caused an embarrassing situation at the final dress rehearsal, for he had gone beforehand to each member of the company in turn and told him to 'Cut out the drama.' Perhaps he was secretly alarmed that he had written such a commercial play. All the dramatic values that we had striven to bring out in rehearsal had disappeared. What was I to do? It was already midnight and tempers were becoming frayed; also I had several hours of scene and lighting rehearsals in front of me—there were seven scenes and four quick changes. Harris, very tired and cross, had already been to me during the last act to protest because Galsworthy had offered him a malted lozenge by way of refreshment, instead of a drink. 'Who does he think he is?' growled George. 'Christ's vicar in the theatre?' In self-defence, as well as for the sake of the play, I was forced to reassemble the weary company, and insist upon their playing the play on the morrow as we had rehearsed it. Galsworthy left the theatre with the nearest approach to a bad temper that I had ever seen in him. It seemed that our close friendship was about to be broken.

In the first-night programme we printed a statement which read as follows: 'In order to satisfy the Lord Chamberlain the word "bloody", used by one of the characters in Mr. Galsworthy's play in a moment of great emotion, has been removed from the spoken text.' This moved a correspondent in the *Sunday Times* to point out that before the war thousands of people had heard Mrs. Patrick Campbell use the same word in *Pygmalion*. 'Is there then', he asked, 'one law for Mr. Galsworthy and another for Mr. Shaw?'

Both plays received a tremendous welcome. Galsworthy, determined nor to be overshadowed by the Barrie to follow, made a brief curtain speech. And, lest the audience might think the evening was over, I stepped forward to remind them that there was more to come. In the morning we awoke to an ecstatic press. For the whole of that day, and extending over the following week-end, friends and staff competed with each other in bringing printed praise to my notice. Many of the reviews referred to the 'star cast', which was an encouraging recognition of our ensemble, but it remained for the *Sunday Express* to give me the deepest personal satisfaction. 'The spirit of team-work will do for the London theatre what the actor-manager system did for it in the past. We are on the right tack at last.' This was certainly blowing the ReandeaN trumpet!

In the midst of all the excitement I remembered to write an apologetic letter to J.G. for my share in the gentle fracas at the dress rehearsal. In generous response I was invited up to Grove Lodge for lunch, where I was met by the largest sheepdog I had ever seen. During the meal, presided over by Ada Galsworthy, all charm and fibreglass, nothing was said about the affair, but afterwards, as J.G. and the sheepdog were seeing me off the premises, I was gravely told 'this must never happen again'. It never did. In all future productions each of us respected the other's territory. In family matters J.G. continued to show his interest, advising me upon such questions as where our sons should be sent to school. Inevitably they followed J.G.'s own scholastic route, going first to Elstree School under the care of the son of J.G.'s great friend, Ted Sanderson, and thence to Harrow.

About this time Max Reinhardt took over and renovated the lovely eighteenth-century Theater in der Josefstadt in Vienna, equipping it with descending and ascending crystal chandeliers to light and dim the auditorium. For his opening production he chose *Loyalties* under the German title of *Gesellschaft*. I must confess to the sin of pride when he wrote for a copy of my prompt book.

13

Alec Rea was so exhilarated by our success with *Loyalties* that he agreed to join George and myself on our annual pilgrimage to the Continent. We went first to Berlin, where Alec soon caught my enthusiasm for the latest lighting equipment, made by Schwabe Brothers under the direct inspiration of Max Reinhardt. We arranged for their chief technician, Herr Reiche, to visit us in London to prepare a scheme for a similar installation at the St. Martin's

From Berlin we went to Prague and Vienna. Eastern Europe was still very disturbed, and there was a great deal of distress in literary and musical circles. An international play agency in London had sent word of our coming to various writers in the hope that they might have plays suitable for us, but in Vienna they shunned our hospitality, at pains to conceal their distress. But in Budapest we met Albert Szermai, a charming Hungarian, who had achieved success with light musical pieces. He accepted our invitation to lunch for himself and two or three of his friends. Alec asked the *maître d'hôtel* to provide the most substantial meal of which the near-deserted hotel was capable. The menu included an enormous sturgeon, produced for our inspection beforehand. At lunch we did most of the talking, our guests being otherwise engaged: altogether an embarrassingly ravenous occasion!

We returned in time for the International Theatre Exhibition at the Victoria and Albert Museum in July, where there was a wonderful display of models and drawings by Gordon Craig and Adolphe Appia, recognised leaders of the new movement in the European theatre, as well as by artists less concerned with scenic design than with colour. A series of lectures was given in connection with the exhibition, to which I contributed a talk on 'The Actor and his Workshop.'* In the course of it I drew attention to the model exhibited by Norman Bel Geddes, a young American designer, for a production of *The Divine Comedy* in Madison Square Garden, New York. He planned to build a vast arena stage (no proscenium) across one corner of the great building with seats in a semi-circle round it, and a huge dome for background. The stage was to be made to sink to cellar level on a lift, where changes of scenery were to be effected in a few minutes of darkness. The project owed something to Max Reinhardt's Theatre of the Five Thousand; it was a fine, imaginative concept that did not get beyond the drawing-board. My comments aroused a curious backlash from St. John Ervine. In and article in *The Observer* he wrote:

> '. . . I protest that the proscenium arch, now so despised by
> theatrical revolutionaries, has been an immense blessing to

* This was subsequently printed and sold at our box-office.

the dramatist. All this contemporary tosh about the need for restoring the apron stage and the platform stage and all the rest of the obsolete paraphernalia of the theatre in process of evolution is spouted by people who have not yet realised that the proper place for an audience is outside the play not inside it. . . .'

The change in outlook since those words were written illustrates the kaleidoscopic nature of the theatre, constantly changing and turning in upon itself, but ever and anon returning to basic patterns. Truly, there is nothing intrinsically new in theatre craft, not even the spotlight!

Eight
In America, too

I

I went to America for the first time in August 1920 to produce both *The Skin Game* and *The Blue Lagoon*, knowing nothing of the conditions I should find when I got there. During the Atlantic crossing on board S.S. *Olympic*, pre-war veteran of the White Star Line, I spent much of my time in the company of Gilbert Miller, just then enjoying his first success as a London manager. He was one of a group of passengers, not all of them theatre men, who appeared to be immediately at home with the ship's daily round, knowing just what to do at what time. Their day began with early-morning gymnastics, held under the watchful eye of an ex-army instructor on the top deck or inside in the gymnasium where the pitch and roll of the ship were uncomfortably accentuated whenever it blew from the north-west. On such mornings you had to be nimble, else you might find yourself flung against an electric horse or camel, ending up with bruised knees or shoulder blades. Gilbert's determined efforts to achieve a much needed reduction in his weight were not helped by the generous meals which he ordered in advance from the French restaurant and which he sometimes invited me to share. His favourite dish, curtly described as a 'rack o' lamb', when brought to table for his inspection, looked enough to satisfy the whole sixth form. But then Gilbert always maintained that the consumption of meat made no difference to one's weight, a view which his appearance at the end of the voyage confirmed, although not in the way he intended.

He was ready with information about all that had happened in the American theatre during and after the war. Its business affairs were now largely in the hands of two theatre-owning circuits, the first run by Klaw and Erlanger, controlled almost six-hundred theatres throughout the States. (I subsequently learned that Klaw had seceded, leaving Erlanger the sole arbiter.) The Shubert Brothers, Sam, Jake and Lee, about whom stories of their 'pinch-hitting' habits were as numerous as the gags in a Marx Bros. film had built up a second empire in competition. Apart from the syndicates, Gilbert cited a number of independent managements, headed by that of Charles Frohman, run by the dead impresario's brother, Dan, but without his flair (Gilbert did much to restore the prestige of the Frohman Office when later he was appointed its direc-tor). The Theatre Guild, emerging from its chrysalis, the 'Province-town Players', was about to move into a theatre built specially for it in the Broadway district. There was, too, Henry Miller, Gilbert's father, an actor of distinction and part-owner of the New York theatre named after him, described by his son as 'the only gentle-man in the business'; also William A. Brady, for whom I was to produce *The Skin Game*.

Independent managers were forced to book their attractions with one or other of the syndicates in order to obtain showings in the big cities. The syndicates in their turn were often compelled to invest in the productions of the producing managers in order to keep their theatres open. Exploitation chasing its own tail! Actors' Equity, under the leadership of Clarence Derwent, a British Jewish actor who before his emigration to America had been a member of the first Horniman Company—I had taken over some of his parts after he left—was busy in the actors' interests. On the technical side production was fully unionised, and demarcation strictly observed; musicians, carpenters, electricians, and property men all jealously guarding their separate functions. I must be careful not to break the rules or dire results might follow. To top off his crescendo of warnings Gilbert told me wild stories of fortunes more often lost than won on Broadway 'at the drop of a hat'. All of this made up rather a frightening picture, yet one that left me unprepared for subsequent events.

2

After checking-in at my hotel and eating a hasty lunch, washed down with ice-water, I set out for the Playhouse on 48th Street,

William A. Brady's theatre where also he had his offices. There I had my first experience of the casual way in which American theatrical managers appeared to run their businesses. The telephone girl, doubling the duties of receptionist, stopped polishing her nails to tell me Mr. Brady was not available just now.

'Oh,' I protested, 'but I've just come from England.'

'Perhaps you would like to see Mr. So-and-So?'

'Yes, I would be glad to see Mr. So-and-So.'

But that gentleman had apparently never heard of *The Skin Game* nor of my contract to produce it. However, with a dismissive flourish of courtesy, he would be happy to tell me as soon as Mr. Brady was available. Where was I staying? Feeling rather forlorn I retired to the Gotham Hotel to await events, wondering whether I should ring up Gilbert at the Ritz-Carlton for comfort, or sit nursing my loneliness. Later that evening Mr. Brady did ring up and in a muffled voice said he would see me at the Playhouse the next morning. Subsequently I learned that the brush-off I had received was a way of concealing his drinking bouts. The introduction of prohibition had led to a vast amount of secret drinking, presumably in resentment against the infraction of American Liberty.

Next morning Brady was all smiles and apologies; he had been 'tied-up' the night before. This tough Irish-American was an intelligent man, who had somehow managed to reconcile his interest in the new drama with the production of some of the most frankly commercial plays to be seen on Broadway. At our first interview he used his Irish charm in an effort to brush aside the clauses in the contract that restricted his freedom of action. But Galsworthy, who always regarded the American theatre as brash and juvenile, had armed me with a stiff contract, giving me, among other things, complete control of the casting. (This contract was to set the pattern for similar arrangements in the future, and to open up a world of opportunity for me). Brady changed his tactics abruptly. Auditions for the cast had been called for the following morning on the stage of the Playhouse. The stage manager would give me a list of people to be interviewed. That was all.

Auditions are hateful affairs. At the best of times they have always made me nervous and uncomfortable. As I faced the little knot of British players with their strained anxious faces on the following morning I felt particularly unhappy. Gilbert had warned me that good English players were hard to come by in New York. Although many had remained in America during the late war, either for financial reasons or of choice, they were like deep water fish stranded in shoal water, gasping for opportunity.

I knew we should have the greatest difficulty in filling some of the important parts. Fortunately, Brady had agreed to 'import' Herbert Lomas to play Hornblower: he proved every bit as good as Edmund Gwenn in the part. I had also been asked to engage an English girl for the Meggie Albanesi part because 'English *ingenues* are unobtainable in New York'. Joan Maclean was in fact a Scots lassie with attractive ways and modest talent. Marsh Allen, one of the first British actors to be interviewed that morning, proved a happy choice for Mr. Hillcrist, but there was no one present who was even remotely possible for Mary Clare's part of Chloe. The audition had proceeded slowly for the first half-hour or so when there was a stir amongst the waiting actors. A well-dressed, well-corseted lady, looking remarkably like Marie Tempest, approached the prompt table, escorted by the stage manager.

'What name?' I asked innocently. The stage manager gasped.

'Grace George,' she said with an ingratiating smile.

'What part?' I asked. She looked surprised.

'I imagine, for the part of Chloe.'

'Would you mind reading a few lines?' She did so. Before she had finished the first page I interrupted her, explaining courteously that I did not think the part would suit her.

'Oh!' she gasped, 'then I shall have to tell Mr. Brady,' and she walked away. Everybody was aghast, for she was an American star of great taste and intelligence and Brady's wife. In fact he had bought the play for her. Soon the story was ringing round Broadway: 'Who's the English guy who's sacked Grace George?' Overnight I had acquired a reputation for toughness that was to cling to me for years; it was far removed from the nervous anxiety with which I approached production on Broadway.

The rehearsals were disordered and nerve-racking, quite unlike the disciplined conditions to which I was accustomed at home. For example, we never knew from one day to the next upon what stage we were to rehearse. Called to one theatre in the morning, we were liable to be sent elsewhere after an hour or so or else summarily ejected to make way for another rehearsal, perhaps a troupe of tap dancers, granted a prior claim by one of the numerous business managers with which the syndicates appeared to be encrusted. There was no rehearsal furniture, just a few bentwood chairs and a packing case or two. To touch the furniture packs neatly piled on the stage for the evening's play was sternly forbidden. Spittoons were available at either side of the stage, but no ashtrays.

When the furniture for our dress rehearsal finally arrived I was warned by a scared stage manager when I dared to adjust the angles at which certain chairs had been set. 'If you do that again,' he said, 'the crew will walk out.' When an actor asked me what he should do while he was kept waiting in a scene, I said, 'Oh, light a cigarette.' He did so. Immediately a stentorian voice yelled from the back of the pit: 'Put that cigarette out!' Then an infuriated house manager strode down the stalls gangway, still yelling. Argument between us rose to top pitch. Finally, I had to obtain special dispensation from head office for the cigarette to be smoked as part of the business of the play. Then the disrupted rehearsal was resumed. No wonder, I thought, that British actors stranded in New York appear so distrait at rehearsal. The stage crews, on the other hand, working short hours for extremely high wages, were both quick and capable.

The Skin Game opened in New York at the Bijou Theatre on October 20th, 1920: the first of many first nights in New York, which always left me baffled by the undemonstrative behaviour of the habitual first-nighters, known as 'the death watch'. I missed the warm welcome of the London 'gallery-ites' or their equally noisy disapproval, which was certainly preferable to this cool attitude of 'Well, show me'. At curtain fall the audiences, preoccupied with the scramble for car and taxi, preferred to reserve judgment on what they had just seen until the all-powerful critics had spoken in the morning. Managers and actors went in mortal fear of newspaper strictures. It was dreary, sitting in a Child's restaurant, sipping coffee and awaiting the verdict of the early editions which were usually on the streets by 1 a.m. Actors brought over from England were anxious about the length of their American engagements, but those resident in America were blasé, and went sensibly home to supper and bed.

In the case of *The Skin Game* the verdict was mixed, many critics holding Brady to be greatly daring in presenting English highbrow drama to Broadway audiences not fully recovered from the brashness of wartime, a view neatly summarised at curtain fall by a well-known writer of children's books: 'A play for adults in New York, how refreshing!' Among the many follow-up articles one from *The New York Herald* pleased me mightily: 'Every character listens with an intentness rare on the New York stage to what the other has to say.' After an equivocal start the play settled down to become the dramatic success of the season.

3

The production of *The Blue Lagoon* for the Shuberts was a comic-opera performance from first to last. Lee Shubert was a quiet little man with hard unrelenting eyes that belied his gentle voice. During a brief visit to London his acquisitive nature had been aroused by our crowded houses. When I pointed out that the scenic effects were an essential part of the entertainment and required most careful preparation, he brushed this aside, as though his signature on the contract were all that was necessary for success. Purchase of the play for America proved to be one of his flights of fancy.

So soon as *The Skin Game* rehearsals were in train I wrote to him from my hotel, asking him what date was set down for *The Blue Lagoon*. I had no reply. So I went round to his office to make enquiries, and found it to be more of a madhouse even than the Brady office. No one had ever heard of *The Blue Lagoon*, let alone of my contract to produce it. 'Mr. Lee'—the name by which he was known to all his satellites—was tied up for the next hour or so. 'Would I wait or call again tomorrow?' I called daily for the next week. Always 'Mr. Lee' was either busy or out of town. I grew tired of waiting about in one or other of his corridors of power, listening to angry arguments over the telephone by members of his staff, who all seemed to be living in a mild state of frenzy lest 'Mr. Lee's' displeasure should put their livelihoods at risk. In the end I retired to my hotel to await a definite appointment.

When eventually we met, it took Lee quite a few minutes to recall the play that he had purchased. When I began to explain the play's requirements he cut me short. There was plenty of scenery in store. One scene that he had in mind was used last season for a musical comedy about the South Seas; it would be just the thing; would I look it over? As to the cast I should see his casting director; he did not bother to give me his name nor in what office he was to be found. Pursuing his economy thought, he said the music and the scenic effects could be done without; technicians were very expensive and to consult them beforehand would be an unnecessary expense; finally, there was no need for a stage manager before rehearsals began. Auditions for the cast would be arranged, but nobody was able to advise me as to which actors were suitable because no one had read the script. In despair I gave up and wrote to 'Mr. Lee', advising a year's postponement, by which time it might be possible to release some of the London cast. The plan would also give time for a new production to be built from our original designs. This was agreed after an exchange of cables with London to obtain postponement of the film production. I left New York with that responsibility postponed for one year.

4

The warmth of American hospitality is proverbial, but I should have had a thin time of it during those first days in New York but for Gilbert Miller's friendliness. He went to great trouble to introduce me to his friends and to people of importance in the American theatre. I particularly remember a visit to Florenz Ziegfeld and Billie Burke at their country home one week-end—I think it was at Great Neck—and being astonished at the luxurious surroundings no less than by the menagerie of expensive pets with which Flo had peopled the place, although watching Billie with some of them made me wonder whether she was as pleased with these proofs of her husband's adoration as he expected her to be. Another clear memory is of a week with Holbrook Blinn—a great romantic actor—and his wife at their farm in Connecticut in late September, and of my surprise at seeing an abundance of ripe peaches still on the trees in their orchard, while higher up the valley the sun had already begun its early-morning battles with Jack Frost. Although American actors appeared to live in a closed world of their own—in snobbish terms they were not 'received' by Society—I made many easy friendships, with no obligation to endure on either side, and found in so much exuberant good nature a relief from the cut and thrust of theatrical Broadway.

In the city the dancing craze was in full spate. In every hotel, restaurant and club, wherever there was space enough, and sometimes ignoring that necessity, men and women of all ages would foregather and, scarce pausing to order supper or dinner, would be out on the parquet floors, rubbing shoulders with their own or someone else's partner. The wartime dancing stars Mr. and Mrs. Vernon Castle had set the trend for Carl and Dorothy Hyson and others who were drawing immense crowds to the more fashionable clubs where business tycoons produced flasks from bulging hip-pockets in open rejection of prohibition. Expensively private dances at the Ritz-Carlton Hotel on Sunday nights, to which I found myself invited, ignored the 18th Amendment even more barefacedly. On all occasions our *ingenue* became my dancing partner. Caught up in the general exhilaration we flung ourselves into all the feverish excitement with zest, and fell irresponsibly, but not irretrievably, in love. That was one emotional battle I did not have to fight alone.

5

Part of the information which Gilbert Miller had poured into my ears during my first Atlantic crossing concerned the developments in lighting that had taken place in America during the war. Without going into a mass of technicalities of little interest to the general reader, it is sufficient to explain that by using metal grids in place of carbon filaments the Americans had developed a range of electric lamps which, when used with appropriate lenses and reflectors, were powerful enough to supersede the open arc lamps still in use in the theatre at home. These spotlights, as they were called, are now in such universal use and for such a variety of purposes that it is difficult to imagine how worthwhile results were obtained without them. Gilbert maintained that they were America's greatest contribution to stage lighting since Edison invented the electric globe.

The new equipment revived my Liverpool dreams. Without counting their cost (until a banker's draft arrived from London to pay for them), I ordered several crates of spotlights of all sizes, together with the new slider-type dimmers that had been developed for controlling the light, to be shipped in great secrecy as passenger freight on my return home in the *Olympic*. It would be exciting to be the first to introduce the new equipment into a London theatre, I thought, but as I watched the men unloading my crates on the quayside at Southampton I was shocked to see precisely similar crates being landed in the name of Gilbert Miller! They were wanted for the St. James's Theatre, while mine were, of course, destined for the St. Martin's.

The sequel to the use of incandescent lamps in place of arcs on the stage came with their use in the auditorium. I am not sure whether I first saw this in America or in Germany, but certainly not at home, where front lighting was still confined to arcs placed at the back or side of the gallery or in the dome of the theatre. Ours

Above *Loyalties*. Capt. Dansey (Eric Maturin) and Ferdinand de Levis (Ernest Milton) confront each other in a famous London club. Other members present played by Dawson Milward, Edmund Breon, J. H. Roberts, Malcolm Keen and Ben Field

Below Barrie's one-act conundrum: *Shall We Join the Ladies?* Puzzle: spot the stars. Answer: all were stars in this play

Above   The street scene in *East of Suez*. His Majesty's Theatre, 1922

Below   The terrace of the House of Commons in *London Life*, Theatre Royal, Drury Lane, 1924

These photographs show the tremendous scale of the scenery employed to induce a sense of the open air into our spectacular scenes. (The Great Gate of Pekin was 45 ft. high and built in low relief.)

was the first theatre to install permanent spots in the auditorium. There was a heated discussion, I remember, between my electrician and an L.C.C. official, a little man with a cherrywood umbrella and a bowler hat, who at first would not agree to the proposal because of the risk of their exploding among the audience. He looked at our baby spots as though they were Mills bombs!

British firms could hardly be blamed for their backwardness in this matter. During World War I they had other things to think about. But I was disappointed when the lamp manufacturers refused my repeated requests to start making the various new types of lamps required for the new lighting techniques now being developed. They said the demand would not justify the expense. Consequently the lamps had to be imported, too. After each visit to New York I brought more of them home. I used to watch the crates being dumped on the dockside at Southampton with butterfly tremors. If my precious lamps were smashed the new equipment would be useless.

6

In the late spring of 1921 when *A Bill of Divorcement* was packing the St. Martin's Theatre in London I received visits from two artists previously unknown to me. One was Allan Pollock, an Englishman, who before the war had been a star of the American theatre. Enlisting in the British Army on the outbreak of war, he rose to the rank of captain and was severely wounded in 1916 at the Battle of Loos. He lay out in front of the enemy wire with half his jaw shot away, unable to make his presence known to the search parties, but he was finally rescued in the nick of time twenty-four hours later. He spent the next three years in various hospitals and rehabilitation centres. Now he was anxious to make his comeback by playing Malcolm Keen's part in New York. He pleaded with me so hard, as though all his hopes of rehabilitation depended upon my consent. His mutilated appearance put me off at first, yet he had a delightful personality and told his story in simple, modest words with just that degree of nervous tension which the part demanded. After consulting Clemence Dane I agreed to let him have the play, provided he was able to find an American management to sponsor the production, because, of course, he had neither the resources nor organisation with which to carry out his plan, just a gratuity and some war savings.

M

My second visitor was Katharine Cornell, a young American actress who had recently been appearing in London as Jo in a dramatisation of Louisa M. Alcott's *Little Women,* in which she had scored a considerable success. Now she had come to ask for Meggie's part in America. She had been in touch with Allan Pollock, and both had been lobbying Clemence Dane. No sooner had agreement been reached on these and kindred matters than I received a visit from an American manager who came smiling and laughing into my office to declare his enthusiasm for the play. This was Charles B. Dillingham, a producing manager associated with Klaw and Erlanger, which Gilbert Miller had told me were superior to the rival Shubert syndicate. Dillingham was not in the least nonplussed when I told him that arrangements had already been made. 'Oh, that'll be all right. I know Pollock quite well. He's a good actor, but he'll have to have a management. I'll soon fix things. Where's he staying? And what are the terms?' And he bounced out of the office chuckling, as though the whole thing were a huge joke. Here was a manager of an altogether different type from those with whom I had done business hitherto.

7

It was almost twelve months to the day that I found myself once again on board the *Olympic,* bound for New York. Once again Gilbert Miller was a fellow-traveller, still doing his exercises before breakfast, still valiantly consuming his rack o' lamb and still my willing mentor, although no longer treating me as novitiate in the business of theatrical management. I was under contract to produce *A Bill of Divorcement* for Dillingham, but first the comic-opera performance in the Shubert office had to reach its climax.

The George Harris designs, complete with scale drawings, meticulously set out as usual, had been forwarded to Shubert well in advance, so I assumed the production would at least be on the way by the time I arrived. But the drawings had been either lost or purposely put on one side, and so nothing whatever had been done. I cabled for the colour sketches hanging in the foyer of the St. Martin's Theatre to be sent out by quickest means. Meanwhile, I did my best to cope with the casting. Fortunately, we were able to release Harold French to repeat his London performance; he was partnered by Frances Carson, a beautiful young woman but too mature for Faith Celli's part, and there were good actors for the rest of the cast.

The Blue Lagoon was the kind of naïve offering to encourage the best (or worst) of caustic comment from the New York critics. The opening night was a shambles. Each succeeding paper that I opened in the small hours of the morning seemed to have something worse to say than its predecessor. Some were downright rude, others preferred ridicule, such as: 'In America we have had actors, too.' Another critic was more subtle: 'We are only just beginning to realise what the war really did in London.' Even the spectacular effects came unstuck, because no one on the Shubert staff had given a thought to the techniques that had brought us success in London. One paper dryly remarked that to make the wind blow in one direction and the driving rain in another produced a weird effect. But it remained for a woman's journal to give our efforts the quietus: 'This is a play for the British leisured classes'. . . . It was just as well that the Clemence Dane play was due in New York a few weeks later, for my stock as the young English producer who had dared to sack Grace George on his first visit was very low indeed.

8

A Bill of Divorcement was the first production in America that I made for Charles Dillingham. As I was to be associated with him upon several occasions in succeeding years perhaps I should here set down my impressions of a unique character, a nineteenth-century theatrical manager strayed into the twentieth. When I met him first Charlie Dillingham was already established as the *beau sabreur* of the Broadway bright lights; handsome, well educated, generous to the point of eccentricity, with a lovely and expensive wife who moved in exclusive New York society. He was an amateur among hard-bitten professional Jewish operators in the theatrical 'exchange and mart'; or, if you prefer, a gentleman rider on the roundabouts of 42nd Street, laughing and joking his way past all the financial red lights until he reached the inevitable crash-barrier. Yet he had undoubted flair that brought him many successes which his extravagant optimism invariably dissipated. When we first met he was in the heyday of his fortune, part proprietor of the Globe Theatre at the very centre of Broadway, where Ed Wynn and other popular comedians earned him several fortunes and where he had his offices from which he hurried to obey frequent summonses to appear before his financial judge, the formidable Abe Erlanger at the New Amsterdam Theatre on 42nd Street.

Pollock and Dillingham between them had secured an admirable cast, headed by Katharine Cornell as Sydney Fairfield and Janet Beecher, a great favourite with American audiences, playing Mrs. Fairfield quite as well as Lilian Braithwaite in London. The rest of the cast were English and included Ada King, sent over to play Aunt Hester. Owing to the delays caused by my struggle with the Shubert management, I had taken little part in the advance preparations, but I was able to rehearse the company for three weeks. The play opened at the Broad Street Theatre, Philadelphia, on the 26th September, 1921, and received thoughtful criticism and high praise for the acting.

When the play opened at the George M. Cohan Theatre on Broadway on October 10th success was nearly snatched from us because of the folly of Abe Erlanger himself. He had foolishly booked the play to open in New York on the same night as three other major attractions, with the result that our play received only brief mention in the Press. There was only $200 in the house on the second night. Erlanger thought he had a failure on his hands, and decided to close the play immediately. He booked another attraction to take its place the following week. But by the Wednesday morning the situation had begun to change and by Thursday evening the manager calculated that the week's receipts would total $15,000, a success largely due to 'Kit' Cornell's performance in Meggie's part, in which she laid the foundations of her eventual stardom. So Erlanger had to find another home for Allan Pollock and his companions. Fortunately, the Times Square Theatre was available and there Clemence Dane's play became the dramatic hit of the season: the second year running that a ReandeaN importation had achieved this distinction. I did not see the New York first night, leaving within days of the Philadelphia opening because of urgent requests from home where preparations for *Will Shakespeare* were well advanced. Consequently, I only learned of Erlanger's goings-on from reading a sharp criticism of it in the *New York Times*. I was not altogether surprised, for it was beginning to dawn upon me that these circuit men with their armfuls of theatres were property-owners and not theatre men at all.

9

The most revered American producer of the immediate post-war years was David Belasco. Indeed, reverence is the aptest description of the regard in which he was held on Broadway, where his name was mentioned with bated breath. I was particularly anxious to meet him because of his greatest reputation as a lighting expert. Once again Gilbert Miller used his good offices to secure me an interview with the great man during my second season in New York. This took place one morning at the Belasco Theatre. There was an atmosphere of religious quiet about the theatre that reminded me of my interview with Hall Caine many years earlier, as I followed a soft-footed attendant into the presence. The room, with its dark velvet furnishings and concealed lighting, was more like a bishop's study than a theatrical manager's office. The clerical atmosphere was accentuated by the dog-collar which I was told Belasco always wore. He invited me to be seated and then began to speak with religious fervour of the mission of the American theatre to colonise the world stage with its high ideals—of which he was evidently the exemplar. Knowing that he had not of late produced any plays of notable literary quality—in fact, hokum would not be too harsh a description for many of them—I found this nauseating. With the arrogance of the newcomer, I considered respect for his audience's intelligence to be a manager's positive duty, forgetting of course, my own lapses!

There was a kind of sentimental 'goo' spread over Belasco's productions that effectively concealed any weakness there might be in the dramas. Nevertheless, I was grateful to him for allowing me to spend many hours with his chief electrician, Hartmann, who was the technical brain behind his theatre's reputation for lighting. I called on this artist-technician every time I went to America and learned much. Upon one occasion he showed me some experiments he had been conducting in the use of reflected light. By directing the spotlights on to reflectors coated with a special paint, and mounting his reflectors on universal joints, he was not only obtaining effects of rare softness, but by adjustment was able so to direct the light that it was impossible to trace its source from the auditorium. Hartmann gave me one of his reflectors and a copy of the paint formula. We installed the system at the St. Martin's, and achieved wonderful effects of intimacy with it.

10

I went back to New York the following year to produce *Loyalties*, crossing in the S.S. *Majestic*, having, in company with other regular migrants, deserted the old *Olympic* in favour of the faster and more luxurious vessel. By this time I knew that all Dillingham productions were sponsored by the Erlanger circuit, but, as I had not yet encountered the redoubtable Abe personally, I feared no ill. On the morning of my arrival I had scarcely reached the Ritz-Carlton—I had promoted myself to that haunt of the rich and successful—when the telephone rang and there was Charlie with his usual chuckle.

'Oh,' he said, 'did you have a good trip?'

'Marvellous,' I said, 'and thank you for the telegram. But what do I do with the roses?'

He chuckled again at my embarrassment and then said: 'Abe wants to see you in the morning.'

'Who's Abe?' I asked.

'Abe Erlanger.'

'What for?' I said rather sharply, mindful of Galsworthy's stern warnings against any interference with the play.

'Oh, he just wants to talk to you,' said Dillingham soothingly.

The following morning I made my way to the New Amsterdam Theatre on 42nd Street and was immediately shown into the great man's presence. I had heard that he regarded himself as the Napoleon of the American theatre. A statuette of that emperor on the desk in front of him seemed to confirm the rumour, but his posture could hardly be described as imperial. A corpulent little man, bald as an egg, he was seated in a swivel chair in his shirt-sleeves, with his feet on the desk, and within aiming distance of a brass spittoon. These highly polished receptacles—it was the special duty of Negro handymen to keep them so—had not yet been banished from America's offices. The shades were down, flapping gently in the hot and steaming draught from the surrounding buildings. Below, the roar of traffic on 42nd Street, with tramcars still adding their quota to the clangour, made conversation sharp and edgy.

'Come in, Barsle. Sit right down. Cigar?'

'No, thank you.' (A pause.) 'Mr. Dillingham says you want to see me?'

'Sure I do,' and he spat into the spittoon. 'You gotta great property there in that *Loyalties*.'

'Yes,' I said crisply. 'It's Mr. Galsworthy's best play so far.'

'Sure, sure, I know that,' he said musingly, and spat again.

I wiped the sweat from my neck while I waited nervously for the purpose of the interview.

'There's just one little suggestion I wanna make.'

'Oh,' I said, immediately mounting my high horse. 'Mr. Galsworthy won't agree to any alterations, if that's what . . .'

Mr. Erlanger interrupted my brusquerie.

'Nah, nah, Barsle, take it easy, boy. I just wanna make a little suggestion.'

'Well?' I said.

Erlanger gazed at the ceiling, mopping his bald head. 'A great property.' Then swivelling his beady bespectacled eyes on me, he added: 'An' I don' want you to miss it.'

Still I waited.

'Yer see, it's like this. We gotta big Jewish population in this city, and they're great supporters of the theatre. Now I don't want them to think this play is anti-Jewish, and . . .'

'It's not,' I said quickly. 'It's a contest between two outlooks . . .'

Before I could say more, he put a pudgy hand forward to stop me. His face reddened. He was obviously angry at my recalcitrance.

'Just listen to me, will yer?' His voice toughened. 'I guess I know more about this little old city than you do. This is a great property and I want us all to have a smash hit. Now, I got this little suggestion.' Again he spat into the spittoon with remarkable accuracy. 'Just a little alteration: nothing more. You've got a contest in there between a Britisher and a young Jewish gentleman.' (Pause). 'An' the Jew wants the money back wot the Britisher's stolen. Right?'

'Well?' I said.

'Now that may offend our Jewish audience and that'ud damage the property. See?'

'What's your suggestion?' I asked. 'I shall have to cable the author,' adding rather gratuitously: 'I'm sure he won't agree.'

'My suggestion is that we change the Jewish part in there into a Scotchman. Now, what d'yer say?'

No cable was sent.

The all-British cast included Charles Quartermaine (brother of Leon) as Captain Dancey, and James Dale as De Levis—a first-class performance, by the way, nearly as good, but not quite, as Ernest Milton's. Other members of the ReandeaN Company sent over for important parts were Lawrence Hanray for Mr. Twisden and Lord St. Erth, and Felix Aylmer as General Canynge.

Loyalties arrived at Dillingham's Globe Theatre in the heart of Broadway on September 27th, 1922. A cordial telegram from David Belasco was especially gratifying. That he had deigned to notice me was final proof of my acceptance into the close fraternity of Anglo-American producers. We received a surprisingly warm welcome from the 'death-watch', less vociferous than in London, but that was just a difference in temperament. By one o'clock in the morning the Press had confirmed the verdict: we had a big hit! There was at that time a certain amount of envy of the more polished style of English acting, and especially a prejudice against what was known as the 'English accent'. It was gratifying therefore that our ensemble was highly praised. 'Everyone in this English company could be clearly heard', wrote more than one reviewer.

Abe Erlanger's fears lest the play be considered anti-Jewish were not realised. The *New York American* went out of its way to deny in bold headlines the existence of anti-semitic feeling, and a prominent rabbi called a special meeting in his synagogue to discuss the characters in the play.

As late as April in the following year, when the company was visiting Chicago, Burns Mantle, a prominent New York columnist contributed a long article to the *Chicago Tribune*, which ended with the gratifying comment: 'I don't wonder that *Loyalties* is the one play they talk most about in the club cars running between New York and points west. . . .'

.   .   .   .   .

I did not enjoy my American successes as much as I might have done because anxiety about *Hassan* was increasing rather than diminishing. Both Mme Flecker and Delius were growing restive under the long delay. To make matters worse Alec had dug his toes in. There were to be no more advance payments to the poet's widow. The third and last of our options would expire next spring. Still keeping my financial blinkers on, I persuaded Dillingham to introduce me to Michel Fokine then living in New York. Over a sumptuous dinner Charlie told the great *maître de ballet* fabulous tales about the play, which he had not read, and about the wonderful ballet music, which he had not heard. I think Fokine was more impressed by the composer's name than by Charlie's ebullience. I was overjoyed when he agreed, subject to reservations as to date, to come to London to compose the ballets. This information helped me to restrain Mme Flecker from bolting with the script of the play in her teeth, so to speak, into the arms of another producer.

Nine
Return to His Majesty's

I

My success at the St. Martin's attracted the notice of the big commercial managements, who began to ask themselves whether this provincial newcomer might not be useful to them. I heard about this from Golding Bright, the leading play agent who represented most of the established dramatists; he also looked after the interests of certain prominent actors and actresses, more as a personal favour than as a matter of business. Thus began a system of personal management that is now a commonplace of the entertainment world. By the exercise of shrewd judgment concealed behind a charmingly casual air he had acquired immense influence with the West End managers. He would sit in his little upstairs office just off Leicester Square, telephoning his advice on plays and players, always benign, always good-humoured, pulling endless strings in a variety of directions and almost invariably to good effect. Outside the theatre he had only one interest, the racecourse, his mental relaxation a study of the Book of Form.

At every first night he was to be seen in his accustomed place at the end of the fourth row of the stalls, wearing white gloves, which he kept on throughout the evening in an attempt to cure himself of the habit of biting his nails. So soon as the curtain rose he would drift into somnolence. The play's chances had already been weighed up with astonishing accuracy before he sold it, tactful indications given as to where the blue pencil was necessary and suggestions made as to the cast. He could afford to await the outcome with calm. He was a unique character in an age that was fast shedding its eccentricities. Golding was also a director of our provincial organisation, the DEE CEE Company (so named after the initial letters of myself and Clift) which we had formed to exploit ReandeaN successes in the provinces. It was to him that I owed my introduction to the commercial theatre.

After the death of Tree His Majesty's Theatre entered troubled waters for a brief period, but it was safe-harboured when George Grossmith, popular star of the Gaiety Theatre, and J. A. E. Malone, former stage director for George Edwardes and later London representative of the Australian J. C. Williamson syndicate, joined in partnership to take over Tree's 'beautiful theatre'. One might have expected 'Gee-Gee', his nickname in musical-comedy circles, to bring the Gaiety policy with him, but it was not so. His secret ambition was to don the mantle of the Chief, whether out of a belief in his own histrionic ability or for purposes of *réclame* was never made quite clear. Rumour had it that his sights were set upon an official accolade. . . .

The new management, having little idea how to achieve their object, Pat Malone, prompted by Golding Bright, sent for me one day to ask whether I would care to produce a play for them. My pulse began to race a bit, but I replied with what sounded to me admirable calm: 'I should be happy to do so, provided of course I like the play.' Not in the least taken in by my cheeky answer, Pat replied with equal calm, 'It's by Somerset Maugham,' after which, taking my acceptance for granted, he went on to describe the play. It was *East of Suez*, a melodrama, set in China. It would give wonderful opportunities for scenery and costume. 'Just the very thing for Harris,' I thought. Oriental crowds, colourful lighting, just the thing to delight a young producer's heart.

'Gee-Gee' and Pat, the most accommodating managers I ever met, wisely left all the casting to Golding Bright and myself, and all the production matters to me alone. Their job was simply to sign contracts. In the cast the Establishment was well represented by Ursula Millard, former leading lady to Lewis Waller, Basil Rathbone and C. V. France; Meggie Albanesi, released to play the leading part of the Eurasian girl, Daisy, and Malcolm Keen and Ivor Barnard came from the ReandeaN Company. Harris, as designer and I as director revelled in our unwonted freedom from financial anxiety. During our continental journey we had discovered in Munich two books full of wonderful photographs of Chinese buildings, temples, etc. These supplied the architectural information we required for the scenery.

2

Maugham began his play with a spectacular street scene, for which he had provided no dialogue, merely a general indication of the activities to be seen in the narrow streets bordering on the Great Gate of Peking. George built the gate in low relief and placed it at the back of the stage; it towered forty feet high, with various shops clustered round it. There were street-lamps complete with modern arc lighting, a Ford motor-car and goodness knows what other realistic details beside. On the flat roof of a café we placed a Chinese orchestra. For music in the Chinese style, to be played throughout this scene and during the various interludes, I turned to Eugene Goossens. He and I went down to Chinatown where, in a crowded pub, Eugene took out pencil and paper and jotted down tunes played endlessly on stringed instruments by smiling Chinese.

The forty or more Chinese of both sexes, engaged to act as shop-keepers and general crowd in the street scenes, were not easy to handle. The majority of them could speak no English. Instructions had to be relayed to them in their own language. If I suggested 'business' to which they took exception all action ceased immediately, like a 'held frame' in a movie, and dozens of almond eyes stared relentlessly at me. However, I was fortunate in having the assistance of Henry Petersen, whose knowledge of Chinese behaviour and ways of thought was invaluable. He was at my elbow throughout rehearsals to relay my instructions and to correct any that might be regarded as loss of face. News of our preparations soon spread beyond the stage-door. The *Sunday Express* wrote a special article, praising the fact that the new group of artists to whom the destinies of the great theatre were about to be entrusted, citing Harris and myself, Eugene Goossens, and especially Meggie Albanesi, 'were all young—young—young!'

3

I was intensely nervous at the first rehearsal as I gazed at the assembled company, seated in a semi-circle, waiting to read their parts. For here was I back on the stage of London's foremost theatre, in charge where formerly I had been general dog's body. I had brought with me one of my stage managers from the St. Martin's, a highly efficient young man, part of whose job it was to read out the stage directions. Of course he had the stage manager's sharp eye for the properties that would be required. In the first act, Daisy, the half-caste, played by Meggie Albanesi, calls upon her English fiancé at his office in Peking, and tea is served. At the mention of tea my stage manager looked up suddenly: 'China tea, I suppose, Mr. Dean? And what sort of sandwiches would you like?' Feeling self-conscious with the distinguished author sitting beside me, I said rather irritably: 'Oh, I don't know. Cucumber, I should think.' Then Maugham suddenly spluttered: 'It's the l-l-last th-th-thing they'd have.'

Throughout the rehearsals he remained withdrawn, neither helpful nor obstructive, never offering advice unless it was asked for. I think he found the whole business tiresome and the actors' arguments rather petty. Yet, when appealed to, he was always ready with the unconvincing response: 'Oh, ex-excellent!' Once I asked him whether I might cut certain lines: 'Wh-wh-why not?' he spluttered. 'The st-st-stage is a w-w-workshop.' The significance of his attitude was that Maugham lacked genuine enthusiasm for the theatre.

All my ReandeaN stalwarts gave splendid performances, although Meggie Albanesi failed to achieve the brilliance of her work at dress rehearsal. She always had a tendency to play emotional scenes with tightened vocal chords and this tendency to overstrain invariably led to throat trouble, particularly when she was 'burning the candle at both ends', as was now often the case. She developed laryngitis. However, with Sybil Thorndike devotedly acting as dressing-room nurse, she managed to struggle through the first night, but had to be replaced immediately afterwards by her understudy, Norah Robinson. Her disappointment was bitter. She knew that, according to her own exacting standards, she had failed. Nevertheless, the critics praised her for a wonderful performance. All agreed her pathos was utterly moving, yet she always protested she had let me down upon that occasion, which was an absurdity. Yet it is profitless to interfere with the self-criticism of an artist.

The play was produced on September 2nd, 1922. The critics were not impressed, although most of them grudgingly admitted the box-office value of the spectacular scenes. The *Sunday Times* began its criticism by noting that 'the stage of this famous and beautiful theatre is once more in the possession of a man of letters', while the *Observer* trumpeted that 'We have now got a play which is a play and not an excuse for scenery and inadequate clothes.' The employment of real Chinese on the stage was meat and drink to the gossip writers, the *Sheffield Mail* declaring that Chinese actors should remain 'East of Suez'.

4

From the very first days of ReandeaN I had lived in a whirl of production, the pressure increasing each passing year. Living at full stretch, alerted to each new crisis, up or down the ladder, began to affect my health. This was remarked upon by Pat Malone as we shook hands on the agreement to produce *East of Suez*: 'You'll kill yourself if you go on like this.' But it never occurred to me to stop or that I should crack up if I did not. This is not a medical history, so there is no need to enter into details. Sufficient to say that after my last visit to America a series of febrile attacks of increasing violence and at decreasing intervals caused such concern to Marguerite Rea, born nurse that she was—she missed her vocation; as the matron of a big London hospital she would have been superb— that she packed me off to various specialists, none of whom could find the answer. Finally, she persuaded 'Tommy' Horder*—she was on familiar terms with many of the distinguished owners of door-plates in Harley Street—to come out to St. John's Wood to observe me alternately sweating and shivering with a temperature of 103 degrees. But the great diagnostician could only say 'You must have a poison factory somewhere.' This led to the operating theatre, where Mr. Walton, a leading surgeon of the day, at the end of what was called an exploratory operation, found nothing. (Later, Mr. Walton received a knighthood, but not for that exploit.) While I was convalescing at my partner's lovely home in Kent I had my worst attack of fever to date, which drove 'Nurse' Marguerite into a frenzy of activity among blood tests and other clinical devices.

The year 1923 was to be one of violent contrasts, beginning in an atmosphere of anxiety and poor health, soaring to a personal triumph and ending in a mood of tragedy that I shared with all my associates. Before it was far advanced, in fact while I was still in hospital, Messrs.

* Later Lord Horder.

Grossmith and Malone—I always thought of them like that, as a firm, never as separate personages—came to see me. I woke up one afternoon to see them standing, one on either side of the bed, Pat Malone, the bluff Irishman, beaming encouragingly at me, while Grossmith, after courteous enquiry, proceeded with much charm and circumlocution to broach the purpose of their visit. *East of Suez* was still doing well, but plans for the future had to be made. And so to the point: 'Would I direct a revival of Arthur Pinero's *The Gay Lord Quex* with himself as the gay lord?' In an inspired moment, induced possibly by a rising temperature, I thought, 'Here is the opening for *Hassan* at last!' After an appropriate show of diffidence I said: 'Yes, I will do it for you if you will let me do *Hassan* immediately afterwards.' In such prosaic language was our bargain struck and the way to fulfilment of my promise made clear. . . .

5

I faced the prospect of rehearsing *The Gay Lord Quex* with a good deal of trepidation, knowing that Pinero had always directed his own plays, and that he had a legendary reputation for strict discipline at rehearsals. As the acknowledged leader of the dramatists of the pre-war era he was still a formidable figure, while I represented the new spirit in the theatre. Gossips were speculating as to how we should get on together, prophesying that the combination of old and new methods would not work and could only result in a blazing row and my early retirement from the scene. But matters did not turn out that way.

The great man agreed that I should rehearse the play for the first two weeks. Then he would descend upon us to inspect our progress. Grossmith was highly nervous at the prospect. On the appointed day Pinero arrived, dressed in a heavy broadcloth over-coat, a square Churchill bowler, and wearing a pair of Sleep's driving gloves. He solemnly mounted the stairs to sit with me in the front row of the dress circle, while Grossmith waited on the stage for the rehearsal to begin. He was positively jiggling with nervousness, quite unable to restrain the toothy smile often featured by caricaturists.

'Are you there, Sir Arthur?' he called out impatiently.

'I'm here, George,' growled Pinero.

'What would you like us to do?'

'I think we'll do the bedroom scene, George; that's the most difficult.'

The rehearsal began. Pinero said nothing for a little while. I was sweating at the palms. Then suddenly he put his gloved hand in front of his mouth, turned to me and whispered in staccato tones:

'I rather think our friend George's made a mistake.'

I made some inconsequent reply and the rehearsal proceeded. When the scene was over, Grossmith looked up expectantly at us evidently anxious for the verdict.

'I'm coming down, George,' said Pinero.

Then turning to me and again putting his gloved hand in front of his face, he murmured:

'Plays the part like a Fulham chemist.'

For the remainder of the rehearsals 'Pin' took charge of the company's elocution, speaking the lines for them with precise Edwardian diction and Victorian emphases. For the women's parts he assumed a high-pitched voice, tossing his completely bald head in the air to indicate annoyance or petulance. Even that fine old actress, Rosina Filippi, was not spared his tutelage. This left me free to supervise the staging of the play, the grouping, the lighting, etc., all of which received high praise, especially Harris's garden scene. Poor George Grossmith, after his encounters with Pinero at rehearsals lost his ebullience and was reduced to an ineffective passivity, entirely contrary to his nature and reputation. Consequently, his performance was mauled by the critics. The play, too, came in for some rough handling. The *Daily Express* suggested that it should be set to music and put on at the Winter Garden. I enjoyed my comparative freedom from responsibility at the rehearsals, which cheated the gossips of their anticipated explosion. Instead, a gold-mounted malacca cane, inscribed 'To B.D. from A.P.', was waiting for me at the St. Martin's box office on the morning of the first performance.

The Fokine Ballet, 'Fair and Dusky Beauties', in *Hassan*, Act 2

Hassan by James Elroy Flecker, music by Delius. His Majesty's Theatre, September 20th, 1923

Above With Michel Fokine, a press release

Right Hassan and Ishak, the court poet, begin The Golden Journey to Samarkand

Below The rescue of the Caliph from the House of the Moving Walls

6

Hassan: *A summary of correspondence, diplomatic and undiplomatic, with Flecker's widow will show how my obligation to the dead poet dogged my footsteps:*

1919

June: Mme Flecker arrived in London expecting a production the following autumn: I explain it is impossible: arrange for the appointment of a well-known agent to draw up agreement with ReandeaN, securing the rights for next twelve months. Mme Flecker receives payment in advance.

1920

April: Mme Flecker asks whether she may dispose of play elsewhere if ReandeaN cannot produce at once. (A very cross letter indeed!) I remind her of her contract.

Nov.: Send Mme Flecker copy of the acting version as requested. She replies, objecting to certain lines: 'Roy would never have agreed to them.' As they are last-minute alterations in the poet's own handwriting I protest. Mme Flecker asks for further payment in advance. This is agreed.

1921

June: Write Mme Flecker I am going to America in autumn: hope to engage Fokine to do the ballets: she asks if I can arrange simultaneous production in U.S.A.

July: Mme Flecker insists upon publication of the play in book form: I warn her to be patient.

Oct.: Write Mme Flecker owing to worsening theatre situation can no longer object to publication of play in German: I agree to see its performance there if told in time.

1922

Feb: Mme Flecker hopes I have not made any final arrangements with Mr. Harris to design the scenery and costumes: I reply that designs well advanced.

April: Mme Flecker asks whether the play can be translated into French before it is produced in London.

June: Mme Flecker asks for further payment in advance: Letter concludes with complaint that ours are under-

N

stamped. Third advance payment made. (Alec Rea says this must be the last.)

1923

May: Inform Mme Flecker preparations for production at His Majesty's Theatre now going forward: she reminds me of poet's desire to have stylised Persian costumes. Telegram from Mme Flecker announcing the first German performance at Darmstadt, May 30th.

June: Mme Flecker reports on Darmstadt production: first half of play too long, complains no Englishman present on first night of her husband's masterpiece: Harris and I fly to Cologne to obtain *laisser-passer* through French lines in the Ruhr; questioning by Senegalese troops, white teeth and bayonets gleaming in light of torches. I report Darmstadt performance dull: Frederick Valk good as Hassan.

July: Inform Mme Flecker auditions for dancers being held. Fokine to make final selection on arrival. Send her the cast list to date.

(Pre-production correspondence ends.)

7

Eureka! *Hassan* to be produced at last! The exhilaration I felt was tempered by knowledge of the mountain of responsibility that confronted me. The Pinero revival at His Majesty's was unlikely to run beyond the summer. Then it was to be *Hassan*, to the production of which Grossmith and Malone were now contractually committed. At last the gremlins that had been flitting in and out of my mind for so long were about to be exorcised in the excitement of preparation. When the piano score arrived from Delius my musical friends assured me that my shot in the dark had found its target. The composer had made an outstanding contribution, notably with the lovely hidden choruses, the Yasmin Serenade and in the final chorale, The Golden Road to Samarkand. I determined upon similar distinction in all branches of the production. The quality of the acting, the richness of scenery, costumes and lighting, all should match the brilliance of Flecker's writing and the seductive beauty of the Delius music. It was the instinct for 'total theatre' that I was later to develop into a theory, although without a comparable opportunity for its exercise.

There were the usual obstacles to be overcome in approaching this grand design. First, the censor: I was told the play could not be licensed because of the torture scene! This caused quite a flurry. I went to see Lord Cromer, the most cultured and enlightened holder of the office of Lord Chamberlain up to that time. We discussed his reader's objections, and in the end he agreed to read the play himself. Later, I was invited to lunch at his house in Harley Street, where I finally convinced him that there would be no attempt at a realistic representation of torture on the stage. He withdrew his objections, and we received the licence.

Next, actors able to give full value to Flecker's rich language must be found: Henry Ainley was selected to play Hassan. No one could speak the words better, I thought. His panache and love of the grand manner would keep the rather loosely constructed play firmly under control. If only he would keep away from the drink! This handsome man, of noble voice and mien, with an infallible ear for the music of words, a cool intelligence, and a sly humour, needed a core of steel to hold his many gifts within bounds. But alas! he was a mass of unco-ordinated impulses that created vicissitudes and eventually destroyed him. He loved to dazzle the other actors with flashes of his genius and then, for no reason that I could fathom, to retire into nonentity for the remainder of the rehearsal. It was impossible to lead or drive him. A gentle nudge as one walked beside him at rehearsal was the only way to keep him in line. That and an amiable conspiracy with his wife, Elaine, to keep temptation away during the trying weeks of rehearsal.

Another fine verse speaker was Leon Quartermaine, whose scholarly approach was very different from Harry Ainley's uncertain vocalisations. His performance of Ishak, the Court Poet, remained a landmark throughout his long career of undeviating achievement. Basil Gill and Malcolm Keen added their magnificent voices to the male chorus, each giving a performance to remain long in the memory of those who saw them. Gill was concerned in a trifling domestic incident involving my youngest son, who was born in this year. When my wife went to register his birth the St. Marylebone registrar remarked with a knowing smile: 'I saw your husband acting the other day.' She later discovered that the boy had been registered as the son of Basil Gill! Our son had to be re-registered at Godalming.

The casting of the two women's parts was less fortunate. Much as I wished Meggie to play Pervanch—her emotional intensity would have given the prison scene almost unbearable force—I knew it would be unfair to my partner to take her away from her current success. Fay Compton, whom I greatly desired should play Yasmin, was also busy elsewhere. However, Laura Cowie and Cathleen Nesbitt did their best with parts for which neither of them was temperamentally suited.

Where were we to find a sufficient number of dancers worthy of the great Fokine? At that time there was no English school of ballet capable of reaching the standards set by the Diaghilev Ballet. I had to send Roger Ould, now my personal assistant, scuttling about the country, to Scotland and to Paris to hold auditions, with Willie Warde, a veteran pantomimist and dancer, to make preliminary choice, from which the final selection would be made by the maestro when he arrived. A number of symphony players had to be persuaded into the orchestra pit. Fortunately, the Goossens family under the baton of Eugene, were at hand to ensure the standard of performance which the composer expected, and indeed demanded.

8

This was George Harris's finest hour. Inspired as much by Mardrus' Persian reproductions as by the play itself, he turned out design after design so rich in character and colour that each drawing was a work of art in itself. Scarce one remains today because of the unaccountable folly of Grossmith and Malone, but more of that later. As rehearsals progressed Harris was here, there and everywhere in and out of paint room, workshop and wardrobe, cajoling the craftsmen into achieving the high standards upon which he always insisted.

A posse of electricians were soon at work up in the fly tower running the extra cables required to create the effects of light and air for which my productions were now becoming known. One experiment is worthy of record to illustrate the makeshifts we sometimes employed. The lenses used in the spotlights of those days frequently cracked because of poor ventilation. I had extension pieces fitted to the front of about a dozen projectors, so that the broken lenses could be set at an angle of 45 degrees to the lamp. Next, we coated the high white walls of the street with a mixture of whitening and ground mica. As dawn broke over the city, the effect of the prismatic light, which the broken lenses produced, striking upon this prepared surface, was so surprising that there were gasps of pleasure from the audience.

As the rehearsals progressed a stream of experts and advisers came jostling through the swing doors in Charles Street on their way to consultation either with myself or with Harris or the stage director. First, the music adviser: who was going to find that strange instrument, the pavillon d'armide, called for in the Delius score? For Harris, there were costumiers, shoemakers, hatters, swordsmiths; for the stage director, mechanical engineers to advise on how to hoist the basket containing the Caliph and his two companions from the Street of Felicity up into the House of the Moving Walls without pulling the scenery over.

By this time Fokine had selected the dancers for his ballets and was putting them through a course of intensive training. His impact upon those eager youngsters was electrifying to watch. Among them was Ursula Moreton, devoted collaborator of Ninette de Valois during the formative years of the Vic-Wells Ballet and later to become ballet principal of the Royal Ballet School at White Lodge, Richmond. During the final week I surrendered the stage to Fokine for the first hour or so every morning, so that he could rehearse in the actual scenery. Among the male dancers was a clever little acrobat. Slow in the uptake, he seemed always to be in trouble, never failing to catch the maestro's eye with his mistakes. One morning, waiting for my own work to begin, I wandered into the stalls during one of these rehearsals. The unfortunate little dancer was once again hauled out in front of the rest of the ballet to receive his daily lecture from Fokine, in scarcely comprehensible English.

'Plees coom here!' screamed Fokine. 'Always you late! Now, watch.' Flinging his arms and extending his fingers, he said: 'Thees is traa-gic.' Then, crouching and doubling up his fingers, he went on: 'And thees ees cawmic. Now, make cawmic!'

9

Now came the dress parades: tedious affairs but often indicative of character. The well-adjusted actor takes the precaution of coming to terms with both designer and costumier beforehand. No matter how many changes he may have, he turns up at his dress parade with costumes properly fitted and complete with all accessories, or at least satisfactory explanations for their absence. The careless or lazy actor on the other hand is usually incompletely dressed and grumbling. At our parade for the male choristers, a tiresome mischief-maker turned up in undervest and shorts, socks and suspenders, and wearing a gorgeous jewelled turban on his head that belonged to someone else. Well pleased with the laughs that his appearance caused in the wings, he was not at all prepared for my sharp rejoinder when he tried to lay the blame for his missing costume upon an embarrassed wardrobe man. A great one for dressing-room laughs, that one: a pity he was not similarly successful with his audience.

Women, too, display different characteristics at dress parades. The principals, called first, chat to designer and dressmaker in warm confidential tones, as though my presence were not really necessary. Among the chorus girls a prude or two, objecting to the exposed bellybutton, drags chiffon out of place to conceal the enormity: 'Don't pull at it like that, my dear,' calls out the dressmaker, 'it's only tacked.' Another girl deliberately puts on her costume back to front just to outface the wardrobe mistress whom she dislikes. A breeze among the assembled 'trades', enlivens the close of the proceedings. 'You said you were going to provide belts and buckles for the soldiers.' 'No, I didn't.' 'Yes, you did. I'm only doing the boots'—an argument sharply terminated by the designer. . . . Thank goodness, it's over at last.

IO

Then the dress rehearsals! Hearing the music for a production for the first time always gave me a special thrill. I liked to watch the musicians filing into the orchestra pit, the shuffling into places while cheerful greetings are exchanged that have nothing to do with music, the tuning of instruments and the checking over of parts with the copyists. Then the conductor taps smartly on his desk and work begins. These preliminaries acquired special significance in the case of *Hassan* because a new work by a distinguished composer played by an orchestra of symphony players under a brilliant young conductor, was about to be heard for the first time.

Now the final rehearsal, those last magical hours when I can still control events somewhat. Tomorrow I must hand over to others, and, like a pilot, scramble over the side before the ship departs. As I sit at my production desk in the stalls, awaiting the stage director's signal that all is ready, I look round at the privileged spectators scattered about the auditorium, all of them either professionally or emotionally involved. I cannot resist a feeling of pride that it is my persistence that has brought them together. In the front row, near the orchestra, sits Delius, an invalid now, dependent upon his wife to lead him to his place. With them is Philip Heseltine, the composer's close friend. Fokine goes to pay his respects to the composer before turning for a final word with Goossens: about the tempi of the ballets? I expect so. Sir James Barrie sits by himself, smoking his biggest pipe and watching the last-minute comings and goings with intense interest. Elsewhere, dotted about the auditorium are little groups of people who have worked on the production, awaiting the final assessment of their efforts. Eugene Goossens, also awaiting the signal to begin, tugs at the collar-stud at the back of his neck, a characteristic nervous gesture that I had often seen before. At last the signal: Eugene taps smartly; the auditorium lights dim out; the overture is begun.

The change in Act One from 'The Street of Felicity by the Fountain of the Two Pigeons' to 'The House of the Moving Walls' has stretched the skills of my highly trained staff to the utmost. In fact, it is one of the most elaborate quick changes that the stage of His Majesty's Theatre has ever seen. All has gone well so far. I remember the old superstition that a good dress rehearsal means a bad first night and vice versa. But now, thank goodness, something goes wrong. The quick change is not quick enough and the wait is longer than the interlude music provided for it. Eugene, reacting instinctively to this common experience at a dress rehearsal, begins to repeat the interlude. Immediately a shrill scream rises from Delius, in fact more a screech than a scream: 'No, no, no, Mr. Goossens. What are you doing? You mustn't play it *twice*!' While the back of Gene's neck flushes crimson at the rebuke I try to soothe the outraged composer, explaining that all will be well tomorrow night, as indeed it was. It is long after midnight before the rehearsal is over. Barrie, deeply moved, congratulates Delius, gives me a silent handshake and disappears. Back in his flat in Aldephi Terrace he sits down to write me a eulogistic prophecy of the approaching night's events. The letter brought to me by his man early in the morning ends with the words: 'Tonight you will have such a night in the theatre as never again in your life.'

II

Somehow the suspense of the first night had to be endured. I walked the streets for hours—at least it seemed so long—thinking of all the things I might have done better and of all the probable mishaps. Would 'Harry' Ainley get stuck in the basket half-way up the wall? He was no light weight. . . . And so on and so forth. . . . I could endure it no longer. I hurried back through the stage-door, discounting the excited looks of the staff, which might have soothed my anxious questioning, shut myself in the manager's office beside the dress-circle and waited, sweating with anxiety. . . . Distant sounds of the chorale told me the ending was near. I could not contain myself, I crept out and stood at the back of a box, watching the audience wrapt in the dying fall of The Golden Road to Samarkand. I could see Gladys Cooper, Gerald du Maurier, Dennis Eadie and many other West End stars standing at the side of the stalls. They had finished their performances earlier than usual so as to be present at our curtain fall.

The applause was deafening. I fled back to the shelter of the office, where I was eventually found by the theatre manager, unsympathetic to my trembling and my tears. 'What are you thinking of? Come at once.' I remember little of my curtain speech, save that I had the wit to say how glad I was that after nearly ten years of struggle, I had been able to keep my promise to the poet. Then I fled back to the office and locked the door, refusing to answer when my wife and her family came to shower me with congratulations. I was sobbing uncontrollably.

Thus, Flecker's play came to the stage of Tree's former theatre after all; to be precise, on 20th September, 1923, before one of the most distinguished audiences that had ever assembled there, including most of the leading dramatists of the day: Arnold Bennett, Alfred Sutro, A. A. Milne, John Drinkwater, H. M. Harwood and Reginald Berkeley; and among the socialites, Lady Louise Mountbatten and her fiancé, the Crown Prince of Sweden, Lady Rhondda, Lord Lee of Fareham, Lord Lathom, Lord Logan, Sir Eric Geddes. It was eight years after the poet's death, and nearly ten since the play first came into my hands.

There were numerous parties after the first night. I attended two of them, scoring bad marks for late attendance at both, one given by Eddie Marsh for Mme Flecker, at the old Pall Mall Restaurant in the Haymarket, and the other at the White Tower, run by that admirable Middle European restaurateur, Stulik. A copy of Flecker's play containing a few notes of music from Delius inscribed inside, and a badly pencilled verse from Maurice Baring, beginning: 'You gave us Pommery and Irish stew . . . Golden eggs from Samarkand.' remains the only memento of that party. Others who signed the book were Lady Diana Cooper, Viola Tree, Compton Mackenzie and Eugene Goossens. My own signature was so unsteady that the first letter of my surname is missing.

12

There were ecstatic notices in both the morning and evening papers. I was particularly glad to read in the *Daily Telegraph* that 'the scenic marvels had not outfaced the literary merit of the work', because the purists, always suspicious of popular acclaim, had been critical of our advance publicity. The atmosphere of Eastern pantomime surrounding His Majesty's Theatre during *Chu Chin Chow* lingered like a mirage in their mind's eye. There had been sneering references to 'the usual camels'. In that matter they were fooled because Harris produced his caravan effect without the use of live animals. He cut tiny profiles out of three-ply wood, painted them himself and placed them on an eccentric track behind the distant sandhills of the last scene, so that, as the pilgrims left The Gate of the Moon, the camel train could be faintly seen, moving with stately pace along The Golden Road to Samarkand.

Among the telegrams waiting for me at the office was a letter from Mme Flecker: 'I must tell you again I never hoped for anything so perfectly beautiful as your production and I know for sure how much Roy would have liked it. . . .' Nevertheless, she maintained her watchful attitude over the play by adding: 'I will come round and see you at your office one of these days. I want to tell you one or two weak points in the acting. . . .'

Of all the praise I treasured most a two-page letter from J.G. He had not been at the first night, being abroad in search of health for Ada Galsworthy. The letter is dated October 10th: 'I saw *Hassan* this afternoon. I thought that for colour, design, beauty and aptness of stage-setting it surpassed anything I have seen on the English stage.' He goes on to criticise with Galsworthian precision the performances of each of the chief characters, and ends with a reminder of that earlier letter in which he had so strongly disapproved of my selection of Delius as the composer: 'The music is extraordinarily mediocre. You were let down there, as I thought you would be.'

Here and there in my booksof press cuttings I come across little reminders of the extent of the play's impact. Quotes from the play are used as newspaper headlines: 'Nowadays men have special need of dreams'; an *Evening Standard* contributor complains it is impossible to obtain a printed copy of the play anywhere; a fancy-dress ball is announced at which all the guests are to appear as characters from the play. Finally, most unusual touch of all, an artist models sets of the principal characters in porcelain: these are now collectors' pieces.

Of course, none of these details emerged on the stupendous 'morning after' when exhilaration was at such a pitch that normal duties kept dancing in and out of my mind like spillikins. Towards noon Pat Malone rang up in great excitement, inviting me to come and see the sights. There was a queue of people waiting to book seats that extended from the box-office right round to the stage-door. Standing with Pat on the first-floor balcony overlooking the Haymarket I was so 'levitated' that I felt like leaping out into the street, certain that no harm would come to me.

Ten
Seldom pleasure

I

Riding the seesaw of success and failure at the St. Martin's was a more exhausting exercise than producing spectacular plays at His Majesty's, possibly because at the latter I had little or no financial responsibility, whereas the ReandeaN cash box seemed always to empty itself as fast as it was replenished. *Loyalties* began to show signs of wear early in that eventful year of 1923. So I replaced it with one of A. A. Milne's graceful light comedies, *The Great Broxopp*, for which Edmund Gwenn and Dawson Milward returned to the St. Martin's; they were joined by Mary Jerrold, Faith Celli, and the senior members of our company who were not already busy at His Majesty's. Meggie Albanesi was not included. Exhausted after five months of playing Daisy in *East of Suez* she had been given leave to visit her sister in America. With such a strong cast I felt certain we should have a success or at all events run long enough for Meggie to have a good holiday and for me to make ready a new play against her return. You see, by this time she had become a pivotal figure in my forward planning. But attempts to dictate the course of events in the theatre usually fail. The Milne play was a flop, the *Evening Standard* unkindly reminding us that 'this is the shortest run an A.A. Milne play has so far received!'

Three days after the play opened we gave a public demonstration of the new Schwabe-Hasait lighting that had been installed during rehearsals to the accompaniment of prolonged daily arguments in guttural German which no one dared to interrupt. All the leading managers, producers and many dramatic authors and critics were invited to it. Although it was obvious that full use of the equipment could not be made in our small theatre, the results were so intriguing that the General Electric Company invited me to become their technical adviser on stage-lighting, although all I had done was to stand on the stage and direct the switchboard operators to produce the full gamut of storm and cloud effects: 'a modest Prospero in spats', a reporter wrote. The critics were cautious, mixing enthusiasm with reminders that the play must come first. Bernard Shaw, greeting me in the lobby at the end of the demonstration, saw no cause for congratulation. Instead, it was: 'I'll take good care ye'll not use any of those contraptions in my plays, young man. The audience would be so busy staring at your clouds they wouldn't listen to my words.' Of course, he was right.

2

The play that I had in mind for Meggie was *The Lilies of the Field*, which I thought was John Hastings Turner's best play to date. In it Meggie was to try her hand at light comedy for the first time. I had been looking forward to my star's return from America, rested and ready for fresh triumphs; but she came back exhausted by an over-enthusiastic welcome on Broadway, and immediately fell ill. The Turner play had to be postponed. I had nothing to put in its place, so, for the first time since we began, the St. Martin's Theatre was 'dark' and the ReandeaN players out of work. The morale of the company, unprepared for this sequence of disaster, was badly shaken. In desperation, I turned to Nigel Playfair, who had recently announced the acquisition of two plays by the Czech dramatist Karel Capek. The first was *The Insect Play* and the second *R.U.R.* If he did not want both plays, I asked him, might I have one of them? He preferred *The Insect Play* for Hammersmith and relinquished *R.U.R.* to me. The play, roughly translated by Paul Selver, had been adapted by Nigel, but his version was crude and unfinished, and required a great deal of further work. So I sat up at night in a tiny furnished flat which I was renting for convenience almost opposite His Majesty's stage-door in Charles Street, literally with a wet towel round my head and cups of coffee provided by my former batman, now demobilised and celebrating his freedom by a certain partiality for the bottle.

We could only afford to keep the St. Martin's closed for two weeks plus two days for the dress rehearsals, so I had to drive the company pretty hard. Everyone backed me to the full. We had a fine cast, with Leslie Banks as the chief robot and Ada King as Emma the housekeeper. This fine actress had long since abandoned her provincial 'charring' in *The Silver Box* and other plays of the Manchester school for which she had won enthusiastic notices everywhere but small reward. She was now a member of our permanent company. As difficult, as cantankerous and as lovable as ever, she saw no reason to change the habits she had acquired during her years as a provincial actress, including her Sunday-night libations of Australian burgundy.

George's scenery was most effective, especially the office set, which had textured walls painted to represent steel. For the robots he designed uniforms made out of buckram, cut in angular shapes and glued on to thick cardboard, painted to look like burnished steel. They were most effective; they were also very heavy. Leslie Banks complained about their weight before the dress rehearsal began, but knowing how actors love to grumble at their costumes before a dress rehearsal, I dismissed the matter from my mind, and went on with the rehearsal. At the climax of the second act the glinting figures of the robots appeared above the parapet, silhouetted against a flaming sky. Clambering through the tall windows at the back, they proceeded to wreck the office to the accompaniment of piercing shrieks from Ada King. The effect was stupendous. I sat back in silence after the fall of the curtain, well satisfied with the effect we had created.

Just then the stage manager poked his frightened face round the corner of the proscenium. 'Oh, sir!' he called out.

'What is it?' I asked, my mind full of the details of the scene.

'Mr. Banks has just fainted.'

'All right,' I said. 'Break for lunch,' an incident which Leslie Banks recalled with delight upon many occasions, but never with malice.

Nearly all the young robots who stormed into that office won successful careers on the stage: Leslie Perrins, Hugh Sinclair and Ernest Digges are names that come to mind. Perhaps the most successful was Hugh ('Tam') Williams, who achieved distinction both as an actor of great charm and sensibility and as the author with his wife of many delightful comedies. He recalled with relish the only line he had to speak in the play, which was also his first on the London stage: 'We are sterile; we cannot beget children.' Later he wondered whether it created 'a kind of trauma which resulted in my having five'.

The reviewers had a great time. One pointed out the social significance of the dramatist's invention; another reminded him of his debt to H. G. Wells; yet another remarked pithily that the play might have been called *Man and Superman* if Bernard Shaw had not already appropriated the title. . . . The robot was the invention of an artist and not of a scientist. Today its blind intelligence has given way to the superior competence of the computer. Nevertheless, the word has passed into our language, and is often used as a term of contempt.

3

Meggie was now sufficiently recovered to begin rehearsing *The Lilies of the Field*. The play contained delightful parts for twin sisters; Meggie played one and Edna Best the other. The appeal of two of the most popular young actresses of the day as twins was undoubted, as the bankers say. The contrast in style between the two added piquancy to the attraction: Edna Best with her crisp, boyish timing set against Meggie's wistful humour and instinctive knowledge of just when to let the audience into her secret. When to this partnership there was added the sharp wit of the veteran actress, Gertrude Kingston, as the grandmother of the twins, the delight of the audience seemed to float about the theatre in waves. The play also gave Austin Trevor an opportunity, brilliantly seized, to lead off in a romantic quadrille. On the opening night at the Ambassadors Theatre on June 5th as the second act was nearing its climax, the terrific explosion next door which signalled the robot attack upon the factory nearly blew down the scenery. Subsequently, we did our best to alter the timing of the explosion by shortening or lengthening the act waits at one or other of the theatres, but more often than not mistakes were made and the actors from the two theatres would compare notes on the effects of the unwelcome simultaneity. Philip Page, the most popular and handsome man in Fleet Street, poured his journalistic wrath upon the play in the columns of the *Daily Sketch*, but I am afraid that was because we stuck to our managerial rule not to admit latecomers until the end of the first scene. Of all the latecomers he was hardest hit by the rule, since it seriously interfered with his somewhat turbulent way of life. Significantly, the only journal to praise our latecomers' rule was *Horse and Hound*, presumably because its readers were accustomed to punctuality at the starting gate. In spite of Page's animadversions, not because of them, the house was crowded at each performance and gave every sign of becoming the most persistent of our commercial successes to date.

4

Turning-points in life are seldom recognised at the time; perspective is absent. It was certainly so in my own case. About the time of *R.U.R.* I received a letter from Miss Kate Phillips, a veteran actress who had appeared with Henry Irving at the Lyceum. She had been giving lessons to the Countess of Warwick's younger daughter, Mercy. Encouraged by successful appearances in the Barn Theatre at Little Easton before audiences that sometimes included Bernard Shaw and H. G. Wells, Mercy now wanted to make a career on the stage. With some reluctance I agreed to see her. She was introduced to me under the stage name of Nancie Parsons. As she had charm and a gay personality, I decided to engage her for a probationary period, a decision fraught with deep consequence for both of us. Nancie made her first appearance on the professional stage as a parlourmaid in *The Lilies of the Field*, her début attended by several members of her family.

The dancing craze was still sweeping the country. Everywhere in clubs, hotels and restaurants on parquet-covered squares in the centre of the rooms men and women of all ages indulged their passionate reaffirmation of vitality after the slaughter of the war. Parties arriving for dinner or supper would scarcely pause to discuss the menu with a smiling *maître d'hôtel* before hurrying to join the jostling throng. The smartest rendezvous in London was the Embassy Club in Bond Street, where Luigi, in impeccable white waistcoat and with equally impeccable manners, conducted the distinguished guests to their favourite tables.

I was not caught up in the craze at first, nor, I think, were any other members of the company except Meggie. The plain fact was that we were too busy rehearsing and playing. Meggie was the exception. She lived an intense emotional life of her own. Dancing gave her relief from tension. Late nights became a habit with her and after the rupture with Owen Nares the habit intensified. I used to tease her about it, saying that she ought to be in bed resting in readiness for rehearsals the next day, but she scoffed at my advice and went her way. Then I had the quixotic notion that, if I took her out at night myself, I might persuade her to keep more reasonable hours. But she preferred gay partners, comedians and jockeys. How I hated those raffish friends! None of them seemed to appreciate the precious jewel of her friendship which they wore in their caps, nor did they understand the toll they were taking of her vitality. Why should they care? She was enjoying herself, wasn't she? I raged inwardly, knowing that nothing could be done.

Meanwhile, Mercy had become popular in the company. Using her stage name, she was Nancie to everyone. It suited her natural gaiety better than her given name and by it she remains in memory. We began to go dancing together. Whether I did so because I, too, was enchanted, or because of increasing anxiety about Meggie's rackety life I am not sure, but on the rare occasions when Meggie and I met at night-clubs, and I urged her to go home, she would turn quite savagely upon me, telling me to mind my own business in language that would surprise no one today, but quite took my breath away.

Throughout the summer of 1923 the conflict of wills went on. Perhaps that is too strong a term, for we were not conscious of it at the time, but the emotional mists are long since dispersed, and one can survey the truth with clarity. Success was buzzing in our ears. Meggie and I went our joint and several ways in theatre and night-club. While she danced away her leisure hours, not so much in dissipation as in a mood of desperation, I gave myself up more and more to a newly discovered gaiety. Then the strangest thing happened. One day in high summer I took Meggie to lunch at the Carlton Grill. I have a vivid recollection of that afternoon. We talked about future plans as we had so often done before. I wanted her to play Juliet, the tragic notes of the part stressed rather than the romantic. She did not think she was beautiful enough. Absurd, I said. What about Ibsen's Nora? A world of possibility there.

Above The *Likes of* 'E Sally Winch and Florrie Small in the plate-smashing scene (Mary Clare and Hermione Baddeley)

Below R.U.R. The robots storm into the office after setting fire to the factory

Above 'I pray you, though you mock me, gentlemen,
Let her not hurt me.'
(Edith Evans, Leon Quartermaine, Athene Seyler, Frank Vosper)

Below 'Is all our company assembled?'
The rude mechanicals: Frank Cellier, Wilfrid Walter, H. O. Nicholson,
Miles Malleson, Clifford Mollison, Alfred Clark

A Midsummer Night's Dream. Theatre Royal, Drury Lane, 26 December, 1924

Then there were the Chekhov parts, although my knowledge of that author was limited at the time to the translations of Constance Garnett. Meggie followed all this in her imagination with enthusiasm. Suddenly it was three o'clock. She would be late for her voice production class.

We jumped into a taxi and drove up the Haymarket, turning into Panton Street on the way to her appointment, still talking excitedly of the future. Then, with no words spoken, the barriers between us were down. We lurched into each other's arms, kissing frenziedly. There was a quality of desperation about the embrace that somehow robbed it of reality. Meggie's eyes filled with tears. I became aware of a pathetic sense of inability to handle her life alone. We would go away together and become great artists of the theatre. We kissed again violently, passionately even, but without love. The taxi-driver protested. Meggie was late for her lesson, and when we met again next day we were shy of each other, afraid of our plan and the pain it would cause. We were both young in such matters.

Somehow or other I have to find the moral strength to write the truth about this episode. Meggie was not offering herself for love—Owen Nares had been the fixed star of her love—but out of the passion for artistic achievement that we shared; perhaps, also, because of a deeply felt need for her own sexual regulation. Basically, it comes down to this: the first thoughts of both of us were for fulfilment in the theatre. I thought I could prevent Meggie from losing that sense of dedication. In my conceit it never occurred to me that she might have similar aims regarding myself. We did not recognise the force that was driving us to extremes. If we had been able to confront it, as it were, we would have become self-conscious, and the current of feeling between us would have been switched off. . . . After our 'Brief Encounter' we perversely went our separate ways, with disastrous results, career-wise, for us both. That is not to say that it would have been otherwise if we had followed our rash impulse. The dualism in our natures would soon have propelled us on to a collision course, although not, I fancy, in the theatre.

5

With two successes running concurrently side by side, confidence of both company and staff in the future of ReandeaN took a leap

o

into the air. Given leadership and a policy in which they believe, actors will always respond. The eagerness of the younger generation to accept financial sacrifice in order to join our company now became almost embarrassing. Young players were stacked up like aircraft waiting to land on the stage of the St. Martin's Theatre. Whimsical friends used to say that the actors thronging the stage-doors in West Street ought to be given identity cards. We also received innumerable written applications. One morning as I was about to leave London to address the Nottingham Playgoers' Society, I opened a letter from a young man who was appearing in the town, enclosing a postcard of himself in midshipman's uniform. A personable young man, I thought, so I decided to stay over and see the matinée the next day. My midshipman proved a disappointment, but presently there entered the 'tatty' stage drawing-room a typical colonel's daughter, armed with a tennis racquet and, believe it or not, asking the inevitable question: 'Who's for tennis!' The girl was obviously talented apart from her English-rose beauty. It was Diana Wynyard! I gave her a year's contract and sent her to join Dee Cee where she played several parts. Before the year was up she wrote to enquire rather naïvely what she should do next. It was unfair to keep her waiting any longer for a vacancy in the ReandeaN Company, so I wrote to William Armstrong urging him to engage her. It was during her years at the Liverpool Playhouse that Diana Wynyard laid the foundations of her career. I was glad to have had some small share in helping her on her way.

6

I decided to push on with a scheme that had been long in mind, which I hoped would add to the reputation of ReandeaN and give further acting chances to our eager company. This was an afternoon theatre to which I gave the name of The Playbox.

Two brochures were issued in connection with the scheme. The Playbox was to be a subscription theatre, giving performances on Tuesday, Wednesday, and Thursday afternoons, from September to May. The plays would be produced in series of three, and a list of those in the first series followed, together with details of a coupon system whereby purchasers of books of coupons could obtain seats at reduced prices. Included in and forming part of each series would be a special Sunday evening performance, to be known as a Gala

Performance, admission to which would be free and for subscribers only.

In the foreword I posed certain questions and proceeded to answer them in explanatory terms. . . . 'How can we get the best results from actors and dramatists if we only produce one or two plays a year, such as has been our recent experience? How can we create a special audience by such restricted means? . . . A special audience can only be created if its wits be subject to constant stimulation. Given a theatre where a company of actors and actresses by constant association develop a feeling for the "ensemble", which is the highest form of theatrical presentation, we believe you would see such a revival of interest in the art of the theatre as no one has dared to hope for in this country.'

Here are some brief extracts from the second brochure, my address to the ReandeaN Company, also printed and circulated among our well-wishers. . . .

'The forthcoming opening of The Playbox affords legitimate excuse for meeting you all together quietly without any of the business side of the theatre being present—just a frank meeting between artists—and for explaining to you the underlying principles which guide my actions as Director of ReandeaN, and which have given rise to the formation of the Playbox. . . . By constant association together, actors can develop an individual standard of technique and a general sense of the ensemble that is nothing short of uncanny. Moreover, audiences can by their enthusiastic co-operation help to build up a really individual theatre, one to which no artistic triumph can be long denied. . . . I look forward to the time when the acting in our Playbox Theatre shall become unique, so vivid as to be unlike any to be seen elsewhere in London.'

I make no apology for the exuberance of these remarks. After all we were a young company, and this was a reflection of the enthusiasm prevailing in our theatre at the time. Nevertheless, I had quite a struggle to overcome my own diffidence because English actors were unaccustomed to such frankness from the management regarding future plans, although of recent years the practice has been widely followed. When I had finished speaking I could not help noting the looks of scepticism on the faces of the senior actors; but there in the front row sat all the younger players, dreaming of the many new opportunities they would be given;

especially, there was Meggie, her face shining with the excitement of it all.

7

I had intended to open The Playbox the previous autumn, but had been delayed by various set-backs. But people had paid good money for their books of coupons and could be kept waiting no longer; we had to keep faith. That is why the experiment began in July, a most unsuitable choice as it turned out.

There was now too much work for one person to handle, so I began to look round for an assistant producer. I was delighted when I heard that my old friend Esmé Percy had returned from Germany where he had been responsible for the entertainment of British troops during the occupation of the Rhineland. I invited him to join us and to play a leading part in the first Playbox production. This was *Melloney Holtspur* or *The Pangs of Love*, an enchanting ghost-ridden love story, which I decided to produce myself. The full strength of the ReandeaN Company was deployed. This now included Mary Jerrold, Laura Cowie and Cathleen Nesbitt, charming actress and an invaluable presence in any company. Masefield was present at all the rehearsals, sometimes dropping hints to the actors that were in marked contrast to the gentle voice and manner of our future poet laureate. For instance, he told Esmé Percy that when the Ghost appeared to interrupt his love scene with Melloney he should bare his teeth and look 'like a dog interrupted at its meals'. The company could make little of Masefield's tenuous fantasy, but, as with every author with whom she came in contact, Meggie aroused his admiration. One phrase in the letter he wrote to her after the performance fills me with infinite sadness whenever I think of it: 'You are going to be the wonder of our stage.'

8

The pressure of alternate success and failure brought in its train an increasing desire for relaxation. Nancie and I closed our ears to gossip and went on dancing. The Countess of Warwick, hearing rumours of my association with her daughter, invited me to Easton Lodge for a week-end to find out for herself how matters stood.

Ours was a fairy tale and I was completely lost in it, so I had no fears about my first meeting with the formidable Edwardian hostess. It was on a hot and sunny August morning that I went down for the Bank Holiday week-end. Leaving the murk of Liverpool Street Station and changing at Bishop's Stortford on to the little branch line to Dunmow, I was met at the private station, built for the convenience of Edward VII and the groups of friends with whom he liked to be surrounded during the sumptuous house parties that were a notable feature of his reign. Blue Gates, the main entrance to the park, was on the other side of the Stortford Road, almost immediately opposite, so the transfer of royalty into the comparative seclusion of a country mansion could be unostentatiously effected. Half a mile further on was a second lodge, where the aged lodge-keeper, running out in answer to a summons, bobbed us a curtsey. The road stretched for a mile or more across a neglected park, full of giant oaks with their main branches fallen or rotted away; it was in a bad state of repair, with great pot-holes ineffectively filled in with loose granite chips which, if taken at speed, jerked one right out of one's seat, and promised early destruction of tyres and springs. The road converged with others from various quarters of the compass upon a spacious yard, lined with stabling in lovely red Tudor brick along one side and a range of Regency cottages on the other, built for the use of huntsmen and grooms. Once a scene of equine activity, the yard was now deserted save for a chauffeur leisurely washing a large black Daimler.

My first sight of the house was a disappointment. Nancie had shown me pictures of it as it was at the beginning of the last century, but in 1847 a disastrous fire had destroyed the central portion. This had been rebuilt at the time of the Gothic revival and remained an unsatisfactory marriage with what was left of the original mansion. Then, in 1918, on the night following the marriage of Lady Warwick's younger son, a second fire destroyed the remaining wing, leaving only the lovely library and some areas of Tudor brickwork as a reminder of the architectural hotch-potch.

The interior of Easton Lodge still reflected some past glories, although not exactly of taste. For example, the main staircase, in white marble was a fearsome substitute for the carved woodwork of the original. Over the fireplace in the Audit Room, where I waited for audience, hung the portrait by William Beechey of Nancie Parsons, a famous courtesan of the eighteenth century, who, after living with the the third Duke of Grafton and other noble personages finally married the second Viscount Maynard, who is reputed to have shared his marriage with certain ducal companions. I wondered more than ever why our Nancie had adopted the name of a lady of such scabrous reputation. Impatient for my first meeting with her mother, Nancie took me into the saloon, a room crowded with Edwardiana: gilt mirrors, enormous Chinese vases with sheaves of pampas grass protruding. Dresden figurines, priceless bibelots competing with the nouveau art of the nineteenth century; at every available stance signed photographs of royal personages, dukes, duchesses and trade-union leaders—profusion without taste, amplitude without dimension. I was received by my hostess in the garden room, a reconstruction of the oldest part of the house wrecked in the 1918 fire. The painted walls bore witness to Lady Warwick's generous encouragement of Edward ('Teddy'), Gordon Craig's son, then at the beginning of his career.

I have a clear memory of that first interview—it was so unexpected. Instead of condescension there was interest; instead of criticism there was tactful enquiry about my work and interests. The habit of interlarding conversation with French words and phrases (and sometimes German) I dismissed as an Edwardian affectation. Later, I discovered that the Countess's knowledge of these languages was firmly based upon the instruction she had received from her governess, a certain Miss Blake, friend and confidante of German princelings and an accomplished linguist.

Soon we were deep in talk about the theatre. Lady Warwick spoke of her friendship with Ellen Terry, of how Ellen used to take part in entertainments in the tithe barn nestling beside Little Easton Church. Upon one occasion she read some of the nurse's part in *Romeo and Juliet*: 'I read Juliet. Of course we were much too old, but then, you see, it was wartime—1915. People came from all over the county, in pony carts and waggonettes and on foot. Mercy must take you to see the Barn. It's quite lovely.' (I now have confirmation of this story from one of Nancie's oldest friends, who was present at the performance, and also at a later performance of *A Midsummer Night's Dream*, with H. G. Wells as Duke Theseus and 'Gyp', his elder son, as Bottom. Bernard Shaw was present as avuncular critic of the young players.) Our talk was punctuated by the screeching of parrots, the chatter of monkeys, and the yapping of dachshunds, some of them so old that their tummies were trailing along the ground. None were house-trained, but Lady Warwick did not seem to mind.

On Sunday morning Nancie took me to Little Easton Church, where generations of her mother's family had worshipped and now lay enshrined in marble and brass. Later I had to be introduced to all Lady Warwick's pets, including a fierce woolly monkey which had already bitten and permanently scarred Nancie's arm. I could not help noticing how Lady Warwick's confident handling of her pets evoked immediate and affectionate response. Next, I was taken on a tour of the wonderful gardens, the sunken garden with its rare water-lilies, the rose garden, the green garden and, finally, to the chain of ornamental ponds, shrouded in tall trees, rare shrubs and exotic ferns. Lady Warwick's grumbles that since the war she had been reduced to eight gardeners where formerly there had been double that number, seemed unimportant in the face of such Edwardian splendour. Indeed, my lasting impression of house and park and gardens was one of uncontrolled amplitude faced by inexorable diminution.

9

Bank Holiday Monday, hot and sunny under a cloudless blue sky: Nancie was early at my window, calling up from the wide terrace beneath. She had come clattering up the stone steps, riding her mother's old hunter. There was something incongruous in the slight, graceful figure sitting astride such a huge animal. The view from the window was intoxicatingly beautiful; I could have gazed at it for hours, but I hastened to join Nancie in the stable-yard. We wandered in and out of the rose garden, carrying the scent of its blooms into the dairy, where thick, yellow cream from the Jersey herd was standing in big earthenware jars, waiting to be turned into delicious butter. The place looked cool and inviting in its white tiles under a thatched roof. I gave myself up to the enchantment of the day and the hour.

Later, I strolled in the park before lunch, while Nancie went about some simple tasks for her mother. The whole countryside was swathed in a pale blue gauze of mist, behind which the distant fir plantation stood up, dark sentinels against the high, bright sky, where larks were singing. Here and there groups of deer were lazing in the tussocky grass. Their leaders looked up with startled eyes as I approached. Soon they were up and away, their white scuts marking their line of retreat into the undergrowth. The ground everywhere was fouled by rabbits, their favourite burrows among the giant roots of the ancient oak trees. There must have been thousands of them. Lady Warwick would not allow them to be shot or trapped. In consequence, fodder had to be provided for the deer almost the year round.

It was the day of the annual flower show, an event that had taken place in a field bordering the gardens for years uncounted, in fact ever since flower-shows were first thought of. I climbed over a fence and went to watch the preparations which had been going on throughout the week-end. The showman who ran the fairground was an old friend of Lady Warwick's. He was busy setting up his side-shows, swings, rocking-horses for the roundabout—no modern variants for him—coconut shies. A traction engine to provide energy for the fair was already puffing smoke from its tall funnel. In the marquees the farmers and cottagers were busy putting the final touches to their exhibits of flowers, fruit and vegetables in readiness for judging by the experts. All the villagers round about competed for the prizes which very properly took first place in their thoughts.

When Nancie and I arrived after a hurried lunch judging had already begun. So, too, had the steam organ, grinding out strident versions of popular songs. The paths across the fields were thronged with villagers streaming towards the ground, the children fanning out ahead, eager to enjoy the roundabouts and swings, while their elders made for the tents to argue over the relative merits of the exhibits and to criticise the awards. We went first to watch the judging—for form's sake, Nancie said. But she was bored and ran across to the fairground, I self-consciously following. I had a vague sense of hurrying after a spirit that I could never capture.

I turned to study the country types swarming through the tents. These are among the oldest heart-lands of the English, the people as remote and unchanging in their outlook as the characters in Hardy's novels. Dialect and accents might vary and be modified but the 'Englishness' was as fixed as the towers of their ancient churches.

When we left the last rays of the setting sun were glistening behind the old oak trees and the blue mist was once again shrouding the landscape. The coloured globes looping the fairground had already been switched on and the younger children taken home, loudly complaining; but the older ones and their boy friends were still swinging excitedly or aiming at the last of the coconuts, shouts of success punctuating the sharp crack of miniature rifles. Meanwhile old wives gossiped and their menfolk crowded the beer tent to drink away their prize money.

Home to a riotous supper! What am I writing? It was not my home, and yet among that young house party I felt it to be so. We were all a little drunk—not with drink, that was always in short supply at Easton—but with the joy of living. While the rest of the party played Consequences and card games in the audit room, Nancie, blissfully happy and unusually quiet, suggested a walk through the gardens. The night was warm and still. We crossed the tennis courts, passed once more through the sunken Italian garden and along the alleys of pleached lime trees in the green garden where at every grassy intersection statuary gleamed white under the rising moon, and down the long avenue to the first of the miniature lakes with its pagoda-like summer house built over the water. We sat gazing at the scene for a long time in silence, and then wandered on to the last of them where water-hens, disturbed by our presence, scuttered over the still water to hide behind the enormous leaves of great clumps of gunnera which completely encircled the lake. For some reason—I cannot think why—I thought of Rostand's *Les Romanesques*. Why this particular play should have come to mind I do not know, for there were no irate parents nor hired bravos to deny us our love. The great harvest moon, copper-coloured, floated over the trees, bathing the woods, the statues, the flowers and ourselves in its mystery. I was committed to a lasting memory.

10

Our capricious climate chose the month of July to inflict London with a scorching heat-wave which played havoc with the West End box-offices. The Playbox had to be closed almost as soon as it was opened, only just managing to survive for the scheduled number of performances—six in all. I think *R.U.R.* struggled on into August, and then collapsed. After its tumultuous start this took us by surprise. We had nothing ready. Fortunately, crisis was averted when Charles McEvoy suddenly came into orbit, dressed much as when I first met him in Manchester fifteen years before: green velveteens with a red handkerchief round his neck in place of a tie; he might easily be mistaken either for a gamekeeper or his natural enemy, the poacher. He was still voicing off-beat opinions in which love of the open road, the hedgerows and the gypsies, were inextricably mixed up with the cloudy idealism of the early Socialists, and always in the same peculiar high-pitched voice, compounded of Cockney and county. I remembered the various plays of his that I had produced, his gentle mockery of my own playwriting and, above all, his advice when I tackled Liverpool: 'Get the ordinary people into the theatre: never mind the high-brows.' The play he now thrust into my hands with a mixture of cockiness and diffidence, as though dreading confirmation of his private doubts about it, had been badly typed on an old typewriter and sheathed in crumpled brown paper. 'Oh dear!' I thought.

The Likes of 'Er proved to be his most successful piece. In different guise and under a different title it was destined to acquire an international reputation; but that story is for later telling. The plot is simple enough. Sally Winch, the heroine, lives in a slum alley in Stepney during the demobilisation period following the ending of World War I. She is waiting, Ruth-like, for the return of her soldier lover. Despite the fact that he has been posted as missing she obstinately believes he will return and refuses other suitors. Among her Cockney neighbours, all of them drawn with humour and sympathy, is Florrie Small, a slum waif whose father, a counterfeiter, has taught her to steal and regularly ill-treats her. Sally takes the child under her care and sends the father packing. But she soon discovers Florrie is both a liar and a thief. When challenged Florrie denies the theft and throws a plate on the floor, whereupon Sally tells her to go on smashing plates if it will relieve her feelings. She watches calmly as one by one her cherished pieces of chinaware are smashed. Finally, Florrie bursts into tears, confesses to the theft, and sobs in Sally's arms. Her complex is broken.

I realised this play would afford wonderful opportunities for my old associates from the Manchester and Liverpool companies. But there was no one young enough to play Florrie Small. By a happy chance, while I was cogitating this problem I read a notice of the performances which the Arts League of Service were giving at the Royal Court Theatre. They had been given a sympathetic welcome by the London critics, especially a child named Hermione Baddeley. On the spur of the moment I decided to go to the final matinée on the Saturday. The child I had come to see was in her early teens, small, dark, thin as a rake, with large eyes set in an impish face. She sang a simple ballad in costume with a parasol. Here was obviously great natural talent. Immediately after the performance I went round to the stage-door and asked her mother to bring the child to see me at the St. Martin's on the following Monday. I gave her a three-year contract with the ReandeaN Company. Florrie was her first part with us. She scored an immediate, a startling success.

The Likes of 'Er was on the short side, so I obtained permission to produce J. M. Barrie's one-act play, *The Will*, in front of it. The contrast between the urbane sentiments of Barrie and the biting Cockney humour of McEvoy was much appreciated both by the critics and the public. Mary Clare, Leslie Banks, Ian Hunter, Ada King, Ben Field, Clifford Mollison, Olga Lindo, in fact the entire company, gave a fine account of themselves. A newcomer to the ensemble was Robert Harris, who had been the Critics' Circle choice to win the Academy medal at R.A.D.A., as well as a year's engagement with us. He acquitted himself well in the Barrie play, to the relief of the critics who thus found their judgment confirmed by the public.

The plate-smashing scene in the McEvoy play acquired considerable fame because it skilfully used the theories of Freud and Jung in an entirely new stage approach to child psychology. There was no doubt about the sensation the scene caused: also, it gave the play a quality of intellectual distinction that otherwise it did not possess. McEvoy writing with sympathy, understanding and always with humour after the First World War foreshadowed a similar stretching of conventional boundaries after the second in what came to be known as the kitchen-sink drama.

II

By this time the general public was showing great interest in our doings, thanks largely to the admirable publicity in the hands of W. R. Titterton, a left-wing poet and journalist of immense enthusiasm who had met Flecker during a poetry session at a Fabian summer school and been accounted the better poet! From the outset I had striven for distinction in the layout of our printing by cutting out unnecessary detail and putting an end to the assortment of type generally used so that the ReandeaN imprint became instantly recognisable everywhere in theatre-land. When Titterton joined us he became editor of the *ReandeaN News Sheet*, a magazine programme

YASMIN?.....

AUBREY HAMMOND.

*Aubrey Hammond's idea of
H. de Vere Stacpoole as Hassan.*

containing in addition to the usual information, articles by the dramatists who were writing for our theatre, and notes by members of the staff. A special number was printed to commemorate the Fourth Anniversary of ReandeaN's existence. It contained articles on various aspects of our work by Arnold Bennett, J. M. Barrie, Clemence Dane, John Galsworthy, John Hastings Turner, H. de Vere Stacpoole and A. A. Milne, concluding with one by Geoffrey Whitworth on the art of George Harris. There were woodcuts by Harris and caricatures by Aubrey Hammond. The inadequate programmes of those days were usually supplied by the concessionaires who ran the refreshment bars, and contained little beyond a list of scenes and the names of the players. Our news-sheet followed the precedent set by Tree at His Majesty's Theatre, but I doubt whether even he could have assembled such a galaxy of authorship within the pages of a theatre programme. Nevertheless, I received a sharp rebuke from Philip Page, who wrote an article reminding me that a theatre was neither a school nor a lecture hall. One wonders what he would have said about the directives on audience understanding sometimes issued by the subsidised theatres of today.

Titterton was on personal terms with a surprising number of famous literary figures. He had no hesitation in calling upon them to take part in a series of debates upon our current productions. The first debate was about *R.U.R.* presided over by the enthusiastic Titterton himself. Among the speakers was Bernard Shaw, who wound up the discussion with all guns firing paradoxes right and left. 'All the people of this audience are robots. . . . Your opinions are a manufactured article imposed upon you from without. . . . Tell me it's the Government's business to make you happy and I say damn the Government's impudence. . . . Let me be a robot for two hours a day and for the rest of the day let me be Bernard Shaw.'

The second debate, with *Melloney Holtspur* under discussion, was presided over by Marie Tempest, and opened by Conal O'Riordan, who declared that the Masefield play was the worst play about ghosts ever written, except one.

'Which was that?' demanded a member of the audience.

'*Hamlet*,' remarked Earl Russell, lounging on a purple sofa at the side of the stage. . . . All this was capital fun and valuable advertisement for us and for our Playbox.

12

I always liked to involve myself in the technical side, and this seems right to me for these men are the engineers and donkeymen, without whose efficiency the ship cannot be brought safely into port. In the ReandeaN Company the heads of departments were encouraged to regard themselves as direct contributors to the success of each production. It was not long before they were given copies of the plays to read in advance, so that they should know the tasks that lay in front of them. The statement that has been made in print that Laurence Olivier initiated this democratic principle when he assumed direction of the National Theatre is incorrect. Our staff became so alert that at the first reading of one of the later Galsworthy plays I was astonished to find them lined up in their white linen coats and soft canvas shoes (I detested noise backstage) with outlines of the scenes taped out on the stage and substitute properties neatly tabled on one side! For productions on the larger West End stages my staff were put in charge of all technical matters, a system that led them to puff out their chests with pride. Upon one occasion I overheard Albert Jones, my stage superintendent, cleverest master of his craft in all London and, incidentally, possessed of the largest pair of hands I have ever seen, explaining with amiable condescension to the head technician at Drury Lane what he expected of him during a forthcoming production. I had two stage directors, A. B. Ince, a tiny little man, scarce more than five-feet tall, of immense energy with the fire of unswerving loyalty in his belly, and W. A. Abingdon, his direct opposite, imperturbability his greatest asset, who was made responsible for the more spectacular productions at His Majesty's Theatre and, later, Drury Lane.

I enjoyed all the activities of production enormously, especially the dress rehearsals, the final one being my superior delight, especially when it was time to begin lighting rehearsals. Not only the heads of departments, but all the staff were intensely proud of our work discipline. A tiny incident, oft-repeated, illustrates the good relations that existed among us. Our rehearsals were often prolonged into the small hours of the morning. The empty theatres became perishingly cold, so I always kept my hat on. But as concentration deepened, I would drop it on a seat somewhere during my peregrinations round the auditorium. At the end of the rehearsal it would invariably be lost, and I would ask someone to find it. Then there would be a great shout: 'Guv'nor's lost 'is bloody 'at again. Anybody seen it?' This would raise a mocking cheer from the exhausted crew, but not much effort to find my lost headgear.

On the day of performance I would rehearse technical details over and over again, often staying until the auditorium lights were switched on and ticket-holders had begun to trickle in. I would go to each dressing-room in turn to give last-minute encouragement. I was never able to sit through my own first nights; there was too much at stake. I preferred to wait, quiet but shaking with nerves, in a nearby restaurant, receiving hurried reports from the staff as to how things were going, and then entering the stage-door just as the curtain was about to fall. Congratulations (or sympathy, as the reception warranted) followed to each member of the company in turn, always disappointed that I had not been there to see it all, sometimes gleefully recalling the success of some special directions I may have given them—'it was just as you said it would be, but oh! why weren't you there?' Then the staff would assemble in my office where I would sit listening to their salty criticisms of each other's work that night. Meanwhile, Paul Clift would be bargaining with the 'libraries' in his office next door, and Alec Rea receiving the congratulations of our 'customers' in the foyer. By these various means, not deliberate but because I liked to do it, we built up a wonderful esprit de corps. The surrender to nerves was a weakness which robbed me of many exciting moments, but it never saved me from the shock of disaster.

The high praise that we were receiving for our productions at the St. Martin's and the Ambassadors—even A. B. Walkley in *The Times*, seldom ecstatic about anything save the more advanced areas of French literature, joining in the chorus of approval—was proof that the standards of ensemble acting that we had set out to achieve were now generally recognised. When to this was added a month or so later the furore over *Hassan*, it really did seem as though the zenith had been reached, from which nothing was going to topple me. The folly of such imaginings in the world of the theatre was to be vouchsafed to me all too soon.

Eleven
Over the hills and far away

I

One effect of the *Hassan* sensation was the special interest which Sir James Barrie showed in my work. Although he had always followed the happenings at the little theatres in West Street with encouragement, this special sympathy seemed to beckon me on to further fortune, but it did not turn out so.

I often went to visit him in his big sitting-room in Adelphi Terrace. From the wide window of the flat there was a splendid view of the river and of the Lion Brewery on the opposite bank. But the flat itself was gloomy in the extreme and made more so by a butler whose sinister presence suggested Mr. Smith in *Shall We Join the Ladies?* They were strangely subdued afternoon sessions, with Barrie seated on the oaken settle on one side of a smoky fire, looking gnome-like in the autumn light, and I, young and ardent and extremely talkative where theatre matters were concerned, on the other. I would sit in silence for minutes at a time, waiting for the little man to say something, the silence broken only by the gurgling of his old briar pipe. Although he spoke little one felt that he saw everything. Sometimes I would miss my cue to leave and would be asked to stay for tea. Then his man would respond to the unexpected occasion by setting out a meagre tea upon a gate-legged table—a few slices of brown bread and butter and a sultana cake— with a slow neatness which added to the strangely oppressive atmosphere. I suspected my host of preferring that most abominable of meals known to the Scots as 'high tea'.

There was at that time a certain mystique surrounding Barrie's name and reputation, a kind of reverence, for which the universal

appeal of many of his plays, especially *Peter Pan*, was mainly responsible. The story of his marriage to Mary Ansell, playing in his
first success, *Walker, London,* and of how he would sit at her bedside
recounting the incidents of the day to a wife longing for a physical
love which he was incapable of giving, and of the subsequent
betrayal of his trust by the young writer he had befriended was
known only within a small circle of sympathy. Perhaps the knowledge
of his impotence and the thought of the runaway wife whose marriage
had never been consummated were the cause of his phenomenal
shyness. Certainly it stimulated a public curiosity that was never
to be satisfied. There was pathos, too, in his yearning for the love
of children. The faded school-cap of a young friend drowned at
Oxford which hung on a peg above his desk may have been a morbid
gesture, but it was there also as a warning that some thoughts
were too precious to be discussed. He seemed to have a nostalgia
for youth and its dreams, and to care less for established success.

2

One autumn afternoon, as we sat together in his flat, Barrie more
than usually silent and depressed, his man announced Sir Sydney
Cockerell, who was director of the Fitzwilliam Museum at Cambridge. I got up immediately.

'No, no, stay where you are,' said Barrie. 'He wants to ask me
for something,' a remark that, judging by the expression on Barrie's
face, was full of foreboding.

Sir Sydney came into the room exuding charm and erudition. The
conversation ranged wide and free upon every subject but the one
that was uppermost in both men's minds. I sat silent, wishing myself out of the way. Presently the conversational preliminaries died
away, and there was silence. Barrie walked up and down the room
between window and fireplace, sucking at his pipe. The moment of
crisis had arrived. Then in a tone of anguish he murmured: 'What
did ye want to see me about?' Whereupon Cockerell began an
eloquent description of Augustus John's portrait of Thomas
Hardy. 'I've seen the picture,' muttered Barrie.

That was a 'middle-stumper' all right, I thought, but Cockerell
continued, undeterred. He was anxious to acquire the picture for
the Fitzwilliam, and described how various friends had suggested
Sir James might like to present it to the museum. Another silence

Above   *Spring Cleaning*. Ian Hunter introduces a not-very-convincing street-walker (Cathleen Nesbitt) to his wife's guests: Edna Best, Cecily Byrne, Nancie Parsons, Denys Blakelock, and Ronald Squire

Below   Peter Pan battles with Captain Hook in U.S.A., 1923: Marilyn Miller and Leslie Banks

Above   Sex confronts Religion on the Island of Pago Pago (Olga Lindo versus Marda Vanne, Malcolm Keen and J. H. Roberts)

Below left   With Somerset Maugham, not exactly 'Singing in the rain'. Cartoon from *The Bystander*

Below right   Switching on the rain!

W. Somerset Maugham's *Rain*. Garrick Theatre, 1925

as Barrie in his carpet slippers trudged the width of the room, gazing first at the smouldering logs in the fireplace and then back at the Lion Brewery through the window.

Finally, he stopped, and in a voice of anguish asked: 'How much?' Cockerell with the utmost delicacy hinted that he thought the figure might be about £3,000. Again that silence: again the gurgling pipe which seemed to be protesting at the enormity of the request. Then, with his sad doe's eyes staring at his visitor, Barrie said: 'I don't think I'd like to do that.' Cockerell left shortly afterwards, discomfited by the blank refusal. Barrie resumed his march up and down the room before turning to me with tears in his eyes to say: 'I don't think they ought to ask me to do these things.' . . . Whatever may have been the final outcome of that interview, the John portrait of Thomas Hardy now hangs in the Fitzwilliam Museum at Cambridge.

3

Barrie's confidence in me continued to grow, so that one day he told me I might revive any of his plays that I wished, with the exception of *Mary Rose*, which was held under contract by the Haymarket Theatre. Once again the siren voice of opportunity was luring me off-course, this time without the excuse of having to fulfil a promise. During the next twelve months it was to lead me into various blind alleys from which eventually I had to extricate myself as best I could.

For some time Golding Bright had been urging me to revive *The Little Minister*, one of the early Barrie plays, and to give Fay Compton the opportunity of playing Lady Babbie. But the play required more stage room than we possessed at the St. Martin's, so I was once again on the look-out for a larger theatre. One inquiry led to another until at Golding's prompting there entered upon the scene the rather sinister figure of Alfred Butt, whose pockets were bulging with opportunity.

Butt began his career as an accountant at Harrods. He transferred his attention to the theatre when Charles Morton, who had built the Palace Theatre as a home for popular opera, got into financial difficulties, and called him in to keep the books. He became Morton's partner, developed a flair for showmanship, and established the Palace as one of the most popular music-halls in Europe: Maud

P

Allan as Salome, Margaret Cooper's Songs at the Piano, Anna Pavlova as the Dying Swan, Herman Finck and his orchestra playing 'In the Shadows'—so popular that it drew men out of the bars to listen to it—it was a formidable list indeed! One of the latest stars to shine in that coruscating firmament was the delightful Elsie Janis, first introduced to Alfred Butt by her terrible mother as 'the only virgin in vaudeville'. By 1914 Butt had acquired or gained control of many of the leading theatres and music-halls in London. His ruthlessness in business made him unpopular, and malicious stories were told about him. Suffering from a curious jerky movement of the head, gossips used to say that was because he could feel the rope round his neck.

At Bright's suggestion I was to go into partnership with this formidable tycoon at the Queen's Theatre on terms that appeared to be ideal. Butt was to provide the theatre and to occupy himself exclusively with the business side of the venture, while I was to reign supreme behind the curtain. The plan was warmly welcomed by the Press. The one element essential to success was missing, namely the plays. I was so greedy for opportunity that I had not realised that Butt expected me to find them, and that all he had to do was control expenditure and nod his approval at our eventual success. The first production was *The Little Minister*, done in association with ReandeaN (November 7th, 1923). Subsequently, plays were to be chosen by mutual agreement and financed entirely by Butt.

While electricians were swarming over the stage. George Harris and I went up to Kirriemuir, which Barrie had used as a model for his village of Thrums, to make sketches of the countryside and of the exterior of the manse where one of the principal scenes is laid. Golding Bright came with us. We went on to Glasgow to interview some Scots actors whom Barrie had recommended. Following my usual practice, the play was cast up to the hilt. Owen Nares, playing Gavin Dishart, refrained wisely, I think, from any attempt to reproduce a Scots accent, but Fay Compton, with the Mackenzie blood in her, had no difficulty. The four elders of the kirk, headed by Norman McKinnel, were all Scots and also the boy, Micah Dow, played by Hector Macgregor, a youngster from Glasgow who had never been on the stage before. We did better in the matter of accents than the original production nearly thirty years earlier when the elders were played by Englishmen, which had caused a Scots member of the cast to protest to Barrie that their accents were absurd. 'I know that,' said Barrie, 'but it's not English either, and the audience won't know the difference.' Hannen Swaffer, wandering in and out of rehearsal in search of titbits of news, a cock o' the walk pecking in the theatrical farmyard, noted that 'Whenever Barrie spoke or made the tiniest gesture, the whole rehearsal would stop immediately, to listen to the words of the great little man.'

The open-air scenes gave wonderful opportunities for atmospheric lighting, of which I took full advantage. When Barrie saw what I had contrived for the first act, the Scotch mist gradually blotting out the sunset over the distant village, and the tiny rushlights appearing one by one in the cottage windows, he remarked wryly: 'Soon actors and actresses will be coming on the stage naked, and the lights will dress them.' The remark was not intended as a prophecy. Yet some producers have achieved this without the use of lights!

Criticism on the whole was adverse. Fay Compton came off best. Owen Nares' restraint in not attempting an accent was praised, and that fine actor Norman McKinnel made the scenes with the elders a joy to listen to. One doubter wondered whether this ancient play would stand up to the modern change of taste: '. . . for one person who can enter into the spirit of Barrie there are a thousand who like to pretend they do'. As for the stage and lighting effects, they were so far in advance of what was customary that some of the critics found them distracting. S. R. Littlewood, the doyen of them all, gave me a sly dig, saying thay my hobby appeared to be 'lights ancient and modern'.

Writing more favourably of the performance than some, the *Morning Post* critic drew a comparison between the acting of Fay Compton and that of the Albanesi. Whereas in Fay's case the audience thought first of the part she was playing and then of her performance of it, the exact opposite was the case with Meggie. People speak instinctively of having seen her in certain parts; 'she lives in the emotions that the part evokes.' Fay Compton, on the other hand, is an actress by instinct. Descended from a line of famous players, she has the theatre in her blood. . . . In spite of a mixed reception the play ran until March, 1924.

4

Free for the moment from bothersome outside commitments—I grumbled at them but really it was all my own fault—and with both ReandeaN productions running strongly in West Street, I looked forward eagerly to the reopening of the Playbox. The next production was to be *A Magdalen's Husband*, adapted by Milton Rosmer and Edward Percy from the novel by Vincent Brown: a rather pedestrian affair, but containing a part for Meggie that would stretch her emotional powers to the full. I was filled with joy at the prospect of working with her again, and selected an especially strong cast from our permanent company to support her—Ian Hunter, Malcolm Keen, Clifford Mollison and Ada King among them.

Meggie appeared to be in splendid form, and obviously glad to be working in 'our' theatre again. I did notice that she tired sooner at rehearsal than was her wont, but I put that down to the gay life she continued to lead, despite the warnings of an ever-widening circle of friends, including some of the dramatic critics. True, there was a look of desperation in her eyes at times, but I thought that was just part of her usual struggle to perfect her part. With her performance as Joan Potten, the village girl, rescued by her lover from the assaults of a drunken husband, who is accidentally killed in the struggle, she was going to take another giant stride forward in her career, I was so elated at the prospect that I was blind to the impending disaster.

We came at last to the dress rehearsal, an unforgettable memory. In the morning I think it was, because all the cast had matinées at one or other of our theatres, the whole company seemed to be inspired by Meggie's acting, giving unusual quality to a very ordinary little play. There was an aura of dedication, of inner communication about the theatre that morning that everyone felt, yet could only express afterwards in a few stumbling phrases. When we reached the last act those of the cast whose parts were done, instead of rushing off to lunch, came into the stalls to watch Meggie, seated at a cottage table, reading verses from the New Testament to her half-witted brother, and ever and anon stopping to listen for the nearby prison clock to strike eight o'clock, the time of her lover's execution. We watched and listened, spellbound. Gradually, the quiet, slightly hoarse voice began to pour its emotion over us, as the pupils of her eyes dilated, making them seem twice their normal size, and the whole personality became charged with explosive force. The effect was shattering. There was silence for a full minute after the curtain fell, and then spontaneous applause burst from the little knot of actors. Then they filed quietly out of the theatre, humbled in the face of a unique experience.

I hurried upstairs to congratulate Meggie in her dressing-room. The moment I appeared she flung her arms round me and burst into tears, as she had so often done before, but this time there was a deeper accent of despair: 'Oh, Basil, darling, I know I shall never play this part. I know it. I feel ill,' and there followed a jumble of incoherent phrases. I had never known her so deeply distressed.

'Nonsense, darling,' I said, as soon as I could control my voice, 'of course you will. It's your greatest performance yet.'

'I can't! I shan't! I shan't! I feel it!' she repeated passionately. I told her again and again of the triumph that awaited her. Eventually, she grew calmer, and I persuaded her to go across to the Ivy where friends were waiting to give her lunch. A quarter of an hour later I went myself to the Ivy to lunch with George Harris. As I told him what had happened I looked across to where Meggie was sitting, unusually quiet and eating very little. Her complexion had a greenish tint. Suddenly I realised that she was very ill indeed. It was as if a cold hand had gripped me by the throat. I went across to her table:

'Meggie, darling, you don't look at all well.'

'I told you. I do feel ill,' she replied wanly.

'Then you're not to play today. I shall put the understudy on. You must go home. Go to bed and rest.'

With unusual docility she agreed and left the restaurant. Later, she decided to go down that afternoon to the Kingsgate Castle Hotel, near Broadstairs, where she often stayed. She was a great favourite with the proprietor. I never saw her again. She suffered a severe haemorrhage during the journey. Luckily, a good Samaritan on the train insisted on taking her to her own home and sent for her family doctor. He advised immediate removal to a nursing home and an operation. Later, he rang me up at the theatre to tell me Meggie's condition was very serious. She had not wanted either her parents or the theatre to be told, but he had insisted.

5

Meggie Albanesi died on December 9th, 1923. She had just passed her twenty-fourth birthday. Her stage career had lasted six years. The memoir that her mother, Maria Albanesi, wrote about her some five years after her death is full of love and tenderness, but shows a complete lack of understanding of the dual nature of her brilliant daughter. The implication in her book that I was partly responsible for her child's death caused me much distress. Information I gleaned from hints dropped by Meggie's intimates gave me some reassurance that overwork was not the cause of her death. Meggie had refused to take even the most ordinary precautions, an attitude of mind that may have been due to her Catholic upbringing. Some time later I met the surgeon who had examined her prior to an operation. She was too ill to undress. He was shocked by her condition. 'She had virtually no inside left,' he said. The result, one supposes, of repeated curetting. Her mother's complete lack of knowledge of that side of her daughter's life, or, alternatively, of her determination to turn a blind eye to it, was patent.

The St. Martin's Theatre and all who worked for it were stunned by the tragedy. The authors, the actors, the staff, all had come to regard Meggie as the gem in our little crown of achievement. To us all it was tragedy because the immense promise of her life had been largely unfulfilled. Beyond our immediate circle, in the world outside, there was a similar feeling of personal loss. As I glance through the books of faded press cuttings I am struck once again by the coverage accorded in national and provincial newspapers to such a brief life.

One of the most perceptive appreciations was written by Christopher St. John in *Time and Tide*:

'She could bring her inner emotion directly to face and voice and body without trick or artifice. . . . She expressed herself, so to speak, in primary colours with a frankness and cleanness that made every character she impersonated seem amazingly simple. One knew she was a person in the great drama of life before she opened her mouth in the mimic drama. . . .'

More succinct but no less eloquent was the tribute from an unknown correspondent in the *Sunday Times*, quoting Edgar Allan Poe's epitaph on Madame Malibran: 'She left the world at twenty-five having existed her thousands of years.'

6

It is no exaggeration to say that I knew genuine grief for the first time. My life in the theatre had been bound up with Meggie's career far more than I had realised. The company, realising this,

December 11th 1923

Dear Mr Dean We would like to offer you our most sincere sympathy on your tragic loss, a loss which is equally felt by us all and we shall be only too pleased to help in all ways to make things as easy for you as possible during this difficult time.

[facsimile of round robin with numerous signatures]

signed a round robin, expressing their sympathy with me and promising me their continued support. This was evidence of the *esprit de corps* that existed among us but it could not make good my loss. I replied thankfully and in like terms in a letter addressed to the company generally and posted on the theatre notice board. The round robin is reproduced here in facsimile.

In July of the following year we gave a special matinée at the St. Martin's Theatre to raise funds for a permanent scholarship at

Another Harris woodcut: Sybil Thorndike and Malcolm Keen

the Royal Academy of Dramatic Art. The list of patrons was headed by the Queen Mother (then Duchess of York). The galaxy of stars taking part was testimony both to the love and the admiration which the English Theatre felt for her achievement: Henry Ainley, Fred and Adele Astaire, George Robey, Jack Buchanan and Betty Chester, Fay Compton, Leon Quartermaine, all the ReandeaN players, and hosts of minor celebrities, scrambling to find a place on our small stage in memory of her.

I commissioned Eric Gill to design a memorial plaque and wrote the inscription for it. This is to be seen on the side wall leading out of the main lobby at the St. Martin's Theatre.

7

Early in the New Year I had to face the melancholy task of presenting *A Magdalen's Husband* with another actress in Meggie's part. This was followed by the promised Sunday Night Gala Performance: free seats for subscribers only. We gave the two verse plays already announced: first *Gruach* by Gordon Bottomley, an imaginary prologue to Shakespeare's *Macbeth*, foreshadowing the future Lady Macbeth's propensity for sleep-walking. Lascelles Abercrombie provided the second piece, *Phoenix*, which he described as a tragic farce. The full strength of the ReandeaN Company was deployed with Esmé Beringer and Sybil Thorndike as guest artists. Sybil's performance as Gruach gave high promise of a future Lady Macbeth. But what should have been a joyous vindication of our poets' faith in poetic drama turned out to be a dull and lifeless performance. The shadow of our recent loss seemed to hang like a raincloud between us and the audience.

For the remainder of that year the story becomes little more than a catalogue of disaster. First, *The Lilies of the Field* at the Ambassadors, failing to recover from the loss of Meggie, gave place in February to Clemence Dane's second realistic play, *The*

Way Things Happen, in which the part specially written for Meggie was played by Olga Lindo. Ada King in the small part of a mother captured major critical attention, but she was not what the play was about. No sooner had this play been produced, than *The Likes of 'Er* at the St. Martin's began to show signs of heart failure. Fortunately, I had an interesting new Galsworthy scheduled there.

Harris woodcut for The Forest

The Forest was an unusual play in that it set out to expose the exploitation of Central Africa by big business in the City. It began and ended with directors' meetings reminiscent of the board-room scenes in *Strife.* Its two middle acts were laid in the African jungle, where an explorer (Leslie Banks) and his expedition were eventually overwhelmed by hostile tribesmen. There was virtually an all-male cast; in addition to our usual players, it included Franklin Dyall, H. R. Hignett (playing a doctor instead of his usual sinister butler), Felix Aylmer and Campbell Gullan. The sole female part, that of a native girl, was played by Hermione Baddeley. Armed with a spear and a terrifying yell she leapt simultaneously on to the back of Leslie Banks and into the hearts of an audience waiting for a repetition of her success in *The Likes of 'Er.* They were not disappointed. As I watched this child of sixteen taking a solo curtain call with the assurance of an established favourite, I wondered whether kind Fortune had presented me with another young star to take Meggie's place. But Hermione's extreme youth stood in the way of her attaining the dramatic power which our plays usually called for. Later she developed a gift of comedy that none of us suspected at the time.

J.G. was unable to attend more than the first readings because Ada Galsworthy dragged him away to the Continent to exercise his nursing skill upon her current indisposition. In his stead, Barrie, commanded to a watching brief on behalf of the author, asked me for a copy of the play and the times of the rehearsals which I sent him. He came to two of them, made no comment and when at the end of the second rehearsal I turned to ask his opinion he was seen disappearing through an emergency exit.

For the forest scenes Harris followed up a suggestion of mine that the tree-trunks should be covered in velvet, overpainted and treated with size to give an effect of tropical damp. The lianas and orchids that hung from the trees were similarly treated and the whole scene back-lighted in pale green and yellow. This made the shallow St. Martin's stage look as deep as that of Drury Lane. The division of dramatic interest between London and tropical Africa proved fatal to the play's success: a play with what is technically known as a broken back rarely succeeds.

Envoi

(*Extract from the memoir* For Meggie *published in the anniversary number of the 'ReandeaN News-Sheet' in 1924.*)

Gone from rehearsal is the sound of her quick, eager step, the slightly raucous laugh, the questioning about her part across the footlights. Vanished, too, her burning vitality, her passionate desire to learn and to extract the last ounce of meaning and emotion out of her part. . . . Meggie was usually first at rehearsal, and always the last to leave. She used often to tell me she preferred rehearsals to performances. That was the true Meggie, honest, hard-working, critical of herself, happiest when her striving spirit had difficulties to overcome, when the creative power within her had full rein.

With each successive production sympathy and understanding grew between us, until at last people behind the scenes used jokingly to talk of Trilby and Svengali. This was absurd. Meggie was always herself, selecting carefully what little help I could give her, rejecting the unsuitable. Throughout her work with us I never once heard her give a false inflection. Meanings she could not feel (for inflections are but meanings expressed) she rejected. Her acting was after the manner of Duse, soaring high and clear above impersonation by presenting emotion in the round, so to speak, it passed beyond the confines of the written word, presenting human emotion abstract yet glorified.

Meggie was the English Rachel not yet come to the fulness of her powers. Hers was not a spirit that burned brightly on the hearth; it roared up the chimney. At last the fierce spirit burnt itself out, longing pitifully for that greater achievement, so well within its grasp, that temperament had denied to her. One might say that she sped, comet-like, across the theatrical firmament, and burnt herself out in exhilaration and divine fire. . . .

Twelve
'Sweet smell of Old Drury'

I

Theatre Royal, Drury Lane: how evocative that sounds—evocative, that is, of childhood memories and of the great figures of our stage. For the greater part of two centuries Drury Lane, like a great flagship, rose and fell upon the waves of popular favour following the emergence and decline of each great acting leader. Lasting success was first achieved there by the Triumvirate, a group of actors led by Colley Cibber, actor, author and eventually poet laureate. It was his boast that tradesmen's bills were promptly paid each week—presumably also the actors' salaries—a unique example of ordered management in a turbulent age. But the most notable outcrop of English acting genius appeared in the person of David Garrick, who threw overboard all previous notions of tragic acting with its accents of formal woe and presented comedy in terms of observed character, vastly different from the sheer buffoonery which it replaced. John Philip Kemble's performances with his sister, the incomparable Sarah Siddons, brought superb declamation and classic dignity to his Shakespearean rôles. With the arrival of Irving at the Lyceum, this primacy was ended. Great actors no longer led the English Theatre from Drury Lane, preferring to use its size and historic significance for their farewell appearances. But as the line of actor-managers died out, even this shadow of former greatness was denied to it. Thereafter, Drury Lane became our national theatre by right of legend only, the home for spectacular melodrama and Christmas pantomime, with the spirit of its progenitor, Grimaldi—once described as the David Garrick of pantomime—lingering on in its harlequinades. 'Hot Codlins' was no longer sung from its boards.

The theatre remained rooted in tradition right up to the time of the First World War. In the aftermath it began to fall out of grace with the public who wanted neither melodrama—they had experienced sufficient thrills in the recent conflict—nor old-fashioned pantomime. Its manager was Arthur Collins, whose policy was a continuation of that pursued by his great predecessor, Sir Augustus Harris. When Sir Alfred Butt joined the board of directors this basically simple policy became subject to conflicting interests. Butt obtained additional capital from his backer, Solly Joel, and stampeded the shareholders into rebuilding and modernising the theatre —work which involved its closure for more than a year. It reopened in April, 1922, with a spectacular drama with music called *Decameron Nights*, which ran for a year. During that time relations between Collins and Butt became strained. The former was tired while the latter was nursing new ideas which he kept to himself.

2

It was towards the end of 1923 that I was propelled into the scene. Four of my productions were then doing well in the West End, and my stock stood high with the commercial managements, higher indeed than my achievements precisely warranted. So there was every temptation to add a fifth theatre to my list of occupancies, if time and opportunity should serve and suitable plays be available. But I was forgetting one of the truths of managerial existence, that to count upon continuing success in the theatre is usually to court failure.

My chief proponent for the Drury Lane arena was Sydney Carroll, a solid Antipodean with a passionate love of the theatre and a gambler's instinct for quick success. Possibly it was this trait in his character that attracted him to the theatre, with its glamour and its sudden changes of fortune, although he also had a sound knowledge of its literature. He began his career as a small-part actor, drifted into journalism and became dramatic critic of the *Sunday Times*. A good man in the theatre. He was a generous admirer of my work. Although I was aware of his partisanship I was astonished when he came to see me one day and told me that Butt was thinking of offering me Drury Lane. It was a tempting prospect, but I demurred at first because I shared the view of my generation that 'Old Drury' was a cumbersome enterprise, lumbering behind public taste. But I gave way to temptation of a still wider opportunity, one for which I was ill-prepared and which was to become my undoing.

During my interview with Sir Alfred I strode about his office, stipulating for complete control over artistic policy, the casting and production of the plays and the engagement and dismissal of all technical staff. I was doing most of the talking while Butt just sat and listened. When I was finally 'hooked' an entirely different set of conditions emerged, which made it plain that only if I met with immediate success would I be free of interference. I received the letter of agreement, signed by Sir Alfred as chairman on January 30th. The appointment was back-dated to January 1st, and was to be confirmed by the board, but I heard nothing for several weeks. But when the current melodrama, most inappropriately named *Good Luck*, which had opened with a tremendous flourish, began to show signs of collapse, a board meeting was hurriedly summoned and my appointment confirmed. A press conference was called, at which Arthur Collins courteously inducted me into the hot seat, where I was left holding the baby, already in an advanced state of dissolution! To complete my induction I was invited to dine with the board of directors at Lord Lurgan's house. Among those present were Solly Joel, who held a large debenture on the theatre, terrifyingly jocund and ruthless, 'Willie' Boosey, reigning power in the world of popular song, and Lord Lurgan, urbane and polished, the most sympathetic of all the personalities I met there. I was too nervous to do more than gulp mouthfuls of the rich food between waves of uncertainty and listen to financial arguments the meaning of which quite escaped me. I left the dinner party without any of that bounding confidence in the future with which my fellow-guests had been courteously toasting me in goblets of champagne.

3

Ordinary caution should have warned me that it was highly dangerous to accept the managing directorship of Drury Lane when neither a policy nor a programme to express that policy had been discussed, let alone worked out in detail. Absorbed in production elsewhere, I had given little thought to the matter beyond cherishing a vague desire to give the theatre true national status by presenting some of our leading actors in Shakespeare and the English classics: Tree's policy at His Majesty's Theatre brought up to date. While my agreement was under discussion Butt had confidently asserted that *Good Luck* would run well into the autumn, which would have given me time to make plans and to secure his agreement. Now the prospect was bleak. The theatre was about to be closed; for how long must depend upon my ability to find a successor.

Here was a bad beginning. There was no time to discuss policy. The theatre's immediate future had to be settled over-night, as it were. The only play immediately available was *London Life*, written by Arnold Bennett and Edward Knoblock, originally intended for the Queen's Theatre. With the authors' agreement and Butt's approval I decided to stage it at Drury Lane. It was an unfortunate decision, for neither Bennett's intimate dialogue nor Knoblock's meticulous craftsmanship was suited to the broad canvas of Drury Lane. However, we took full advantage of the varied opportunities for spectacle which the play afforded: a reception in Grosvenor Square at the height of the London Season, a *fête champêtre* with playing fountains and a display of fireworks (which went wrong on the first night), and the terrace of the House of Commons with members in full fig. To secure the necessary breadth of performance, the play was cast partly from the older generation of actors, including Henry Ainley, Lilian Braithwaite, Graham Browne (Marie Tempest's husband), Gordon Harker and Mary Jerrold.

Rehearsing on that vast stage was intimidating at first. Then I remembered what Sir George Alexander had said to me when I went to see him about recruiting actors for the garrison theatres during the recent war: 'Drury Lane has a unique quality: it flatters the good actor and damns the bad one.' Ainley was always unreliable at rehearsals. Upon one occasion, just after lunch, we began on the big scene between him and Lilian Braithwaite on the terrace of the House of Commons. This ended with a tremendous curtain speech for Ainley. He had been too bored to rehearse it in the morning, and seemed just as distracted after lunch. But presently, Bennett marched on to the stage, bowler hat on the back of his head, thumbs in the armholes of his waistcoat, followed by Knoblock, his faithful Boswell. Both were smoking large cigars. As soon as he saw Bennett approaching, Ainley launched into the curtain-speech, regardless of cues, leaving Lilian Braithwaite mute and astonished. The speech was delivered with such magnificent gusto that at the end one could almost hear applause reverberating round the vast empty theatre. There was a moment's quiet as Ainley feigned surprise at the author's sudden appearance. Then came Arnold's spluttered comment: 'Th-th-that's a bloody fine speech!' . . .

To mark the change of management the tawdry posters and programmes with their ill-assorted typography were done away with, as at the other theatres in my charge. In their place we issued a programme and news-sheet on the cover of which in place of the conventional 'Alfred Butt and Basil Dean present. . . .' there appeared the simple statement:

The Actors of the Theatre Royal, Drury Lane,

in

LONDON LIFE

Inside there was a facsimile of the patent and charter granted to Thomas Killigrew in 1662 by Charles II. All this was part of my plan to remind the audience of the theatre's historic past.

Arnold contributed a short article, 'Writing for Drury Lane', in which he explained how the play had been written expecially for that theatre, an astonishing piece of duplicity on his part, at which I must have connived. A mix-up over seats for the first-night shows the childish delight Bennett took in being the keen man of business. He'd been sent the usual author's box and four complimentary stalls. When he wrote for three more stalls he was asked to pay for them, which drew a strong protest from Bennett: this was the first time he had ever been asked to pay for seats for the first night of one of his own plays. Referring to the article in the programme, he wrote:

> 'It is 700 words long. I am about the highest paid journalist in the country, and I never take less than 1/6d. a word for my work, whatever it is. I was therefore making a present to the Board of fifty guineas, whereas the Board is refusing to give me £5. worth of stalls, plus a box worth I suppose a few guineas. The article cannot possibly do me any good. It can make no difference whatever to the success or failure of the play, and I have written it solely to oblige the managers. This morning I have withdrawn the article.'

Such attention to financial detail made him an excellent foil to Nigel Playfair during the historic years of his management at the Lyric Theatre, Hammersmith.

Contrary to Bennett's prognostications, *London Life* had a mixed press. 'No horse-races, no burning houses, or falling roofs, no sea voyages', complained the *Daily Telegraph*. *The Times*, deceived by the title was full of lament because 'we had hoped to escape from Arnold Bennett's potteries for once'. I have always thought that Bennett's early success in collaboration with Knoblock, followed so quickly by his individual achievement with *The Great Adventure*, led him to the false conclusion that playwriting required only a small amount of creative effort. But the theatre does not readily give up its secrets to those who approach it in an attitude of condescension. The response at the box-office was so poor that at the chairman's behest the company took half-salaries after the first fortnight. The play closed on July 5th after a run of five weeks. My first Drury Lane production had been a disastrous failure.

4

The second closure of Drury Lane, coming so soon after my appointment, was a terrible blow to my plans. Time! Time! That was what I needed. Time! But that is rarely vouchsafed to the unwary.

When my appointment was first mooted I had begun to think in a general way of suitable historical subjects to supplement the Shakespeare programme. One such subject was the French Revolution, an idea inspired by Reinhardt's production of Georg Büchner's *Dantons Tod* which I had seen in Berlin. Much of the play's significance had escaped me because of my imperfect knowledge of German, but I had been left with the exhilaration of having seen a great play. Nevertheless, I thought Drury Lane deserved an original work, not a translation.

I asked Louis Napoleon Parker to prepare a scenario on the subject. As the leading pageant master of the day he was an obvious choice. Also, I thought if I could persuade Hilaire Belloc, whose knowledge of French history was considerable, to collaborate with him, a really worthwhile play might emerge. Both authors seized upon the idea with alacrity, but each wished to prepare his own scenario with a promise of interchange later. What followed was a model of non-collaboration. Parker completed his first draft in Italy and on his return sent it to Belloc, who had meanwhile retired to Somerset, since when all attempts to get him to break author's silence had

Q

failed. Our need of the play was now so urgent that I decided to bring matters to a head, and persuaded the two authors to meet in my office at Drury Lane. It was a stiflingly hot afternoon in July. Belloc arrived first, demanding a brandy and soda almost before wc had shaken hands. I sent for Mr. Webb, the house manager, and told him to open his liquor store. Pouring himself a libation from the full bottle Belloc proceeded to give us a vivid account of life in Paris under the Terror; Parker, vainly adjusting his box of hearing aid, heard scarcely a word! The two authors departed after I had extracted a renewed promise of collaboration. Belloc's brandy and soda remained untasted.

The prospects for my programme of English classics were brighter. The first production would be *The Taming of the Shrew*. Ainley as Petruchio and Gladys Cooper for Katherine would be a notable conjunction of stars! Then at Christmas *A Midsummer Night's Dream*, produced with scenic splendour and the Mendelssohn score—a good way to break with the pantomime tradition. Further ahead, I planned a production of *The School for Scandal*, done in a manner as close to the original production at Drury Lane in 1777 as research and Harris's skill could make it. Cyril Maude had already agreed to play Sir Peter with Fay Compton as Lady Teazle and Ainley as Joseph Surface. Alas! Harry was engaged in a lively correspondence with the board's secretary regarding non-payment for two cases of whisky he had bought during the run of *London Life*, and when a bill from a famous tailor in Savile Row for a complete outfit of modern clothes for the same play landed on the chairman's desk, it did not predispose him in favour of Harry's engagement as our leading man. The arguments that followed must have ruffled Harry's feelings considerably, for after I had obtained the board's reluctant approval I was confronted with a telegram from Harry refusing to play any more parts at Drury Lane! . . . All this while I remained blissfully unaware of the chairman's adamantine opposition to the production of any but obvious box-office attractions.

5

Half-way through August and still no play! This in spite of the efforts of authors' agents, raiding their dusty shelves in search of forgotten masterpieces. The search was by no means confined to the ranks of the great unacted. William Archer submitted the scenario of a play about Ancient Rome. When Butt mildly suggested the play lacked humour, Archer replied with an essay on the futility of 'comic relief'. Among the novelists who sought the Midas touch of success at Drury Lane were Phillips Oppenheim, Eden Phillpotts, Sax Rohmer and Winifred Holtby.

Out of the general gloom one afternoon there emerged John Barrymore with a suggestion that he should play *Hamlet* at the Lane. For a brief moment I thought this was the answer, but the great actor was without resources or organisation of any kind. My proposal that Drury Lane should finance the proposition further enraged the board. Butt thought I'd gone mad. (In the following spring Barrymore gave his memorable performance at the Haymarket.) About this time, too, I received several long telegrams from C. B. Cochran in France, telling me of a wonderful idea that he had for Drury Lane. But as he could not tell me what it was until terms had been agreed, I had to point out that the directors could not be expected to buy 'a pig in a poke'. The negotiations came to nothing.

As for the *Danton* project, the authors had been busily engaged in cutting each other's work to ribbons, the game of battledore and shuttlecock ending when Parker submitted a final version, from which most of Belloc's dialectics had been removed. The records show that in August, 1924, the board agreed to sign the contract, but the play was finally lost in the smoke of battle over the future of Drury Lane which overwhelmed us all in the autumn.

Towards the end of August Butt departed for Deauville in Solly Joel's yacht, whence he wrote to me protesting that he was ready to return as soon as I had found a play, adding that the problem of 'Drury Lane must be solved—otherwise it will become a public scandal'. This was all very well, but how? One could not claw plays out of the sky. Such exhortation seemed only to deepen the mental void into which I had fallen, as I gazed day after day at that empty auditorium.

In desperation Butt, still shunning the prospects of Shakespeare, agreed to the showing of Douglas Fairbanks' latest super-film, *The Thief of Bagdad*. This at least would pay the rent. It would also set me free to fulfil my obligations in America. This was not a case of running away from an intractable problem, for Golding Bright, always my firm support in business affairs, had expressly stipulated in my contract that I should be free not only to continue working for my own company and for Butt at the Queen's, but also to produce any of the plays of J. M. Barrie in America: stipulations that spelt out overconfidence in each half-sentence.

6

A backward glance at what had been happening at the Queen's reveals a similar story of disaster. The only bright spot in my series of Walpurgis-nights was provided by my encounters with Walter Hackett, a dramatist to whom I had turned after a series of failures with other authors. To begin with, nobody had warned me that he shared with Sheridan the distinction of being the laziest dramatist on record. To save himself trouble he always wrote the same play, varying the plot each time with a few new twists, but always including the same part for his wife, Marion Lorne, a charming comedienne of limited resource, who was always given situations of embarrassment from which to extricate herself with fluttering eyelashes. Hackett's ideas seldom progressed beyond the first act. He sold the remaining acts by verbal exposition. Subsequent delivery took place act by act, sometimes a few pages at a time. Thus, we began to rehearse *Pansy's Arabian Night*, without the last act. Angry expostulation brought forth nothing better than evasive chuckles and promises for the morrow, never fulfilled. Butt knew better than to come to the first night. Instead he sent me a telegram, hoping that 'our patience will be rewarded with at least one big success', which was reasonable enough, seeing that he had urged me to do the play after reading the first act. It was withdrawn after three weeks. Walter Hackett retired to the South of France to escape Butt's wrath.

The red light had been winking at me for a long time now, but judgment was blinded by a maelstrom of conflicting influences. However, at last I had the sense to realise that drastic steps must be taken to climb out of the pit of disaster into which I had fallen. I suggested to Butt that our partnership at the Queen's should be ended. He agreed. I had never been at ease in the arrangement, and for Butt it must have been sheer misery.

Interlude: America

I

The main purpose of my visit to America was to produce *Peter Pan*
for Charles Dillingham who had managed to persuade Barrie to
let him revive the play in America, where the legendary figure of
Maude Adams had kept it in shadow for more than a decade.
Barrie had consented only on condition that I was to direct it,
whereupon Dillingham had offered me a production in the autumn
of 1924 which I had accepted out of hand. My undertaking had now
come home to roost. There were other compelling reasons for
my flight to America at this time. After months of indecision my
wife was about to sue for divorce. There would be hateful publicity.
Nothing I could say or do in court or out of it would extenuate my
behaviour in the eyes of the public. Yet there were reasons of
temperament and circumstance that made the break-up even now
seem inevitable. Moreover, after months of indecision and a bad
conscience about personal affairs, added to the strain of the last
six months, my health was showing signs of wear. It was imperative
that I should get away. I left for New York on September 17th in
S.S. *Majestic*, taking George Harris with me. At a last-hour meeting
before we sailed Sir Alfred seemed to favour my plan to produce a
Midsummer Night's Dream at Christmas. Naturally I was delighted,
and confirmed my enthusiasm in a hasty letter posted from Cher-
bourg. There were good friends on board. Eugene Goossens on
his way to take up his appointment as conductor of the Eastman
Orchestra in Rochester, N.Y., Somerset Maugham, friendly but
wary of deck-tennis, preferring shuffle board, and his companion

of that time, Gerald Haxton. I steered clear of Haxton as much as possible.

By the time we reached quarantine I was fit and well again, but quite unprepared for the shock that awaited me. Shortly after I went to Drury Lane Pat Malone told me quite casually that he had sold the American rights of *Hassan* 'lock, stock and barrel' to A. L. Erlanger. The deal included the scenery, costumes, everything, even Harris's designs which, strictly speaking, were not his to sell. I told him it was a crazy arrangement. To begin with, our production could not be fitted into any of the cramped stages in New York. More important, the secret of our success had lain in my ability to weld all the elements of production into some degree of artistic unity—speech, music, light and movement—like the conductor of a symphony. Without such unity the production would fall apart as a rather ill-adjusted spectacle. However, all I could extract from Malone was a verbal promise that I should supervise the production, provided I had the time. Obviously, in view of my position at Drury Lane, no contract could be signed, but Erlanger would wait for me as long as possible. In August I heard rumours that the production was going forward without me. I sent a cable to Erlanger asking him to wait, but received no reply.

So much for the past history of the affair. Now, as I leant over the rail enjoying the September sunshine, Eugene came hurrying up to me with the early-morning papers. 'My God!' he exclaimed. '*Hassan* was produced last night.' 'Let me see,' I said. The notices were dreadful. The performance had been a shambles, wrongly cast and badly directed, so ill-prepared that one critic caustically asked why the word 'props' was painted on the side of the ladder used to rescue the Caliph from The House of the Moving Walls. I could not read any more. My eyes were full of tears. George came up and read them. His language was unprintable. At the landing stage Dillingham's man was waiting to help us through Customs as usual. 'No good, I'm afraid,' he said in response to my look of misery. 'What else could you expect?' I replied, swallowing hard.

The whole affair had been misconceived from the start. Abe Erlanger, that preposterous Napoleon of the post-war American theatre, seeing an opportunity to acquire fame and to save my fee had decided to direct the play himself. First, he went to work on the script, cutting out most of what he could not understand, which was considerable. He attended rehearsals dressed—as seemed to him appropriate for such an important assignment—in a football sweater and cap, and armed with a referee's whistle to keep the chorus in order. Since the stage of the Knickerbocker Theatre would not accommodate the London scenery, it was either cut down or left in the theatre alleyway.

Dillingham, ever cheerful in the face of disaster, treated the whole thing as a tremendous joke, including the cable he sent Malone immediately after curtain fall: 'HASSAN PASSED PEACEFULLY AWAY AT 10.45 TONIGHT.' When he saw how distressed I was he begged me to go and see what I could do to put things right. This I refused to do. The play ran for ten days only. Dillingham had so admired the London production that he had taken up a fifty per cent interest in the American rights; he lost it all.

2

Dillingham quickly threw off the effects of the *Hassan* débâcle— it was just another gamble gone wrong—and turned his attention to the preparation of *Peter Pan*. I had already discussed the production in some detail with Barrie before I left London. I was determined to present the play exactly as he wished. He had made some minor corrections in the script, mainly to remove the verbal moss that had grown over it through the years. Otherwise the production would keep within its established convention. This was important because Gilbert Miller during one of our Atlantic crossings had warned me of the legend surrounding Maude Adams, the Barrie actress of America, especially adored as *Peter Pan*. This was why the Frohman office had never attempted to revive any of the Barrie plays. Fortunately, the responsibility for casting the new Peter had been taken off my shoulders, Dillingham having already obtained Barrie's consent to Marilyn Miller, star of the recent musical comedy, *Sally*. She had a 'girl-boy' personality and figure, danced enchantingly, not as a ballerina but better than the majority of girls in American musicals. But oh dear! That voice! It sounded like a corncrake. But she was eager to learn. I spent many hours teaching her to speak properly. Several of the cast came over from England, including Leslie Banks to play Captain Hook and Edward Rigby for Smee. Other British members of the cast were players resident in New York.

For the first time in America I had not to worry about the

technical side of the work. George took all that off my hands. We rehearsed in Dillingham's own theatre, the Globe. This was a great advantage because the impresario's offices were above the front of the theatre. George and I went there every day after rehearsal to discuss progress with Charlie, while Vera Murray, his personal assistant, was learning to make tea in the English way. The outer office of the Globe Theatre became known on Broadway as Harris's tea-rooms.

Peter Pan opened in Buffalo and came to the Knickerbocker Theatre in New York two weeks later. Appreciation among the critics swung sharply between those who were old enough to enjoy memories of Maude Adams and younger members of the fraternity, able to look at the performance without any conflict of memory. Alex Woollcott epitomised the former view when he wrote: 'Marilyn was followed by a shadow which could not be nipped off by all the nursery windows in Christendom ... the shadow of Maude Adams.' George's work came in for high praise, especially his ship scene, the model for which was later shown at various theatre exhibitions, and is now in the Mander and Mitchenson Collection.

Waiting in my cabin aboard the *Majestic* before we left for home was a marconigram which read as follows:

'YOUR PRODUCTION OF PETER PAN HAS AMERICA'S HEARTFELT SYMPATHY. MARILYN MILLER IS TERRIBLE YOUR PRODUCTION IS WORSE.

SYDNEY SOLOMON'

I could not recollect ever having met Mr. Solomon. Evidently, I had offended him deeply. A day or two later another marconigram, this time from Marilyn Miller, joyously announced record-breaking figures at the box-office. At least it was good to know that the company would have a successful season on Broadway. And so it proved.

Thirteen
'My Christmas dream'

I

The devious courses that Butt and I pursued before Shakespeare
was allowed to return to Drury Lane in the guise of Father Christmas
must now be set down. George and I began to plan the production
on the outward voyage to New York. A cable from Clift was waiting
for me on landing. The film at Drury Lane was a great success. Good!
That was one anxiety the less. I sought out Michael Fokine, dined
with him and Mme Fokine in their apartment on Riverside Drive
and persuaded Fokine to join me once more in production. A cable
to Butt on October 1st gave him the glad tidings, followed two
days later by an enthusiastic letter, setting out my general scheme.
This was not to be a Shakespearean production in the ordinary
sense. The full text would of course be used and Mendelssohn's
music, but there would be more colour and movement than usual:
two ballets by Fokine and a wood scene which would change in full
view of the audience to one of enchantment, after the manner of the
transformation scenes of long ago. I had no hesitation in stressing
the commercial possibilities of what I hoped he would regard as a
substitute for the usual pantomime.

Meanwhile, other intentions were at work. Soon after my arrival
in New York I received a telephone call from Lee Ephraim, a
London agent visiting New York on the look-out for plays. He had
been asked to get into touch with me about a musical comedy
called *Rose Marie*. Within the same hour I received a cable from
Butt, asking for a report on the play. After seeing *Rose Marie* I
cabled that it had excellent music and wonderful dancing, but I

did not fancy it for Drury Lane. I admit there was something of the Nelson touch in this.

Next, on October 6th I received an angry reply to my cable about Fokine. I had no right to engage him; the board had not agreed to a Christmas production of *The Dream*; they were unlikely to do so. (This reference to the board was camouflage. The directors were completely in Butt's hands, or rather in the hands of Solly Joel, who held not only the purse-strings but virtually the entire purse.) On October 17th a letter from Butt confirmed the board's rejection of my *Dream* plan. Also he wanted to know why I had suggested *Rose Marie* to Malone for His Majesty's. The answer was simple. Ephraim had already offered him the play and I had volunteered to back up his opinion, but on receipt of Butt's letter I sent for Ephraim and told him Drury Lane was interested and must have first refusal. This information I forwarded to London, at the same time requesting an immediate decision on my plan, otherwise I should have to cancel my arrangement with Fokine. To this letter I received no reply. Butt was obviously keeping me in the dark. It was humiliating to have to go to Fokine and tell him matters were not yet settled. But I had not given up my battle for the 'soul' of Drury Lane. Eventually I was to win a Pyrrhic victory but lose the final campaign.

2

On the voyage home George and I argued the problem to the point of satiety. In New York, Lee Ephraim was negotiating on Butt's behalf with the American management. Yet it would be impossible to conclude negotiations in time for a production of *Rose Marie* at Christmas. It was a miserable and anxious voyage. By the time we landed at Southampton, we were well into November, the Fairbanks' film had begun to fail, and it was obvious that *Rose Marie* could not be got ready in time. Butt realised this, too, and decided to let me have my way, but on terms that would enable him to rid himself of his troublesome prelate. At my first interview with him, yes, I was to be allowed to produce *A Midsummer Night's Dream* at Christmas, but only if I agreed to hand him my written resignation as joint managing-director, to take effect only if the production failed; if it succeeded the document was either to be destroyed or returned to me. Meanwhile, it would remain secret, locked in Sir Alfred's safe.

Somehow or other Sydney Carroll got to hear of this. He came to see me.

'Whatever made you give up that contract?' he demanded furiously.

After listening to my side of the story he said:

'You should have told me about this before you wrote your letter. I'd have dealt with Butt all right. After all, it was a contract for a period of years at a large salary.'

I was shrewd enough to guess that if *Rose Marie* were a success— as indeed it was—it would not be long before Butt would point out the impropriety of my taking a large salary for doing nothing and would suggest a nominal one. But I was young and keen. I had no desire to lapse into a sinecure position at Drury Lane.

Butt's reluctant consent to my *Dream* plan carried with it no promise of co-operation. Instead, he raised a series of minor objections. On casting: When I suggested Henry Ainley for Bottom the reply was that he did not agree; he suggested instead George Hayes, who had recently played the part at the Old Vic. When I pointed out that Lilian Baylis was unlikely to release him I was told to buy out his contract—and for a liberal sum! Of course Miss Baylis refused to consider the idea. When I secured Frank Cellier, Miles Malleson, Clifford Mollison, H. O. Nicholson and Alfred Clark for the 'rude mechanicals'—as fine a group of character actors as had ever been assembled for those parts—doubt was expressed about their competence, especially Alfred Clark. A large irritation began to form in my mind: What on earth did Butt know about casting a Shakespeare play? But wait a moment! Had he not taken the precaution of going to see the Old Vic production while I was in America? As I intended to have the lovers' parts played in a lighter comedy vein than was usual I engaged Edith Evans, Athene Seyler, Frank Vosper and Leon Quartermaine—a breakaway from tradition that was a great success. The chairman raised objections to their salaries, especially Quartermaine's. He suggested Phyllis Neilson-Terry for Titania, but she could not be released in time, which was all to the good because it secured us a well-graced performance from Gwen Ffrangcon-Davies, complemented by a well-spoken Oberon from Robert Harris.

Next, on production: Butt said the fee I was paying George Harris, (£250 as against £300 paid to him for *London Life*) was too high. He had no conception of the work involved nor of the short space of time in which to finish it. Within four weeks George executed over four hundred sketches, complete with half-inch details, costume designs and properties, a display of virtuosity that I think has never been exceeded.

On publicity: When I decided to continue the policy of providing a programme and news-sheet Butt protested that this would cut down the amount of advertising space and was more expensive to produce. He countermanded my instructions and told the theatre manager to prepare a programme on the old lines. I heard of it quite by chance: this would not do at all. I managed to hold up things while I fought and won my battle for a magazine programme. It contained a special article about the play by G. K. Chesterton, and a brief history of productions since Shakespeare's day, written by W. R. Titterton.

The children required for the ballets were provided by the Italia Conti School, that seemingly inexhaustible fountain of juvenile talent. Always contumacious, Italia Conti fought furious battles— with me about rehearsal hours, with parents about meals and with the Education officer of the London County Council about schooling: 'Don't you realise that fairies have to be trained?' she screamed.

3

Rehearsals began on November 29th, less than two weeks after we landed at Southampton, in an incredible flurry of question and answer by cable, telegram and telephone. How many of the cast were able to attend the first week of rehearsals? When would Fokine sail? Had his passage money been paid? What was the number of his labour permit? He would not budge without it. Why was Eugene Goossens lingering in Rochester, N.Y., when he was so urgently needed to consult with Herman Finck? For all this frenzied correspondence Dillingham was the willing post office. After an agonising silence I received a radio message on December 8th from the *Mauretania*, forwarded through Plymouth: Fokine would be at the Savoy Hotel that night.

It was a new experience for me to work in an atmosphere of hostility after being surrounded by so much enthusiasm. My only supporters were the technical staff I had brought with me. I loved my work-people for their integrity, their rough encouragement and, above all, their humour. The fact that I had always maintained close contact with them now paid off. These men knew that something was

in the wind, affecting the future not only of their boss but of themselves. So Jock, the Scottish flyman, Morgan, the Welsh property
master, and Albert Jones, master carpenter, now promoted to be
stage superintendent, he of the giant hands—all graduates of the
ReandeaN 'technical college'—were determined to see the guv'nor
through. As fast as George's scale drawings arrived, they were
seized upon and carried off into the workshops, where the circular
saws, the planing and morticing machines were soon humming.

I intended to use the theatre's facilities to the full. As usual
in my spectacular productions, with emphasis laid upon light and
space, an enormously high cyclorama was rigged, with painted
draperies to represent the forest hung at the sides and in front of it.
This entailed heavy work, especially up aloft, where Jock performed
prodigies of hard work and endurance, rigging heavy blocks and
tackle. When all was over it was his boast that he had not left the
theatre during the final thirty-six hours, content to take snatches of
sleep among his ropes and pulleys—a fantastic achievement.
Electricians swarmed on the gantries, rigging my special lighting
equipment. All the mechanical contrivances on the stage floor had
to be renovated. Gaping holes would suddenly appear at the actors'
feet. 'Stand back!' the stage manager would shout as the engineers
began to raise one of the big hydraulic lifts. Demands from the
actors for quiet had to be ignored. In normal circumstances they
might well have refused to go on rehearsing, but all I think were
caught up in the magic of the occasion. After all it was forty years
since an original production of Shakespeare had been staged at
Drury Lane. There was no time to theorise about the production. I
had an instinctive desire to unify all the elements into what I had
come to regard as 'total theatre'. As background or foreground to
all this, whichever way you care to look at it, there was that judge of
the High Court trumpeting my domestic faults as he granted my
wife her decree nisi.

There was a final flurry of anger from Butt when he learned that
the production would not be ready in time for the customary
opening on Boxing afternoon. But I was adamant, for that would
involve a dress rehearsal on Christmas Day, which was out of the
question. It would be a superhuman task to get the play on at all.
As it was we were still rehearsing on Boxing afternoon until within
a few minutes of curtain time, dealing with last-minute emergencies,
such as re-timing music cues and so forth. It is impossible to describe the tension during those last-minute preparations. Every now

and then it would break and swirl about the stage in gusts of hearty laughter or furious argument. . . . Already I could hear the audience taking their places, chattering and laughing. I doubt whether many of them thought the return of Shakespeare to Drury Lane after forty years—ninety in the case of this particular play—a momentous occasion; just a joyous climax to their Christmas fun.

After my usual tour of the dressing-rooms I waited in the wings until the first notes of the overture, then shook hands with the stage managers and went out into the street, feeling slightly sick. I walked alone—even George had deserted me—in such anxiety that each minute seemed like an hour. I went to my usual table at the Ivy, too nervous to eat anything, then out into the street again. At last I could endure the suspense no longer and went back into the theatre by the stage-door. None of the staff spoke to me—they were too busy, but I knew by the way they looked at me that all was well so far. I crept behind the huge cyclorama and listened to the roars of laughter at my 'rude mechanicals'. That scene always goes well. But the finale as the fairies take possession of the palace after the Duke and his court retire to their nuptial beds—how would that go? I had contrived a technically difficult effect. The white marble walls and columns of the palace were to become transparent as Titania, Oberon and attendant fairies, grouped in a kind of ghostly frieze, were raised on our largest hydraulic lift at the back. Their appearance at the top of the great steps was timed to coincide with the opening bars of music for the final Fokine ballet. This had made a sensation at the last dress rehearsal. How would it go tonight? Prolonged applause: that must be the Duke's exit. Now the introductory music for the—What is all the commotion about? The great cyclorama is billowing in all directions—and all these scurrying feet —What has gone wrong? I am powerless to intervene, yet unable to keep away, like a witness to a road accident. One of the valves of the hydraulic mechanism had jammed, leaving my frieze of fairies two feet below the level of the top steps. Stage managers and stage-hands rushed back and forth, lifting the girls up, children first, up, up! Give me your hands! Hurry, children! Bundle them into the scene by any and every means! Quick! Group along the topmost platform. Oberon hoists Titania by the armpits. All are in position as Herman Finck desperately plays the music cue for the third time. Phew! A narrow squeak! I feel as limp as a rag, and have to be more or less propelled on to the stage by excited stage managers to face the storms of applause that followed soon afterwards.

4

Looking through the press notices so many years later, I am struck by the fact that both the right and left of critical opinion accepted that I had deliberately chosen to produce the play as a Christmas spectacle and, apart from inevitable points of criticism, declared that the experiment was a success. I was particularly happy that James Agate in the *Sunday Times* drew attention to the three constituent parts of the play, the romantic, the fairy, and the low comedy of the mechanicals and how I had succeeded in drawing them together into a coherent whole. A. B. Walkley in a delightful essay in *The Times* found no such synthesis but much else to admire. Both the *Observer* and the *Manchester Guardian* accepted the production for what it was, and E. A. Baughan in the *Daily News* declared unequivocally that there were many ways of producing Shakespeare, and as a Christmas production this one had succeeded. The Swedes evidently agreed with him, for Herr André, Director of the Royal Opera House, invited me to Stockholm to make a similar production there. It remained for the weeklies to provide the lees of dissent after the heady draughts of praise. Francis Birrell took me to task for faulty diction, while another purist went so far as to set out phonetically how certain words should be pronounced. Language is a living thing that changes with each succeeding generation. Shakespeare's actors would be well-nigh incomprehensible today; so, too, would we have difficulty in 'taking in' the talk of Dickens' London, so, too, do I have difficulty in understanding the speech of the younger generation on television.

Sir Alfred Butt was spared the annoyance of attendance on the first night. He had gone to America to see *Rose Marie*, leaving Lord Lurgan as the sole but sympathetic occupant of the directors' box. However, the secretary to the board had been asked to prepare a report against the chairman's return. In this he made grudging admission of our success, but did not think we should run beyond the end of February. *Rose Marie* had already been announced for early March, so this was no prophecy.

The box-office response astonished my critics. One of the Manchester papers announced on January 17th that £6,000 had been taken in the previous week of nine performances and that the matinée the previous day had amounted to £700. These were big figures indeed for that time. It did not surprise me therefore when audible protests were made in the pit and gallery during the last week of February because of the play's withdrawal.

5

Throughout the rehearsals I was uncomfortably aware that my resignation lay in Alfred Butt's safe. I suspected that he had no intention of returning it to me, whether or not I succeeded with *The Dream*. I grew so accustomed to the idea that I was astonished (flattered in a negative kind of way) when the contents bills of the evening papers splashed the news: 'Dean resigns from Drury Lane.' In spite of my failure I had aroused sufficient public interest for the Press to take the matter up in a big way. There were statements and counter-statements. In defensive interviews I talked vaguely about the status of Drury Lane as a national theatre. The Press pounced upon this at once. Did this mean a subsidy from the Government? asked the reporters. I said! 'Not necessarily. That might lead to inter-ference in the theatre's internal affairs.' This was an evasive answer because it must have been obvious to everyone that it was impossible to turn Drury Lane into a national theatre without government subsidy. In considering this prevarication allowance must be made for the public attitude towards any form of state aid for the theatre at this time. Bernard Shaw's view that a national theatre was a tangible asset in the balance sheet of national well-being was generally regarded as special pleading, and among the die-hards as a crime against the State! The *Yorkshire Post* put it succinctly: 'Sir Alfred Butt wants to earn dividends for his shareholders, Dean wanted it to become a national theatre with a policy. Winston Churchill* will tell him promptly that the country has no money to spare for intellectual luxuries at present.' So we can see the extent to which the climate of public opinion has changed.

Looking back on all that happened, it is clear that when I was appointed the old theatre was at the parting of the ways. I have no doubt at all that if I had had the wisdom and the experience to carry Sir Alfred Butt with me, and if the idea of subsidy had been ripe for public acceptance, I might have succeeded in my attempt to wean Drury Lane away from a purely commercial outlook. For a

* Then Chancellor of the Exchequer.

brief period the theatre did regain its national status, when it became the general headquarters of E.N.S.A. during the Second World War. It is a curious fact of theatrical history that it was largely E.N.S.A.'s influence upon national morale that brought about a change in public outlook towards the theatre, and made politically acceptable the demand for government support. Although the present Arts Council of Great Britain which is responsible for the distribution of Government subsidy did not spring from the loins of E.N.S.A., but grew out of its smaller neighbour, C.E.M.A., the basic ideas were first put into practice by the larger organisation. Because it was not directly sponsored by a government department E.N.S.A. became a casualty at war's end.

.   .   .   .   .

When it became known that I was to leave Drury Lane I remember Albert Jones saying in the kindliest tones:

'Never mind, guv'nor, you'll be back.'

'Why do you say that, Albert?'

'Because every producer works in a theatre three times.'

I had not heard this quaint superstition before. In my own case the carpenter's prophecy was to be fulfilled in course of time.

R

Fourteen
The end of the beginning

I

My departure from Drury Lane lightened the burden of responsibility somewhat—burdens are heaviest when they are unsuccessfully borne. But I soon found myself involved in production once more, assisting at the birth of the new influences that were stirring the London stage. Three plays produced about this time expressed in varying degree the changing attitudes, particularly in matters of sex. They were *Our Betters* by Somerset Maugham, which had so shocked Alec Rea when it was offered to us in 1923 that he refused to let me accept it; Noël Coward's *The Vortex*, and Frederick Lonsdale's *Spring Cleaning*, the third in the trilogy, which I was about to produce at the St. Martin's. After hawking his play round various London managements Lonsdale had taken it to America, where in spite of an indifferent production it had scored a notable success. I bought the play for the St. Martin's but, because of Alec's strong objection to what he regarded as its risqué element, it was to be presented by our Dee Cee Company. There was the usual tussle over censorship. The play's reputation for daring, acquired on Broadway, was such that it needed all Freddie's persuasive eloquence to secure a licence.

I began rehearsals immediately after Christmas. Freddie had a reputation for a sharp tongue, but he was amiable enough towards me, possibly because I had secured Ronald Squire for the leading part. Freddie and Ronnie were close friends and spent much of their time exchanging intimate jokes from which the rest of us were excluded. Several members of our permanent company were in the cast, including Cathleen Nesbitt as the prostitute, Mona, euphemistically described in the programme as 'the strange lady'; Cecily Byrne as the wife, Ian Hunter as the husband, and Edna Best, with shingled head, an eye-glass, a twelve-inch cigarette holder and mannish clothes to represent a young woman of aberrant sexual tendencies. These externals were as much as the censor would permit of reference to lesbianism. Serious study of sexual perversion was strictly taboo in the theatre of that time. In any case, such a study would have been beyond Edna's comprehension; she relied upon Freddie's witticisms and her off-beat 'get-up' to make a considerable impact.

Freddie, a white muffler round his neck, no overcoat, although it was bitterly cold, and trousers half-mast to expose white socks, spent much of his time wandering about the theatre, culling opinions from small-part actors, understudies, cleaners, as the fancy took him: 'What d'you think of it? Not much good, eh? Poor stuff!' Then with an air of simulated surprise: 'You like it? More fool, you!'

It was like old times to see the distinguished first-night audience crowding into the lobby of our theatre once more. Many authors were present, in fact most of Freddie's contemporaries. The play received such a vociferous reception that I was forced to rush the author on to the stage to make a bow in the usual abashed-author manner. But I had scarcely disappeared into the prompt corner again before I heard Freddie say: 'Thank you very much, ladies and gentlemen. Now Sir Butt would like to speak to you.' Amid much laughter he then dragged me out to add my thanks to his and to say how glad I was to be back in my own theatre, at which there were loud 'Hear hears!' The turn-round in my fortunes was a reminder, if any were needed, of how swiftly the kaleidoscope revolves in the theatre.

The play precisely caught the mood of the moment; it received an ecstatic press, with scarcely an adverse note to be heard amid the general acclamation. One critic compared the author's wit with that of Oscar Wilde; another retorted that Wilde never wrote anything so good, which was absurd. Hannen Swaffer provided a jeremiad in the *People* that is an amusing contrast with present attitudes: '. . . we are back in the days of a drama even worse than that of the Restoration period'. After further pontifications 'Swaff'—as we used to call him—ever with an eye upon circulation, quoted the author as saying: 'This thing is growing to such an extent that if it is not checked perversion may become the ordinary habit and custom of the age'—which reads like a quotation from a Restoration polemic. Actually, the play skirted round the subject, holding it up to ridicule rather than giving it serious thought. Before the opening night Freddie had been rather diffident and modest, claiming only that it was an amusing comedy. After the press notices, he gave interviews in which he declared portentously that his play was intended as an awful warning against a growing social evil.

Success at this time meant much to Lonsdale, despite his pretended disregard of money. He was for ever enquiring how things were going at the box-office, and wandering in and out of the auditorium to judge the laughter and applause. Upon one occasion he slipped out through a door at the back of the dress circle into the corridor where he encountered a playgoer who had just done the same thing. The man looked at Freddie and said:

'Can't you stand it either?'

'No,' said Freddie, 'but you see I wrote it.'

'What difference does that make?' the man replied. 'Come and have a drink.'

Freddie was unreliable in business matters. Unlike Walter Hackett, he made little attempt to charm the bird of resentment off the tree with good humour; he preferred silence. For example, the contract for his next play after *Spring Cleaning*, made with our Dee Cee Company and which I was to produce, was never carried out, despite frequent letters from Clift demanding its fulfilment. Meeting him in the lobby of the St. Martin's Theatre one day I was astonished that he pretended not to know me, an aloofness which he maintained for the rest of his life. After a while the reason for his attitude dawned upon me. In a recent interview I had committed myself to the view that Coward rather than Lonsdale might come to be regarded as the Sheridan of our age. I felt that Lonsdale's writing was dominated by his love-hate for such established institutions as the British aristocracy. Freddie certainly had a long memory for grievances·

Spring Cleaning was produced on January 29th, 1925, and ran for 262 performances, first at the St. Martin's and later at the Playhouse. Once again, as in the case of *Our Betters*, Alec's innate Puritanism had deprived ReandeaN of the box-office success that it so urgently needed.

2

One morning shortly after the opening—I'm not sure it wasn't the next day—Rea walked into my office and announced without any preamble that our agreement had expired some months ago. I stared at him in surprise for, to tell the truth, I had forgotten its existence. What did this sudden remark portend? My dismissal? ReandeaN had been in financial straits for some time past, due to my incurable habit of trying to do too much with too little. No doubt Alec had grown tired of dipping into his personal fortune to keep us in funds. Well, I should not complain: he had been a wonderful partner and a sincere friend. But no! All he intended was a renewal of our agreement for a further five-year term—this time by a simple exchange of letters. My basic salary was to remain unchanged at twenty pounds per week, but I was to have a larger share than before in the contingent profits. But there were no profits! Fortunately I had been able to augment my salary by the production fees that I had received elsewhere; otherwise I should have been unable to meet my family responsibilities, even then when the British pound still had a sterling ring to it, albeit made of paper.

In the course of the discussion that followed Alec impressed upon me the absolute necessity of achieving financial stability, otherwise he could not go on. I knew that the only way to secure this was by producing a thumping box-office success. But that will-o'-the wisp rarely surrenders itself at the first grab! For my part I was pinning my hopes upon the production of *Rain*, the dramatisation made by two Americans of one of Somerset Maugham's short stories, originally called 'Miss Thompson'. Perhaps a word or two is necessary to explain how I became involved in this highly speculative venture. The play was produced in New York with Jeanne Eagels in the part of Sadie Thompson. Both play and performance made a sensation. When I arrived to produce *Peter Pan* it was still the talk of the town, and a mad scramble to secure the British rights was going on. These were owned by Sam Harris, an astute Broadway producer, who was demanding the most extravagant terms for both play and star. (He had promised Eagels that she should play the part in London.) After seeing the play I thought that here was an outstanding chance of commercial success, so I decided to join the competition. Dillingham offered to help with the negotiations, although he did point out that, if Jeanne Eagels were to be insisted upon, the play could not be done in London for another year at least, possibly two. However, he managed to persuade Sam Harris that ours was the only management to whom the play could be safely entrusted!

Both Alec and manager Clift had serious misgivings about the cost of the enterprise. However, I persevered. Dillingham introduced me to Joseph Bickerton, one of Erlanger's smart lawyers who arranged the agreement with Sam Harris and signed it eventually on our behalf on February 4th. On the following day Alec and I exchanged our letters of agreement. There was no significance in the juxtaposition of dates. On the 11th I left for America in the *Aquitania*—with Alec's rather anxious blessing.

The change of emphasis in management, indicated by the appearance of Dee Cee on the theatre's posters, did not go unnoticed. Coming so soon after the flurry of excitement over Drury Lane the curiosity of the Press was aroused, so it was no surprise to find a bevy of reporters waiting for me on the jetty at Southampton, eager to ask leading questions about my uncertain future. I replied that I was quite happy and I hoped others were, too: a cryptic remark that kept everybody guessing, as I intended it should. 'What was I going to America for?' 'Oh, just to look around,' I said airily. They left me after that, and turned their attention to more important passengers. But the New York reporters continued the chase, one well-known theatrical paper going so far as to declare that my partnership with Rea was ended, and quoting its London office as authority for the statement. This I firmly denied, but I could not help wondering what rodents were busy at home while my back was turned.

3

My wife obtained her decree nisi in December. Nancie, released from her small part in *Spring Cleaning*, went off on a pre-marital tour of Italy with her closest friend, Olga Tufnell—a twenty-first birthday treat from her mother—while I faced my gamble over *Rain* with the future of ReandeaN as the stake.

Jeanne Eagels had already decided not to come to London to play Sadie Thompson. I should have to discuss the position with Maugham. To obtain his approval of my alternative would not be easy. In such matters as casting Maugham had a habit of pretending indifference until the last moment when he would suddenly pounce, with a decisive yea or nay that was usually an expression of personal like or dislike. The play had acquired such an astonishing reputation and the impact of Jeanne Eagels' performance was so tremendous that when it was known that she was not coming to London after all there was curiosity, not to say competition, among our own actresses as to the final choice.

Foremost among the younger actresses whom I thought suitable for the part was Tallulah Bankhead. After a brief stop-off on Broadway this talented American had descended upon the post-war British theatre with all the grace and a touch of the ferocity of the big cats. She appeared first with Gerald du Maurier in a play called *The Dancers*, written by himself and Viola Tree. With her golden hair flying in the wind, husky voice, a soft Southern accent and utter scorn of convention, she had become, almost overnight, the idol of all the up-and-coming generation of working girls, who saw in her the embodiment of their dreams of a free life. The squeals of delight at her every appearance foreshadowed the modern 'Beatlemania', but were a handicap to critical evaluation of her talent. This she had in plenty, although often wasted through lack of dedication.

The more I thought about it the more convinced I had become that she was the right choice. Although comparatively inexperienced for such a big emotional part, she would be an undoubted box-office attraction. She was desperately eager for the part, even offering to go to New York to see Jeanne Eagels' performance. This impressed me. Finally, I said I would engage her to play the part, but that my choice was subject to the approval of the author whom I hoped to meet in America. I asked her to write to me, confirming that she understood the position. I also jokingly reminded her of her promise to see the Eagels' performance, if Maugham consented.

On arrival in New York I proposed Tallulah to Maugham as promised, reminding him that, although inexperienced, she was a box-office draw. I did not add that casting her might save my financial bacon. Maugham was the last person to be moved by a sentimental appeal of that kind. He expressed no view one way or the other and left the next day for Washington. Two days later Tallulah rang me up from her room in the Hotel Gotham, where I was staying. She had just arrived in the *Berengaria*. When I told her that the author had gone to Washington she decided to follow him there and persuaded me to go with her. This was a mistake in tactics, for Maugham disliked being pestered by women. Importunity proved fatal to Tallulah's chances.

4

While all this was going on I had been busy with preparations for a revival of *The Little Minister* for Charles Dillingham. He had seen my London revival of the play and liked it. He asked me to make a similar production in New York with Marilyn Miller as Lady Babbie. But when I arrived *Peter Pan* was still playing to big business in Chicago. So Ruth Chatterton was chosen for the part, with her new young husband, Ralph Forbes, as Gavin Dishart. Ruth had great charm as an actress, although momentarily out of favour with the public. I thought her too mature for Lady Babbie, and Ralph Forbes unsuitable for Gavin Dishart because of his height. I wrote to Dillingham, who had retired to French Lick, a health resort in Indiana, objecting to these arrangements. All I got in reply was a brief note pointing out that Owen Nares was taller, adding, with his incorrigible whimsy, 'Besides, aren't you forgetting that everything has gone up since the war?' By way of postscript, he hoped that Vera Murray 'isn't cheating on the tea'. Really! Charlie was irrepressible. The revival was unfavourably received by the New York press; it played to only moderate business and did my reputation no good. I had failed to realise the extent to which the plays of J. M. Barrie had dated, and found myself 'out of phase' with the public.

Determined to use every endeavour to save ReandeaN, I took a good look at the Broadway scene to see what other plays I could buy. I was much attracted to the work of the Theatre Guild. Both the plays and the standard of production seemed to be more alive than anything to be seen in London. But the Guild proved extraordinarily difficult to deal with when it came to negotiating for the British rights of two of their successes: Eugene O'Neill's *Desire under the Elms* and *They Knew What They Wanted* by Sidney Howard. I had already met Sidney and his delightful wife, Clare Eames, and we became good friends. Through his good offices I was made an honorary member of the Coffee House, a kind of lunch-time version of the Garrick Club in London, a delightful oasis at the centre of New York City, where one met authors, journalists, painters: American hospitality at its simplest and warmest. Sidney's play had just won the Pulitzer prize and was a huge success. He was naturally anxious for it to be seen in London. Between us we managed to persuade the Guild to give ReandeaN a twelve-month option, pending the grant of a licence by the Lord Chamberlain, when we were to pay the Guild $2,500 in advance of royalties. It was a condition of the contract that Pauline Lord was to be given the option of playing her part in London after the New York run was over—the Jeanne Eagels' situation all over again. So far as the licence for *Desire under the Elms* was concerned, it was agreed that I should tackle the Lord Chamberlain in person. If this were successful I was to have the play for London. With these treasures in my pocket but still without a decision regarding Sadie Thompson I sailed again for home where personal happiness and professional anxiety were awaiting me in about equal measure.

5

Nancie and I had little opportunity to enjoy each other's company during the year of my association with Alfred Butt. This was hard upon her for she was in the very springtime of happiness. However, her letters from Italy had been full of excitement at the pictures and art treasures she was seeing for the first time. Olga, a girl of discernment in artistic matters, gave poise and background to her gay and restless spirit. The girls visited Milan, Florence, Rome and Naples, a journey not without incident for it was unusual in those days for two young girls to travel about the Continent by themselves. At Assisi they found the monks hard to shake off; in Rome the recommended hotel thought them a poor risk, so the taxi-driver took them to a pension where the duenna insisted upon escorting them home at night. Money ran out in Naples; they thought to borrow some from Gordon Craig (optimists!) who had invited them to Rapallo, but he was no longer there when they arrived. The return journey was accomplished on a diet of buns!

Now that we were both home again we spent as many week-ends as possible at Easton Lodge, driving down after the show on Saturday nights, laughing and teasing each other along miles of virtually deserted country roads. Sometimes Nancie would fall asleep on my shoulder, only to be jerked awake when I stopped the car at Blue Gates, main entrance to the park, so that she could fetch the key from its hiding-place. A quarter of a mile further on she would stumble out again to unlock the inner lodge gates. Then the bumpy drive across the park to a waiting tray of hot milk and sandwiches. A decanter of whisky, usually half-empty, stood at a discreet distance, placed there by Lady Warwick herself in evident awareness of family dangers! She had no need to worry on my account; Nancie's company was sufficient stimulus. Then I would creep silently along the guests' corridor, past the big mahogany doors, each with its little brass frame to hold a card with the guest's name, and each surmounted by a miniature knocker in the shape of the Maynard crest for the guest's reveille. Now the little frames were mostly empty of cards, which gave the silent corridor a depressing air, as of festivity long abandoned.

The last butler and the last footman must have departed long since, but maids of varying degree, all in starched cap and apron, still passed along that corridor to perform their early-morning ritual, which I often watched, lying awake, but with all radical impulses comfortably asleep. First, a discreet ratatat on the door, then cup and saucer upon a silver tray placed at the bedside; next a match to the pine logs in the large old-fashioned grate, soon roaring up the chimney; next, a white blanket laid over the hearth-rug, and a large hip-bath upon it. Next, the processional part of the ritual: the maid swiftly returning with 'tweeny' or houseboy as acolyte, each bearing hot water in copper cans, so brightly polished you could see your face in them! At last the final apostrophe: 'Your bath is ready, sir,' delivered in a tone of such gentle firmness that you took it as a warning that male guests were expected to be 'down' for breakfast. (Was I dreaming? Had I ever been a provincial actor, living in one room in Ackers Street, Manchester?) I was often lazy and tempted to decline my rôle in that secular baptism. Yet the alternative! Those cavernous baths with their mahogany sursounds and two-tier mounting blocks; how did the plump, the middle-aged and the arthritic climb into them? There was, I realised, a measure of historical interest in these proceedings, for was I not witnessing the last flickers of life as it was lived in 'the stately homes of England' (Noël had not yet written the song) in good King Edward's reign?

It was difficult to get away from week-end visitors. Sometimes upon a warm Sunday afternoon Nancie and I would wander through the Italian garden down to the lower lake where, in a pagoda-like summerhouse, built out over the water, we would picnic from a tea-basket thoughtfully provided by the housekeeper, and dream away the gentle afternoon. Once our idyll was interrupted by Lady Warwick, extolling the beauties of her gardens to John Galsworthy, week-ending with H. G. Wells at Easton Glebe; he had walked across the park to pay her his respects. After a phrase or two about the weather—it was a glorious afternoon in late summer as I remember—and an offer of our lukewarm tea politely refused, they continued their stroll along the herbaceous borders, then in full splendour, Galsworthy whispering cautionary words about the danger of allowing Nancie too close an association with myself!

6

Spring Cleaning was still playing to full houses when I returned from America. So I had to find another home for *Rain*. Eventually, I chose the Garrick Theatre. The news that Sadie was still not cast had preceded me, and interest in the outcome now spread to the public. Was Tallulah going to play the part or not? If not, where would I find an actress with sufficient emotional power to do it justice and with the necessary box-office appeal? I asked myself the question a dozen times as the rehearsal date drew near. When would Maugham finally make up his mind? He came to the first rehearsal and sat in the stalls, watching Tallulah but making no comment. He came the next day too, but by this time his agent had told me privately that Maugham did not want Tallulah to play the part. I had a painful interview with her in my office, and she left in tears. Our loss was Noël Coward's gain, for at short notice, almost the next day, she slipped into partnership with Edna Best in *Fallen Angels*, and made an enormous success.

I began to consider the possibilities of actresses who were not stars. The part was so spectacular that it might well add another to the British constellation overnight. Among the younger members of the ReandeaN Company was Olga Lindo, who had played varied parts with us with mounting success. While I was in America she had been loaned to another manager to play the leading part in a comedy drama at the Vaudeville Theatre. She made a sensational success. . . . After seeing the performance Maugham agreed that she should play Sadie Thompson.

May 12th, 1925: A spring evening, fine and clear, the stars shining in competition with London's 'bright lights'; the lobby of the Garrick Theatre crowded with eager first-nighters; Galsworthy, John Drinkwater, H. G. Wells, Arnold Bennett, half the top literary 'scene' seemed to be there; playgoers, exhausted by their all-night vigil had been admitted into pit and gallery an hour or two earlier.

All the senior members of the ReandeaN Company, apart that is from those already busy with *Spring Cleaning*, were in the cast, and all gave first-class performances: Malcolm Keen, as the Reverend Davidson, Marda Vanne, an invaluable recruit from South Africa, as his wife (a most sensitive performance), J. H. Roberts as Dr. McPhail and Hilda Bruce-Potter as the doctor's wife, while Barbara Gott gave such a remarkable performance as the wife of the American trader that she won a paragraph of praise from Arnold Bennett. But what of Sadie Thompson, upon which all depended? Well, Olga Lindo was an actress of great competence but no sex appeal: she was what used to be called a critic's actress. She scored a triumph that night and had to make a curtain speech in response to persistent applause, especially from the higher-priced seats, a reversal of the usual order of things. Yet in spite of that applause and the columns of praise subsequently lavished upon her I knew that I had fallen into grievous managerial error in not insisting upon Tallulah, knowledge that was confirmed by the overheard remark of a 'galleryite': 'When it's a real success we applaud louder than this.'

The rain installation, which had caused the fire authorities grave misgivings because of the risk of short-circuiting the lighting system—they had insisted upon sand everywhere in impressive quantities—performed so well that in the interval one man in the lobby was overheard complaining of our wretched English spring, a clear case of hypnosis: And Arnold Bennett wrote in the *New Statesman* that on leaving the theatre he had half expected to find soaking pavements and not a taxi in sight.

No ReandeaN production received better notices, yet after a run of 150 nights, first at the Garrick and later at the St. Martin's, we were left with production expenses barely repaid and no profit at all. I believe I could have overcome Maugham's objection to Tallulah if I had insisted, but I was not single-minded at the moment of decision. My timidity brought about the end of ReandeaN, whereas it was courage and determination that had wrought our original success.

7

While Nancie and I were away, the family lawyers had been busying themselves with legal matters concerning our forthcoming marriage. Now Lady Warwick decided that we must have an engagement party, for which purpose she placed Easton Lodge at our disposal for the long Whitsun week-end while she tactfully withdrew to Scotland: sufficient proof, if any were needed, of the welcome she was extending to our plans. Nancie wanted our first party to be a feast of wit and wisdom! We made out a list of all the people we knew in the worlds of music and the theatre. It was a formidable total. We invited them all, forgetting that acceptance meant a stay at Easton of three nights. Many of those we asked had professional engagements and could not come, but it was still quite a party. I have not a list of those who accepted, but writing from memory and with the help of a faded photograph* taken on the steps of the main terrace, here are the names of some who were there: Eugene Goossens and his first wife, 'Booney', Jascha Heifetz, Noël Coward, Gladys Calthrop, Harriet Cohen, Gwen Ffrangcon-Davies, Olga Lindo, J. H. Roberts and his wife. Eugene Goossens and I had remained good friends ever since our first meeting in Liverpool at the time of the *Titanic* disaster. Through him I had met many of the younger musicians who clustered round the Diaghilev Ballet and the Beecham National Opera. I found Gene's quiet, cynical humour as stimulating as the advice he gave me on musical matters. Included in the photograph, too, are Charles Dillingham with Marilyn Miller and her husband, Jack Pickford (brother of Mary), who drove down on Whit Monday. What fun it was! We were childishly excited, watching the guests arrive at various times during the first day. Some came by train and had to be met at Bishop's Stortford. Noël and Gladys, with Gene Goossens and 'Booney' as passengers, drove down late after the play.

There was the usual anxiety about the weather. If only it would stay fine! Our guests would then find plenty to do: tennis (two hard and two grass courts), a lovely countryside with ancient villages sufficiently deserted to make motoring through them still a pleasure: I'm making this read like the brochure of a holiday. Alas! Sunday afternoon and evening were wet and dismal. So we congregated in the audit room where Noël organised a series of games with pencils and pieces of paper, a type of recreation at which he seemed adept; 'Consequences' is the name of one of the games we played. Others played bridge. Later, in the saloon, Eugene and Noël took turns improvising on the piano: Quite a concert! I cannot remember

* It is amusing to compare this picture with the one taken at the same spot of one of Lady Warwick's parties for King Edward VII.

whether Harriet Cohen played for us on that occasion, but I think she did. Monday was a glorious day, warm and sunny. The guests soon organised themselves into groups, some for tennis, some for a visit to 'H.G.', others to roam in the park and enjoy the sunshine.

Remembering the old lady's phobia about alcohol I had ordered several dozen bottles of white wine, recommended to me by the local grocer, forgetting that neither wine nor soft drinks, even though home-made and of delicious flavour, were satisfactory substitutes for a good whisky and soda. I was worried lest some of our male guests should wander off in boredom to the pub in Dunmow, which was a Maynard property. Lady Warwick would certainly hear about that. By Monday evening the monotony of my 'wine list' had begun to pall and what I had feared took place. Gene and Jascha disappeared, returning late with several bottles of whisky, and one of cointreau for 'Booney'. They played snooker with disastrous results to the cloth of the billiard table.

8

Back in London after the Whitsun recess there were more problems to be faced. The advance booking for *Spring Cleaning* was dropping—a sure sign of failing health—and the success of *Rain* at the Garrick was equivocal; it was not going to rescue my partner from financial despond. Yet somehow or other ReandeaN had to pull itself out of the mud by its own overdraft. Earlier in the year Galsworthy told me he had written a new play called *The Show* which he had promised to Leon M. Lion, presumably in compensation for his disappointment over *Loyalties*. But now Lion had gone on a long tour of South Africa, and J.G. was growing impatient. Here seemed to be an opportunity exactly tailored to our needs. Surely a new play by John Galsworthy at the St. Martin's, home of his previous success, was our answer. J.G. agreed to cancel his tentative arrangement with Lion, and Alec, with the utmost reluctance, opened his private purse once more to our necessities.

Galsworthy was unwell during the casting of the play and unable to come to the office. Instead, he wrote me voluminous letters, sometimes two a day, giving his views on this actor or that actress. One of his recommendations was decidedly novelistic. Recommending Elissa Landi, he wrote: 'There is a touch of the leopard in her face, a leopard mother whose kittens are threatened.' As befitted the occasion I secured the strongest cast of which our resources were capable, including many of those who had appeared with success in earlier Galsworthy plays. Leslie Banks, Ian Hunter, Clifford Mollison, Felix Aylmer, Ben Field and Robert Harris among the men; outstanding among the women were Haidée Wright and Hermione Baddeley, returned to the fold after a brief flirtation with the Co-optimists, the company in which she had discovered her true métier.

On May 30th, when casting was all but completed, J.G. wrote to tell me that the doctors had diagnosed his continued fever as paratyphoid B., so he would be unable to come to the rehearsals. However, on the whole he thought it best that production should go on. From the Beach Hotel, Littlehampton, during convalescence, he wrote in regard to one scene: 'You can't give too much attention to the demeanour and little movements of the characters when they are *not* speaking', a direction that reminded me of 'Maria' Tempest's well-known expertise with a newspaper whenever she thought it was time to distract the audience's attention from a fellow-player.

July 1st was an unforgettable day. Quite early in the morning Nancie and I were married at the register office in Covent Garden after an exciting chase round and round the market by reporters. Lady Warwick with characteristic munificence had smothered the gloomy room with flowers. Then at night the first performance of a new Galsworthy before an audience distinguished in the extreme, Bernard Shaw and Rudyard Kipling, two literary giants of major influence facing one another in opposite boxes. The reception was mixed, the gallery having decided to turn it into a welcome for our marriage, while the stalls looked on silent and somewhat perplexed. When I stepped forward, mistaking the generous applause for approval of the play, I was awakened to reality by a shout from the gallery: 'Couldn't he give us a better one than this?' After the performance the players from both theatres assembled on the stage and presented us with some delightful wedding gifts, including a silver salver with the signatures of every member of ReandeaN engraved upon it. Truly, a day so crowded with events and emotions that it is impossible to disentangle them all.

The Show opens with a police inspector making enquiries into the suicide of an officer with a distinguished war record, followed in by a reporter on a similar quest. Only a few days before, the tragedy had occurred in real life—a distinguished soldier having committed suicide after seeing *Rain*. Although that was no justification for the coroner's animadversions about gloomy plays, it did not help us. On the day of the opening while I was getting married, my first wife received no less than twenty-two telephone calls from newspapers in search of 'news'. These two happenings served to underline the reality of the author's theme, although how he could have hoped to achieve success by attacking two of our most sensitive institutions, the Press and the police, seems incomprehensible today: yet in the circumstances in which I then found myself I doubt whether I would ever have had the temerity to refuse a new Galsworthy play.

The Press was so hostile that there seemed neither space nor inclination to make more than passing reference to the acting. *The Times* with its usual caution wrote that 'we bow to the moralist but miss the artist'. Next, 'an unpardonable libel on the police and a malevolent if slightly pathetic attack on the Press', came from the *Daily Express*. The *Daily Chronicle* headlined its notice 'Galsworthy's worst play', while the *Westminster Gazette* said it was his 'best play since *The Silver Box*'. So where were we? It did not take us long to find out. The next morning the box-office telephones were silent.

After a hurried glance at the bad notices Nancie and I set out for Beer in South Devon in my new Lancia car, with tired nerves and a considerable hangover. After we had been driving for an hour or so in the bright sunlight the mood of exhilaration passed, and I was struck by a sudden premonition. Even though ReandeaN should survive the present financial crisis, relations with Alec were never going to be the same. This and other wandering anxieties took away much of the joy of our honeymoon.

9

The Show was causing us such grievous loss at the St. Martin's that so soon as we returned from Devon I made arrangements to transfer *Rain* there from the Garrick as soon as possible. Alec was away at the time, but a few days later he walked into my office with the same rather shy manner that he had worn upon a previous and happier occasion, and asked for the return of the letter of agreement he had given me a few short months before. I was so stunned by this *volte face* that all I could say in reply was: 'Oh, very well!' In the discussion that followed I reminded him of the two plays upon which we had paid considerable sums in advance of royalties. One was Noël Coward's *Easy Virtue*, the other was *They Knew What They Wanted*, the licence for which had recently been granted and the payment due under the contract made to the Theatre Guild. Alec was upset but determined. So far as the Coward contract was concerned, this should be disposed of to another management. The Guild contract was not transferable. He finally closed the discussion by saying firmly that he was not prepared to finance any more ReandeaN productions. Instead, the St. Martin's was to be let either, as in the case of *Spring Cleaning*, to our own Dee Cee Company, or to any similar organisation willing to produce plays upon sharing terms. Considerate as always, he saw no reason why I should not continue to occupy my office at the theatre, at all events until I could find accommodation elsewhere.

After Alec had gone I sat at my desk for a long time. This then was my premonition. The watershed of friendship that had kept my professional and private life moving in parallel had been washed away in the cross-currents of emotion set up by my second marriage. It was only now that I realised the personal basis upon which Alec had supported me. He had always been a close friend of my first wife's family—indeed, I met them through his introduction—and so he had come to look upon ReandeaN as a kind of family affair. He never regarded himself as the professional entrepreneur; rather he was an amateur of the theatre in the exact sense of that word. Now I was to drift into the uncharted world of finance with no sea-anchor of money to hold me to a course. Spasms of the money neurosis implanted in me as a child began to stir as I closed my desk and went out to lunch.

The following morning Clift came into my office. Blushing violently as he adjusted his pince-nez, and with a cherubic smile, he said:

'What *do* you think? Alec has just offered me your contract. Shall I take it?'

'Of course,' I replied. 'Why not?'

No further conversation on that subject passed between Clift and myself.

.   .   .   .   .

Overheard in the Ivy Restaurant: Mrs. Patrick Campbell to Marie Tempest (not yet a Dame): 'I hear Basil Dean has left the stage and joined the aristocracy'—a quip so far removed from the truth as it was possible to be.

s

Interlude: A home
ancient and modern

We decided to make our home, Nancie and I, at Little Easton Manor, in Essex. I had purchased the house from the Maynard Estate on condition that the money was used to augment the younger daughter's portion, to which Nancie was entitled on marriage, and that the whole sum be placed in trust for her and her children.

Restoring an ancient manor house that has lain neglected, or put to misuse, for centuries, is a most expensive hobby. But if, as in the case of Easton Manor, it has both historical and family associations, it offers a unique reward. Gradually, as the work goes on, such a place can acquire a special influence over those who care for it enough to spend years restoring its self-respect. It was so with me. I thought at first the work would be completed in at most twelve months, but I was to spend twelve years on the task, aided and abetted by my artist friends, during which time the old house exerted more and more of its happy influence over me.

First then, and in part justification of the foregoing, some facts about the history of Easton Manor. A house or, more accurately, a fortified manor had existed on the site as far back as the eleventh century, even earlier, for in Roman times men lived and worked there. We found evidence of this in the walls of the ancient cellars which were built of Roman brick, material obviously remaining on the site from former occupancy. Indeed, the original Latin name for the church and village, Estaines Parva (Estaines meaning East of Stane, or Stone Street, the paved Roman road leading through Dunmow to the garrison town of Colchester), is further proof of this. At all events, the flint walls, forming the outer parapet to the present garden mark the site of a fortified manor that once stood on the fringe of the ancient Hainault Forest, remains of which were still to be seen in Easton Park until the Second World War when many oak trees reputed to be more than eight hundred years old were blown up to clear runways for an American bomber squadron. A moat surrounded both the manor and the little forest chapel that in later centuries was built up by successive benefactions into the church which stands, today, crammed with fine brasses, frescoes and lordly tombs, a museum of local medieval history.

Estaines was much favoured by the Plantagenets, who liked to go hunting and hawking in the surrounding forest. Here in 1460, so the legend runs, Edward IV spent part of his honeymoon with Elizabeth Woodville, the beautiful widow for whose sake he absented himself from the wars and quarrelled with Warwick 'the King-maker'. Once it boasted a Plantagenet Princess, Isabella, as its chatelaine (1483). In the following century Sir Arthur Throck-morton records in his diary* two visits that he paid to relatives living there.

The house came into the possession of the Maynard family in Elizabethan times when Henry Maynard, knighted by Queen Eliza-beth when Secretary to Lord Treasurer Burghley, acquired the estate from the family of de Louvain, last of a succession of Norman families that had held the property since Domesday. Thus began the connection with the county of Essex of a family that continued to grow in rank and wealth through the centuries, rising from knight-hood to barony and, finally, to viscountcy. The early Maynards though conservative of their rights and duties, were thrusting and ambitious men, so it is not surprising that they found the medieval manor incompatible with their style and dignity. And so Easton Lodge, the 'big house', came into being, with the help, it is suspected, of much of the building material, carved beams, stonework, etc., of the earlier dwelling.

My first sight of the place was most depressing. Growths of ivy smothered the leaded casements and chimneystacks. Little cast-iron pillars supported the Regency roof to a Victorian front door with red and blue glass panels. It was no surprise to learn that for years this rump of a house had been used as the estate office. As I stared rather ruefully at my purchase I began to wonder what sort of a bargain I had made.

* See *Raleigh and the Throckmortons* by A. L. Rowse.

Fortunately, there lived not far away a certain Marquis D'Oisy, who was said to be descended from one of the oldest French families, some said that of Cardinal Richelieu. Although he had never been to France, could not speak a word of French, and had an atrocious Cockney accent, he was, by tacit consent, known throughout the district as 'the Marquis', yet I never heard him lay claim to any title. Lady Warwick used to say he came not from any foreign land but from the East End of London. He was a strange creature altogether, very tall and thin, emaciated almost, with a squeaky voice and a chin beard: an obvious homosexual. He lived with a Scottish henchman called John in a tumbledown cottage so primitive that one had to bend almost double to get through the door. Lady Warwick once murmured mischievously to me: 'If you ever go to lunch with the Marquis he'll give you nasturtium leaves and violets to eat.' Nevertheless, she had done her best to help him and now suggested I should employ him to supervise the restoration of the manor.

The Marquis was well acquainted with both fact and legend regarding the house. As he led me round the property on a sort of treasure hunt, his long nose twitching with excitement, like huntsman after fox, I caught something of his zest for restoration. He began by tracing the lines of the great hall and the 'fire', its red brick chimney-stack still standing, smothered in ivy at one end. He also showed me the entrance to an underground passage to the church, long since blocked up, which enabled hunted men to seek sanctuary in the church. To test his story I asked the gardener one day to dig down below the flowers and the winter-planted vegetables. There, sure enough, were the brick footings extending the length and breadth of the garden, just as the Marquis had said.

The inside of the house, what remained of it, had been ravaged by Victorian adaptation to menial use. Rusty iron fire-gates with marble surrounds hid the open hearths. Victorian wallpaper covered the old walls. An antiquated bathroom with uncertain water supply, a door to the 'loo' with blue glass panels, and a Wedgwood lavatory pan with blue figures, replacing an earlier earth closet, completed my catalogue of horrors. Toadstools grew out of the walls of the dining-room and kitchen.

The Marquis was not a whit disturbed by all the mess, poking his long shepherd's crook through rotting plaster and tearing away accumulations of Victorian wallpaper to show me where original oak beams might be found. And there they were. In two small rooms we found beneath the deal boards the original oak floors, fastened with the original hand-cut nails, and still valiantly resisting the depravity of dry rot.

After two days of discovery it was decided to begin work at once. There lived in the village of Little Easton an excellent local builder, who understood how to handle oak with respect and when not to meddle with age. He knew, too, about that distinctive Essex craft known as 'pargetting', a method of ornamenting exterior plaster with all manner of attractive design, according to the whim of the craftsman. So the Marquis, combining his antiquarian zeal with natural good taste, made plans and drew sketches that would have made a qualified architect shudder but which Mr. Pickford, after scratching his head with the brim of his bowler hat, pocketed with the obvious intention of relying upon commonsense and local tradition. So prices were fixed—to be many times exceeded, needless to say—while Nancie and I watched and waited and finally went off to America, confident that all would be well.

Fifteen
Swings and roundabouts

I

The production of Noël Coward's *The Vortex* at the Everyman Theatre, Hampstead, in November 1924 was an event of high importance in the English theatre. Plays of such outstanding quality that they are able forthwith to establish the reputations of their authors and to influence the future course of contemporary drama make their appearance every decade or so. *The Vortex* is one of these, Stanley Houghton's *Hindle Wakes*, and, more recently, *Look Back in Anger* are other examples.

By mischance I lost the opportunity of sharing in this notable historic happening. This was the way of it: On September 4th, 1924, Constance Collier wrote to Sir Alfred Butt, telling him that she had a play by Noël Coward, called *The Vortex*, which she would like to do immediately after the run of *Our Betters* at the Globe. As Sir Alfred was away at the time the letter was sent on to me at Drury Lane and answered in my absence by my assistant, asking for the script to be forwarded for consideration on my return. Understandably, Miss Collier did not reply.

The production made such a tremendous stir that as soon as I got back from America and in spite of my many distractions at Drury Lane, I rushed up to Hampstead to see it. What a lucky spurt of energy that was! Not having seen Noël since he played an angel in my production of *Hannele* at Liverpool in 1913, I was astonished at his assured touch both as author, director and actor. Here was a formidable talent. His technique was as clear-cut as a diamond, although perhaps a trifle unrelenting. The big scene with Lilian Braithwaite in the last act surpassed in nervous intensity anything

I had seen on the stage before. He told me how Lilian had replaced Kate Cutler in the mother's part at the last moment, a circumstance that encourages the fantasy that there is always a good fairy to watch over the birth of a play of major importance. I doubt whether any other actress of Lilian's day could have caught so admirably the folly and the shallowness of the character. Incidentally, that performance opened up for Lilian a whole range of parts she had never before attempted, prolonging her career by at least a decade. The décor had been provided by Gladys Calthrop, a close friend of Noël's, whose shrewd commonsense, cultured mind and good taste must have greatly influenced his early years. The settings were of exceptional taste and originality, especially one scene with a wallpaper made of newspapers pasted on to canvas and varnished. (Before she was allowed to repeat this effect in New York Gladys had to join the paper-hangers' union.) The whole production struck a note of youthful integrity quite new in the theatre of that time. I went back to my anxieties at Drury Lane deeply stirred by what was obviously going to be a new influence in the theatre, and sad that I was not to share in it. My regrets were premature.

In the following spring Joseph Bickerton, the New York attorney who had drawn up our *Rain* contracts arrived in London to represent Sam Harris at the first night. He immediately asked to see *The Vortex*, which by this time had been transferred to the old Royalty Theatre in Dean Street, Soho, where it was having a highly successful run. Bickerton was so excited by the play that he came into my office the next morning wanting to buy it for America. I introduced him to Noël who was reluctant to entrust himself and his play to an unknown manager. Whereupon Bickerton offered to take me in as a joint producer, with the special task of re-directing the ensemble scenes which Noël felt needed outside supervision. And that was how I came to be associated with Noël's early career as a dramatist: a fortunate circumstance for me in many ways.

2

We left for America on August 12th. Once again I found myself in S.S. *Majestic*, not alone this time, but in the gayest of company. In addition to Noël and his adoringly sensible mother, there were Gladys Calthrop and Lilian Braithwaite of our Company. Also on board were Eugene Goossens and his wife, 'Booney', Michael Arlen and Leslie Howard *en route* to produce *The Green Hat* with Katherine Cornell, and Ruth Chatterton busily planning the American production of *The Man with a Load of Mischief* with Ashley Dukes. Above all, Nancie was with me. Excited by her first experience of ocean travel and having no professional anxieties, she gave herself up to the fun of what was virtually a wedding trip. All on board seemed to be bounding with energy and happiness, or was that just a reflection of my own feelings? As the great ship pitched and rolled her vast shape through the summer Atlantic, we passed our time between noisy deck games and twice daily immersion in the marble-pillared swimming-pool below. At night-time it was dancing, card games or gossip, the while American dowagers and business tycoons, returning from trips abroad, stared askance at 'those noisy theatre people'.

We arrived early in the morning. Bickerton was nowhere to be seen, but there was an unexpected landing-stage welcome from Charlie Dillingham, followed by tea in his office brewed by Vera Murray. Only then did I learn that Bickerton had sold much of his interest in *The Vortex* to Mr. Erlanger, with whom, as usual, Dillingham was associated. This I took as a storm warning. Sure enough, within days I received a request to attend with the author at the office of the great panjandrum. Charlie came too, hoping as always to soothe ruffled tempers with a display of whimsy.

Noël has described that interview in *Present Indicative*. To that account I need add little, save that it exactly recalled my interview with Erlanger over *Loyalties*. But what was sticking in the little man's gullet this time was not an imagined affront to Jewry but a still more unpardonable assault upon the sanctity of mother-love. Bearing in mind the New York production of *Hassan*, I shuddered when Erlanger offered to attend rehearsals and to 'straighten out the last act'. Of course Noël refused his surgery, so Bickerton, emerging from his 'decontamination centre', took back the Erlanger-Dillingham interest and resold it to Sam Harris which for practical purposes left Messrs. Bickerton and Dean in control of the production, and that in effect meant myself alone; altogether a satisfactory outcome.

3

There is no need to retell the story of Noël's triumph on the first
night at the Henry Miller Theatre in New York. His success was
instantaneous and stupendous, with the critics and the usual 'death-
watch' of first-nighters standing in their places to acclaim the
emergence of a new personality in the theatre. The Press notices
were equally overwhelming. The only sour note was sounded by a
cub reporter, airing his elementary French: '*Jambon avec sauce
piquante*'—a total irrelevance amid the paeans of praise. What is of
relevance to my own story, or so I think, is the manner in which this
dauntless young artist of the theatre stood up to the pressure of
overnight success. In the ensuing weeks it was fascinating to watch
him grasping it by the throat to make it sing his tune.

Noël was certainly quick off the mark in his determination to
win the race. He insisted that Bickerton and I should give a party
for him at the Embassy Club after the first night. This we were
delighted to do. He seemed to know by instinct the right people
to invite, although the Social Register was a book not yet opened
to him. He provided us with the list of guests, which included most
of the younger set who mattered in the theatrical and artistic life
of New York. The published list of those present was a striking
indication of the impression Noël had so quickly made. The party
was a huge success, receiving its English cachet when Lady Diana
Cooper arrived unexpectedly, sailing with calm beauty through
the noisy throng to add her cool congratulations. Noël asked Nancie
to be the hostess—a formidable assignment for a young woman
of twenty-one on her first visit to America—but she carried it
off with a poise that delighted us all.

.　　　.　　　.　　　.　　　.

This was the last time that I had any business dealings with Dillingham, although I often called upon him during subsequent visits
when I was busy with film matters. So now is the appropriate moment
to pay tribute to a kind and generous friend. Our relations were invariably pleasant; more than that, he made them happy occasions.
There was always a cablegram of welcome addressed to me on
the ship, a courier at the pierhead to see me through Customs,
baskets of fruit and books waiting in my cabin on departure days and,

most decisive of all, a laugh and a joke to welcome me in his office. I cannot recall any occasion when Charlie was not chuckling at some oddity or other that had struck him, even as he dictated first-night telegrams to friends and enemies alike: 'Love and kisses, Charlie.' His end was conventional, which sounds heartless; yet it was so, following the curvate career of so many theatre gamblers. No longer able to command success, his theatre sold and all his resources spent, Dillingham lived through the darkening years before the Second World War alone in a single room at the Astor Hotel, paid for by friends. Strange that he should have chosen to end his days within sight but no longer within sound of the box-offices of Broadway.

4

A few weeks before we all left for America I dashed into what used to be my office and found Clift closeted with a quiet young man, discussing what to do about a play that he had written, for which a licence had just been refused. The young man's name was John Van Druten and his play *Young Woodley*. Clift, adjusting the pince-nez on the bridge of his nose and drawing in his breath with a gently sucking sound—procedure he invariably adopted when the matter in hand demanded caution—began to explain that he had been considering the play for our Dee Cee Company, but had been told unofficially that it would not be licensed. It was surprising that I, as chairman of the company, had been told nothing of this. While Clift was talking I began to wonder whether 'Foxy', his nick-name among the actors, was due solely to a rufous complexion. The quiet young man smiling anxiously at me across the table was obviously upset, for this was his first full-length play, upon the success of which he had set high hopes of escape from the drudgery of solicitor's offices, and lectures upon legal matters at a university.

For some time now, ever since *Hassan* in fact, my relations with the Lord Chamberlain's office had been cordial. Upon more than one occasion Lord Cromer, whose interest in the theatre was genuine not evoked by the duties of his office, had invited me to discuss ways of modifying the schedule of restrictions set out for the guidance of that secretive and oracular body, the Advisory Board. However, secret diplomacy had got me nowhere in the negotiations for a licence for *Desire Under the Elms*. In an unofficial letter to me, dated July 2nd, Lord Cromer committed himself to the view that this was 'just the sort of American play that should be kept off the English stage'. In such a climate of opinion a play by an unknown author about the sexual difficulties of schoolboys would stand no chance at all. Polite society swept such problems under the carpet or held them to be non-existent. A thought now struck me. Since *Young Woodley* was to be expelled from England, why not enter him for America? I broke into Clift's commiserations with the author and said I would take the play to New York; if it succeeded there, I would tackle Lord Cromer personally about it on my return.

A further thought: I had recently made the acquaintance of George C. Tyler, another Broadway manager out of the Erlanger stable, who was visiting London in search of plays. Now supposing he liked Van Druten's play—Clift was praising it very highly—why not produce it with him? I put the proposition to Tyler who jumped at the chance of presenting a play with what he called 'a noo sex angle'. He wanted the part for Glenn Hunter, the young American star who had recently scored a big success in the film of *Merton of the Movies*. But he did agree to cast the remaining parts from among the British actors resident in America. After pulling a long face, he also agreed to engage Gladys Calthrop to design the décor, consoling himself with the thought that he would not have to pay her transportation costs. I remember well how Gladys would come to me at rehearsals to describe her frantic efforts to secure the correct scenery and furnishings. A newcomer to the professional theatre, she found it difficult to compromise her impeccable taste in the face of the hugger-mugger scramble of Broadway in the twenties. In the end, against all odds, she did provide me with backgrounds reminiscent of an English public school.

I had quite a struggle at rehearsal to achieve a semblance of uniformity among the variety of British-American and American-British accents that confronted me. Glenn Hunter's air of tired juvenility put me off at first, but beneath it I discovered a talented actor of great personal charm. All the British actors in the cast had this tired look about them, as though exhausted by the strenuous life of Broadway. Of the Americans only Helen Gehagan, a beautiful Irish-American, who played the schoolmaster's wife, brought natural freshness to the performance.

Young Woodley began its year-long career in America at Boston, Mass., towards the end of October 1925. It came to the Belmont

Theatre, New York, on the night of November 2nd, when Glenn
Hunter received an audience ovation, and on the following morning
a critics' ovation, too, rivalling that given a few weeks earlier to
Noël and his *Vortex*. Some of the first-night audience in the back
rows guffawed at the more tender passages between Glenn and
the schoolmaster's wife, perhaps thinking they were still watching
Merton of the Movies. For this they were rightly castigated by all
the leading columnist-writers, who made great play, too, with the
Lord Chamberlain's ban. One of them neatly combined criticism
and comment by saying: 'Whereas the Lord Chamberlain decided
that *Young Woodley* was not fit for British audiences, I have a horrid
suspicion that American audiences were not fit for *Young Woodley*'
... This was number two in my score during that season of American
success.

5

During our talks in London about *Young Woodley* George Tyler
surprised me by suddenly announcing that he was going to make
a production of *The School for Scandal* in the autumn for American
schools and universities. 'What an extraordinary fellow,' I thought,
'with his shabby clothes and fierce resentment whenever production
costs are mentioned, as though all the world were plotting to rob
him of his just reward.' Yet there was no denying his passion for
the theatre, as he sat there talking about his recent tour of the principal theatres of Western Europe in a hired car: highly expensive, no
doubt! He appeared to have forgotten all about *Woodley* as he
explained how difficult it was to find American actors capable of
speaking eighteenth-century English properly. He was wondering
whether he might borrow some of the ReandeaN players, adding as
an afterthought that perhaps I would like to direct the production
for him? I at once thought of the plans George and I had made for
staging the play at Drury Lane after the manner of its first production there in 1777. Tyler's suggestion would give us the chance to
put our ideas into effect, as well as providing new opportunities for
some of the ReandeaN Company which, alas! was now in process
of disintegration. I accepted it but when I proposed to bring
George Harris with me Tyler objected because of the transportation
expenses, another quirk of character.

The cast was made up of American and British players in roughly equal numbers. George provided a wonderful array of costume designs which stood out brilliantly against the sober backgrounds. The play was lighted by candlelight, ostensibly from three crystal chandeliers (the trouble George and I had in ferreting out craftsmen able and willing to assemble the glass into a semblance of eighteenth-century design!). All this, coupled with the minuettish movements and stylised gestures that I imposed upon the players provided a pastiche of the original production so far as one could conjecture it.

Tyler wanted to open in New York but so great was the prejudice among managers against anything that suggested culture that none would let him have a theatre, save at an outrageous rental. Undeterred, he defiantly bought the Knickerbocker Theatre for one performance on a Sunday night, 'so as to catch the critics', he said. Columns of erudite criticism followed, the *New York Times* going so far as to publish a lengthy extract from Lamb's essay on the play. . . . The reception in universities and schools entitled me to notch up my third win of the season.

6

Easy Virtue was one of the plays which ReandeaN had bought and which Alec wanted me to dispose of elsewhere. Noël had been pressing me for some time to take over the contract. We decided with Bickerton's help to try for an American production and, if this were successful, I agreed to do it in London. Our disagreement with Erlanger proved fortunate, for now we felt free to accept an offer from Gilbert Miller to present the play at the Empire Theatre where he had recently taken charge of the Frohman interests. The Empire had always been run with dignity and taste, like the Haymarket Theatre in London. This would help to sustain the countryhouse atmosphere of Noël's play. Thus once, and once only, did I see my name in print associated with that of the great American impresario, Charles Frohman.

The play was a cheeky borrowing from *The Second Mrs. Tanqueray*, with Noël's dialogue and a Paula decked out in modern clothes to alleviate the conventional situations. There is no need to recount the plot; the reader will know it already or at least can make a close guess at it—so, too, at the stock characters. These we cast up to the hilt, bringing over two more members of the now dispersed

ReandeaN Company for important parts: Robert Harris for the well-meaning husband of the lady with a past (re-named Larita), and Marda Vanne as his mannish, elder sister. His mother, with female stiff upper lip, was played by Mabel Terry-Lewis with all the sureness of touch of a Terry. Among the bevy of young friends and neighbours to join in the party in the last act were Lilian's daughter, Joyce, playing her first part, and Joan Clement Scott, grand-daughter of the doyen of Victorian dramatic critics, whose ideal was Henry Irving. The star was Jane Cowl. How we succeeded in engaging her interest in the play I cannot recall, but this beautiful, capricious and faultlessly theatrical star was exactly suited to the part of Larita. She was probably well aware of the truth of Alexander Woollcott's subsequent remark about the play: 'It will prove a whacking success; it always has been.'

The scene was set in the hall of a country mansion, not quite one of 'the stately homes of England' of Noël's later song, although it did have a grand staircase to provide effective entrances for Jane Cowl. No special features otherwise, save for a statuette of the Venus de Milo conveniently placed at the foot of the staircase for Jane to hurl a book at as the curtain descends upon the second act: 'I always hated that damn thing.' The climax came rather too early for my liking. Jane's coloratura performance made it extremely difficult to maintain interest in the last act. Noël blamed her for overacting the scene, but to expect her to do otherwise was like expecting a starving cat to leave the fish alone.

The critics had a rare time with Noël. Alan Dale called the play 'Cowardly Pinero', inept because the outstanding characteristic of Noël's career has been a sustained contradiction of his surname. In my view three factors saved the production from banality. First, there was Noël's wit. Next, there was Jane's performance, which was so outstanding that it brought immediate success to the box-office. Finally, there were the dance scenes in the last act. Noël complained at the time that I polished them nearly out of existence, but I was secretly gratified when several New York critics pointed out that it was my management of them which saved the last act from collapse. It was now that I began to develop the meticulous timing of ensembles for which I became known in subsequent years. This was the last of the four productions that I made during that New York season.

7

The influx of plays and players from Britain was especially notable that season. This circumstance attracted the attention of the newsmen who were soon hot on the trail for news and views. When they came to see me I was particularly irked by the censoring of Eugene O'Neill's *Desire Under the Elms*, by the similar fate apparently awaiting Sidney Howard's *They Knew What They Wanted*, and by *Young Woodley*'s virtual expulsion from Britain. The only result of my complaints at home had been a newspaper campaign against 'dirty plays from America', which so infuriated me that I had told reporters at Southampton that I intended to call a public meeting on my return to protest the charge. In New York my criticisms were even more emphatic: 'the future of the English-speaking Theatre lay in America', etc., etc. Noël backed me up strenuously. No doubt our comments were ill-timed, but there! we were excited by the fizz that was part of the Broadway scene, mistaking it for artistic merit. On the other hand we had some justification because of the outstanding work of the Theatre Guild whose standards of choice, presentation and performance were way ahead of our own. Both *Heartbreak House* and *Back to Methuselah* were produced in New York before they were seen in London. Ashley Dukes, another member of the British 'posse' went to work more subtly but made similar noises. Michael Arlen, whose *Green Hat* had been produced successfully the night before Noël opened in *The Vortex*, kept out of the controversy, pursuing a course towards social success, for which he had special aptitude.

Our praise of the Theatre Guild naturally attracted the attention of its directors, who saw no reason why they should not profit by this British accolade. They invited all three of us, that is to say Noël, Ashley and myself, to address a public meeting of their supporters one Sunday evening in the Mecca Temple, a large hall of Italianate design recently opened on 52nd Street. The building was crowded, not all Guild subscribers by any means, but all had paid for admission. No hospitality was offered to us either before or after the event, which drew adverse comment, *sotto voce*, from Noël, who saw no reason why the Guild should make profit out of us in this way. He was the prize attraction and spoke first, wittily and well. I followed, rather ponderous, but listened to with attention.

When it came to Ashley's turn he got into the most dreadful muddle, trying to calculate how much the Theatre Guild would make out of the proceedings and what it cost visiting Englishmen to live in New York City. This raillery the audience found unfunny.

A week or two later we were the speakers upon a more formidable occasion, a luncheon given by the Book and Pen Club in the huge banqueting hall of the Hotel Biltmore on Madison Avenue. I have never seen so many women together in one place either before or since: two-thousand all told, I was assured by the publicity man. As guests of honour we were seated upon a raised dais, placed along one side of the hall where we could be kept under close observation by a thousand pairs of staring eyes. I found myself sitting next to Fred Kerr, a fine old English actor, then playing on Broadway; he had come with his daughter, Mollie, a member of our *Vortex* company. Fred was noted for his acerbity, usually sweetened with a spice of humour, as on this occasion. Glancing at the sea of upturned faces, he growled out: 'Only wants bars in front of the table and the picture's complete.' Serving of the lunch was carried out at top speed, with whistles blown for change of course. Then there arose such a din and clatter of plates as made conversation impossible. Chicken followed the grapefruit, ice-cream the chicken, then the coffee, all at lighting speed—more a gymnastic than a gastronomic exercise. Unwise to dilly-dally or let go one's knife and fork for then all was lost, or rather, the chicken was last seen with others disappearing through swing doors in care of a file of waiters.

8

Ever since my arrival on the London theatre scene I had been over-strained, over-stretched, 'over-everything', and the subsequent difficulties had induced in me the habit of introspection. Now, in a way I find difficult to define, I felt released in spirit. This I put down to Noël's gay and indomitable outlook upon life, which had a great influence on me.

All sorts of little cameos of memory come to mind as I sit and ponder those hectic days. There was the morning when I called to see Noël before rehearsal. He was living in a duplex apartment belonging to Mae Murray, the film star, in the Hôtel des Artistes on New York's West Side. It was finished 'all accordin'': interior

Left The last portrait of Meggie Albanesi

Right As Daisy in *East of Suez*

Below *The Lilies of the Field*. Meggie lets her hair down, metaphorically speaking—with Gertrude Kingston, Edna Best, Austin Trevor

The memorial plaque by Eric Gill which I presented to the St. Martin's Theatre

wrought-iron gates, Spanish style, to guard against intruders to the upper part, electric flambeaux leaning from the walls at dangerous angles, and cushions with enormous swags everywhere—an ensemble accurately described by Noël as early Metro-Goldwyn-Mayer. Its sole merit in Noël's eyes was undoubtedly the grand piano, where on this particular morning George Gershwin was seated, playing sections of his 'Rhapsody in Blue' which Paul Whiteman had brought out at Carnegie Hall the previous year. Noël, enraptured, was excitedly demanding repetition of passages he particularly liked, sometimes tapping out rhythmic movements—one could hardly call them dance steps—which he was obviously storing up for use in later work. The vitality and enthusiasm of those two young men at the beginning of notable achievement was exhilarating to watch and listen to. I was shockingly late for rehearsal that day.

What other cameos were there to hold up to view? Oh, yes! there was the night Ashley Dukes was having supper with us. Noël told him that George V after seeing Marie Tempest in *Hay Fever* had been heard to remark: 'I may be old-fashioned but I do like these clean plays.' Ashley, whose moderate success had been somewhat overshadowed by Noël's, made acid rejoinder: 'You might give a special performance of *Easy Virtue* for President Coolidge. He's an old-fashioned playgoer, too.' 'Why not Queen Mary?' grinned Noël.

Then there was 'the case of the opera hat', to borrow Mr. Sherlock Holmes' phrasing: The use of this type of headgear was virtually over, although Gibus still had his shop at the corner of St. Martin's Lane and Trafalgar Square. Now I never had any luck with my headgear; it always looked battered or out of date. My opera hat was no exception. One evening we were rattling down Fifth Avenue, four of us, Noël, Gladys and myself—I forget who the fourth was, probably Nancie. We were on our way to some party or other, appropriately dressed for the occasion, I with my battered old opera hat. Suddenly Noël looked at me with a wicked grin: 'Basil, why will you wear that awful hat?'

'Don't you like it?' I said.

'Certainly not,' replied Noël briskly.

'Very well,' I replied, and threw it out of the window into the middle of Fifth Avenue.

'That's better,' said Noël, nodding approvingly, 'you're coming on fast!'

T

9

The feeling of exhilaration that possessed me on first arriving in America never failed to recur in subsequent years. The tempo of living seemed to be growing faster all the time. New York in particular was sizzling with vitality, flexing its muscles in anticipation of America's eventual rôle as a super-power. The city was being rebuilt at an increasing pace. The rat-tat-tat of pneumatic hammers could be heard on every hand, rivetting together vast steel frameworks soon to be cocooned into new hotels, apartment houses and theatres, yes, *theatres*! At the height of the boom New York possessed more theatres than any other capital city, all of them built on inadequate sites, with insufficient stage space, the one dimension essential to efficiency.

Nancie arrived in America with a bundle of introductions from her mother. Most of them were useless because the names had long since disappeared from the Social Register. But at least one friend from the past remained, old Mrs. Post, member of the most exclusive circle of American society, at whose head sat Mrs. W. K. Vanderbilt. Mrs. Post welcomed us with haughty grandeur. Almost before we had sat down in her Louis Seize apartment she looked at Nancie and cried out: 'Gracious me, child! Whatever made you marry someone on the stage?' Before Nancie had time to more than swallow her surprise she shook her head at me, adding: 'Besides he's much too old.' It was impossible to protest at an Olympian attitude so obviously genuine and involuntary. Also, it would have made no difference if I had! While the China tea, properly made for once, was being served, Mrs. Post melted a little. 'Because of your beautiful mother,' as she put it to Nancie, she arranged for us to be received by Mrs. Vanderbilt. On the appointed day as we stood on the steps of the brownstone mansion on Fifth Avenue, soon to be demolished to make way for the new Rockefeller Center, waiting for audience, I felt as nervous as though before a royal presentation. Presently the outer doors were slowly opened by a footman in livery and knee-breeches, who passed us on to a major-domo who in turn ushered us into the presence where Mrs. 'Willie K.' sat enthroned. The old lady chatted graciously, enquiring after Nancie's friends and relations she had known in Edwardian days. It was astonishing that, in the supposedly classless American society, these old ladies should still be gazing at an aristocratic view that had long since disappeared over the hill.

Other introductions brought us nearer to our own generation. We were frequently entertained by Philae and Clifford Carver. Clifford was at that time chairman of the Finance Committee of the Metropolitan Opera. We sat with them on the Golden Horseshoe, noting the glittering assembly and how so few of them managed to arrive on time and how so many more departed before the end to join the wild scramble to pick out their own limousines from the unbelievable muddle of traffic that always ensued.

Time, or the lack of it, created its own imperative: at the end of rehearsal, find taxi, rush to the hotel, change into white tie and tails: a janitor, whistling desperately, finds another taxi at the last moment; arrive at the dinner party at the last acceptable minute, the martinis are half-molten ice, a full course dinner eaten at speed, into the host's car to join the queue waiting impatiently to make their way to theatre or opera, arriving just in time to scramble, tense and nervous, into one's seat to spend the first act recovering equanimity: such was theatre-going during the boom years.

The smart café society was a different set again. Noël seemed able to swallow its poisonous sweets without damage to his mental digestion; but he soon abandoned its popularity in favour of quieter friends and deeper appreciation. Our stay among the bright lights was just long enough to note the ever-increasing rejection of pro-hibition. The number of speak-easies was greatly increased, more closely guarded than ever before by gorilla-faced men, peering through little wickets in the steel-studded doors at visitors waggling their cards of admission, no words spoken.

Most of Nancie's generation, the heirs to tobacco and other fortunes, and their sisters and girl friends, seemed to live in a state of frenzy induced by drinking spirits often of dubious origin. One notable party-giver was Schuyler Parsons whose wealth, I believe, derived from sugar. A myopic little man, he was excitedly drinking away his fortune and inviting a wide circle of friends to share in the process. He was always the most exhilarated member at his own parties. It was at one of them, given in his large apart-ment on Park Avenue, that we met for the first time Fred and Adele Astaire. I was very attracted by Adele, with her frank open face and wide generous mouth. We danced quite a lot together. Then as the party grew noisier some of the guests pushed us into a large cupboard beneath the staircase of the duplex apartment, intending to leave us there long enough presumably to cause gossip. Instead, we spent our time banging on the door—not so much as a single kiss exchanged! I can still recall Fred's anxious look at his sister when we emerged.

It had not been much of a wedding trip for Nancie. I did not want her to miss her share of the social round, but she had to come to terms with theatre obligations which occupied so much of my time. Afterwards I realised what a splendid show she had put up.

At last the day came for us to return home. We had been four months away. In that time I had produced four successes, which was a record for an English producer on Broadway. We left America in the *Mauretania* on December 17th, longing for a sight of our future home and eagerly discussing plans for its furnishing. We arrived in time to spend Christmas at Easton Lodge.

Sixteen
Tallulah at the St. Martin's

I

While I was in America Paul Clift, from his new position as general manager for Alec Rea, strove mightily to restore prosperity to the St. Martin's. *Rain*, transferred from the Garrick, lasted only for one month; it was followed in quick succession by three productions by outside managements, only the last of them, *The Ghost Train*, outlasting the contractual period of one month. This ingenious thriller began its run late in November and was puffing merrily into popular favour when I returned. Unfortunately, Clift, in his other capacity as managing director of our Dee Cee organisation, had signed contracts with an influential author for the presentation of his new play at the St. Martin's within a certain date. But he had omitted the usual extension clause for *The Ghost Train* which had to move on to another station. Thereafter, it had a unique career, 'ghosting' its way from one theatre to another and then back again in a manner appropriate to its title but confusing to the public.

My position at the theatre remained ambiguous and the outwardly friendly atmosphere that prevailed between Paul Clift and myself did but add to the ambiguity. Relations with the staff throughout the ReandeaN years had been so close that they could not understand why I no longer gave them clear and definite instructions about forthcoming productions, nor why I continued to occupy that small office at the end of the passage. Yet complete severance was not possible, seeing that I was still chairman of the Dee Cee Company. That organisation had grown enormously of recent years, passing from the exploitation of our own London productions, sometimes with their original casts, to the presentation of West End stars in their recent successes. This was just show business, and extremely profitable, being ably managed by Paul Clift, but my heart was not in it. It was a far cry from the ideals with which we had set out a few short years ago.

It was no part of Clift's plan that I should produce the new play, but as chairman of Dee Cee I refused to be brushed aside. So, hastily swallowing my Christmas dinner—time being so desperately short—I sat down to prepare our latest acquisition. And so that was how I found myself early in the New Year rehearsing a play that I had not chosen, one which I thoroughly disliked. The final incongruity in this strange affair was my occupation of an office at the other end of the corridor from where I had used to work.

The author of the play was Sir Patrick Hastings, a leading advocate at the English Bar and until recently Attorney-General in the Ramsay Macdonald Government. The most formidable cross-examiner of his day, he possessed an acute sense of dramatic values, and impeccable timing for the definitive question. These qualities he took with him into the business of playwriting which the wide circle of friends whom his devotedly enthusiastic wife gathered round him regarded as an amiable eccentricity. Mary Hastings was a woman of great charm and extravagant habit. Pat was a lavish spender, too, and immensely popular at the Garrick Club where he enjoyed sardonic exchanges with Seymour Hicks and Frederick Lonsdale, scoring as many hits as they did. As part of his defensive armour against criticism Pat used to declare that he wrote his plays solely to make money. Perhaps that is why success so often eluded him. Although his dialogue was terse and sharpened with caustic humour, none of his characters ever seemed to come alive. A confirmed realist whose plays lacked all reality: that must be the final verdict on his 'hobby'. Another foible which his friends learned to accept was a disarming brusquerie towards guests at the lavish dinner parties which Mary arranged for him at their flat in Hay Hill, Berkeley Square. Punctually on the hour Pat would announce to the assembled company: 'It's ten o'clock: All you people must clear out now. I've got work to do.' The party would break up precipitately, Mary always protesting with an air that failed to conceal her secret acquiescence, for she knew the immense amount of work which Pat had to get through to maintain the huge income that she so assiduously spent.

The play *Scotch Mist* was Pat's second attempt to reach his Eldorado. The first act opens in the London home of a wealthy

Cabinet Minister and his dissatisfied wife. She and some of her friends—all slightly unreal characters—are exchanging witticisms when they are interrupted by the arrival of an old 'flame' from Africa, who in despair of his suit had sought the wide-open spaces in the accepted manner. He invites the husband to his Scottish castle for a fishing trip and the wife, surprisingly enough, insists upon going, too! In the second act, while his other guests are away fishing, the host and the wife go for a walk on the moor where they are overtaken by a Scotch mist, hence the title! They seek shelter in a hut where the heroine uses all her sex wiles and the hero, like St. Anthony, fights off temptation. Alas! the Scotch mist fails to disperse; indeed, it grows thicker. So the lovers must pass the night together, the lion lying down with the lamb, so to speak. I have small recollection of that last act, save that, as in all such stories, love conquers all. It remains for the husband to conclude this woeful drama with the comment: 'Well, goodbye! But don't think you can come back to me, because you can't!'

The cast: the part of the dissatisfied wife gave me the opportunity to draw Tallulah Bankhead into orbit, a chance I had so disastrously missed in casting *Rain*. As a box-office personality she might yet pull the St. Martin's out of the financial mire. This she very nearly did, but not quite. Godfrey Tearle was ideal for the strong, silent hero.

The production: a generous patron of the theatre at that time was Lord Lathom (Ned to his friends), who dissipated a large fortune in various theatrical ventures. One of them was an interior decorating business, in which Mary Hastings was an enthusiastic partner. The décor of our first act was undertaken by this firm which later received the hallmark of fashionable approval in Syrie Maugham's white carpets and white painted leather chairs.

The rehearsals: my sole recollection of these is of a clash of personalities, not as one might suppose between author and cast—indeed Pat spent much of his time telling the actors what a bad play it was and how good they were, possibly seeking reassurance against his worst fears!—no, the clash was between Godfrey's noble love-making and Tallulah's ravishments, or rather his wife's view of the latter. Godfrey at that time was married to a beautiful Irish actress, Mary Malone, 'Mollie' to her friends, who was intensely jealous. But Godfrey's handsome features aroused no interest in the volatile Tallulah. Nevertheless, Mollie attended every rehearsal, watching lynx-eyed. She made her feelings so obvious that everyone in the theatre viewed the progress of this tea-cup comedy with secret amusement. When the time came to allot the dressing-rooms Mollie told the stage manager that Godfrey would prefer to dress at the top of the theatre, next door to the wardrobe-room, where he would get more fresh air, leaving Tallulah to occupy the star dressing-room on the ground floor. At the final dress rehearsal I was astonished to find Mollie seated in the middle of the front row of the stalls; so, too, was Tallulah. When we came to the *scène à faire* in the second act she suddenly let go and played with such abandon that poor Mollie was reduced to tears. It was as if her Godfrey were being raped before her eyes. When the curtain came down I rose from my place to go on the stage to give notes. Before I had time to do so Tallulah poked her head round the corner of the pass-door, glanced at Mollie and then at me, chuckling gleefully: 'All right, Basil? Good thing I had me drawers on, wasn't it?'

After the tremendous advance publicity, largely conducted by Mary Hastings herself—not always with discretion—it must have given poor Pat a shock to read the opinions of the critics, many of whom were his personal friends, the critic of the *Morning Post* remarking conclusively: '*Scotch Mist* is one of the worst plays I have ever seen.' Tallulah's contribution fully justified my belief in her ability to draw uncommitted playgoers to the box-office. She was given a rapturous reception by the gallery at every performance as she blew them repeated kisses, ending with what was fast becoming her signature tune: 'Bless you, darlings.' Miss Frances Ross-Campbell in the small part of a Scottish housekeeper caused derisive laughter from the gallery on the first night when she said: 'If ye must talk, talk sense.'

The sensation in the second act saved the play from financial disaster. Various religious bodies contributed to this result. Several London vicars made the play the subject of Sunday-morning sermons, which woke up an otherwise dormant box-office. When the Bishop of London joined the outcry, and his 'Clean up the Stage' Campaign Committee announced that its request to the Lord Chamberlain 'to revoke the play's licence' had been refused and that in consequence the matter was to be raised in the House of Lords, queues at the box-office became inevitable. If the good bishop were alive today and could be induced to visit one of the current 'permissive' plays he would die of apoplexy before the first act was over.

2

A *succés de scandale* rarely has a long life in the theatre. So, although the box-office was busy enough to warrant my paying a short visit abroad, it was no surprise to find on my return that *Scotch Mist* would soon have to be replaced.

Now, although the theatre was no longer my direct responsibility I was determined to meet our obligations so far as the two plays I had originally aquired for ReandeaN were concerned. *Easy Virtue* was no problem. Noël and I had already agreed, following its success in New York, to bring Jane Cowl to London with as many of the British members of the cast as wished to return home. This would not be for some time yet since the play was in the full tide of its American success. There remained only Sidney Howard's play, which had been in the pipe-line for more than a year now. There had been quite a struggle over the censorship. The play is set in southern California and deals with the efforts of an illiterate Italian immigrant wine-grower to obtain a wife by 'postal vote', as it were. I knew that the tough characters and racy dialogue would afford a rich harvest of blue pencillings for our censor. I told Sidney I felt sure I could overcome the censor's objections, given time, but it was several months before I was able to send him a list of the emendations that were demanded before the licence was granted. They appear nonsensical today, but then British censorship was always dragging its feet in the wake of advancing public opinion. The following notes taken from the correspondence illustrate this:

'Jo, 'ee sleep with everyone'—*Alter* to 'Jo, 'ee's been with everyone' (a less pleasant expression in any context).

Again: 'Toni, 'ee's not too old for 'avin keed'—*Alter* to 'for 'avin' family'. All 'God damns' to be removed. And so on and so forth.

After keeping us waiting for some months Pauline Lord finally decided upon a season in Chicago, followed by an extended road tour. Our option was now running out, and the Guild were pressing for immediate fulfilment. I was anxious to keep faith with Sidney, so the only solution was for me to take over the contract and to present the play myself at the St. Martin's, to which Alec offered no objection. Thus we were faced with the bizarre situation of Alec and myself signing contracts with each other, with Paul Clift acting as witness for both of us. I was safely over the first hurdle in my race to beat the Guild's time limit.

The next obstacle was finance. Now it so happened that during the rehearsals of *Scotch Mist* I had made the acquaintance of George Ansley, a member of a well-known banking family, who at that time was a junior barrister in Hastings' Chambers. He and Pat were great friends, and when Pat was busy in the courts Ansley would come along to the rehearsals to represent him. He became interested in the theatre and volunteered to finance my next production. In the end Ansley found one-third, James K. Hackett, the American star, a friend of Sidney's, one-third, and I the remainder of the money. Thus I managed to scramble over my second hurdle without mishap.

Next, there was the seemingly impossible high jump on the casting. Although I knew it was impossible for British actors to give convincing representations of 'way-out' American characters, I secretly welcomed Miss Lord's decision not to come to London because I thought we needed an American actress previously known to our audiences. In fact, I was thinking all the time of Tallulah Bankhead. I wanted her to play Amy. Here I ran into difficulty because both the author and the Theatre Guild were violently opposed to the idea. After a tussle I overcame their objections, and gave Tallulah one of the great chances of her career, which she seized with both hands. There were two other outstanding performances in the American production which I despaired of being able to duplicate: Toni, the Italian vineyard proprietor, played in America by Richard Bennett, and Joe, the charge-hand, played by Glenn Anders, whose deceptively casual technique foreshadowed the methods of Marlon Brando. Both actors gave really star performances, so I engaged them for the London production of *They Knew What They Wanted*.

In his letters written about this time Sidney expressed very strong views about the manner in which stars would twist a play out of shape in pursuit of audience response, even after it had achieved success on the first night. When he heard that I had engaged Richard Bennett he wrote me a long letter about this, warning me of the dangers to come: 'Dick will of course sob a great deal, but no one minds Dick's sobbing. Don't let him make speeches in London. He always gets drunk and talks about his wife.'

Through the Dillingham office I made arrangements for the two stars to arrive on the first day of our rehearsals. Glenn Anders did so, but Richard Bennett cried off at the last moment, sending me a doctor's certificate by cable, the only time I have ever received such a document by those means. I was now in a difficult situation. Where could I possibly find an actor capable of representing the Italian proprietor of a Californian vineyard? In the end, by what trick or chance or memory I cannot now recall, I gave the part to Sam Livesey, father of Roger Livesey, who had spent so much of his time touring in an old melodrama called *The Village Blacksmith* that everyone had forgotten what a fine actor he was. His performance won universal praise, especially from Ivor Brown in the *Saturday Review*, who included me in the encomium for having the circumspection to cast Livesey in the part. I had taken my highest jump successfully.

Tallulah set to work enthusiastically, putting herself entirely in my hands and accepting without protest my careful discipline at rehearsals, a process she had never before encountered. Her approach to the part was intelligent—no surprise that!—and conscientious even to the dressing of the part. Amy was after all a poor drab, discovered by Toni in a 'spaghetti joint' in Chicago. Her appearance in a wedding dress in the course of the play was an obvious opportunity for display by anyone as fashion-conscious as Tallulah, but she did not fall into the trap. She went off to buy the cheapest clothes she could find, but she wore them with such distinction that one of the women's papers accused her of over-dressing the part. Our publicity man, seizing an opportunity to exercise his office, announced that all her clothes—wedding-dress, two cotton frocks, three pairs of hose and one hat, cost six pounds in all.

There was a tremendous rush for seats for the first night of this much-talked-of American play with the unusual title. All the regular ReandeaN patrons were there as a matter of course, and a fair sprinkling of Tallulah's fans beside. I was a little anxious as to how her noisy followers would take Tallulah's attempt at a character part of such serious intent. I need not have worried. Her performance was restrained, sincerely felt and accurately characterised throughout. The audience rose to it with surprise and delight, while the fans, taken aback at first, gave her a riotous reception from which the usual hysteria was notably absent. Indeed, the applause after each act was so prolonged that the audience wondered why there were no curtain calls. When I was a young actor we used to gauge our success by the number of 'curtains' we received at the end of each act. 'How's it going? How many calls?' we used to ask when other actors returned to the dressing-room. But on this occasion we adopted the usual American practice, and held all calls until the end of the play.

This is now almost universal, but it was adversely criticised at the time, one paper saying that the man responsible for raising the curtain must have fallen asleep.

Hitherto American plays had not had a high reputation among London critics, possibly because only the more obvious commercial 'vehicles' ever made the journey, but they gave generous welcome to Sidney's play, naming it as the finest example of post-war dramatic writing to come out of America: a verdict headlined in one popular paper as: 'A good American play at last.' St. John Ervine ended his notice in the *Observer* on a note of unconscious irony: 'The St. Martin's is itself again; the home of plays for intelligent people.'

Tallulah had now scored two box-office hits. So it seemed that my judgment was correct and that she might yet prove to be the star to guide me into financial haven. But I made no allowance for the rifts in her character. Born in the American deep South, grand-daughter of a Senator, with a touch of aristocratic arrogance, possessed of great beauty, much wit, and an instinct that told her the surest passport to American hearts, and, incidentally, to the front page of the newpapers, was never to be dull and only to shock with distinction, she yet lacked a sense of dedication that alone could overcome her lack of basic training. She was always an amateur—in the better sense of that term—approaching the theatre, and indeed each aspect of life, as an experiment, quickly to be dropped when unsuccessful. She once told me how as a child she used to rehearse gestures and facial expressions by herself in a long mirror, a form of narcissism fatal to integrity. This encouraged her later habit of giving performances of herself as her admirers saw her. Thus she passed from one extravagance of behaviour to another. Now she is gone, leaving a glitter of star-dust but no void in the ranks that she once graced.

A few days after the opening the *Daily Sketch* headlined an article 'REANDEAN NOT DEAD', in which they announced that new Rean-deaN productions were to be looked for shortly—a *canard* for which I was not responsible. My hopes began to revive that I might yet persuade Alec to reverse his decision not to produce *Easy Virtue* and thus save the day even at this eleventh hour and a half! I pondered the matter for several days and then waylaid him at the stage-door of the theatre as he was about to leave for his house in the country. It was a humiliating position for both of us. While Marguerite Rea sat in the car and Payne, the chauffeur, stood respectfully by, and actors came and went, I pleaded my cause, reminding him that *Easy Virtue* was a big success in New York, and of the money we had already spent on it. Alec was obdurate, his only comment being: 'Whoever takes it over ought to pay ReandeaN something for having held the baby for so long.' My hopes died that afternoon. But the next day I found a new resolve: I would seek affiliations elsewhere.

Interlude: Moscow

For some time now the English stage had been buzzing with exciting stories about happenings in the Russian theatre; stories of new theatres, new production methods, new plays and, above all, of new audiences packing the theatres every night. Oliver M. Sayler, an American theatre enthusiast whom I had met in New York, had recently published a book on the subject. His account of his experiences in Moscow during the early days of the revolution was fascinating. I was anxious to see things for myself and, if possible, to be the first English producer to do so, but cultural contacts with the Soviets were non-existent; it seemed a hopeless proposition until a chance meeting with the Soviet Minister of Labour, then on an official visit to this country, threw opportunity in my way. Lady Warwick, ever with ear attuned to the siren voices of the Left, had invited the Russian Ambassador, Mr. Bogomoloff, to bring the Minister down for the week-end. I raised the subject over dinner with little hope of a favourable response, but to my surprise no objections were raised. The Moscow authorities were anxious to establish some contacts with this country, particularly in cultural matters. Arrangements were quickly completed between the Foreign Office and the Russian Embassy. Accompanied by George Harris, I set out for Moscow on January 29th. We took the precaution of hiring enormous fur coats and capes from Moss Bros., in which attire we were duly photographed saying farewell to Tallulah Bankhead at the stage-door, much to the amusement of the staff.

We reached Russia by way of Berlin and Riga. In Berlin we were shocked by the apathy of the audiences and the shabbiness of the productions. The love of music and drama of the old liberal Germany that I had known before the war was gone. Disillusionment had set in. In the Kurfürstendam district sleazy night-clubs were crowded with men dressed as women, and with women in trousers, smoking cigars and cigarettes from long holders. Such a public display of sexual inversion was then unknown in England. I had a brief talk with Reinhardt, defeated by events and contemplating flight to America, with Leopold Jessner of the State Theatre, whose fondness for acting at different levels had earned for his tiers of steps the nickname of 'jessnertreppen', and with Ernst Toller, the Communist dramatist, whose *Masse Mensch* had recently been given a private performance in London. Altogether a depressing visit; we were glad to leave.

Derutra, the Russian travel agency in London, had given us 'soft' or first-class tickets and a letter guaranteeing us places on the 'train diplomatique', which left Riga at midnight twice a week for Moscow. Arriving at Riga on the appointed day with an hour or two to spare, we looked out for the consular official who had been asked to meet us, but the station was deserted. It was ten o'clock at night and bitterly cold. However, we marched confidently into the station-master's office to secure our reserved seats, only to be told that the 'train diplomatique' had been cancelled the previous week. No 'soft' seats were available on the train that had taken its place, and, of course, the station-master refused to give us 'hard' seats when our tickets said 'soft'. After some angry exchanges over the telephone with various people at the Russian Consulate—none of them spoke intelligible English, so I carried on with a mixture of bad French and worse German, which made them very cross indeed—the station-master was persuaded to allow us to travel 'hard' on the substitute train. We were given a tiny compartment to ourselves. It had two narrow wooden benches with upright backs. George said it would be like sleeping on the larder shelf, a misleading description seeing that the restaurant car went out of action soon after we left Riga. We subsisted on ham sandwiches and frequent mugs of hot tea brought to us by a kindly conductor. The engine was incapable of more than twenty miles an hour, and stopped every hour or so to take on wood. Sometimes there were longer stops for engine repairs. Gazing at the beauty of dawn among the snow-covered pine and birch forests was a novelty that soon palled. Thereafter, George spent the time sketching vigorously—picturesque wooden villages under snow and occasional figures—while I shifted uncomfortably on my wooden bench, watching the changes of light upon an otherwise monotonous landscape. Thirty-four hours after leaving Riga we arrived in Moscow early in the morning. On the platform to receive us was Minister of Labour Schmidt and several officials. They must have known of our progress all the way, although at times we seemed to be lost in the wilderness.

The city was beautiful under snow, with a great red sun rising above the Kremlin. We were taken to the hotel reserved for visiting foreigners, where our passports and letters of introduction were taken away, presumably to see that they contained nothing subversive. In the afternoon the documents were returned by a foreign-office man who told us to present our letters of introduction in person on days to be arranged. In the evening we were escorted to the Bolshoi Theatre to see a ballet called *Semiramis*. I have no memory of the performance, only of the scarlet and gold magnificence of the huge auditorium, to which a black-coated trade delegation, some thirty or more, sitting trance-like on gilt chairs in the imperial box, added a sombre note. We returned to the hotel to find our luggage had been searched. The sense of being spied upon was exciting in a curious way.

The next morning a personable young woman from the Russian Tourist Bureau presented herself at the hotel. She was to be our guide, interpreter and friend for the period of the visit. She spoke perfect French but answered all our questions in patient, imperfect English. Our first letter of introduction was to Lunacharsky, Minister of Education, who included among his other responsibilities control of all the Moscow theatres. He was housed in a large building full of scurrying clerks and apple-cheeked peasant women carrying brooms and pails of water. Russian police dressed in the uniform of the Revolution, black blouse and top boots, and armed with revolvers, lounged in every doorway, most of them with cigarettes drooping between their lips. Lunarcharsky was a pleasant, professorial type, who talked at us for an hour and a half on the importance which the Soviets attached to the theatre, a discourse variously interrupted by telephones, clerks with documents, and frequent cups of tea from the samovar in the lobby outside, brought in by an old peasant woman in a shawl.

The Minister grouped the Moscow theatres under three heads: the revolutionary Theatre of the Left, led by Meyerhold; the less advanced Theatre of the Centre, represented by the Kamerny

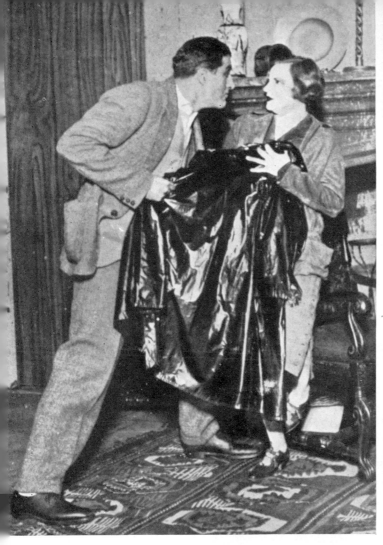

Above left Tallulah defends her honour in *Scotch Mist*

Above right *They Knew What They Wanted*. She bought it off the peg for £3.10.0!

Below Pat Hastings contemplating further *dramatis personae*

Above A royal occasion at Easton Lodge, June 1886. Among the guests:
T.R.H. the Prince and Princess of Wales and the Princess Royal, Lady
Randolph Spencer Churchill, Lord and Lady Charles Beresford, Sir
William Gordon Cumming, Baron de Rothschild

Below Our engagement party taken on the same spot. Among the guests:
Eugene and 'Booney' Goossens, Harriet Cohen, Noël Coward, Jascha
Heifetz, Charles Dillingham, Jack Pickford, Marilyn Miller

Theatre under Tairoff, and the Theatre of the Right, led by the Moscow Arts Theatre and its various offshoots. When I asked him if the Revolution had thrown up any outstanding dramatists he replied 'many'. Later we learned that the Minister recently had seven or eight plays of his own running in Moscow at the same time, which had moved his colleagues in government to protest. . . . We left the office, carrying Lunacharsky's pass admitting us to all theatres and cinemas in the city.

I decided to make notes of all that happened to us. It was just as well I did, for there followed such a jumble of interviews, conferences, speeches and eager questioning by actors and staff assembled to greet us at each theatre that one day's impressions tended to erase those of the day before. Little remains in memory: only these few notes.

Our next introduction was to Olga Kameneva, in charge of the Office for Cultural Relations and wife of the President of the Moscow Soviet. An interesting personality, dresses in black velvet; smokes incessantly and peers at me through pebble lenses. She understands English but refuses to speak it herself. She evades my questions about Stanislavsky and the Art Theatre; instead, talks volubly about the Theatre of the Revolution (her special interest), the Red Army Theatre, the Theatre of Satire, and so on. Evidently we are to be plunged straightway into the headiest part of the theatrical ferment, the Theatre of the Left. Before we leave I am asked if I have any other introductions to Soviet leaders: I produce one to Leon Trotsky which she immediately seizes and promises to deliver. When I asked her about it later on she became evasive: he was not in Moscow, he was ill, etc. We never met him. Subsequently we heard he was already on the run from his implacable enemy, Stalin.

At Madame Kameneva's own Theatre of the Revolution a mock trial, directed for her by Meyerhold, is being presented, using the most advanced production methods; actors dispersed among the audience, mainly working class: an old woman with a basket of groceries plops down in the seat beside me; she follows the action of the play with shouts of approval or disapproval—I'm not sure which—a form of audience participation, of which the current 'nouvelle vague' would heartily approve. At the Red Army Theatre, a play about the 1905 revolution; a caricature of the late Czar is greeted with howls of derision. In the Theatre of Satire an actor impersonates Trotsky so to the life that he is greeted with loud cheers.

At Meyerhold's theatre, originally a music-hall, no curtain, no

U

draperies or scenery of any kind, stage-hands encouraged to lurk at corners of the stage to watch the show; artists, too, waiting to make their entrances. Something theatrical in this flaunting un-theatricality. We are told the actors are called every morning for a daily work-out in a nearby gymnasium. Physical fitness is certainly necessary for actors continually running up ladders and leaping from rostrum to stage in the effort to add dimension to their per-formances. The play is an absurd melodrama called *The Cry of China*; propaganda against the gunboat diplomacy of Britain. At the back of the stage is a vast girder mast, and what purports to be the quarter-deck of the British gunboat, *Cockchafer*. At certain moments this contrivance is made to advance and to swing the muzzles of two large guns over the audience with menacing effect. In front of the gun-boat is a tank of real water, and nearest the audience, platforms and steps for the incidents on shore. The British captain strides about his quarter-deck smoking an enormous briar pipe. When an Ameri-can guest leaves the ship he has a dispute with a Chinese boatman, falls into the water and is drowned. The captain demands two Chin-ese lives in place of his guest. He attends the public execution with a squad of marines to see justice done, still smoking his pipe.

Meyerhold received us at his theatre the next morning, seated at the head of a long table surrounded by members of his company, and representatives from every department of the organisation, including wardrobe and box-office staff. All rose and bowed stiffly as we entered; it was very impressive. Then he began a formal address of welcome. I realised with a shock that I had prepared nothing in reply. This grey-haired professorial man of about fifty had a fanatical eye and an eager, impulsive way of expounding his theories. The conference lasted an hour and more. We left wondering whether Meyerhold's dogmas would take him farther than his political bosses might welcome. And this is what happened.

Next, to the Theatre of the Centre, in particular Tairoff's Kamerny Theatre, to see Oscar Wilde's *Salome*, and Eugene O'Neill's *The Hairy Ape*, realism and expressionism successfully combined. At another theatre in the group, name illegible in my notebook, a comedy illustrating the backwardness of the peasantry; it is given before an audience of Red Army officers. The impromptu entertain-ment with refreshments back-stage, planned for us after the per-formance, was cancelled after much embarrassed whispering among the actors; they felt they might be accused of wasting public funds.

The Jewish Kamerny Theatre also belonged to the Centre group:

Jewish plays, making fun at their religious legends and idiosyncrasies. Granovsky, a brilliant producer, helped by Mark Chagall, Rabinovitch and others. Unfortunately, he is away ill, but we are given wonderful action photographs of the company.*

At last to the Theatre of the Right, mainly the Moscow Art Theatre and its studio. First, to the Art Theatre itself: *The Storm* by Ostrovsky. I am given the seat of honour in the stalls; it has *Constantin Stanislavsky* engraved on a brass plate on the back. I feel very proud. Then, on successive nights, *Tsar Fyodor* and *The Blue Bird*, amazingly good technically, considering the production is eighteen years old. (The Russian theatre does not alter its productions, and the names of the original producers remain on the programmes even though they are no longer alive.) Greatest treat of all, we see the original production of *The Cherry Orchard* with Mme Knipper (Chekhov's widow), Moskvin, Katchalov, Dubenin and the rest.

In the first flush of the revolution the authorities sent a commissar to take general charge of the Art Theatre and to censor the choice of plays. Courageously, the distinguished artists who had led the company to international renown rebelled. Stanislavsky took to his bed, but leading players, led by Mme Knipper, put on their coats and caps and went to Lunarcharsky to tell him they preferred imprisonment to interference with their freedom as artists. They were left alone after that—more or less.

To the Second Art Theatre to see Chekhov's nephew playing Hamlet and Malvolio, the latter's final discomfiture replaced by a scene of reconciliation with the Countess and much kissing of hands, while Toby Belch and Andrew Aguecheek are hauled off to prison. Asked how this could be, Anton Chekhov replied warily that it is not in accord with Communist ideas to permit the Countess's steward to be defeated by a pair of unworthy knights!

The Theatre of Vachtangoff, named after Stanislavsky's most brilliant pupil, was originally a mansion of forty rooms, occupied by three aristocrats and forty servants, so the actors tell us. It was bought by the maestro and converted into the First Studio of the Art Theatre. An enchanting place, nobly-proportioned rooms used as studios, foyers and work-rooms. See a performance of *Princess*

* Granowsky wrote me some months later (November 13th) asking what chance of success his theatre would have if it paid a short visit to England. I replied on January 10th on my return from America, but I was not sufficiently encouraging either to him or to Mme Kamenseva who had a similar project in mind for the Second Art Theatre.

Turandot, played as a charade by ladies and gentlemen of a house party in evening dress with music played on combs. Great fun, but not much revolution about it.

.   .   .   .   .

Notes become confused as time grows short, and more and more engagements are thrust upon us: visits to museums and art galleries fill brief gaps in our schedule. The Bakhrunin Theatre Museum: the finest in Europe. A unique collection, ranging from models of early religious theatres to the designs of the first Italian artists imported for the Imperial Ballet, from the actual costumes of the earliest serf actors to the complete wardrobe in the reconstructed dressing-room of Vera Komisarjevska, greatest Russian actress, who died of plague in Tashkent while still a young woman: original manuscripts of Tolstoy, Turgenev, Dostoievsky, and Pushkin. Wonderful treasures! the lifework of one man now living in a portion of his former mansion, state custodian of his own treasures.

Time only for one art collection, housed in Morosov's former palace: priceless French impressionists crowding the walls and stacked in corners three and four deep.

'Where have all these come from?' I gasp in astonishment. 'They have been collected from various palaces and houses in Moscow,' our young lady replies tactfully.

'Oh, I see. Pinched,' I mutter thoughtlessly.

She looks round frightened, poor girl. George pokes me in the ribs:

'Be careful, or you'll get yourself arrested.'

.   .   .   .   .

What else is there ere I close my notebook? Few impressions of the social scene outside our circle of professional interest: just glimpses here and there of shabby people shuffling by in the snow or waiting outside Lenin's tomb; a gang of ragged urchins, crawling out of a giant sewer—are they male or female?—and being chased across Bolshoi Square by a burly Cossack policeman. They look like animals as they run screaming away. The deathly silence in the deserted streets at night. The constant grumbling of my companion about our monotonous diet. I explain that our hosts are doing their best, but ham omelettes, caviare, vodka and tea for nearly three weeks on end was an unexpected revolutionary diet.

Our last Saturday afternoon—we leave tonight for Warsaw—

Stanislavsky has invited us to see the work of his Opera Studio. A performance of Act I of *The Czar's Bride* is staged for our especial benefit by students from the Conservatoire. They act and sing their rôles simply and truthfully in the tradition of the Arts Theatre. . . . Stanislavsky autographed a copy of the English edition of *My Life in Art* which I brought out from England, inscribing it to me and to the St. Martin's Theatre Company.

Most of what we saw and heard has little relevance today, although the attempts of Meyerhold and others to bring audiences and players into communion has a certain parallel with what is now going on in the English-speaking theatre.

We left a city where everybody seemed to be talking incessantly. smoking incessantly, drinking incessantly (tea mostly; samovars bubbling in every government hallway), convinced that beneath all the exuberance lay the seeds of future artistic growth. Strange that such an outburst of vitality should have failed to inspire any drama of international consequence. Perhaps Anarchy is better for artistic expression than Conformity!

Seventeen
Early Coward

I

Three essentials to my survival as an independent manager were plays, money with which to produce them, and a theatre to put them in. All three fell into my lap like plums shaken from a tree. First the plays: my work with Noël in America had been so successful that without much question we drifted into an association that led to my producing most of his early work. Next, the money: George Ansley's modest venturing with Sidney Howard's play had been successful; at least, he had got his money back. This must have whetted his appetite, for after prolonged negotiation he and his brother formed a City syndicate to finance my productions, beginning with *Easy Virtue*. Ansley insisted, and I agreed, that I should find part of the finance myself. He thought it would restrain my tendency to extravagance, and I thought it was the only way in which I could retain the final say in artistic matters. Ansley was extremely businesslike, which was reasonable enough, but his training both in the courts and in the City did not help him to understand the unconventional ways in which agreement was reached between manager and manager, and sometimes between manager and actor. (I write of the time before the days of the ubiquitous agent.) Many business procedures that theatre people took for granted, and still do, appeared slipshod and almost incomprehensible to Ansley. For example, he could not understand that, although contracts might specify the precise date on which a new production should open, there were often postponements of one or two days because plays were not quite ready. In such cases forfeits were sometimes claimed to meet the theatre's standing charges. This Ansley regarded as most unbusinesslike. Every experienced manager knows it is less expensive in the long run to postpone a play than to open with it ill-prepared. I had to agree to each theatre contract being countersigned by him on behalf of the syndicate. Surveillance went too far when he wanted to substitute Elissa Landi for Joyce Carey in *Easy Virtue*. A tart reply to my cable to Noël on Capri put an end to that. The syndicate worked well for a number of years and I am glad to think that the final balance-sheet came out on the right side, in spite of one or two nasty turns of fortune.

Miss Violet Melnotte, proprietress of the Duke of York's Theatre, got wind of the break-up of ReandeaN and approached me with a suggestion that I should make her theatre my 'home' in future. Like so many manager's plans when first mooted, her offer was wide and generous. It is only when contracts are drawn and the day-to-day commerce of the theatre begins that difficulties arise. Miss Melnotte was a retired Edwardian actress; with hair dressed *à la* Pompadour and a formidable manner, she guarded jealously the property left her by her husband for the benefit of her only son. Wary at first of the large promises she made I agreed in the end to produce three plays at the theatre on sharing terms. When news of the success of *Easy Virtue* in America reached her ears, she accepted it as the first production under this arrangement. . . . And so the last of my three essentials, namely a theatre, had plopped firmly into place.

While I was busy with my plans Noël, back from his American success, went off to various countries of the Mediterranean, returning in time to be present at the provincial opening of *Easy Virtue*, which took place at the Opera House, Manchester, on May 31st, four days after Jane Cowl and the returning British players arrived from New York—a considerable logistic feat, come to think of it.

It was sixteen years since I had last been in Manchester as a member of Miss Horniman's Company. In that time several of the principal theatres had disappeared, the Theatre Royal and the Gaiety among them; even Flanagan's Queen's Theatre in another part of the city had gone, replaced in the same area by an over-large opera house. I was shocked that the seed sown by Miss Horniman during those strenuous years at the beginning of the century should have borne no fruit at all. At a mass meeting of all Manchester's amateur groups which I was invited to address I was openly critical. A unanimous resolution was passed, pledging support for the establishment of a civic theatre. I was secretly gratified when the *Manchester Guardian* devoted its first editorial the next morning to support of my remarks, but the evening papers indignantly denied my criticisms, claiming 'all's well'.

Before we opened *Easy Virtue* there was quite a fraças about the title. The theatre management wanted us to alter it because they thought the Manchester Watch Committee might object to *Easy Virtue*. (At a small cinema almost next door to our theatre a film was being advertised called *Flames of Passion*.) Noël suggested we should present the play without a title, which we did, although it was already advertised to open in London as *Easy Virtue*. This was a shrewd suggestion because it aroused gossip and brought us publicity.

Jane Cowl was reputed to be the daughter of a stage-door-keeper. Whether or no that was true makes no matter. Her star quality seemed to twinkle more brightly away from her natural habitat, which was theatrical Broadway. In other terms, to watch her perform in company with our young English players was like observing some exotic flower, say the amaryllis, rearing its lovely head above an English meadow of buttercups and daisies. Her whole attitude to life was theatrical in the extreme. Never for one moment did she allow herself to relax from being on show. Everything must be done, every situation tackled according to the expected behaviour of a great star. She possessed a full-toned well-modulated voice which spoke from the mind rather than the heart; dark, lustrous eyes and a beautiful figure. Her gestures seemed to possess a certain over-drive that gave exceptional emphasis and yet avoided extravagance. Only her hands may have betrayed her plebeian origin, for these she kept permanently encased in black gloves—at least I never saw her otherwise. During the reception after the first night in London the stage became strewn with flowers; they were for Jane Cowl rather than for Noël's play. She had reminded playgoers of the great days of the Edwardian theatre. She was ably backed up by splendid performances from Marda Vanne and Mabel Terry-Lewis. James Raglan played the part that had been taken in America by Robert Harris, and there were good performances from other British players, including Adrianne Allen and Joyce Carey, but first and last it was Jane's night.

The derivation of the play was as obvious in London as it had been in New York, and commented upon no less humorously, the *Daily Mail* crisply remarking that Noël had 'put Paula Tanqueray into a short skirt and a shingle'. The box-office success which the newspapers prophesied was fully achieved. Jane's outburst at the end of Act 2 became the talk of fashionable London. Society turned out in force, led by the Duke and Duchess of York. Before the days of Royal Film Premières American actresses had few opportunities of meeting the King and Queen. Jane was overwhelmed with excitement when she received an invitation to the Royal Garden Party. She prepared to make a great effect with her presentation bow. When the moment came she was disappointed not to be immediately recognised and was about to announce herself, but unfortunately the Queen had already passed. Later, one of the ladies-in-waiting told Her Majesty that Jane was a well-known American actress. To make amends, the Queen postponed her journey to Sandringham the following day and went to see Jane's performance, taking King George, loudly complaining, with her. Thus did Jane achieve the summit of her social ambition.

.   .   .   .   .

On Friday, October 1st, Jane left the cast, sailing back to America the following morning, ostensibly to fulfil a New York engagement but actually because it was her policy never to outstay her welcome anywhere. In this she showed a complete disregard for the interests of the play and the company. Grizelda Hervey, who had been painstakingly understudying her throughout the run with little hope of appearance, went on for the last performance too late to achieve more than a satisfactory report from the stage manager.

2

Over at the St. Martin's it looked as though Sidney Howard's play was going to end its run at the height of the summer season, before August, in fact. This was a serious embarrassment for Alec who was planning a production of *Berkeley Square*, adapted from a Henry James's story by John Balderston and J. C. Squire. It was likely to prove expensive, so Alec had no wish to present it during August. Instead, I agreed to produce the second of the three Coward plays I had earmarked for Miss Melnotte's contract at the St. Martin's.

The Queen was in the Parlour, Coward's first excursion into the world of romantic fiction, took him to Ruritania, there to nod a greeting to Anthony Hope and to help himself to some of that author's plot while he wasn't looking! The play—a tale of undiluted love, Noël's expression, not mine—had all the ingredients of popular romance, with Noël's wit and taut emotional writing to aerate the dish. . . . In Paris a royal personage from the kingdom of Krayia is about to forsake all and marry her handsome lover, when lo! enter an emissary from that far country—a full general, no less—to summon her to resume her public responsibilities and ascend the vacant throne. Shall love or duty prevail? She returns. A prince from a neighbouring country offers to share her royal burden, not at the call of love but of duty. Very Teutonic that! In the last act he stands by her side at the palace windows to calm a dissatisfied and rebellious populace while her despairing lover shoots himself in her bedroom off-stage. (An incident reminiscent of one of Gertie Millar's lovers who shot himself in her dressing-room at the Gaiety Theatre during the run of *Our Miss Gibbs*.)

The play was given various titles to begin with, none of which Noël really liked. Finally, he asked me for my suggestions, and I proposed *Bitter Sweet*. But in the end he decided upon *The Queen was in the Parlour*, and *Bitter Sweet* became the title of his first big musical success. Our play was superbly acted by the strongest cast that I had yet assembled, either for Coward or any other dramatist. It included Madge Titheradge in the leading part of Nadja, supported by Francis Lister as Sabien, the lover, and Herbert Marshall as the prince. C. M. Hallard, a popular West End actor ever since his handsome juvenile days, 'queened' it admirably as General Krish, all charm and insincerity, the perfect drawing-room general. Lady Tree played a garrulous Grand Duchess, startling us all daily at rehearsal with incisive comment—she needed no direction from me. Ada King captured much of the critical attention and all of the fun by her performance as a prim English secretary who takes a night off to visit a smart café in the Principality. I found great satisfaction in working with Madge Titheradge, a superb actress, who threw herself enthusiastically into the work of preparation. We found ourselves in accord at all points.

Noël was anxious that Gladys Calthrop should design the production, but as she had not yet acquired sufficient expertise in technical matters, George Harris offered to place his wide knowledge of such things at her disposal. The result was outstanding, and set Gladys Calthrop well on the road to her subsequent achievements.

On the opening night the critics gathered in the bar after the first act to discuss what they would do to Noël for his obvious plagiarism of Anthony Hope. But I find nothing reprehensible in it. All artists borrow from each other and inevitably. Neither Shakespeare nor anyone else is exempt from this charge. What does it matter if the subject of a play be as old as the hills, provided its treatment be new? In Noël's case the charge of plagiarism is easily dismissed by his modern point of view and his wit. In this instance, before the critics had time to sharpen their pencils, Noël forestalled them by making one of the characters in the next act refer to General Krish as a first cousin of Colonel Sapt: After all Noël had precedent as when Oliver Goldsmith compares a situation in *She Stoops to Conquer* with one in Farquhar's *The Beaux' Stratagem*.

The overnight success of the play was confirmed by the morning notices. Those who had been chiding Noël for writing unpleasant plays now turned to deep discussion of his new rôle as a romantic. Even *The Times* approved his abandonment of what it called the customary cocktail society. St. John Ervine in the *Observer* remarked that 'The Queen was not in the Parlour. She was in the soup and very nearly in the brothel.' Surely a most unmannerly comment? Desmond MacCarthy, most considerable dramatic critic of his day, wrote two columns of careful criticism in *The New Statesman* a week or so after the play had been produced, in which he drew attention to Noël's fine rhythm of emotion, concluding with the remark: 'There is an artist in him.' This must have pleased Noël mightily.

When *Easy Virtue* closed at the Duke of York's *The Queen* was transferred there on the following Monday, despite squeals of disappointment from the box-office manager at the St. Martin's at the loss of good business. But it played to even bigger figures in its new home until the November fogs took their revenge of Miss Melnotte for her meanness. Her theatre had no central heating, and was notorious for its draughts. In the last act Madge Titheradge, always delicate, had to stand for some ten minutes beside the tall palace windows, which were unglazed. Gusts of icy, fog-laden wind, blowing in from the stage-door, gave the unfortunate Madge laryngitis and later bronchitis. I was in America by this time but I received bi-weekly reports from Clift, whom I had appointed to represent me. At his suggestion the windows were glazed with talc to restrain the draughts. This was an improvement but it came too late. Madge was off for two weeks, which, surprisingly, made no difference to the business at first—in fact, it went up!—but later, when news of her absence got abroad, support began to dwindle. On the night she returned business fell still further, which suggests a weakness in the theatre's publicity department. The play finally closed just before Christmas after giving every sign of prolonged popularity.

3

More than twelve months were to elapse before I produced any more Coward plays in London. In the interval several events took place that were of importance in my life and career. First of all there was the production of *The Constant Nymph*, the dramatisation of the Margaret Kennedy novel which I made in collaboration with the author. This took place at the New Theatre in September, less than a month after the first night of *The Queen was in the Parlour*. I shall write about this in the next chapter. Then in the following March I took offices at No. 5, John Street, Adelphi, next door to those once occupied by Gordon Craig. Thus the end of my partnership with Alec Rea became public knowledge.

Then in April, Somerset Maugham asked me to direct his latest comedy, *The Constant Wife*, in which Ethel Barrymore was already appearing with immense success in New York. The play had been acquired by Horace Watson for the Haymarket Theatre, with Fay Compton and Leon Quartermaine in mind for the leading parts. I was not consulted in this casting and accepted it at its face value because of their long record of success together. But quite early in rehearsals I discovered they were not well suited to their parts, either of them. Maugham's cynical comedy called for the lightest of treatment. Fay's comedy style was too arch and Leo was too pedantic. Thus began a series of misjudgments that, taken altogether, were to prove disastrous. The rest of the cast were quietly competent, but not outstanding, save in one instance. Heather Thatcher, the musical comedy actress, previously associated with Leslie Henson and George Grossmith, made an unexpected hit in her first straight comedy part, using her monocle and her Winter Garden technique with great effect.

The play could not be given at the Haymarket because of the persistent success of another production. So Watson took the Strand Theatre for it. This was an unfortunate choice because the Strand is a difficult theatre for all but the broadest effects. The tally of misjudgments was mounting. Next, an extraordinary managerial blunder ruined the performance on the first night. In those days rope barriers cordoned off the stalls from the pit, now called pit-stalls as befitting the improved status of the occupants. These barriers were advanced or put back according to the demand for seats in the stalls. For a 'new Somerset Maugham' the advance booking was so heavy that the box-office was told to book the front of the customary pit-stalls as stalls. Unfortunately, parallel instructions to move back the rope barriers were forgotten. Consequently, when ticket-holders for the additional row of stalls arrived they found their places already taken by people who had been waiting in the pit queue since 8 a.m. The 'pitites' refused to budge and violent arguments ensued. Horace Watson had to go on the stage and appeal to the usurpers to give up their places to those waiting with reserved tickets in their hands. Maugham and his wife sat in a stage-box, dismayed, while the argument was going on. It was twenty minutes before adjustments were made and the audience finally settled in their places. The effect on the actors can well be imagined. Already suffering from the usual first-night nerves they were put completely out of countenance by the fraças. The performance became slow and uncertain, and lacked the bright finish that Maugham's comedies demand.

The nerves of the audience, already frayed by the row before the play began, were further exacerbated by the restless gallery. Open disturbance broke out when Fay Compton stepped forward at curtain fall to make the usual speech of thanks. She mistook a shout of 'Shut up' from the gallery as intended for her. So she turned to the uneasy rows of stalls and pointedly thanked the 'civil members' of the audience. At once loud booing broke out in the gallery; usual epilogue to a disastrous evening in the theatre.

When the notices appeared it was obvious that the mood of the play had been misinterpreted, although the suggestion of Restoration comedy in the play's title should have been a pointer to the author's intention. Critics demanded querulously: What do these modern writers know about marriage? The evening papers were more concerned with the row in the pit although that, too, had a touch of Restoration behaviour about it. St. John Ervine in the *Observer* did point out that neither the play nor the players had been given a fair chance. He suggested the critics should be invited to see the play again in two weeks' time. But Horace Watson preferred to pocket his pride and lose the cash. When I saw a revival of the play at the Arts Theatre after the last war and watched the crowded audience manifestly enjoying themselves I could not help reflecting how all concerned had contributed by a series of misjudgments to the ultimate débâcle.

4

When *The Queen was in the Parlour* ended its run Madge went away to recover from the effects of her prolonged stance before those draughty palace windows. She and I had worked in such close accord that we were anxious to continue the association, but the play Noël intended for her was not yet begun, so it behoved me to find one in the meantime. I did not want her to pass out of our orbit, even temporarily. The play chosen was *The Happy Husband*, a light comedy by Harrison Owen, an Australian journalist working in London. It was produced at the Criterion Theatre on June 15th, 1927, having been previously tried out in the country. In the cast with Madge were Mabel Sealby, second girl at Daly's Theatre during the great epoch of George Edwardes' musical comedies, and recently married to my friend and assistant, Roger Ould; Lawrence Grossmith, younger brother of George and a much better actor, although not so reliable; A. E. Matthews, whose charm and persistent juvenility in *The Silver Box* I had so envied. He had created the part of Jack Barthwick when he was approaching forty!

Such a cast would probably have carried this light comedy to success in any event, but what gave it outstanding attraction was the appearance of Charles Laughton in the part of a middle-aged American. Laughton was twenty-five at the time and he had made little impression on the West End stage since leaving R.A.D.A. where he had won the Bancroft Gold Medal the year before. In an interview before the opening night, indulging in prophecy for the first and only time in my life, I said that Laughton 'would astonish everyone. . . .'

The praise he received for his performance was certainly not due to his simulated American accent, but rather to instantaneous recognition that a character actor of the very first rank had emerged. Such recognition in depth, so to speak, remains unique in recent annals of the stage. When he was asked about his accent Laughton replied with admirable truth: 'I have never been in America and have only

met one real American in my life.' It was a triumph of tact when
one of the few Americans in the audience on the first night declared
afterwards, 'We sure speak the same as you Britishers.' Laughton's
sensational success brought crowds to the box-office almost immediately.

In addition to the success of the production at the Criterion
Theatre, for which the papers gave me exceptional but unmerited
praise, the play made a wide appeal to continental audiences. By
the time it reached its fiftieth performance we were able to announce
that this light comedy would shortly be running in six countries at
once, including the United States, where Gilbert Miller was to
do it in conjunction with myself; in Berlin under Max Reinhardt;
in Paris by the Edward Stirling English Players, and in Australia
by J. C. Williamson. Thus, a play intended as a stop-gap both
fulfilled its purpose and brought useful grist to my mill.

5

The Criterion Theatre was still playing to capacity when Noël
brought me his next two plays, as promised: *Home Chat*, intended
for Madge Titheradge, and *Sirocco*, an earlier play now considerably
revised, for which he was anxious I should engage Ivor Novello.
But first of all *Home Chat*: this was a light comedy, written in Noël's
brightest manner, but decidedly thin, which was not surprising
seeing that he announced that he had written it in a week—an
injudicious form of publicity. The extraordinary thing about this
play is that whereas I remember well all that went on in connection
with the production of his other plays I can recall little about this
one. Only a few irrelevant details, such as that the pit and gallery
queues began to form outside the theatre at eight o'clock in the
morning. It is a mistake to regard such a degree of advance interest
as an augury of future success. Word-of-mouth disapproval can
cause the longest queue to melt away overnight.

Home Chat was cast as usual up to the hilt. Besides Madge, the
cast included George Relph, whom I welcomed with special warmth,
remembering our struggling days with the raggledy-taggledy
Maclaren Company on tour; Marda Vanne, Helen Spencer and George
Curzon, all representing the younger generation, while Henrietta
Watson, Nina Boucicault, a veteran actress of great charm, who

alas! forgot her words on the first night, represented an earlier period.

Much of the ill-natured criticism that Noël suffered at this time was brought on by his youthful display of indifference to public opinion. Apart from his statement that he had written the play in one week only, his sang-froid on the opening night was mistaken for conceit and alerted the galleryites for counter-tactics. He sat in a stage-box in full view of the audience, reading telegrams handed to him by a deferential secretary: 'Coo! 'E don't even open 'em 'isself,' remarked someone best described in Dickensian style as Fat Lady to her neighbour in the gallery.

At the end the curtain descended to a storm of booing. I was not present because, following information from my staff, I had taken cowardly refuge in the Ivy Restaurant. Noël on the other hand faced the booers with adroit courage. When Fat Lady, voicing the feeling of the meeting, shouted: 'We expected better,' he replied: 'So did I!' However, he did have the grace to pay his tribute to the actors, especially Madge. His first nights were already attracting fashionable audiences, with the foyers awash with famous names; this kept the gossip columnists busy. After *Home Chat* smart society made up for its disappointment by trooping off to a riotous supper party at Mrs. Syrie Maugham's house in Chelsea, where Margot Asquith (Lady Oxford) arrived late wearing a period costume of the eighties, complete with bustle, to dance period waltzes into the small hours with Mr. 'Frankie' Leverson.

Even in their hostility the critics were not unanimous in the items they picked out for condemnation. For instance, St. John Ervine said the beginning was execrable and the end exquisite, whereas *Truth* with rival candour declared the opening to be 'as brilliant as anything he has ever done'. Perhaps the *Daily Mail* summed up the general tenor of critical remark in a sentence: 'The acting was of the best, the play was Noël Coward at his worst.'

.   .   .   .   .

Madge Titheradge was an actress, first, last and all the time; an impulsive warm-hearted creature, so highly charged with emotion that she had been known to faint from excess of it, even at rehearsal. All actresses gifted with the power to express great passion seem to be short of stature. Rachel and Albanesi are two instances that come to mind. Madge was no exception, making up for her lack of height with a husky full-toned voice inherited from her father,

Discussing *Easy Virtue*
with Jane Cowl and
Noël Coward, a press
release

The Queen was in the Parlour. A royal tea-party, but the Prince prefers
brandy and soda (C. M. Hallard, Madge Titheradge, Lady Tree, Herbert
Marshall)

The Constant Nymph. The Sanger sisters: Edna Best, Helen Spencer,
Elissa Landi
New Theatre, September, 1926

George Titheradge, an Australian leading man whose voice had such power that Madge once told me he was able when in full song to set the glass lustres along the front of a dress circle a-tinkle. She was singularly free from jealousy or sense of rivalry with others, and often in later years made suggestions of more suitable stars than herself for the plays I had under consideration. Her second marriage, quite late in life, to an over-sentimental American, who proclaimed the happiness she had brought him upon every occasion, suitable or unsuitable, brought peace to her also. When last I went to see her at her home in the country, she was virtually bed-ridden, a martyr to arthritis, but still as gay and interested in my concerns as ever.

6

Sirocco was produced at Daly's Theatre on November 24th, just one month after the production of *Home Chat* at the Duke of York's, and more than thirty years since a 'straight' play had last been seen there. (That was when Augustin Daly, the American manager who gave the theatre its name, presented Ada Rehan in Shakespeare.) The events on the first night of *Sirocco* were so startling that for many years thereafter the name became a synonym in theatrical circles for disaster; one actor to another: 'How was it last night, Bill?' 'Sirocco, old boy.'

Contrary to what might be supposed, it was not a bad play, better written than *Home Chat*, which perhaps is not saying a great deal. True, Noël had written it in America some years earlier, before *The Vortex* in fact. Consequently, its sentiments were immature, but he had recently spent some time carefully revising it. It was not one of those plays expressing a new outlook upon society which always arouse strong public reactions, yea or nay. We must look elsewhere for the reason why the disturbance on the first night possessed such an emotional quality.

Although my memory of the actual performance is thin—I snatched only hasty, nervous glances at the stage from the back of the dress circle at the beginning of the performance—my recollections of all that preceded it and of the aftermath are all too clear. Noël's success both as actor and dramatist had been so swift that it had attracted the attention of the news gatherers as inevitably as bees seek the honey. Ever since *The Vortex* his jaunty interviews,

x

in which wit, courage and impertinent remarks about the established order were skilfully mingled, had caught the eye of the public. They were something quite different from the usual prosaic theatre reportage, but the captions to some of the early press photos, showing him in a silk dressing-gown embroidered with Chinese dragons, sitting up in bed dictating correspondence were injudicious to say the least, causing vague feelings that this young man was winning success too easily and too fast.

As to the performance itself: the leading parts were played by Ivor Novello and Frances Doble. Both possessed great physical beauty—yes, beauty is the correct attribute for both players—but neither had sufficient acting experience to sustain the play's climax which, as in nearly all Noël's early plays, came at the end of the second act. Ivor was known at that time principally as a gifted composer of popular melodies, beginning with the famous wartime song, 'Keep the Home Fires Burning', but the public had refused so far to take him seriously as an actor, although he had achieved some success in silent films, with a profile to rival Rudolph Valentino. When, in deference to Noël's pleading, I cast him for the leading part, I was conceited enough to imagine I would be able to teach him enough technique to sustain the difficult love scenes, leaving the rest of the part to his natural charm and grace of manner. Even at the zenith of his career, when everything he touched brought him reward, Ivor remained an exhibitionist on the stage. I did not allow for the resentment that gallery first-nighters always display whenever they feel they are being imposed upon. In some subtle way those ardent people feel that the accolade of popularity is theirs alone to bestow.

The audience was restive before the play began. Noël sat in a stage-box with his mother and Gladys Calthrop, opening telegrams as usual, while posses of his and Ivor's friends, come to give the play a joyous send-off, invaded the stalls twittering like sparrows, and disturbing the sedate stall-holders. The gallery sat impatient for the fun to begin. Soon currents of feeling began to flow between the different groups in the stalls and the unusually lively gallery. Before I left the theatre to begin my customary vigil in a nearby restaurant it was already clear that we were in for a stormy evening.

There was an Italian fiesta in the second act, ending with a passionate love scene between Ivor and Frances Doble. Noël greatly praised my production of it although afterwards he claimed that I polished it too much—the director's usual search for effectiveness. When one has exceptional trouble in bringing a dramatist's work to life it is either because there is something wrong with the writing or because of fundamental weakness in the playing, as in this case. On the first night when Ivor began the difficult climax of the scene, the audience rejected it totally. At every kiss the gallery made sucking noises, while the stalls wished themselves anywhere but at Daly's Theatre. Finally, when in the extremity of passion Ivor and Frances rolled on the floor together the gallery broke into little gusts of laughter—a situation sufficient to unnerve the most experienced players.

Following my usual custom I returned to the theatre via the stage-door towards the end of the last act. As I stood in the wings on one side of the stage I saw Noël standing in the prompt corner opposite, waiting, I presumed, for the customary reception. (In fact, he had come through the pass-door to persuade the stage manager *not* to raise the curtain!) Had I been beside Noël much of what followed might have been avoided. Mistaking the dull roar I heard for applause and cries of 'Author' I waved to the stage manager to raise the curtain and for Noël to take his call. But the more I waved to him to go on, the more violently he shook his head. I could, of course, hear nothing above the din. Finally, and for quite a different reason from what I supposed, Noël went on to face the music. He was greeted with boos and cat-calls which came from all parts of the house. He led Ivor forward, thinking his popularity with the gallery would quieten things down, but Ivor could not make himself heard. Then Frances Doble was led forward. There was a momentary hush while people stared incredulously. Surely this beautiful creature wasn't going to make matters worse with a speech? With a beaming smile she clasped her hands in ecstasy and cried out: 'Ladies and gentlemen, this is the happiest night of my life!' This was received with shrieks of incredulous laughter, at which I lost my head completely and went on to the stage in a fury. There was a momentary silence as people waited to hear what I had to say. I began: 'Ladies and gentlemen, if there *are* any gentlemen in the house . . . ?' And then the kettle boiled over!

The next morning and for days afterwards sensation became a word o'erworn in relation to this affair. Reporting a state of near-riot in a West End theatre left little space for constructive criticism. Most of the papers betrayed a certain amount of spiteful glee at the downfall of this over-confident young man. One would-be Daniel announced that *Sirocco* marked the end of the Coward boom, and

Herbert Farjeon reported somewhat extravagantly that Noël's dramatic sermon on passion had been greeted by an excited and divided audience with a demonstration without parallel in a West End theatre. Somerset Maugham, on the other hand, who had once described Noël as the great English playwright of tomorrow, said he saw no reason to change his opinion. Perhaps he realised better than Farjeon that the outcry was no more than a challenge to a young writer of courage and wit. Turning the pages of my books of press-cuttings the other day, I came across at least one voice of generous defence, written for *Lloyd's Weekly News* by the young Percy Cudlipp, still with his way to make in Fleet Street, castigating the 'nobodies' for their envy and spite on 'that dreadful night'.

Sirocco ended my association with Noël as dramatist. I am sorry that it closed upon such a sour note so far as the public was concerned. All four plays fall within a category that might be described, after the fashion of an art catalogue, as 'Early Coward'. Many critics failed to realise that the borrowed plots were but exercises in the development of a striking new talent. Noël was in fact giving what used to be called drawing-room comedy a much needed face-lift. The reputation for writing unpleasant plays which he acquired in the process was ridiculous. Although he has always been sharp-eyed for the social scene, his plays are never salacious, and their wit is undeniable.

I look back upon those two or three years spent in close association with Noël Coward as among the most fruitful in the early years of my career, not because he knew more about the 'arts and crafts' of the stage than I did—a good deal less in fact—but because of his sense of dedication, a sentiment we so strongly shared that each fed upon the other. At rehearsals he would nudge me in excited approval whenever I suggested stage 'business' that he liked. This was tremendously encouraging. Nothing is more disturbing than to feel cold draughts of disapproval blowing down one's neck from an author seated at the prompt table. His attitude of defiance towards adverse publicity could only be sustained from the basis of complete self-confidence. His ability to make swift decisions, not always the right ones, this, too, was infectious. I don't know whether he thinks he gained anything from our experiences; I know I did. I was sad that the sufficiency of his genius took away the need of my help so soon, depriving me of the opportunity of sharing in his later triumphs.

Eighteen
'The Constant Nymph'

I

Whenever I have come face to face with good fortune I seem always to have accepted it with reluctance, as though a 'polter' were there to deny the intuitions within me. I recall the doubts and hesitations that shook me before I went up to join Miss Darragh in Liverpool. Similar hesitancy was to lose me a considerable fortune later on. In the present case the suggestion that I should dramatise Margaret Kennedy's best-selling novel came from Curtis Brown, just then building up the fortunes of his literary agency. Many up-and-coming playwrights, attracted by his energy and sympathetic personality, were entrusting their work to him. This inevitably brought C.B. into contact with ReandeaN, the management he thought most likely to respond to new impulses. It was through him that we obtained the early plays of Clemence Dane, John Galsworthy, John Hastings Turner and others.

At regular intervals C.B. would invite me to lunch at the Devonshire Club in St. James's Street, and always when he had a play he wanted to sell me. He would arrive, usually ten minutes late, puffing and blowing as he leapt out of his taxi full of plans and ideas. I remember a particular occasion when he was elated because he had just settled the publication of Lloyd George's war memoirs. Gulping a glass of sherry, he proceeded through a hurried and indifferent lunch to survey the field of future possibilities: each of us was possessed of different but related daemons of work.

At another lunch C.B. said quite casually: 'I want you to read one of my new novels, *The Constant Nymph*. It's by a woman.'

'I haven't time to read novels,' I replied grumpily.

'Well, you must read this one. It's a great success. I think you ought to dramatise it.'

I promised to read the book and then forgot all about it. That was in the early summer of 1925. Then in September while I was in the last stage of rehearsing *The Vortex* at the Henry Miller Theatre in New York, the house manager came to tell me one morning that someone wanted to speak to me in the lobby. I always hated being interrupted at rehearsal, but in this case I hurried out, curious to know who it could be. It was Curtis Brown, still puffing and blowing, holding a copy of *The Constant Nymph* in his hand.

'Have you read this yet?'

'No,' I said.

'Well, you must, and quickly. Miss Kennedy is getting impatient.'

I said I would but there was so much going on both professionally and in my private life during that fabulous season in New York that it was quite impossible until I was once more on board ship bound for home.

Within hours of my return C.B. was on the telephone, demanding rather fiercely whether or no I had read 'his' book. Yes, but I had not yet made up my mind about dramatising it. C.B. exploded. To be truthful, I was diffident about my playwriting powers after so long an interval. Margaret Kennedy had already rejected one version, prepared by a well-known novelist, and this increased my doubts. Moreover, the novel's delicacy of feeling and modes of thought were an expression of the author's own personality; they should not be tampered with. My first meeting with Margaret Kennedy confirmed this view. She had a lucid mind, and was unlikely to accept any tampering with the inner truth of the characters and situations she had created. Success could only be achieved by collaboration, but I had not collaborated with anyone since 1912 when Barry Jackson and I wrote the children's play, *Fifinella*. That had been a success, so why not try again? When discussing a contract with C.B. I told him I wanted Margaret's touch over the whole thing, and was prepared to reduce my share of the royalties accordingly. Eventually matters were so agreed.

2

While I went off to Russia with George Harris, Nancie plunged into the fun of equipping and furnishing Easton Manor which she carried through with her usual gaiety and with the help of her mother's extravagant advice. On my return we drove down each week-end to view progress on the work of restoration, proceeding all too slowly. I remember one frosty Sunday morning in March. We sat, side by side, hand in hand, on an ancient seat at the bottom of the garden, gazing down the long red brick path at the chimney-stacks and leaded windows, no longer encumbered with ivy. A massive new oak porch had not yet acquired its front door, so we could see right through the house to the blue distance where the village of Little Easton lay enfolded in green pasture-land. The birds were in spring song, and there were daffodils in the park: a blissful contemplation of our future home.

After a brief holiday in Italy we moved into the manor in the late spring where I was soon hard at it, dramatising *The Nymph*. Margaret and I had agreed upon a simple plan of work. I was to draft the scenario and send it to her act by act, including such of the dialogue from the novel as I thought suitable for the stage (in the end we used a surprising amount) while Margaret was to sketch out the additional scenes that I thought necessary. Letters and drafts of scenes went back and forth between us at frequent intervals, although often delayed, in Margaret's case, by a serial she was completing for an American magazine, and in mine by the usual turmoil of production. There were so many characters and such a multiplicity of incident, especially in the early part of the book, that to weave all into a coherent pattern for audience under-standing was a difficult technical problem. I omitted from the scen-ario Sanger, the eminent musician, whose mixture of genius and promiscuous habit had brought 'Sanger's Circus' into existence. Apart from the insuperable difficulty of representing musical genius on the stage, the part would have been a short one because of his death early in the story, and therefore unattractive to an important actor. I believed his unseen influence could be greater than in a brief appearance. I was overjoyed when Margaret agreed. Galsworthy, an admirer of the novel, took an avuncular interest in our progress. Lunching with me one day soon after I had completed the scenario, he was quite upset when I told him that Sebastian, one of the most original characters in the novel, was also to be cut out. I wrote at once to Margaret, suggesting she reinstate the boy, if she saw fit. Instead she gave clear and concise reasons why I had been right to cut him out. (I have the letter before me now.) This was Margaret's great strength; she would not be swayed from her clearsighted view either of character or story, a quality especially valuable in maintaining the truth of her most important creation, that of the Nymph herself, into which she had projected a good deal of her own personality and childish recollection. (This integrity was important later on when we had to deal with film executives.) Encouraged by Margaret's sane and practical answers to my queries I sat down to write the first act. The old facility that I had possessed years ago of seeing characters in the mind's eye and hearing them speak came quickly back. I managed to finish the first act before Jane Cowl opened in *Easy Virtue* in London.

3

In the first flush of pride in our country home Nancie and I delighted to have our friends down for the week-end. On the Sunday following Jane's opening we invited her and her husband whom she always referred to as 'Mr. Klauber', never as 'my husband', to lunch. Klauber was an unassuming little man upon whom Jane relied to look after her travel arrangements, a most efficient courier and baggage-man. But his efficiency fell apart on this occasion. Jane rose late when she set forth in a hired car to follow the route I had written out for her. Growing impatient at the length of the journey, she stopped the car whenever she espied a nearby telephone kiosk and sent Mr. Klauber to make profuse apology and to seek reassurance: were they really on the right road? Altogether there were three such bulletins. Nancie and our week-end guests, Eugene and 'Booney' Goossens and Mabel and Roger Ould made huge fun of this royal progress, but our new cook fumed. Jane arrived finally just before three o'clock with tears of protestation in her beautiful eyes, followed by Mr. Klauber who had a non-speaking part in the scene that followed, played in warm June sunshine by Jane, swathed in black velvet with long black gloves which she kept on throughout the visit.

During the course of lunch I happened to mention that I had just finished the first act of *The Constant Nymph*. Jane at once went into ecstasies about the book, turned pleading eyes upon me and begged to hear what I had written. After an appropriate show of reluctance on my part, we all sat round the open hearth in big easy chairs while I read the act. I was quite bowled over by the reception it got.

'Oh, you must go on with it, you simply must,' declared Jane. (As if there were any doubt about that!) The others all joined in. I was especially struck with Gene's approval. His opinion I valued greatly. In the early evening we took Jane up to Easton Lodge to call upon Lady Warwick. She had expected us for tea. 'Madre' to me now, a name I never liked but upon which she insisted, watched Jane repeat her performance of woeful apology with well-concealed incredulity. After a brief stroll among the herbaceous borders Jane returned to London, well satisfied with the impression she had made.

Encouraged by the reception of my first act, and especially by Margaret's approval of what I had cut out, I found little difficulty in constructing the remaining acts. Margaret wrote unfaltering dialogue that rarely had to be reshaped for stage purposes. By early July the play was virtually finished. I wrote Tessa's death scene in lyrical mood one Sunday evening while across my yard the cracked bell of Little Easton church summoned elderly villagers to evensong. Margaret altered scarcely a word of it. The preceding scene in the artistes' room at Queen's Hall, where Lewis and Tessa decide to run away, did not come together so easily. We each wrote a version, but neither was satisfactory. Perhaps we were reluctant to see characters with whom we were living so intensely take the fateful step! In the end, I persuaded Margaret to come down with her husband (she had married David Davies the previous year) for a week-end, so that we could hammer out a solution together. They enjoyed swimming in the lake and playing tennis, and then on Saturday evening Margaret and I settled down to work while David went up to bed. We became so engrossed that we did not notice how late it was getting until suddenly the study door opened and there was David, in a long white nightshirt, glaring at us.

'Margaret,' he said testily, 'isn't it time you came to bed?'

'Don't be silly, David,' she retorted, 'we must finish this scene. Go back to bed. I'll follow you as soon as we've finished this,' and she turned abruptly to the page. David retired without another word. The sudden apparition in his nightshirt made me think of Malvolio disturbing the revellers. Margaret would have made an admirable Maria, but I was no Sir Toby.

When the play was finished I asked Eugene Goossens to compose the music for the opera charade in the first act, which culminates in a duet sung by Teresa and Lewis Dodd, for which Margaret had written the love poem: 'When thou art dead.' Gene said he would like to do it but had no time before leaving for America, where he was conductor of the Rochester Philharmonic Orchestra. I pressed him hard, so he agreed to try on board ship. He kept his word. The manuscript which I received shortly before rehearsals began was amusingly inscribed as follows:

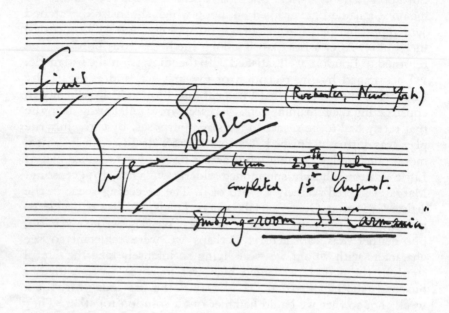

Whenever I mention the play to older playgoers they begin to hum Tessa's song which suggests that composers are not always dependent upon their surroundings for inspiration.

4

Before the play was finished I was already looking round for a suitable theatre. We should need a big one with a good stage, because with a long cast and several big scenes it would be expensive to run. The New Theatre would be ideal. This was part of the mini-empire of theatre management founded by Lady Wyndham. As Mary Moore, enchanting actress of Edwardian times, she had been the stage and business partner of the equally enchanting Charles Wyndham. Following years of success at the Criterion Theatre, they had built out of the proceeds two theatres back to back (Wyndham's and the New), where by shrewd judgment and hard bargaining they had established the fortunes both of her own and the Wyndham families. Now the old lady was in process of handing over the management to her son, Bronson Albery. I had spoken to him about the dramatisation and he had shown great interest in the idea. He asked me several times how the work was progressing. When it was finished I sent it to him. Within forty-eight hours he rang me up to say that they would be delighted to have the play at the New Theatre.

Casting was not going to be easy. There were twenty-one important parts and three smaller ones, all characters needing to be fully realised. Everything had to be done in a hurry. The play was finished early in August and by the middle of the month it was in rehearsal. The two principal parts, Tessa and Lewis Dodd, Sanger's musical protégé, had been my first consideration. Before beginning the dramatisation I had thought vaguely of Tallulah Bankhead for Tessa, but, as the work progressed, I began to doubt whether she would fit into the closely integrated ensemble that I had in mind. Anyway I could not come to terms with her. A lucky escape! Edna Best, who was touring in a comedy called *Innocent Anne* for our Dee Cee Company, was my next thought. I managed to persuade my fellow-directors, backed up by Edna's own pleading, to release her. As Tessa she was to make the outstanding success of her career.

Not quite trusting the reactions of my friends, I sought professional reassurance from Noël. I sent him a copy of the play to get his opinion. He had, of course, known of the project from the start. Within hours, or so it seemed, he rang me up in a state of considerable enthusiasm. He was so delighted with it that he volunteered to play Lewis himself.

'Will you really?' I asked. 'That would be wonderful.'

'Well, say the first four weeks, just to give it a start,' he replied.

I could scarcely believe my ears. Such a swift reaction, coming within hours of Bronnie's acceptance of the play, quite bowled me over. Noël was certain to be extremely popular at the box-office, yet his offer was something of an embarrassment because I had more than half-promised the part to John Gielgud, although I was nervous about this since at that time he lacked the experience to lead a complicated ensemble. I had to go to him and explain the circumstances and ask him to agree to understudy the part for the first four weeks and then to take it over when Noël left. He generously agreed to let me out of my moral obligation. So Noël was to be Lewis Dodd.

I did not expect to meet with similar good fortune in casting the remaining parts, yet it turned out so. Many of the disbanded ReandeaN Company were still available, including Mary Clare (a superb performance of Linda, that people chuckled over for months afterwards), Cathleen Nesbitt, beautiful and intelligent as Florence, better than any of those who played the part in succeeding months and years; Cecil Parker as her father, Aubrey Mather, and Margaret Yarde. To complete the trio of Sanger children I cast the beautiful Elissa Landi (Antonia) and Helen Spencer whose fragile charm was just right for Pauline. Additional members of the ensemble were Marie Ney, Harold Scott (who had yet to make his name and fortune at the Cave of Harmony); Tony de Lungo and Keneth Kent.

There had been no time to consult Margaret about the cast. Besides she was a virtual stranger to the theatre world. However, as soon as Noël's decision was announced, she wrote to me saying that she wished she had been consulted, adding the naïve comment: 'I've a feeling that young playwrights should best steer clear of one another's plays.' But she was soon caught up in the magic of the theatre and the enthusiasm of the actors. From first to last I heard not another word of criticism from her. My exceptional good fortune with the casting illustrates an occasional circumstance to be met with in the theatre, wherein everything seems to move inevitably to a successful conclusion.

5

The first reading was like the first day of a new term in 'the sixth', everyone excited by the play and delighted to be back. I felt I should never be able to achieve a better ensemble than that which was about to perform the highly complicated scenes in the first act. We lived with the smell of success throughout those exacting rehearsals: how well I recall Noël's angry complaints as the seemingly endless repetitions, which synchronisation of voices and movement on the crowded stage made necessary, got upon his nerves. Edna set an example of tireless dedication but Noël frequently gave way to temperament. Upon one occasion he made a terrific scene in front of the whole company, resigned the part and strode magnificently to the emergency exit which was padlocked. So, after an awkward pause and some tactful manœuvres on Margaret Kennedy's part, rehearsals were resumed. Margaret by the way was doing invaluable service, chatting to the actors and spreading tact like a family doctor dispensing pills.

A particular cause of Noël's frustration was the corncob pipe I asked him to smoke in place of cigarettes. This was in an attempt to get away from the smart-set atmosphere that he had presented hitherto. One morning, enraged because in trying to light the pipe he had somehow managed to singe his hair, he hurled the offensive article across the stage, whereupon I immediately sent the stage manager out to buy a new one. In all fairness I must add Noël generously acknowledged the effectiveness of the final result.

During the final dress rehearsal I noticed Mrs. Patrick Campbell seated in the front row of the dress circle, nursing her dog. I wondered what she was doing there, for she had certainly not been invited by me. I assumed that Noël had asked her. I did not speak to her during the rehearsal because I was more than a little scared of what she might think of the play. At the final curtain, as I hurried towards the stage to give the usual notes, she stopped me on the staircase:

'Beautiful play, Mr. Dean,' she murmured in her most seductive tones, 'beautiful play, and how bad Noël is! I *must* go and tell him.' An example of her delight in perverse judgments, for Lewis Dodd turned out to be the best performance in character that Noël had yet given.

6

The Constant Nymph was produced at the New Theatre on September 14th, 1926. The preliminary announcement aroused a great deal of public interest because the novel had appealed to both highbrow and lowbrow, which is not always the case with best-sellers. Moreover, Noël Coward, the remarkable young man on the theatrical trapeze, was to play a leading part. All things considered, it was not surprising that by lunchtime pit and gallery queues were stretching round three sides of the theatre. Some gossips reported that ten pounds had been offered for a stalls seat; others noted that people began to take their places twenty minutes before curtain rise, a marked departure from the late arrival habit then prevalent. All of which goes to show that this was to be quite an occasion.

Everything had been rehearsed at the top pitch of hurry and excitement, so I found myself 'on deck', giving last-minute instructions while the audience were filing into their places. The curtain was hastily lowered as I handed the ship over to the stage director for safe launching. I made my usual round of the dressing-rooms, and then went to the Ivy Restaurant to sit glumly with George Harris, too exhausted to say much. He soon left me, unable to keep away from contemplation of his handiwork. I returned to the theatre in time for the last scene. I was so gripped by the simple tenderness of Edna's death scene that I lost all sense of my share in its creation: I was at one with the audience in their acclamation until the manager fetched me to join the company on the stage. There were sixteen curtain calls, followed by a prim 'thank you' from Margaret Kennedy.

Many of the critics, especially those of a literary turn, had come to the theatre anticipating disaster, and were not afraid to confess it in their notices. *Punch*, for example, began by giving three reasons for its forebodings: first, a best-seller rarely made a dramatic success; second, the novel seemed to him an undramatic proposition, and, third, he had felt no confidence in the cast I had announced. Then he confessed he had been wrong on all three counts. James Agate and St. John Ervine each contributed two columns to their respective papers. Reading their notices again after so long an interval, one is surprised not so much by the fact that each so exhausted the vocabulary of approval that one could have exchanged sentences between the two articles without disturbance of the context. Edna Best's personal triumph was trumpeted in numerous headlines. I liked best the *Manchester Guardian*'s comment upon her death scene: 'Dying in her pain as quietly as she lived in her life.' Noël, too, received lavish praise for his character performance. Why then did he denigrate it in his autobiography? Perhaps it was because he felt it was not an extension of his own personality. The *Morning Post* kept pace with the other papers in its generous allowance of space, adding with a sense of social propriety the names of distinguished personalities present, including a clutch of leading authors: H. G. Wells, John Galsworthy, Arnold Bennett, Somerset Maugham, Hugh Walpole, and Mrs. Belloc Lowndes. Maugham wrote to me in terms of unusual enthusiasm, welcoming me to 'the fraternity of British dramatists', while Galsworthy added helpful criticisms to

his over-all praise . . . Lady Wyndham was there, of course, to witness the vindication of her own sure judgment in telling 'Bronnie'
to accept the play at once.

7

The American sequel to this ecstatic success was an altogether
unhappy affair. George Tyler, back from his usual breathless round
of continental theatres, admiring much but buying little, was present
at our first night and in my office the next morning to remind me
of the casual promise I had made to him in New York the previous
autumn that he should have the first refusal of the American rights.
He offered me the most generous terms and said he wanted to produce as soon as possible. I knew there was an unusual amount of
advance interest over there because old Mrs. Post had already written
to Nancie: 'My dear little girl'—not the real Nancie at all—'I hear
your husband has a new play. When does it come? Where can I
get seats?'

I thought Tyler was rushing things too much, for it was already
mid-September. However, he began to insist upon what I suppose
the lawyers would call 'specific performance'. Caught off balance by
overwhelming success and forgetting managerial caution I signed
a contract with Tyler. Shortly afterwards I realised my blunder.
I had forgotten my promise to produce *This Was a Man*, Noël's
latest play, which was to have been the second of my three productions for the Duke of York's. Much to my chagrin the Lord Chamberlain had refused it a licence, so Noël and I had agreed to put it
into cold storage for later production in New York. Following
Noël's offer to play Lewis, we had agreed to put the production off
until November. I could hardly expect him to agree to a second
postponement. *The Nymph* could not possibly be produced before
December at the earliest. However, Tyler still insisted, so I gave
in. The truth was, I suppose, that we were both over-greedy for
success, a reminder of what happens in the old fable of the dog
with a bone crossing a bridge and seeing his own image in the water
beneath.

Noël preceded me to New York to begin the search for a leading
lady for his new comedy, but nobody showed much interest in it.
An omen? Possibly, but I suppose the real truth was that we were
too late cn the ground. Glamorous stars like Ina Claire were already

engaged. In the end we persuaded Francine Larrimore to accept the part. She gave an efficient but, to my mind, unattractive performance. We engaged a strong cast to support her which included Auriol Lee, Nigel Bruce and A. E. Matthews ('Matty').

In *Present Indicative* Noël attributes the failure to my production. Matty on the other hand comes nearer the truth when he states in his autobiography that he was the cause. What he does not say and what Noël did not know was that the turmoil in which this charming comedy actor was living during the rehearsal period made success impossible either for him or for the play. He occupied an apartment in the St. Hubert Hotel on 57th Street. I had taken a similar apartment on the floor immediately above him. The St. Hubert was old-fashioned by American standards, built round a central well, which acted as a kind of speaking-tube, especially in hot weather when people slept with windows wide open and shades down. Now Matty was at this time deeply involved with two women, living with one at the St. Hubert and receiving angry visits from another after rehearsals were over. This led to nightly altercations which rose and fell like the waves of an angry sea beneath my window. I found it impossible to sleep. Matty fared worse, coming to rehearsal so exhausted that finally I suggested as tactfully as I could that he should put an end to the situation, otherwise he would never know his lines.

'My dear chap', he blandly replied, 'what else can you expect between two women?'

Anyway, as I had foreseen, Matty knew less about the play at the final dress rehearsal than when he'd begun. He mumbled through his part, guessing at cues and creating an effect as though he were saying the part backwards. Exasperated beyond all restraint during the second act I shouted at him from the back of the stalls: 'Louder and funnier, Matthews,' which brought about his final and utter collapse.

Fashionable New York turned out in force on the first night. The theatre was jam-packed with celebrities, a tribute to Noël's success the previous season. After the second act, traditionally regarded by American first-nighters as the highlight of a theatrical evening, the stalls emptied into the inadequate lobby there to exchange views and make dates. Alas! Few of them returned for the last act; they preferred supper at Twenty-One. Café society has a notoriously short memory.

'Tie it for me,
Tessa.'

Above left   Noël Coward as Lewis Dodd
Above right   John Gielgud in the same part
Below left   The German Tessa: Elisabeth Bergner
Below right   The American Tessa: Beatrix Thomson

Above *The Constant Nymph*.
Life at the Karindehutte:
Rehearsing Lewis's Opera-
Charade

Centre Supper afterwards

Below Lewis shocks Florence's
musical soirée, Strand-on-the-Green

8

After the Coward fiasco I turned to what I wrongly expected would be the easier task. When I told Noël we were going ahead with *The Nymph* he said we were making a big mistake: I should wait until the next season and present the play with Edna in her original part.

We finally decided upon Beatrix Thomson for Tessa. She refused to come unless a part could be found for her husband, Claude Rains. Except for his lack of stature I felt he would have made an admirable Lewis, but Tyler had set his mind upon Glenn Anders, a likable actor who had already succeeded with me in London, but who to my mind was more like a cowboy from the Middle West than a young musician from Britain. In the end Claude Rains played Roberto.

Tyler had a peculiar method of casting his productions. It was a kind of dragnet system. He would let it be known among the agents and in theatrical circles generally that he was casting. Out of the ensuing flood of applicants he expected to find suitable artists at the bottom of the net. In my case he channelled the flood over to me, sometimes with little bits of paper, office memos, on which he had scrawled the names of the parts for which he thought the applicants suitable. He grew impatient at my continued rejection of his suggestions and so eventually the stream became a trickle. Neither of us had made allowance for the difficulties we should meet with in filling the long cast of conventional and unconventional characters, none of them types familiar to American actors. 'Not another cent,' he interrupted, when I suggested sending to England for some of them. I had forgotten his phobia about paying the transportation expenses of actors imported from Britain. I had the greatest difficulty in persuading him to pay the expenses of George Harris, who was to design the production, as well as for Beatrix and Claude.

Now I come to a very strange story indeed: while Beatrix Thomson was still on the high seas I began the task of knitting together the players already engaged, getting them to read their parts aloud and showing them how the clichés of technique some of them were using could destroy the truth of the ensemble, much as Lee Strasberg was to expound his theories in the Actors' Studio years later. During

Y

one of these occasions the late Moss Hart arrived with one of George Tyler's chits, recommending him for the part of Jacob Birnbaum. He was small and thin and, like many youngsters hanging on to the fringe of the theatre, engaged in a desperate search for opportunity. I thought him most unsuitable and brushed aside his application with some impatience. In his autobiography, written forty years or so on, Moss Hart uses the incident to protest at the cruelty I was inflicting upon actors seeking employment—a good story but untrue. He had mistaken a rehearsal for an audition. The actor's engagements were not at stake.

During this anxious time Paul Clift was looking after the two plays I had left running in London. He wrote regularly, once, sometimes twice, a week, giving me full information about what was going on. At first it was a tale of success all the way: 'The *Nymph* is doing such heavy business that the New Theatre had put up a third box office in the lobby to cope with the rush for seats'; '*The Queen was in the Parlour* at the Duke of York's is keeping up well with the overflow from the New Theatre queues, those who can't get in to see Noël act can at least walk down the road and see his latest play.'

The play was presented at the Selwyn Theatre, New York, on December 9th, 1926. I can remember nothing of the performance, which is not surprising, for Nancie's baby was born two days later, on December 11th at Swan House, Chelsea, which Lady Warwick had rented for a short season. I was thinking of an altogether different kind of nymph. The notices were poor. Although the acting was praised, it was evident that, lacking the peculiar charm of Edna Best and without the precise characterisation of the London ensemble, the play had failed.

Looking back on that brief season, I realise how fortunate I had been on earlier visits to have had managers like Gilbert Miller and Charles Dillingham to deal with. They commanded the respect and goodwill of the actors and technicians they employed. Especially, too, they afforded a measure of protection against the cheese-paring and corner-cutting with which office staffs sought to impress their bosses. The fact is I never got used to the helter-skelter of Broadway, nor could I reconcile myself to the fact that none of my American productions reached the standards achieved in London. I suppose that is only an excuse, but it has substance.

9

While I was away Curtis Brown had sold the play to Sweden, Denmark, Holland, Italy and Germany. I was particularly interested in the latter because the Berlin impresario, Barnowsky, had secured Elisabeth Bergner to play Tessa: She was a popular Viennese actress who had made a tremendous success in *Saint Joan*. The German agents assured me that I should be welcome at the first night, ultimately fixed for February 12th. I was delighted to accept, never having lost my *schwärmerei* for the German theatre since those early days spent at the feet of Max Reinhardt. Barnowsky was a cheerful, pleasant manager, running his two Berlin theatres on sound commercial lines. The company, too, was friendly and pleased to see me, although nervous of my presence at rehearsal, all save Bergner who awaited my comments after the first dress rehearsal with charming indifference. So far as I could judge from my limited knowledge of German the translation had been faithfully carried out, although the atmosphere in Act One, Sanger's Circus, seemed to be heavily sentimental when it was not melodramatic. The gay inconsequence and amoral attitude of the family circle of Margaret's conception were missing in the performance. But what really shook me was that Bergner seemed to understand the character of Tessa not at all. The misinterpretation was most marked at the end of the musical party in the second act. Whereas in London when Lewis Dodd played the *Dead March* in Saul while the outraged guests stalked out of the room, Tessa rounded upon his bad manners which brought Lewis to a sudden realisation of her as a person, not a child: he 'saw' Tessa for the first time. In Berlin Bergner appeared to egg him on, finally joining him in a mocking chorus. After the rehearsal I went back-stage to explain to Bergner that this was not in Tessa's character. She was very charming and promised to remove the offending business. I thought the whole production was what the Germans call *kitsch*. It received poor notices from the Berlin critics, but had a successful run, due largely to the immense popularity of Elisabeth Bergner with the Berliners.

Now that the play was running simultaneously in London, New York and Berlin, we exhibited playbills from the other capitals outside the New Theatre. Later on, Giraudoux adapted the play for France where it was produced by Louis Jouvet under the title of *Tessa*. It was an artistic triumph for Jouvet, both as director and for his own performance as Lewis Dodd. A pity it was not produced in time for us to add a Paris playbill to the others outside our theatre.

Early in March Margaret and I gave a party on the stage of the New Theatre to celebrate the 200th performance. Looking through the list of those present, it seems as though the entire West End stage was there, as well as a surprising number of prominent Liberal statesmen, including Mr Asquith, accompanying Margot and 'Puffin', together with Lord and Lady Londonderry. They must have been invited by Margaret. There was the usual crowd of 'socialites', always keen-scented for worthwhile occasions—a plentiful supper, served Tyrolean fashion in our *Karindehutte* set, an impromptu cabaret arranged by Harold Scott, Elsa Lanchester and Hermione Baddeley, during which the guests thronged the stalls, and, finally, dancing on the stage. I well remember Margot steering me across patches of uneven floor—a sad reversal of function!—while she voiced trenchant criticism of the London theatre. . . . And that's all about *The Constant Nymph* for the time being or nearly so at any rate!

10

Before I left for America I received a telephone message from a certain Major O'Bryen whom I had not previously met, saying that he wished to bring his principal, Michael Balcon of the Gainsborough Picture Company, to see me. They came the next day and sat in my office discussing the possibility of Gainsborough Pictures making a film of the play. 'Bill' O'Bryen was managing and looking after public relations for Balcon and his Gainsborough Pictures, which was an organisation having studios at Islington. I remember the occasion well. Balcon, young, dark and handsome; O'Bryen with a record of extraordinary dash and bravery in the late war, picking up military crosses as ordinary people might pick up sixpences, both bubbling with enthusiasm for our play.

C.B. had given up trying to persuade an American company to buy the film rights, because of the opposition of the Hays Organisation to the subject. Knowing this, I was converted to the Gainsborough proposition without much discussion. As the talk proceeded I had an idea: Why shouldn't I make the film myself? I knew nothing about film-making, and made the suggestion on a sudden impulse, without regard to the consequences. After the shock of my suggestion had died away, it was agreed than an experienced film director would have to be appointed, but that I should be associated with him as an adviser on the acting and to keep the story on the right lines. . . . I must leave to a second volume all the adventures and mishaps that followed upon that sudden whim, which was destined to deflect my career from its main course and turn my private life upside down.

I I

Amid all the excitements of inter-continental presentations and gay parties, I was not allowed to neglect my domestic responsibilities Lady Warwick saw to that. She had given up her brief tenancy of Swan House and gone back to Easton Lodge, taking Nancie and our daughter with her. Arrangements for the christening were now taken in hand, a matter to which Lady Warwick attached greater social significance than perhaps we, the parents, did. She invited Bernard Shaw to become the child's godfather. I thought this a strange notion but made no demur. Recently I came across Shaw's reply:

2nd March 1927
Ayot St. Lawrence, Welwyn, Herts.

My dear Lady Warwick,

My letters have gone astray; but I gather from my secretary by telephone that you want me to godfather your grandson. I am tempted to make the disgraceful reply that I had much rather father your son; but that excuse, however true, is superfluous, because I am eternally disqualified from sponsorship by the fact that I do not believe either the Apostles Creed or the Church Catechism; and as for the doctrine of original sin I abhor it, and would do anything in my power to turn the infant against it.

I should simply register him, taking care not to give him any names that would tar him with doctrines that he might grow up to detest, or that might raise expectations that he might not be able to fulfil. It is bad enough to have a famous grandmother (a thing that can't be helped) without having a famous godfather as well. He might want to write plays. Mozart's unfortunate son wanted to be a musician, and would have been thought a very good one had his name been Muggins.

Call him Kingmaker Raggedstaff: then they will expect something from him; but they won't know what.

faithfully,

G. BERNARD SHAW.

The sex of the child had been changed in the telephone message from his secretary, Blanche Patch.

Knowing nothing of this letter, only that Shaw had refused, I asked my old friend Roger Ould to become the godfather. The child was to be called Tessa, and so, inevitably, her sponsors on the female side were Margaret Kennedy and Edna Best. She was christened by the Rev. Conrad Noel, a prominent Socialist parson of the day, in his parish church of Thaxted in Essex. It was a bright frosty morning in March with the pale sun lighting up the religious banners and pictures with which Conrad Noel had enriched his beautiful church. After the ceremony we all motored back to Easton Lodge for lunch: a serenely happy party in beautiful surroundings, ecclesiastic and secular. Thus my daughter was launched upon what I believe to be her happy and successful life.

Retrospect

Surveying my early success with ReandeaN, I do not conceal from myself that the slaughter of World War I had destroyed a generation of possible rivals, leaving me with a clear field. To begin with, I held no particular views on the problems either of acting or production. It was only after the loss of Meggie that I began consciously to direct my thought towards developing the technique of the ensemble. The critics began to make reference to what they called my perfect casting. Seeing that all the members of the ReandeaN Company played a wide variety of parts, this showed misunderstanding of what I was trying to achieve. Casting was not for me solely a question of suitable personality, nor of height, voice nor experience. In the course of time I found out that I possessed the ability to gauge elements in an actor's personality that were hidden from him and to draw them out at rehearsal, so that the actor and the character he portrayed became close-fitting like glove to the hand. Oftentimes the actor remained unaware of this part of the rehearsal process. Perhaps this partially explains why actors sometimes complained of the discipline of my rehearsals. It certainly led to occasional difficulties with those who found themselves unable to accept wholeheartedly the essential principle of the ensemble, which is that the interpretation of the whole work shall be greater than the sum of all the parts. Nevertheless, we succeeded in great part, all of us working together, in creating a rapport that brought distinction to individuals as well as a corporate pride that remained in the memory of those who shared in it.

The personalities of the players in our permanent company are sharply etched in my memory: Mary Clare, warm-hearted, emotionally gifted and with a delicious Irish humour; Cathleen Nesbitt, distinguished and dedicated to the cause of intelligent theatre; Edna Best, pert, commonsensical, always true to the limitations of her own talent; Ada King, in poor health, grumbling but relentless in the pursuit of truth—the finest character actress of her day; Leslie Banks, good actor, with a gruff humour sometimes inconveniently exercised; J. H. Roberts, pessimistic, retiring, etching his characters with the delicate strokes of a true artist (What a wonderful Mr. Chips he would have made!); Malcolm Keen, whose magnificent voice compensated for occasional lack of understanding of the subtleties of character, and his enthusiastic wonder when these were explained to him; Ian Hunter, imperturbable, undeniable charm never consciously exploited; Marda Vanne, young but already with an ability to draw character in firm, well-defined strokes; Clifford Mollison, incisive and sharply humorous; Robert Harris with his splendid voice—there were never any complaints from the audience that my actors could not be heard; Austin Trevor; Ben Field; Olga Lindo; and many more, the names streak across the page as I write.

Such success as I achieved went to my head, not so much in causing complacency or conceit as in impelling me forward in the search for perfection. Perfectionist is a dirty word these days, but when it was applied to me, tauntingly sometimes, I regarded it as a professional accolade rather than as criticism. The weakness of perfectionism lies in its disregard of other claims, be they of persons or things. Two examples of my obstinacy in this regard occur to me. One was in respect of *Hindle Wakes*, offered to me by its author, Stanley Houghton, while I was controller of the Liverpool Repertory Theatre and passed on by me to Miss Horniman because the Liverpool Theatre had no Lancashire players in its company, an action which our chairman mistook for lack of personal judgment on my part. The other was my recommendation of *Rose Marie* for His Majesty's Theatre rather than for Drury Lane, where I wrongly supposed Alfred Butt to have acquiesced in the policy I had laid down. In the case of *Hindle Wakes* I was justified by results; in the case of *Rose Marie* I was not.

The ending of ReandeaN was not a good thing for either partner. Alec Rea, its financial head, loved the theatre, not because he was a playwright *manqué*, not because of some professional *diva* whose interests he sought to advance, but for its own sake. Yet he never really understood it, and his judgment of plays was poor, as the subsequent record shows. He was suspicious of plays breaking fresh ground, especially if they revealed Leftist tendencies, a surprising trait in a member of a distinguished Liberal family. His rejection of Shaw's *Heartbreak House* was a case in point. Generally speaking, the plays he produced during the remainder of his tenancy of the St. Martin's Theatre with Paul Clift as his manager, lacked distinction and brought only limited commercial success. Yet he deserves high place in the annals of the English Theatre, for as Patrick Hastings pointed out in his autobiography: 'ReandeaN was virtually the last organised management under a private patron.'

The parting was largely my fault. I should have restrained my impatience to conquer on so many fields at once, realising that it might lead to the criticism that I was disregarding first loyalties. Too many of the enterprises that I began in a spirit of enthusiasm failed because I did not make allowances for the lesser enthusiasm of others. The search for perfection at a time when standards were steadily declining often got me into hot water, laying me open to charges of extravagance. Yet more than once I proved the truth of Sir Herbert Tree's dictum that 'showmanship is the art of judicious extravagance'.

Had we remained together, Alec and I, we might have accomplished something of lasting good. Yet I am not sure. All things are fleeting in the theatre. Reputations glow and fade as rapidly as do the lights on the scenery. All that is left of our enterprise is a Meggie Albanesi Scholarship at the Royal Academy of Dramatic Art and a bundle of playgoers' memories that I am assured remain vivid to this day. When all's said, I owe Alec Rea an incalculable debt, for without his warm friendship and loyal support during my early struggles I might not have achieved anything very much.

Index

of principal persons and plays